JDK 1.4 Tutorial

D1797599

JDK 1.4 Tutorial

GREG M. TRAVIS

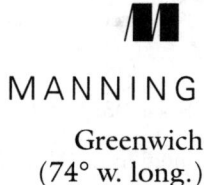

MANNING

Greenwich
(74° w. long.)

For electronic information and ordering of this and other Manning books,
go to www.manning.com. The publisher offers discounts on this book
when ordered in quantity. For more information, please contact:

Special Sales Department
Manning Publications Co.
209 Bruce Park Avenue   Fax: (203) 661-9018
Greenwich, CT 06830   email: orders@manning.com

©2002 by Manning Publications Co. All rights reserved.

No part of this publication may be reproduced, stored in a retrieval system, or transmitted,
in any form or by means electronic, mechanical, photocopying, or otherwise, without
prior written permission of the publisher.

Many of the designations used by manufacturers and sellers to distinguish their products
are claimed as trademarks. Where those designations appear in the book, and Manning
Publications was aware of a trademark claim, the designations have been printed in initial
caps or all caps.

⊖ Recognizing the importance of preserving what has been written, it is Manning's policy to have
the books they publish printed on acid-free paper, and we exert our best efforts to that end.

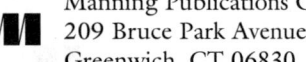 Manning Publications Co.   Copyeditor: Andy Carroll
   209 Bruce Park Avenue   Typesetter: Tony Roberts
   Greenwich, CT 06830   Cover designer: Leslie Haimes

ISBN 1-930110-45-6

Printed in the United States of America

1 2 3 4 5 6 7 8 9 10 – VHG – 05 04 03 02

To Susan

contents

preface

In the summer of 1995, I moved to New York City to work at a web start-up. On my first day of work, I saw Netscape for the first time; by the end of the day, I had written my first applet, a trivial graphics program I called Thingy.

Thingy just drew a bunch of lines from the cursor to the edge of the screen. You moved the cursor, and the vortex moved along with it. Interactive! I announced the creation of Thingy at the company meeting, and, to my surprise, everyone cheered. I had no idea what the big deal was. I had never used the web before that day, and I didn't know why it was exciting, or why it was boring enough that a program like this could enliven it. Apparently, being able to run a program inside a browser was a big deal. A very big deal.

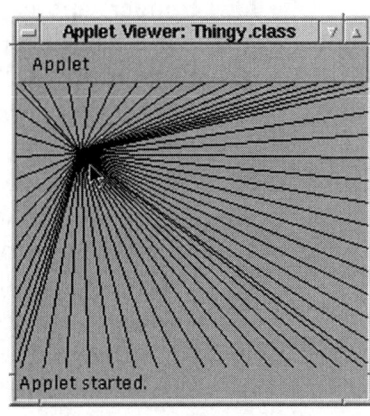

For a while, that was what Java was all about—putting moving images inside pages in a fairly static medium. Java competed against other enlivening technologies, trading moderate complexity for generality, and becoming a very hot resume item in the process.

However, our start-up had realized at an early point that Java wasn't just for the client side. Java was also an excellent server-side language—an application language. For all its flaws, Java seemed to be exceedingly well designed. It felt a lot like C++, but *less*. I had come close to being a C++ evangelist at my previous job, but even I had to admit that I got a headache every time I tried to write C++ code. Java, on the other hand, almost never gave me a headache. On the contrary—it was eerily *fun*.

We heard that the designers (James Gosling and his team) had used a simple design rule: *if you don't know how to do something really nicely, leave it out*. What an excellent rule! Play to your strengths. Why do lots of things badly when you can do a few things nicely? Quality isn't just including good stuff; it's also knowing when to cut the bad stuff.

Java benefited from the fact that it ran in a place where no programs had run before—inside the browser window. The novelty of this made up for the fact that it was slow and used a lot of memory. It didn't allow for the time and space optimizations that C and C++ allowed. But that was okay—it was a different class of language. It occupied a special niche, one that had been sought by other truly high-level languages with commercial pretensions, such as SmallTalk and Eiffel.

And so Java thrived. Easy to use, portable (except maybe the GUI stuff), good for beginners and experts alike. It became a very famous language. Relatives of mine who had never touched a computer asked me if I knew Java and were pleased when I said that I did. Eat your heart out, SmallTalk! Take that, Eiffel!

Once Java was firmly ensconced in the canon of programming languages, its designers increasingly turned their attention to speed. It had gained popularity because of its simplicity, and that simplicity had brought a certain amount of sluggishness; now it was time to make up for that.

The last few versions of the JDK have focused on making Java more complete, faster, and—let's not be shy—less simple. The simple stuff is still there, but more sophisticated elements are falling into place. They might be harder to use, but it's worth it if they improve performance. Java always had a nice learning curve, and the curve has retained its gentle slope. You can start with the basics and move on to the more complex stuff when your projects demand it.

JDK 1.4 is another step on this path. It includes a variety of new features, some of which have been available in prototype form, but all of which are now firmly part of the Java platform. These features are not yet available in most browsers, but if you use Java for true application development, you'll want to learn how to use them right away.

acknowledgments

This is my first book. Not surprisingly, it was a lot harder than I thought it would be, even though I had thought I was prepared for it to be harder than I thought it would be. However, I was fortunate to be surrounded by the extreme competence of the folks at Manning Publications. Many thanks to Marjan Bace, the publisher, for approving the book and helping to define its goals; similarly, hearty thanks to my first contact at Manning, Dan Barthel, for his help both during and after his formal association with Manning.

Particular thanks to Alex Garrett, who with endless patience shepherded the book, and its accompanying code, through a brutally accelerated development and revision process. Thanks also to Lianna Wlasiuk, who served excellently as interim editor early in the project.

Thanks, in fact, to everyone at Manning who answered my questions, pointed out my typos, corrected my spelling, marshaled my reviewers, refined my thinking, or, in fact, actually edited, re-edited, copyedited, revised, read, reread, proofread, typeset, designed, marketed, produced, or otherwise created my book: Syd Brown, Susan Capparelle, Andy Carroll, Lee Fitzpatrick, Leslie Haimes, Chris Hillman, Ted Kennedy, Elizabeth Martin, Mary Piergies, Sherry Roberts, Tony Roberts, and Helen Trimes. Double thanks for doing everything on a very tight schedule. If I've left out anyone, either through accident or omission, please accept my apologies.

Heartfelt thanks to those who read and reviewed the book independently, serving both as expert witnesses and test subjects: Brian Doyle, Al Giacomucci,

Ian Griffiths, Jasen Halmes, David M. Karr, Stephen Kelvin, Carl Muckenhoupt, Andrew Silis, Jon Skeet, and Itai Zukerman. I would particularly like to thank Ian Griffiths, who went over the book with a fine-toothed comb, lending an expert's brain and a proofreader's eye.

Outside the world of book publishing, I would like to thank Kieron Murphy for commissioning many technical articles from me, effectively jump-starting my writing career. Thanks to Jim Blandy, Bob Geitz, Chris Gernon, Steve Hawley, Chris Koch, Tom McHugh, and Rich Salter for teaching me computer science. Thanks to Mark Cline, wherever you are, for teaching me to program in the first place.

Thanks and apologies to friends and family who found me scarce during this project.

Finally, endless thanks to Susan E. Beal, Esq., for her love and patience (and even a bit of proofreading) throughout the writing of this book, and more thanks to Hume Beal for his purring and enthusiasm.

about this book

The JDK 1.4 release of the Java programming language from Sun Microsystems represents a substantial step in Java's progress. Some of the new features are packages that have been in use for some time but have not yet been part of the core Java platform; other features are completely new.

Whatever their origin, these features extend Java's capabilities, encapsulating complex functionality behind simple abstractions. Some of the features help integrate Java further into the host operating system, providing direct access to services that had previously only been accessible to native code.

This book is decidedly code-centric. The central feature of each chapter is a program or set of programs that demonstrate the subject of the chapter within a complete, real-world program. Although each chapter starts with an overview of its topic and outlines the main classes and methods of the crucial packages, it does not duplicate information that can easily be found in the Java documentation. Thus, this book should be considered a by-example companion to the comprehensive documentation.

As you peruse the chapter descriptions that follow, you may notice that this book does not rigorously cover all topics. I consider a number of topics too broad to be covered in any useful way in a book of this kind; such topics generally need their own book. These include CORBA (including the new Portable Object Adapter (POA) Object Request Broker (ORB)), XML, the Java Cryptography Extension (JCE), and the Java Authentication and Authorization Service (JAAS).

At the time this book was being prepared, it did not seem possible to acquire a driver that supported enough JDBC 3.0 features to make testing possible. Rather than write from a position of ignorance, and include possibly spurious code listings, I decided not to include a chapter on this important topic.

Sadly, the Generics (parameterized types) feature was, in the end, not included with JDK 1.4 as originally promised. This controversial addition to the language looks like it will be included in JDK 1.5 for sure, and you can download an early-access version of it from Sun. However, since it requires a change to the compiler, it can't really be said to be a part of JDK 1.4 and so is not discussed in this book.

Who should read this book

The ideal reader of this book is an intermediate or expert Java programmer who needs to use the new features of JDK 1.4. I've tried to include enough introductory material that beginners will also find this book useful; however, this book will not teach you to program—it assumes you already know how.

This book is intended to guide the reader through the essentials of most of the new packages, libraries, and features in the JDK 1.4 release of the Java programming language from Sun Microsystems. It is intended to be *comprehensive*, but not necessarily *complete*. I'm assuming that once you've learned how to use an API, you will be comfortable digging into the documentation supplied by Sun, and that you can explore some of the more obscure features of these new APIs on your own.

How this book is organized

Each topic is given its own chapter, except for the New Input/Output (NIO) library, which is given two chapters. Some of the chapters provide a comprehensive review of an entire package because that package has been added to the core Java distribution for the first time. For these topics, the chapter begins with a conceptual overview that describes the classes and the intentions behind their design. Then, each major feature of the package is discussed in its own section.

Other chapters touch on the new features of an already-familiar package. In these cases, little time is spent explaining the package as a whole. Rather, each new feature is given its own section, which serves as a kind of "mini-chapter."

Each chapter (or "mini-chapter," in the case of chapters covering familiar packages) can be read on its own. It is assumed that you will read the book in any order, and dependencies between the chapters have been minimized. Cross-references have been provided where necessary.

Particular emphasis has been placed on the creation of quality *code examples*. The sample programs in this book are intended to be useful, self-contained, and reusable; they are designed to fully exercise and illustrate a new feature, set of features, or API. Some of them might seem a bit overlong, but I felt that it would be better for the programs to be complete and useful than to be concise. You don't have to read every line of every program—only the parts that strike your fancy. Use the annotations to find your way around the code, and remember, you won't have to type the programs in—you can download them. (More about that shortly.)

A chapter-by-chapter outline of the contents of the book follows.

Chapters 1 and 2—Basic and Advanced NIO

NIO, or the *New Input/Output API*, presents the concept of the *channel* as an alternative to the *stream*. Channels allow for efficient, buffer-based input and output—buffers are used to read data from, and write data to, channels. *Direct buffers* provide direct access to system input and output buffers and thus offer the potential for transferring data from one channel to another with a minimum of data copying.

NIO makes it possible to circumvent the potential inefficiencies of Java's stream I/O architecture, with the possibility of great gains in speed. The channel paradigm is not as simple to use as the stream paradigm, but judicious use of it in cases where I/O speed is essential can help Java applications achieve the throughput of applications written using native low-level I/O APIs.

NIO also offers asynchronous I/O via *selectable* channels, fashioned after the `select` Unix system call. Select is a powerful way to perform asynchronous I/O, allowing you to handle a large number of connections at a single time. This goes a long way in making Java the language of choice for creating high-end Internet servers.

This topic is divided into two chapters. Chapter 1, "Basic NIO," covers the fundamental classes used in the NIO system: channels and buffers. It also has a section on file locking. Chapter 2, "Advanced NIO," discusses powerful features based on the basic classes, including memory-mapped files, asynchronous I/O, charset translation, and network interfaces.

As examples, these chapters contain a simple channel-based TCP/IP forwarder and a select-based implementation of a chat (instant messaging) system.

Chapter 3—Java2D

Two new Java2D-related features are described in this book: the *Print Service API* and a new *Image I/O Framework*.

The *Print Service API* gives your application full access to the set of printers available on a computer, as well as the full range of printing options available on each printer. It is intended to supersede the `java.awt.print` package. Document classes allow you to create printable objects in a variety of formats and submit those documents to printers that support these formats. Listeners allow your application to track the progress of the print job so you can report back to the user.

The *Image I/O Framework* takes Java another step away from the Web-centeredness it started with. It used to be difficult to load and save images; with the new API, this is easy. Images can be saved and loaded in a variety of formats, and there's no need to mess with annoying `MediaTracker` objects.

This chapter includes an example implementation of a print dialog box, and a program for generating professional-looking graphs for displaying web server statistics.

Chapter 4—Java Web Start (JAWS)

You may have found yourself envying programmers who have created applications that automatically update themselves when new releases are available. With *Java Web Start (JAWS)*, you can stop being envious. JAWS is not just an API, but also a system for automatic download and installation of Java applications. Each time a JAWS application is executed, the JAWS runtime checks the application's web server and downloads any new code or data resources automatically. Although existing Java applications can run inside JAWS without modification, the JAWS API provides mechanisms for controlling the way the JAWS runtime behaves, as well as special secure methods for accessing system resources, such as the local disk and the system clipboard.

When Java was first released, one of the exciting ideas was the possibility of being able to deploy complex, full-featured applications via the Web. Browser security models prevented applets from saving themselves to disk, though, and this idea fell out of favor. Now JAWS can be integrated into popular browsers via the Java Web Start plug-in. This allows a user to download and install a complete application with a single click. Downloaded applications are saved between invocations. A comprehensive security model completes the picture.

This chapter comes complete with a simple drawing program that makes comprehensive use of the JAWS system, including accessing the local disk, printing, controlling the browser, and accessing the system clipboard. The Java Network Launching Protocol & API (JNLP), which is the technology underlying JAWS, is also discussed.

Chapter 5—Logging

The *Logging API* provides a mechanism for programs to report about their behavior. More importantly, it provides a way to turn logging messages on and off after an application has been deployed in the field, greatly aiding in application maintenance.

Logging is hardly a new feature—in fact, many logging systems have been created for Java. However, the JDK 1.4 release standardizes this API in order to provide a consistent and reliable mechanism. Widespread use of the Logging API will mean that it will become much easier for applications to be maintained and debugged after they have been deployed.

The example programs in this chapter demonstrate the ability to *customize* the logging system. A custom *handler* redirects logging messages to a logging window (complete with a central control window), and a custom *formatter* provides an alternative logging format that takes up less space than the default format.

Chapter 6—Assertion facility

The new *Assertion facility* provides a way for a programmer to litter the code with "sanity checks." Assertions are like error checks, except they can be turned completely off, and they have a simpler syntax. Because they are so brief, they are very convenient, and there's no reason not to use them liberally.

Assertions can be turned on and off even after the software has been released. When assertions are off, they don't use system resources, but they can be turned on whenever the software seems to have a problem. With assertions turned on, the software is much more likely to find, and report on, its own bugs.

Assertions are important enough that the developers of Java felt it was worth adding new syntax to the language. For large-scale applications, assertions are crucial to maintaining software throughout its release cycle.

Chapter 7—Exceptions

While we're on the subject of errors, there are a couple of nice surprises in JDK 1.4 in the area of *Exceptions*.

The new `StackTraceElement` object allows a program to access each stack frame of an exception's stack trace, giving you access to the source file, method, and line number of each frame in the stack trace. Previously, you had to parse the stack trace output; now you can get at this information directly. You can even synthesize your own stack frames in special circumstances.

Chained exceptions allow for the fact that it is common for one exception to trigger another. In these cases, the initial exception was lost, unless the programmer took pains to stuff the old one inside the new one. This stuffing procedure has been formalized, since it has proven to be so common. Each `Throwable` can now have a *cause*, which is another `Throwable`.

The sample program in this chapter uses `StackTraceElements` to provide a more detailed stack trace—one that lists the source-code context of each frame in the stack trace.

Chapter 8—Collections

The *Collections Framework* has a number of useful new features. Besides some list-manipulation utilities in the `Collections` class, we find implementations of `Map` and `Set` that remember the order of their elements, unlike regular `Maps` and `Sets`. Additionally, the new `IdentityHashMap` class presents a way to circumvent an object's idea of equality, which can be very useful when, for example, traversing a graph of objects.

The ordered `Map` and `Set` classes are demonstrated by a program that searches for files in a file path, and `IdentityHashMap` is illustrated in a program that traverses an object graph.

Chapter 9—Regular expressions

The *Regular Expression*, or *regex*, facility, brings an incredibly useful feature to Java. Common in Unix tools, and vastly popularized by Perl, regular expressions are considered by many programmers to be an indispensable part of their toolboxes. Programmers accustomed to regular expressions, as well as the increasingly common `split` and `join` functions, will be happy to see that Java now has them as well.

To illustrate regular expressions, this chapter includes an HTML templating system and a simple lexical analyzer.

Chapter 10—The Preferences API

The new *Preferences API* provides a standard way for Java applications to store and retrieve preference information. Preference information generally consists of customizations and settings, often user-specific, that are useful but not essential to the execution of the application.

The Preferences API interfaces with any preferences facility that exists within the underlying operating system. In particular, some implementations store preference data in the Windows Registry. (Later implementations will presumably store it in Application Data directories.)

This chapter presents an example program called `PersistentWindows`, which uses the Preferences API to automatically track a user's changes to its window layout.

Chapter 11—The Java Secure Socket Extension (JSSE)

The *Java Secure Socket Extension* (JSSE) complements the already formidable Java cryptography architecture with a full implementation of the SSL suite of protocols. The JSSE framework is a generalized framework for secure socket communications over any protocol, while the `SunJSSE` security provider implements the algorithms and protocols for standard SSL communications.

There have been SSL libraries for Java for a while, but SSL is now a component of the main Java platform. This makes it easy to create programs that communicate with SSL-enabled systems such as secure web servers; it also makes it easy to create complete client/server systems that can communicate with complete secrecy. Tools and APIs for the creation and manipulation of encryption keys round out the picture.

To illustrate secure communications, this chapter includes a simple secure web server and a secure client/server system for credit card verification.

Typographic conventions

Code is displayed in `courier font`. Annotations are placed off to the side and are sometimes continued below the code.

```
public void hello() {
  System.out.println( "Hello." );
}
```

❶ **Here's where we print "Hello."**

❶ Here's some more information about the printing of "Hello." Printing "Hello." might seem trivial, but it's very important to do this.

By *code* we mean any textual material that is (or could be) the actual input to, or output from, a computer program. This also includes names of classes and interfaces such as FilterOutputStream and Preferences, methods such as System.out.println() and hello(), variables such as i and nextValue, and, in general, any short piece of text that is created by machine production or meant for machine consumption.

Italics are used to emphasize a new term the first time it is used, and also for emphasis. Callouts are used for particular emphasis:

WARNING This is a callout. It might be a *Warning*, a *Note*, a *Definition*, or something else. It's meant to grab your attention.

Source code downloads

Most of the programs are too long to be conveniently entered by hand; the book's web site, at http://www.manning.com/travis/, has all of the code available for download.

author online

When you purchase *JDK 1.4 Tutorial*, you also get free access to a private web forum run by Manning Publications where you can make comments about the book, ask technical questions, and receive help from the author and from other readers.

To access the forum and subscribe to it, point your web browser to http://www.manning.com/travis/. This page provides information on how to get on the forum once you are registered, what kind of help is available, and the rules of conduct on the forum.

Manning's commitment to readers is to provide a venue where a meaningful dialog between individual readers and between readers and the author can take place. It is not a commitment to any specific amount of participation on the part of the author, whose contribution to the Author Online forum remains voluntary (and unpaid). We suggest you try asking the author some challenging questions, lest his interest stray!

The Author Online forum and the archives of previous discussions will be accessible from the publisher's web site as long as the book is in print.

about the cover illustration

The figure on the cover of *JDK 1.4 Tutorial* is a woman of late eighteenth century Armenia, attired in an ornate and beautiful dress. While the details of her life and position are for us lost in historical fog, there is no doubt that we are looking at a woman of wealth and high social standing. The illustration is taken from a Spanish compendium of regional dress customs first published in Madrid in 1799. The book's title page states:

> *Coleccion general de los Trages que usan actualmente todas las Nacio-nas del Mundo desubierto, dibujados y grabados con la mayor exacti-tud por R.M.V.A.R. Obra muy util y en special para los que tienen la del viajero universal*

which we translate, as literally as possible, thus:

> *General collection of costumes currently used in the nations of the known world, designed and printed with great exactitude by R.M.V.A.R. This work is very useful especially for those who hold them-selves to be universal travelers*

Although nothing is known of the designers, engravers, and workers who colored this illustration by hand, the "exactitude" of their execution is evident in this drawing. The Armenian woman is just one of many figures in this colorful collection. Their diversity speaks vividly of the uniqueness and individuality of the world's cultures and regions just 200 years ago. This was a time when the dress codes of two regions separated by a few dozen miles identified people uniquely as belonging to one or the other. The collection brings to life the sense of isolation and distance of that period—and of every other historic period except our own hyperkinetic present.

Dress codes have changed since then, and the diversity by region, so rich at the time, has faded away. It is now often hard to tell the inhabitant of one continent from another. Perhaps, trying to view it optimistically, we have traded a cultural and visual diversity for a more varied personal life. Or a more varied and interesting intellectual and technical life.

We at Manning celebrate the inventiveness, the initiative, and the fun of the computer business with book covers based on the rich diversity of regional life of two centuries ago, brought back to life by the pictures from this collection.

Basic NIO
(New Input/Output)

This chapter covers
- The New I/O system
- Doing I/O with channels and buffers
- File locking

The New I/O (NIO) API introduced in JDK 1.4 provides a completely new model of low-level I/O. Unlike the original I/O libraries in the java.io package, which were strongly stream-oriented, the New I/O API in the java.nio package is *block-oriented*. This means that I/O operations, wherever possible, are performed on large blocks of data in a single step, rather than on one byte or character at a time.

The New I/O API libraries are elegant and well designed, but their very nature represents a trade-off: some simplicity has been sacrificed for potentially enormous gains in speed. One of the major sources of speed improvement is the introduction of *direct buffers*. Where possible, data in these buffers is not copied to and from intermediate Java buffers; instead, system-level operations are performed on them directly. Although the implementation necessarily differs from platform to platform, these direct buffers can potentially permit Java programs to have I/O performance at or near that of programs written in C or C++.

The New I/O API also offers a platform-independent form of *nonblocking I/O*. This simplifies multithreaded I/O programming and can enable programs to efficiently handle a large number of connections to data sources and sinks.

The New I/O API model coexists peacefully with the original I/O libraries from the java.io package. In fact, to a substantial degree, the original I/O libraries have been rewritten to take advantage of the New I/O API.

Application programmers will not be forced to rewrite any of their code—existing applications written against the original APIs will continue to work as before. However, you might consider using some of the new features of the New I/O API to speed up any performance bottlenecks you find in your programs. Mixing old- and new-style I/O code is not trivial, but it is possible to do cleanly and effectively.

This book divides its NIO coverage into two chapters—chapter 1, "Basic NIO," and chapter 2, "Advanced NIO." Chapter 1 covers channels and buffers, as well as file locking. These should give you a good understanding of the basic classes used throughout the NIO system. Chapter 2 introduces you to the more advanced features, such as multiplexed I/O; these make use of the ideas presented in this chapter.

1.1   *Doing I/O with channels and buffers*

Channels and buffers represent the two basic abstractions within the New I/O API. Channels correspond roughly to input and output streams: they are sources and sinks for sequential data. However, whereas input and output streams deal most directly with single bytes, channels read and write data in chunks. Additionally, a channel can be bidirectional, in which case it corresponds to *both* an input stream and an output stream.

The chunks of data that are written to and read from channels are contained in objects called *buffers*. A buffer is an array of data enclosed in an abstraction that makes reading from, and writing to, channels easy and convenient. Buffers are often large, reflecting the fact that the I/O paradigm used in the New I/O API is oriented toward transferring large amounts of data quickly.

Most of the input and output streams in the original I/O libraries have been re-implemented to use channels as their underlying mechanism. This means that when you do old-style I/O programming using these stream classes, you're using channels without realizing it. Since programming with streams is conceptually simpler than programming with channels, you can continue to use streams if you find that your program is fast enough. However, channels provide the opportunity for great speed improvements, and some applications are actually easier to write using channels.

In this section, we'll learn how channels and buffers work, and how they differ from streams.

1.1.1 Getting a channel from a stream

As mentioned previously, many of the streams in the java.io package have been re-implemented using channels. It's easy to get the underlying channel that implements a stream, using the getChannel() method:

```
FileInputStream fin = new FileInputStream( infile );

FileChannel inc = fin.getChannel();
```

If you examine the documentation for the original java.io.* classes, you'll see that a number of the classes have been augmented with a getChannel() method:

- java.io.FileInputStream
- java.io.FileOutputStream
- java.io.RandomAccessFile
- java.net.Socket
- java.net.ServerSocket
- java.net.DatagramSocket
- java.net.MulticastSocket
- java.net.SocketInputStream (private)
- java.net.SocketOutputStream (private)

You'll notice that InputStream and OutputStream do not have getChannel() methods. This is because streams *in general* do not have to be implemented in terms of an underlying channel object. Streams that are directly associated with operating system features like files and sockets generally are implemented as channels, while pure-Java streams such as ByteArrayOutputStream and FilterInputStream are not.

1.1.2 Creating a buffer revision

Before you can do any kind of I/O on a channel, you need to have a buffer to do it with. A buffer is an object that contains an array of data, and allows that data to be used for reading from, and writing to, channels.

Creating a buffer is easy. Here's how you create a ByteBuffer:

```
ByteBuffer buffer = ByteBuffer.allocate( 1024 );
```

This method takes a single argument—the size of the underlying array. This value is called the buffer's *capacity*. Once a buffer is created, the capacity never changes. The best size for a buffer depends on the application. A larger buffer can allow for faster throughput, but takes up more memory, while a smaller one may degrade performance slightly, but uses less memory.

You'll notice that we didn't use a traditional constructor here. This is true in general: buffers are either allocated using the static allocate() method, or created from an existing byte array using wrap(). They are never constructed directly by the user.

You'll also notice that we've created a ByteBuffer. The java.nio package also contains IntBuffer, ShortBuffer, FloatBuffer, and so on. There are, in fact, buffer types for each of Java's primitive types. There is a class called Buffer, but it is abstract—you can't create one. (Buffer is the abstract superclass of all the buffer classes.) A buffer is always a buffer *of something*. In the following sections, we'll use this ByteBuffer to illustrate how to do basic channel I/O. In section 1.2.6 we'll learn how to use the other types of buffers.

NOTE   Since the ByteBuffer is by far the most common, and most important, of the buffer classes, we will assume that any buffer we are talking about is a Byte-Buffer unless otherwise specified.

1.1.3 Reading from a channel

Now that we've seen how to create a buffer, we'll see how we can read from a channel into a buffer. In many ways, reading from a channel into a buffer is like reading from an InputStream into an array, using one of the bulk-read methods in the old java.io package.

The old read() method looked like this:

```
public int read( byte[] b, int off, int len );
```

This variant on the `InputStream.read()` method allowed you to read a number of bytes into an array all at once. In a sense, this approach to using streams is the precursor to the channel-oriented method of the New I/O API.

Here's the method we use in the new API:

```
public int read( ByteBuffer dst );
```

You'll note that there's only a single argument to this method. This is because the three arguments from the old-style `read()` call, as well as a number of other things, are all wrapped up inside the `ByteBuffer` object.

You'll also note that this new `read()` method returns an integer, just like the old one. The meaning of this value hasn't changed: it's the number of bytes that were successfully read. In both cases, this value is limited, because the `read()` method will only read as many bytes as can fit in the available space. In the old method, the available space was `len-off`; in the new method, the available space is equal to `buffer.remaining()`. (More about this in section 1.2.3.)

Note that if you read from a channel that is only open for writing, a `NonReadableChannelException` will be thrown.

1.1.4 *Writing to a channel*

Now that we've read some data from a channel into a buffer, we can write that data out to another channel. This is done—surprise!—via the `write()` method of a channel. And, as with reading, writing a buffer is similar to doing a *bulk-write* from the old `java.io` classes. Here is the old `write()` method:

```
public void write( byte[] b, int off, int len );
```

Again, the three arguments to the old-style write are replaced by a single argument, which is a buffer, in the new `write()` method:

```
public int write( ByteBuffer src );
```

In this new method, you'll see an important difference that you don't see with the `read()` methods: the new `write()` method returns an `int`. The old `write()` call was guaranteed to write all the data or throw an exception. There were no valid conditions under which it would write only *part* of the data and return. This is not the case with the new `write()` method. It returns the number of bytes that were written.

And as with reading, if you write to a channel that is only open for reading, a `NonWritableChannelException` will be thrown.

1.1.5 *Reading and writing together*

The CopyFile program (see listing 1.1) illustrates the entire process of copying all the data from an input channel to an output channel.

Watch out for a couple of new methods—flip() and clear(). These methods are used any time a buffer is both written to and read from—which is almost all of the time. After reading from a channel into a buffer, you call buffer.flip() to prepare the buffer for being written to another channel. Likewise, once you've finished writing the contents of a buffer to one channel, you call buffer.clear() to prepare it for being read into again. More about this in section 1.2.4.

Make sure not to confuse reading from a buffer with reading from a channel: reading from a channel means reading data *from* the channel, and putting it *into* the buffer. Likewise, writing data to a channel means getting data *from* a buffer, and writing it *to* a channel. See section 1.2.2 for more details.

Listing 1.1   CopyFile.java

(see \Chapter1\CopyFile.java)

```java
import java.io.*;
import java.nio.*;
import java.nio.channels.*;

public class CopyFile
{
  static public void main( String args[] ) throws Exception {
    String infile = args[0], outfile = args[1];
    FileInputStream fin = new FileInputStream( infile );
    FileOutputStream fout = new FileOutputStream( outfile );

    FileChannel inc = fin.getChannel();
    FileChannel outc = fout.getChannel();

    ByteBuffer buffer = ByteBuffer.allocate( 1024 );

    while (true) {
      int ret = inc.read( buffer );
      if (ret==-1) // nothing left to read
        break;
      buffer.flip();
      outc.write( buffer );
      buffer.clear(); // Make room for the next read
    }
  }
}
```

A full understanding of this program—including an understanding of the `flip()` and `clear()` methods—requires that we learn more about buffers. The next section will describe how buffers work, and how they are used in practice.

1.2 Understanding buffers

Under the original I/O API, the `read()` and `write()` methods of the stream classes took primitive Java types—ints, floats, and so on, as well as arrays of ints, floats, and so on—as arguments. The management of these variables and buffers was up to the programmer.

In the New I/O API, these primitive types are never written directly to channels. Buffers are always used as the intermediaries. Buffers can also handle many of the tasks that used to have to be done by hand—keeping track of how much data has been read, making sure there's enough room in an array for the data to be read into, and so on. And buffers themselves have an I/O interface, because data must be put into and taken out of buffers.

This section will go over the details of how buffers store data and how they are used to transfer data to and from channels.

1.2.1 Creating buffers

As mentioned in section 1.1.2, buffers are never created using constructors. There are two ways of making a `ByteBuffer`: via the `allocate()` methods, and via the `wrap()` methods.

`allocate()` creates a fresh `ByteBuffer` and allocates the memory required to store the data. `allocateDirect()` does the same thing, but it attempts to allocate the required data area as direct memory. (See section 1.2.8 for more about direct buffers.)

The two `wrap()` methods create a new buffer by wrapping an existing array—or a portion of an existing array—in a `Buffer` object. Note that that this doesn't make a *copy* of the data—the data in the buffer and the data in the array are the *same data*. Any modifications to the buffer will show up in the array, and vice versa.

1.2.2 get() and put()

Generally, buffers are used to transfer data from one channel to another. The `read()` method of one channel puts data into a buffer, and the `write()` method of the other channel takes the data out of the buffer. However, buffers also have methods that can be used to fill and drain them "by hand." These are used when you want to put particular pieces of data into a buffer, or to extract the data and use it for something. These methods are called `get()` and `put()`.

It can be confusing to consider the buffer get() and put() methods along with the channel read() and write() methods, because they are backwards: when data is *read from* a channel, it is *written to* a buffer. Likewise, when data is *written to* a channel, it is *read from* a buffer. You read from a buffer using the buffer's get() methods, and you write to a buffer using the buffer's put() methods.

There are two kinds of get() and put() methods: *relative* and *absolute*. Absolute methods take an index parameter, which lets you choose the position in the underlying array at which you want to read or write. In contrast, relative methods do not need an index parameter—they use the next value or values in the array after the last one that was used. Relative methods are more commonly used, since they can be used to fill or drain a buffer sequentially.

There are five basic put() methods. The methods listed here are for ByteBuffer, but each of the Buffer classes has these methods. Of course, the arguments to the corresponding methods of DoubleBuffer are double-based, rather than byte-based, but otherwise they are the same.

- put(byte b)—Put a byte into this buffer
- put(byte src[])—Put the bytes from an array into this buffer
- put(byte src[], int offset, int length)—Put a portion of the bytes from an array into this buffer
- put(ByteBuffer src)—Copy the contents of another buffer into this buffer
- put(int index, byte b)—Put a byte at array offset index (starting from zero)

Of these five methods, the first four are relative, and the last one is absolute.

There are four get() methods:

- get()—Get a single byte from this buffer
- get(byte array[])—Fill an array of bytes with bytes from this buffer
- get(byte array[], int offset, int length)—Fill a portion of an array of bytes with bytes from this buffer
- get(int index)—Get the byte at array offset index (starting from zero)

Of these four methods, the first three are relative, and the last one is absolute. Note that there is no get(ByteBuffer) method. You can accomplish the same thing with put(ByteBuffer).

In addition to these methods, ByteBuffer also contains a set of methods for reading and writing other primitive Java types. In each case, a call to one of these methods can be considered equivalent to calling the single-byte get() and put()

methods one or more times, with the bytes involved making up the value of the primitive type. More on this in section 1.2.7.

1.2.3 *Buffer state values*

In the previous sections, we saw how to read from and write to a buffer, but we never really found out what was going on inside the buffer. If you'll recall, the inner loop of the CopyFile program listed in section 1.1.5 was, schematically, something like this:

```
inc.read( buffer );
buffer.flip();
outc.write( buffer );
buffer.clear();
```

What's noteworthy about this is that our code doesn't seem to have to keep track of how many bytes were read and written each time. This is something the buffer does for us automatically.

Buffers take care of such things using a number of *buffer state values*. These are values that reflect the current state of the buffer as it is used for various reading and writing tasks. They keep track of how many bytes have been read or written, how many more can be read, how much room there is to read more, and so on. These are summarized in table 1.1 and are explained in further detail in the following sections.

Table 1.1   The state of each buffer is represented by three values. These values change as the buffer is read from, or written to, indicating progress through the buffer. In this way, a buffer keeps track of the reading or writing process.

State value name	What it is
position	The index into the underlying array of the next read (or write)
limit	The index into the underlying array of the first element that should not be read (or written)
capacity	The size of the underlying array

Buffer position

The buffer position specifies the next entry in the array that will be used for reading or writing:

- If the buffer is being written to (which means that it is being used for a channel read), the buffer position points to the location where the next byte will be stored.

- If the buffer is being read from (which means that it is being used for a channel write), the buffer position points to the next byte to be read.

In both cases, each time a byte is read or written, the value of the buffer position increases by the length of the item written. The position cannot become greater than the value of the buffer limit. If the code tries to execute a read or write that would make the position greater than the limit, a `java.nio.BufferUnderflowException` or `java.nio.BufferOverflowException`, respectively, is thrown.

Buffer limit

The buffer limit is the amount of data in the array. It defines the first array slot that should *not* be used for reading and writing. It is different from the capacity: the capacity of an array specifies how much data *could* be put in it—that is, how much could potentially fit. The limit specifies how much has actually been put in the array.

If the buffer is being written to, the limit specifies the array element after the last array element that can accept a value. In this case, the limit is generally set to be equal to the capacity of the buffer, so that the entirety of the underlying array will be used.

If the buffer is being read from, the limit specifies the array element after the last array element that can be read. The buffer limit might be equal to the buffer capacity, which means that the buffer was filled with data before reading started. The buffer limit might also be less than the capacity, which means the buffer was only partially filled when reading started.

Buffer capacity

The buffer capacity is equal to the size of the underlying array. Even if the array is only partially filled with data, the capacity refers to the *entire array*, including both the used and unused portions. The capacity of a buffer never changes.

NOTE   Each buffer has a method called `remaining()`, which returns the number of slots left that can be read or written. This value is equal to `limit()` `- position()`.

1.2.4 *flip() and clear()*

Buffers are commonly used to read data from one channel and then to write that same data out to another channel. In this case, the buffer alternates between being written to and being read from. The `flip()` and `clear()` methods are called between these reads and writes, in order to prepare the buffer for each new phase in the process. The following sequence describes the process in detail.

At the beginning, the buffer is brand new. Its limit is set to its capacity, and its position is set to 0 (as shown in figure 1.1).

In figure 1.1, the underlying array has a length of 8. The position is set to 0, while the limit and capacity values are set to 8. The limit *looks* like it is too large, since, technically, it points past the end of the usable area of the array. But if you'll recall, the definition of the limit is that it is the first slot that *shouldn't* be written to.

The read() method of the source channel is then called, and it places some data in the buffer. This data may or may not fill the buffer. The limit is still set to the capacity, while the position has advanced (see figure 1.2).

Some more data is read from the channel and placed into the buffer. The buffer position advances further (see figure 1.3).

The writing phase is now over. buffer.flip() is called to prepare the buffer to have its data read (see

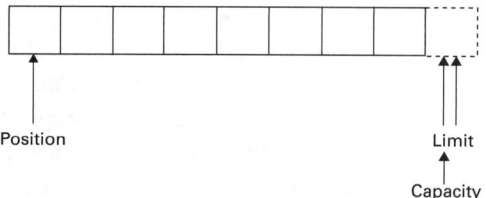

Figure 1.1   When the buffer is initialized, its position is set to 0, and its limit and capacity are set to the length of the array.

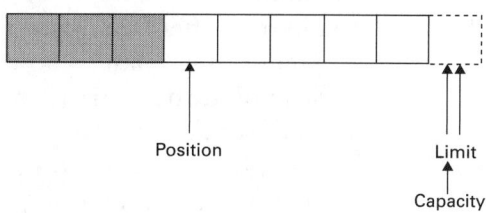

Figure 1.2   After writing some data, the position has advanced, while the limit and capacity are unchanged.

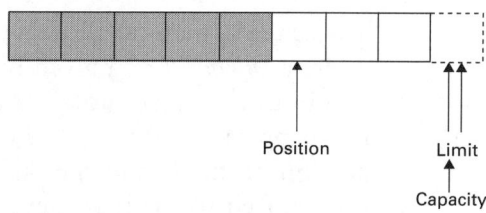

Figure 1.3   After writing more data, the position has advanced further.

figure 1.4). (You can think of the flip() method as flipping a switch between reading and writing modes. Buffers don't actually have reading and writing modes—you can mix read() and write() calls freely. However, it is very common to use a buffer in the way we are using it here—you do some reading, flip the buffer, and do some writing.)

In order to prepare for reading, the value of limit must be changed. Before the call to flip(), the buffer was being used as an empty area into which data could be put; the limit value specified the end of this empty area. Now that flip() has been called, the buffer is being used as a source of data, and the limit value now specifies the end of this valid data. This limit value is equal to the value that position had before `flip()` was called.

Next, the buffer is passed to the `write()` method of the destination channel, which in turn reads some data from the buffer (see figure 1.5).

The reading process continues until the position reaches the limit, at which point there is no more data in the buffer (see figure 1.6).

The reading phase is now over. At this point, the `clear()` method is called (see figure 1.7).

The position is set to 0, while the limit is set to the capacity, leaving as large a space as possible for use in the next writing phase.

1.2.5 *slice() and subbuffers*

The `slice()` method allows you to create a *subbuffer* of a given buffer. A subbuffer is just another buffer that happens to share its data with a portion of the data in the buffer it was created from. It is, nevertheless, a separate buffer with its own position, limit, and capacity. The subbuffer does not have to start at the first element of the original buffer.

When `slice()` is called, it takes the current position and limit values and uses them to define the new subbuffer. The capacity and limit of the subbuffer are set to be the limit of the original buffer, and the first element of the subbuffer

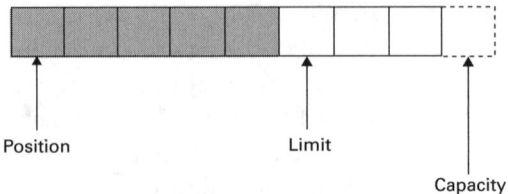

Figure 1.4   After calling `flip()`, the limit is set to the old value of position, and the position is set to 0.

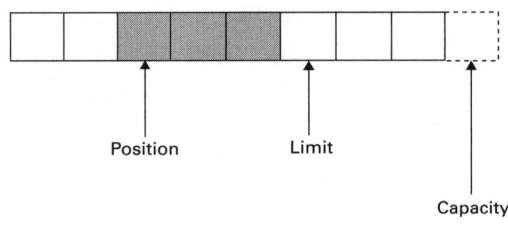

Figure 1.5   The reading process begins—as bytes are read, the position advances.

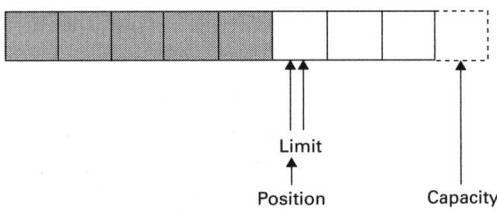

Figure 1.6   All of the data has been read, making position=limit.

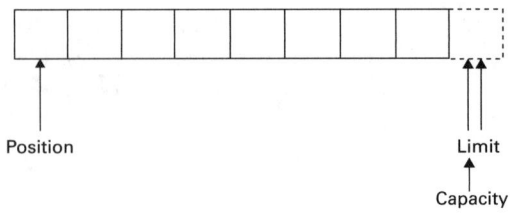

Figure 1.7   After `clear()` is called, position is set to 0 and limit is set to capacity.

corresponds to the element at value *position* within the original buffer (see figure 1.8).

In figure 1.8, the subbuffer corresponds to the second through fifth elements of the original buffer, inclusive. This corresponds to the following code:

```
ByteBuffer original = ByteBuffer.allocate( 8 );
original.position( 2 );
original.limit( 6 );
ByteBuffer slice = original.slice();
```

The individual data elements pointed to by the two buffers are in fact the same data. Thus, any change to the shared data in one buffer will be immediately reflected in the other.

1.2.6 *Buffers of other types*

ByteBuffers are the most basic form of buffer, and it is used throughout the New I/O API. However, it is possible to have buffers of other types. In fact, there is a type of buffer for each primitive Java type. Each of these types is a subclass of Buffer.

A buffer of a non-byte type stores values of that type, the way that a ByteBuffer stores bytes. Each buffer type has five put() methods and four get() methods, just like a ByteBuffer (see section 1.2.2), except that these methods work with their particular type rather than on bytes.

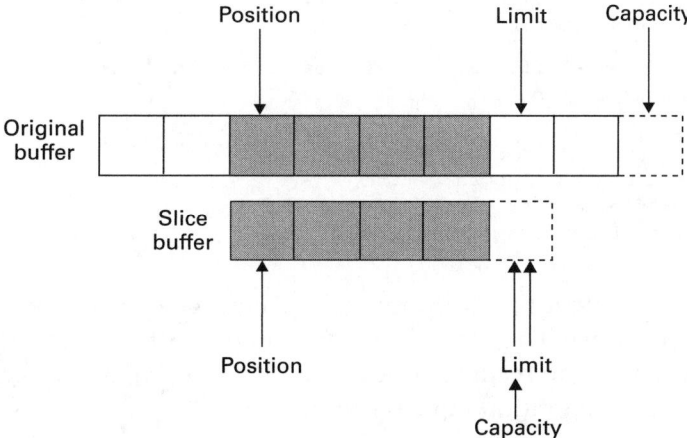

Figure 1.8   A slice buffer shares a subsequence of the original buffer. It has its own position, limit, and capacity values and does not have to start at the same position as the original buffer.

Underlying each typed buffer is a `ByteBuffer` that contains the raw bytes from which the values are built. The float values and the byte values are merely different views onto the same stream of bytes, as shown in figure 1.9.

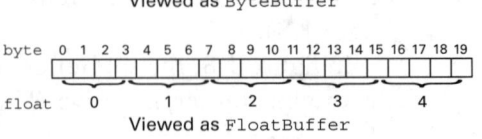

Figure 1.9 The same underlying data can be viewed as a `ByteBuffer` and as a `FloatBuffer`.

Creating a typed buffer is easy. For example, to create a `FloatBuffer`, you call the `asFloatBuffer()` method of `ByteBuffer`:

```
ByteBuffer buffer = ByteBuffer.allocate( size );
FloatBuffer floatBuffer = buffer.asFloatBuffer();
```

Since you have access to both `buffer` and `floatBuffer`, you can access this data as bytes or as floats. Note that you have *two* buffers here, each with its own position, limit, and capacity values.

Suppose, for example, you wanted to read a series of floating-point values from a channel: you could read from the channel into the `ByteBuffer`, and then read the floats from the `FloatBuffer`. Since these two buffers point to the same data, the floating-point values in the `FloatBuffer` are made up of the bytes in the `ByteBuffer`.

```
float floatArray[] = new float[floatArraySize];

FileInputStream fin = new FileInputStream( file );
FileChannel fch = fin.getChannel();

ByteBuffer buffer = ByteBuffer.allocate( floatArray.length*4 );
FloatBuffer floatBuffer = buffer.asFloatBuffer();

fch.read( buffer );

for (int i=0; i<floatArray.length; ++i) {
  floatArray[i] = floatBuffer.get();
  System.out.print( floatArray[i]+" " );
}
```

It's important to remember that the position and limit values of the two buffers are *independent* of each other. This means, for example, that although the `FloatBuffer` might be exhausted by the reading process, the `ByteBuffer` is still ready to read from the beginning—its position value is still 0.

1.2.7 *Reading and writing other types from a ByteBuffer*

There is another way to read floating-point values from a stream of bytes. `Byte-Buffer` has a number of convenience methods that allow you to read values of other types—floats, shorts, and so on—directly from a ByteBuffer. This is particularly useful if you want to read a set of mixed-type values from a buffer.

Figure 1.10 illustrates a series of mixed-type values packed into a single ByteBuffer.

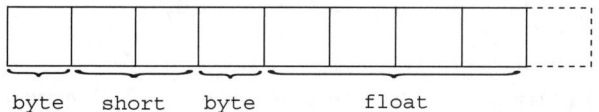

byte   short   byte   float

Figure 1.10   A series of mixed-type values packed into a single `ByteBuffer`

The code that reads this series of values is as follows:

```
FileInputStream fin = new FileInputStream( filename );
FileChannel fch = fin.getChannel();
ByteBuffer bb = ByteBuffer.allocate( 32 );
fch.read( bb );
bb.flip();
byte b0 = bb.get();
short s0 = bb.getShort();
byte b1 = bb.get();
float f0 = bb.getFloat();
```

The choice of whether to use typed buffers, such as FloatBuffer, or the typed accessor methods, such as ByteBuffer.getFloat() and ByteBuffer.putFloat(), depends on the homogeneity of the data involved. A FloatBuffer consists entirely of floats, and so is good for reading banks of uninterrupted floating-point data. A ByteBuffer, on the other hand, might be ideal for reading file headers that contain data of different types.

WARNING   The default byte order of a ByteBuffer is big-endian*, but this can be changed using the ByteBuffer's order(ByteOrder) method. The order() method can be used to find out the ByteBuffer's current byte order. You can find out the platform's native byte order with the ByteOrder.nativeOrder() static method.

---

*The terms *big-endian* and *little-endian*, borrowed from Jonathan Swift, refer to two different methods for ordering bytes within a multi-byte value. The big-endian methods puts the most significant byte first and the least significant byte last; thus, the 32-bit hexadecimal value AABBCCDD is stored with the AA byte first and the DD byte last. In contrast, the little-endian method would store the DD byte first and the AA byte last.

1.2.8 *Direct buffers*

Direct buffers are buffers whose underlying data arrays are allocated in such a way that I/O operations can be performed considerably faster. Typically, data that crosses the boundary between the Java Virtual Machine (JVM) and the underlying operating system has to be copied to or from a Java array to an array within the JVM before it can be passed to the operating system (see figure 1.11).

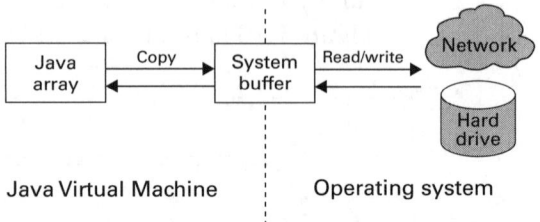

Figure 1.11   When writing from an array or nondirect `Buffer`, data must be copied to an intermediate buffer before it can be written to disk. Depending on the operation, even more copying steps may be required.

Direct buffers, however, allocate their data directly in the runtime environment memory (see figure 1.12).

Although the actual implementation of direct buffers differs from platform to platform, it is expected that any reasonable implementation will take pains to reduce copying of data in direct buffers. These buffers should reside as close to the operating

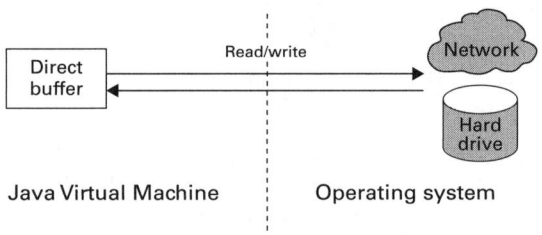

Figure 1.12   Direct buffers use system buffers for their underlying storage. In some operating systems, this means that no copying is necessary for reading and writing data—the data is transferred directly to and from the disk.

system as possible, to reduce the number of copying steps as much as possible.

You might be tempted to allocate all buffers as direct buffers, but this would be a bad idea. Direct buffers should only be used for buffers that will actually benefit from the speed increase. Direct buffers generally cost more to allocate, and may require more system resources during their lifetimes. Again, this depends on the implementation.

NOTE   Direct buffers do not contain *faster memory*. They simply contain memory that can be accessed directly by the runtime system and/or the underlying operating system, so that data that is passed in and out of the JVM will not have to be copied, thus saving time.

Allocating a direct buffer is trivial. Instead of calling

```
ByteBuffer buffer = ByteBuffer.allocate( 1024 );
```

you call

```
ByteBuffer buffer = ByteBuffer.allocateDirect( 1024 );
```

This is the only way you can create a direct buffer. Note that you clearly can't use the wrap() methods, because they explicitly construct a buffer using an array that is within the JVM—a Java array. Similarly, the array() method, which returns the underlying Java array of a Buffer, if any, will not work for a direct buffer, since there is no underlying Java array.

To demonstrate the speed advantage of direct buffers, let's try modifying the CopyFile program from section 1.1.5 (listing 1.1) to use a direct buffer instead of a regular buffer. The modification is shown in listing 1.2.

Listing 1.2   from FastCopyFile.java

(see \Chapter1\FastCopyFile.java)
```
FileChannel inc = fin.getChannel();
FileChannel outc = fout.getChannel();

ByteBuffer buffer = ByteBuffer.allocateDirect( 1024 );

while (true) {
  int ret = inc.read( buffer );
  if (ret==-1)
    break;
  buffer.flip();
  outc.write( buffer );
  buffer.clear();
}
```

On the system used to test the code, copying a 16-MB file with CopyFile took nine seconds, while copying it with FastCopyFile took about 4.5 seconds—a 50% savings!

1.2.9 *Example: TCP/IP forwarding*

Let's take a look at buffers in action in a program that does TCP/IP forwarding. This is a perfect application for buffers, because it's mostly about transferring data, rather than processing it.

TCP/IP forwarding

Forwarder is a simple TCP/IP forwarding program. It forwards
TCP/IP connections coming into
the forwarding machine to any of a
number of destination machines.
Data that is sent from the source
machine to the forwarding
machine is *forwarded* to the desti-

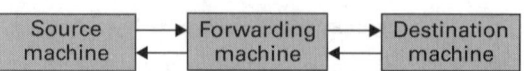

**Figure 1.13   Packages from the source machine are
forwarded to the destination machine by the forwarding
machine. Response data from the destination machine
is likewise forwarded, sent back to the source
machine.**

nation machine. Response data from the destination machine is sent back to the
corresponding source machine (see figure 1.13).

The idea here is to simulate a connection that does direction from the source
machine to the destination machine. The forwarding machine acts as an intermedi-
ary. It forwards the data between
the machines and tries not to interfere otherwise, much as an Internet router does (see figure 1.14).

It's important to understand
that this is a TCP/IP forwarder, not
an IP forwarder. That is, the forwarding is happening at the level

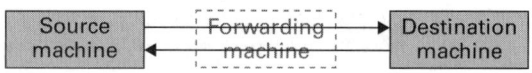

**Figure 1.14   The forwarding machine seeks to
simulate a *direct connection* between the source and
destination machines. It forwards the data but does
not modify it in any way.**

of TCP virtual circuits, rather than at the IP packet level. This means that the forwarder cannot act as *transparently* as an Internet router. For example, data arriving
at the destination machine is marked as having come from the forwarding machine,
not from the source machine. Some connections will have a problem with being
forwarded in this way, but many will work fine.

One use for a program like this is as a simple *firewall*. The forwarding machine is
set up as the only machine that is accessible from the Internet. A set of other
machines are connected to the firewall; these are said to be "behind" the firewall
because external machines can only reach them by crossing through the forwarder
firewall (see figure 1.15). The forwarder can completely control which connections
will be accepted and which destination machines they will be forwarded to.

Configuring the forwarder

A *configuration file* is used to define what ports will accept connections, what destination machines they will be forwarded to, and which source machines they will be
accepted from. The configuration file looks like this:

```
100    panix.com              80
110    panix.com              23
5555   www.w3c.org            80
```

The configuration file is defined more completely in the notes following listing 1.3.

To use this program, you must specify the name of the configuration file on the command line, as follows:

```
java Forwarder forwarder.cfg
```

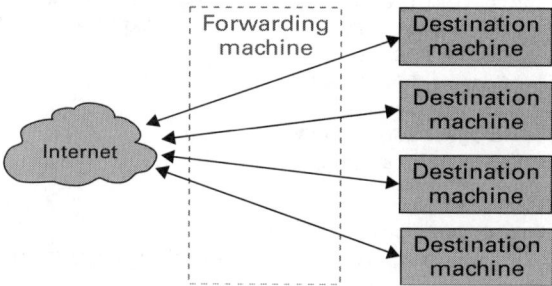

Figure 1.15   The forwarder can be used as a firewall, protecting machines hidden behind the forwarding machine from direct Internet access. Connections to the destination machines must be explicitly allowed by the forwarder.

Source code

Let's take a look at the source in listing 1.3.

Listing 1.3   Forwarder.java

(See \Chapter1\Forwarder.java)

```java
import java.io.*;
import java.net.*;
import java.nio.*;
import java.nio.channels.*;
import java.util.*;
import java.util.regex.*;

public class Forwarder
{
  static private final int bufferSize = 0x4000; //BUFFER_SIZE

  // Defines the format of the config file lines
  private static final int LOCAL_PORT_POS = 0;
  private static final int HOSTNAME_POS = 1;
  private static final int PORT_POS = 2;
  private static final int SOURCES_POS = 3;
```

```
public Forwarder() {
}
public void readConfig( String configFilename )        ❶ Parse the
    throws IOException {                                    configuration file
  FileReader fr = new FileReader( configFilename );
  LineNumberReader lnr = new LineNumberReader( fr );
  while (true) {
    String line = lnr.readLine();
    if (line==null)
      break;
    Pattern pattern = Pattern.compile( "\\s+" );       ❷ Use regular
    String strings[] = pattern.split( line );              expressions to parse
    if (strings.length < SOURCES_POS) {
      System.err.println( "Config file syntax error at "+
                          configFilename+":"+
                          lnr.getLineNumber() );
      System.exit( 1 );  // Any syntax error and we quit
    }

    // First, the local forwarding port
    int forwardingPort = Integer.parseInt( strings[LOCAL_PORT_POS] );

    // Then the destination address
    InetAddress destAddress =
      InetAddress.getByName( strings[HOSTNAME_POS] );

    // Then the destination port
    int destPort = Integer.parseInt( strings[PORT_POS] );

    // Finally, zero or more permitted sources
    InetAddress sources[] = new InetAddress[strings.length-SOURCES_POS];
    for (int i=SOURCES_POS; i<strings.length; ++i) {
      sources[i-SOURCES_POS] = InetAddress.getByName( strings[i] );
    }
    AddressSet allowedSources = new AddressSet( sources );

    addForward( forwardingPort, destAddress,           ❸ Add a forward for
                destPort, allowedSources );                each config line
  }
}
public void addForward( int forwardingPort,            ❹ Set up a forward
                        InetAddress destAddress,
                        int destPort,
                        AddressSet allowedSources ) {
  InetSocketAddress destSocketAddress =
    new InetSocketAddress( destAddress, destPort );
  ForwarderListenerThread flt =
    new ForwarderListenerThread( forwardingPort,
                                 destSocketAddress,
                                 allowedSources );
```

```
      flt.start();
}

class ForwarderListenerThread extends Thread
{
    private int forwardingPort;
    private SocketAddress destAddress;
    private AddressSet allowedSources;
    private HashSet forwardsConnections = new HashSet();

    // Used to prevent shutdown while listening is
    // in progress.
    private Object connectionsLock = new Object();

    // Have we already shut down?
    private boolean shutdown = false;
    private ServerSocketChannel ssc;

    public ForwarderListenerThread( int forwardingPort,
                                    SocketAddress destAddress,
                                    AddressSet allowedSources ) {
        this.forwardingPort = forwardingPort;
        this.destAddress = destAddress;
        this.allowedSources = allowedSources;
    }

    public void run() {
        try {
            ssc = ServerSocketChannel.open();
            ssc.configureBlocking( true );
            ServerSocket ss = ssc.socket();
            byte anyIP[] = { 0, 0, 0, 0 };
            InetAddress forwardingHost =
                InetAddress.getByAddress( anyIP );
            InetSocketAddress isa =
                new InetSocketAddress( forwardingHost, forwardingPort );
            ss.bind( isa );
            synchronized( connectionsLock ) {
                System.out.println( "Listening on "+isa );
                while (true) {
                    SocketChannel source = ssc.accept();
                    InetAddress connectingAddress =
                        source.socket().getInetAddress();
                    // Check to see if incoming connection is from
                    // an approved host
                    if (allowedSources.contains( connectingAddress )) {
                        SocketChannel dest = SocketChannel.open();
                        source.configureBlocking( true );
                        dest.configureBlocking( true );
                        dest.connect( destAddress );
                        ForwarderThread forwards =
                            new ForwarderThread( this, source, dest );
                        ForwarderThread backwards =
```

➎ Handle a forward

➏ Listen on the forwarding port

● Accept an incoming connection

➐ Set up forwarders for the new connection

```
            new ForwarderThread( this, dest, source );
          forwards.start();
          backwards.start();
          forwardsConnections.add( forwards );
        } else {
          System.out.println( "Connection from "+
                              connectingAddress+
                              " refused" );
          try {
            source.close();
          } catch( IOException ie ) {
            System.err.println( "Problem disconnecting "+
                                "rejected connection from "+
                                connectingAddress );
            ie.printStackTrace();
          }
        }
      }
    }
  } catch( AsynchronousCloseException ace ) {
    System.err.println( "Closed forward "+this );
    // We don't call shutdown here, because this
    // exception is triggered by the close() call
    // inside shutdown -- this exception is a *result*
    // of shutting down, not an instigation to do so.
  } catch( IOException ie ) {
    System.err.println( "Exception forwarding "+this+": "+ie );
    ie.printStackTrace();
    shutdown();
  }
}

synchronized public void shutdown() {
  if (shutdown)
    return;

  try {
    System.out.println( "Closing "+ssc );
    ssc.close();
  } catch( IOException ie ) {
    System.err.println( "Error closing "+ssc );
    ie.printStackTrace();
  }

  synchronized( connectionsLock ) {
    for (Iterator it = forwardsConnections.iterator();
         it.hasNext();) {
      ForwarderThread ft = (ForwarderThread)it.next();
      System.out.println( "Closing "+ft );
      ft.shutdown();
    }
  }
```

7 Set up forwarders for the new connection

● **Shut down this ForwarderListenerThread**

● **Close the ServerSocketChannel**

8 Close all Forwarder-Threads for this port

```
      shutdown = true;
  }

  public void remove( ForwarderThread ft ) {
    if (forwardsConnections.contains( ft ))
      forwardsConnections.remove( ft );
  }

  public String toString() {
    return forwardingPort+"-->"+destAddress;
  }
}

static class ForwarderThread extends Thread {
  private ForwarderListenerThread flt;
  private String description;
  private SocketChannel from;
  private SocketChannel to;
  private boolean shutdown = false;

  public ForwarderThread( ForwarderListenerThread flt,
                          SocketChannel from, SocketChannel to ) {
    this.flt = flt;
    this.from = from;
    this.to = to;

    Socket fromSocket = from.socket();
    Socket toSocket = to.socket();
    description =
      fromSocket.getInetAddress()+":"+fromSocket.getPort()+
      "-->"+
      toSocket.getInetAddress()+":"+toSocket.getPort();
  }

  public void run() {
    try {
      ByteBuffer buffer = ByteBuffer.allocateDirect( bufferSize );
      while (true) {
        from.read( buffer );
        if (buffer.position()==0) {
          System.out.println( "Closing on zero read: "+this );
          break;
        }
        System.out.println( this+" read "+buffer.position() );
        buffer.flip();
        while (buffer.remaining()>0) {
          int r = to.write( buffer );
          System.out.println( this+" wrote "+r+", remaining "+
                              buffer.remaining() );
        }
        buffer.clear();
      }
      shutdown();
```

❾ Remove a dead ForwarderThread

❿ Handle a forwarded connection

⓫ Copy bytes from one end of the connection to the other

```
      } catch( AsynchronousCloseException ace ) {
        System.err.println( "Closed forward "+this+": "+ace );
        shutdown();
      } catch( IOException ie ) {
        System.err.println( "Exception forwarding "+this+": "+ie );
        ie.printStackTrace();
        shutdown();
      }
    }
    public void shutdown() {          ⬤  Shut down this
      if (shutdown)                        ForwarderThread
        return;

      try {
        from.close();                      ⑫  Close both ends of the forward
      } catch( IOException ie ) {
        System.err.println( "Error closing from of "+this );
        ie.printStackTrace();
      }

      try {
        to.close();                        ⑫  Close both ends of the forward
      } catch( IOException ie ) {
        System.err.println( "Error closing to of "+this );
        ie.printStackTrace();
      }

      shutdown = true;
      flt.remove( this );                  ⬤  Remove this Forwarder-
      System.err.println( "Closed forward "+this );   Thread from the parent
    }                                          ForwarderListening-
    public String toString() {                 Thread
      return description;
    }
  }
  static class AddressSet {                ⑬  Represent a set of hosts
    private Set addresses = new HashSet();

    public AddressSet( InetAddress ias[] ) {
      for (int i=0; i<ias.length; ++i) {
        System.out.println( "as "+ias[i] );
        addresses.add( ias[i] );
      }
      System.out.println( "address set size "+addresses.size() );
    }

    public boolean contains( InetAddress ia ) {
      if (addresses.size()==0)
        return true;
      return addresses.contains( ia );
    }
```

```
    }
    static public void main( String args[] ) throws IOException {
      String configFilename = args[0];

      Forwarder forwarder = new Forwarder();
      forwarder.readConfig( configFilename );
    }
}
```

❶ The configuration file specifies each local port that will be forwarded. For each local port, it defines the remote hostname and port that the local port will be forwarded to.

❷ Here, we use the regular expression facility in the `java.util.regex` package. The `Pattern` object represents a string pattern to look for—in this case, we are looking for any white space. The `split()` method searches the string for every occurrence of the pattern and divides the string in those locations, producing a set of smaller strings. The white space is not included in the smaller strings.

❸ A forward is created for each line in the configuration file. As an example, the following line forwards port 5555 on the local machine to the web server at www.w3c.org:

```
    5555    www.w3c.org             80
```

This results in the configuration shown in figure 1.16.

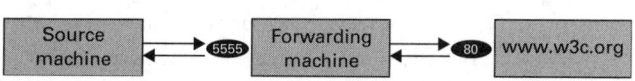

Optionally, you can specify a list of hosts at the end of the line. Only

Figure 1.16 The forwarder is configured to forward traffic on local port 5555 to port 80 at remote machine, www.w3c.org.

hosts from this list can connect to the forwarding port; all others will be rejected:

```
    5555    www.w3c.org             80    192.168.0.1 127.0.0.1
```

Here, `192.168.0.1` is an address on our local network; `127.0.0.1` is the loopback address, referring to the same machine on which the forwarder is running. If you do not specify any hosts at the end of the line, all hosts will be accepted.

❹ `addForward()` sets up a forward from a local port to a remote host and port. A `ForwardListenerThread` is created for each forward; this thread runs in the background, listening on the specified local port for an incoming connection. If this incoming connection is allowed, a pair of `ForwarderThreads` will be created to handle the connection.

❺ A `ForwarderListenerThread` handles a single forwarded port. Each port that is forwarded by the forwarder has its own `ForwarderListenerThread`. This object is responsible for listening on the local port and accepting incoming connections to that port. Each time a connection comes in, the `ForwarderListenerThread` creates a pair of `ForwarderThreads` to handle the connection—one for each direction of the communication. When a `ForwarderListenerThread` is shut down, it shuts down all the `ForwarderThreads` that it has created.

❻ The `ForwarderListenerThread` listens on the address `0.0.0.0`, which is the any address. This means that an incoming source connection can be made against any IP address assigned to this machine.

❼ Each connection is handled by a pair of `ForwarderThread` objects—one for the forward direction and one for the backward direction. The forward direction goes from the source machine to the destination machine, while the backward direction goes from the destination machine to the source machine.

❽ This method can be called either by this class or by another class. Shutting down a `ForwarderListenerThread` means closing the socket used for accepting new connections, but it also means removing all existing connections that are currently being forwarded through this port.

❾ Calling this method removes the `ForwarderThread` from the set of currently open threads. This method is called by a `ForwarderThread` when it terminates on its own. This happens when either the source or destination hosts close the connection. Generally, both `ForwarderThreads` in a pair are shut down at the same time.

❿ Each forwarded connection is handled by a pair of `ForwarderThreads`, one for each direction of the forwarded connection.

⓫ Inside the `ForwarderThread`, data is copied from one end of the forwarded connection to the other using a `ByteBuffer`. In each step, `from.read()` is called to read as much data as possible into the `ByteBuffer`. This amount is limited by the amount of available data and by the size of the `ByteBuffer`. The `ByteBuffer` is passed to `to.write()`, which writes all of the data to the outgoing connection, either in one step or in a series of steps inside the `while()` loop. (Multiple steps might be required since this is a network connection, and limits on the size of network buffers can cause a partial write. In contrast, our CopyFile program in section 1.1.5 (listing 1.1) can safely assume that every write will block until all the data is written, or an exception will be thrown.) Note that `flip()` is used after the `read()`, and `clear()` is used after the `write()`, as described previously in section 1.2.4.

The advantage of using a `ByteBuffer` over a simple byte array is that a `ByteBuffer` keeps track of how much has been read or written during each phase of the transfer. It respects the capacities of the underlying arrays, taking care never to try to read more than can fit, or to write more than there is to write. In short, it takes care of the housekeeping that we normally have to take care of ourselves, and since the `Buffer` code has been extensively tested, it's more likely to work the first time.

⑫ `shutdown()` handles shutting down a `ForwarderThread`. Both the from and to `SocketChannels` are closed, for good measure. Generally, when one of a pair of `ForwarderThreads` is shut down, the other shuts down automatically, as well, because the `SocketChannels` have both had their `close()` methods called.

⑬ An `AddressSet` represents a set of hosts. In this program, it is used to specify the set of hosts from which a source connection will be accepted. An empty `AddressSet` accepts all hosts.

1.2.10 *Doing I/O with channels and buffers*

The channel-and-buffer approach to doing I/O is different than the stream-oriented approach that has been the mainstay of Java programming since the beginning of Java.

The stream-oriented approach provides flexibility and convenience. All streams have, more or less, the same interface. Creating a subclass of an `InputStream` or `OutputStream` can be as simple as overriding a single method—`read()` or `write()`, respectively. Filters allow for arbitrary transformations on the data passing through a stream without complicating the situation for the source of the data, or for its destination. Streams count on the fact that all data is, at the lowest level, built from chains of bytes.

The channel-and-buffer approach has a different focus. Channels and buffers deal in *bulk data*. Here, *bulk* means that the data is dealt with in large pieces, and *data*, as opposed to actual Java *bytes*, means that the low-level data isn't manifest. This approach encourages the use of behind-the-scenes trickery to greatly speed up data transfers. And that's really the whole point of the bulk data approach. In particular, raw data does not have to be stored in actual Java `byte` arrays; it can be stored in low-level memory buffers. Here, low-level can simply mean that the buffers are allocated from the user-space heap within the JVM process, or, in some cases, the buffers can be system-level buffers that are shared between kernel and user processes using memory-paging techniques. In any case, allowing the implementation to use special buffering methods allows for optimizations that would not be possible if the data was stored in regular Java arrays.

However, this bulk data approach also means that the data must truly be hidden behind a complete abstraction barrier. Since every implementation can implement the buffers differently, the data cannot be *manifest*—it cannot be accessible directly as data. It can only be accessed through methods—`get()` and `put()`—which transfer data between the hidden behind-the-scenes implementation and a manifest Java variable or array. (It's true that non-direct buffers can reveal their underlying Java arrays via the array() method, but since this method is only available for non-direct buffers, it should be considered as something of an optional feature, at least as far as the core metaphor is concerned.)

Thus, the channel-and-buffer abstraction represents a *broadening* of the hidden portion of the I/O process. More computation is put behind the abstraction barrier so that more of it can be optimized on a per-platform basis. This means, potentially, more work for the implementers, but the payoff is clear: Java programmers now have access to an I/O system that can provide as much throughput as the underlying operating system and JVM will allow; at the same time, the system has a safe and complete abstraction barrier—any code written against the NIO library is going to be portable, at least to the extent that underlying implementations are correct. Custom JVMs, built to take advantage of special operating system features—or even hardware features—are conceivable; the most demanding I/O systems can now conceivably be written in Java, given the right system support.

Of course, the NIO libraries are compatible with the old I/O libraries. In fact, they are more than compatible—the old libraries have been re-engineered to use the NIO abstractions in places where this is appropriate. Let's face it—channels and buffers are cool, but they don't have the same brilliant elegance as the stream metaphor. However, you can freely mix stream-oriented and buffer-oriented I/O in the same program.

As we continue through this chapter (and the next), keep in mind that many of these I/O innovations are intended to integrate the Java I/O systems more fully with common operating system features. Next, we'll take a look at file locking.

1.3 *The File Locking facility*

File locking makes it possible to lock entire files, or regions of files, in order to prevent other threads or processes from accessing those files. If the underlying operating system has native file-locking capabilities, then the Java implementation will use them. As a result, the behavior of the File Locking facility is platform-dependent. However, it is possible to use the facility in such a way that the behavior will be the same on all platforms.

1.3.1 *Types of locks*

It's important to understand that file locking doesn't necessarily prevent the file—or the portion thereof—from being accessed. A lock that does so is called a *mandatory* lock. There are also *advisory* locks, which do *not* prevent the region from being accessed. Instead, advisory locks prevent other locks from being acquired on the same region. These terms are not Java-specific.

It might seem that only mandatory locks would be useful, but in fact advisory locks serve nearly the same purpose. If all programs that access a particular file agree to acquire a lock on a region of a file before changing it, then advisory locks are enough, because only one such lock can be had at a given time. Using this kind of lock is rather like using the synchronized keyword in Java: synchronizing on an object means acquiring an advisory lock on that object. Such a lock doesn't prevent other threads from modifying the fields of the object; it only prevents other threads from acquiring locks. (This is the definition of *advisory lock.*)

The File Locking facility also supports two varieties of lock called *exclusive* and *shared.* Exclusive locks are like the locks provided by the synchronized keyword: they prevent other threads from acquiring a similar lock. Shared locks, on the other hand, do not. Multiple shared locks can be acquired at the same time, but they prevent exclusive locks from being acquired.

TIP   It is a common practice to use shared locks for reading from a file region, because multiple threads can safely read the same region without interfering with each other. Likewise, it is common practice to use exclusive locks for writing to a file region, because multiple threads *cannot* safely write to the same region without interfering with each other.

The fact that shared locks prevent the acquisition of exclusive locks fits in with this: while threads are reading from a region, no other threads can write to it.

The exclusive versus shared distinction is completely separate from the mandatory versus advisory distinction—they are orthogonal distinctions. Thus, a mandatory lock can be exclusive or shared, and so can an advisory lock.

1.3.2 *Using locks*

File locks cover a contiguous region of a file. This region can be the entire file, as shown in figure 1.17.

Or it can be a portion of a file, as shown in figure 1.18.

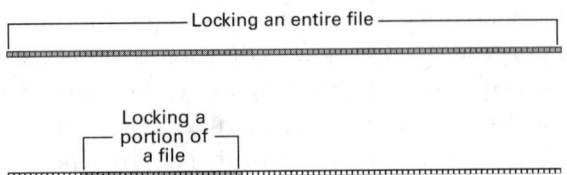

Figure 1.17   A lock can be acquired over the entire region of a file.

Figure 1.18   A lock can be acquired over a portion of a file. This portion must be contiguous.

It's possible for multiple regions of a file to be locked. If they are exclusive locks, they must not overlap; attempting to create overlapping exclusive locks within the same JVM will throw an `OverlappingFileLockException` (see figure 1.19).

Shared locks can overlap with other shared locks, but not with exclusive locks. Attempting to create an exclusive lock and a shared lock that overlap throws an `OverlappingFileLockException` (see figure 1.20).

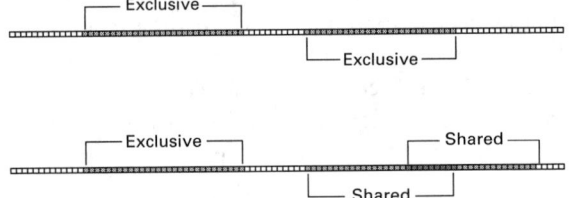

Figure 1.19   Multiple exclusive locks can be acquired within the same file, but they must not overlap.

Figure 1.20   Shared locks can overlap with other shared locks, but they cannot overlap with exclusive locks.

Some operating systems do not support shared locks. In such cases, it is not an error to request a shared lock, but the lock that is returned will be an exclusive lock. The type of a lock can be determined using its `isShared()` method.

1.3.3 *Acquiring locks*

To create a lock, you need a `FileChannel` object. Once you have one, there are two ways to acquire a lock: the `lock()` methods will block until the lock is acquired, and the `tryLock()` methods will return `null` if the lock cannot immediately be acquired. Otherwise, the `lock()` and `tryLock()` methods are identical. For simplicity, only the `lock()` methods will be discussed.

The `lock()` method takes three arguments: a starting position (measured in bytes from the start of the file), a length (measured in bytes), and a `boolean` telling whether the lock should be shared (`true`) or exclusive (`false`):

```
FileOutputStream fout = new FileOutputStream( "abc.txt" );
FileChannel fc = fout.getChannel();
FileLock fl = fc.lock( 20, 20, false );
```

There is also an argument-free convenience method that locks an entire file. The following two code fragments are equivalent:

```
FileOutputStream fout = new FileOutputStream( "abc.txt" );
FileChannel fc = fout.getChannel();
FileLock fl = fc.lock();

FileOutputStream fout = new FileOutputStream( "abc.txt" );
FileChannel fc = fout.getChannel();
FileLock fl = fc.lock( 0L, Long.MAX_VALUE, false );
```

Locks can be released in two ways: via the `release()` method, or by closing the `FileChannel` associated with the file. Once a lock is released, exclusive locks that overlap the region can be safely acquired.

1.3.4 *Portability issues*

Locks created in one process may or may not interfere with locks created in another process—this depends on the implementation and the nature of the locking facility of the underlying operating system. In some cases, two processes can lock the same region of the same file; in other cases, the thread attempting to acquire the second lock will block until the first lock is released. If the operating system does, in fact, support inter-process file locking, then locks created in a Java process can interact with locks created by a program in some other language; operating system–based locks are generally language-neutral.

Although there are a number of variables that depend heavily on the underlying implementation and on the underlying operating system, it is possible to use the File Locking facility in such a way that it is portable across all platforms. The following rules will ensure portability:

- Use only exclusive locks
- Treat all locks as *advisory*—assume that acquiring a lock on a region of a file does not prevent that region from being accessed in any way
- Assume locks only affect other threads within the same process

Although these restrictions prevent the use of many of the features of the File Locking API, they should be sufficient for many purposes. Locks used under this discipline are not unlike the locks used by the `synchronized` keyword—exclusive, advisory locks that only work inside a single Java process. Such locks have proven sufficient for most purposes and can be used to build more sophisticated locking mechanisms.

1.3.5 *Example: a simple database*

This section describes a program called SimpleDatabase. SimpleDatabase is a tiny API for storing fixed-length blocks of data, called *slots*, indexed by number in a flat file (see figure 1.21).

A SimpleDatabase has a get() method and a put() method, each one taking a slot number as an argument:

```
public void get( int slot, byte data[] )
public void put( int slot, byte data[] )
```

The idea is that multiple SimpleDatabase objects will be in use at the same time in separate JVMs. The only concurrency guarantee provided by SimpleDatabase is that each get() and put() operation be *atomic*. That is, each time a slot is written, it is written *completely* before any other thread or process can read or write it. It is possible that one thread or process will immediately overwrite the data that was just written by another thread or process, but at no time will a slot contain data from one data block and data from another data block at the same time.

To test this, the SimpleDatabase program contains an inner class called SimpleDatabaseTester, which reads and writes data blocks very quickly to the slots of a SimpleDatabase. Each data block consists of a single byte repeated over and over, which makes it very easy to tell if a slot has been corrupted by an

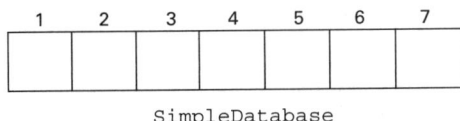

Figure 1.21 A SimpleDatabase **is a flat file containing a set of fixed-length data slots.**

incomplete write. After each read, the SimpleDatabaseTester checks to make sure there has been no data corruption.

You can specify the number of slots in the database, and the size of each slot, by changing the constants in the source code, which is presented in listing 1.4.

Listing 1.4   SimpleDatabase.java

(See\Chapter1\SimpleDatabase.java)

```
import java.io.*;
import java.nio.channels.*;
import java.util.*;

public class SimpleDatabase
{
    static public final int NUMSLOTS = 64;
    static public final int SLOTSIZE = 1024;
    private RandomAccessFile raf;
    private FileChannel fc;
```

```
public SimpleDatabase( String filename ) throws IOException {
  File file = new File( filename );
  boolean exists = file.exists();
  raf = new RandomAccessFile( file, "rw" );
  fc = raf.getChannel();

  if (!exists) {
    byte b[] = new byte[SLOTSIZE];
    for (int i=0; i<NUMSLOTS; ++i)
      put( i, b );
  }
}

private FileLock getLock( int slot, boolean shared )
  throws IOException {
  long position = slot*SLOTSIZE;
  long size = SLOTSIZE;

  FileLock lock = fc.lock( position, size, shared );
  return lock;
}

public void put( int slot, byte data[] ) throws IOException {
  try {
    if (data.length != slotSize)
      throw new IllegalArgumentException( "Data wrong size: "+
                                          data.length );
    FileLock fl = getLock( slot, false );
    synchronized( raf ) {
      raf.seek( slot*slotSize );
      raf.write( data, 0, slotSize/2 );
      Thread.yield();
      raf.seek( slot*slotSize+(slotSize/2) );
      raf.write( data, slotSize/2, slotSize/2 );
      raf.getFD().sync();
      Thread.yield();
    }
  } finally {
    fl.release();
  }
}

public void get( int slot, byte data[] ) throws IOException {
  try {
    if (data.length != slotSize)
      throw new IllegalArgumentException( "Data wrong size: "+
                                          data.length );
    FileLock fl = getLock( slot, true );
    synchronized( raf ) {
      raf.seek( slot*slotSize );
      raf.read( data );
    }
  } finally {
```

● Open the file for read/write and get the file's Channel

❶ If the file is new, clean it out

❷ Create a lock for the given slot

❸ Lock a slot and write data to it

❹ Lock a slot and read data from it

```
      fl.release();
    }
  }

  public void close() throws IOException {
    raf.close();
  }

  static public class SimpleDatabaseTester        ● Test program
  {
    private Random rand = new Random();
    private final int NUMSLOTS = SimpleDatabase.NUMSLOTS;
    private final int SLOTSIZE = SimpleDatabase.SLOTSIZE;
    private SimpleDatabase sd;

    public SimpleDatabaseTester( SimpleDatabase sd ) {
      this.sd = sd;
    }

    public void test() throws IOException {
      byte buffer[] = new byte[SLOTSIZE];
      int numOps = 0;
      while (true) {
        if (rand.nextInt( 100 )<50) {
          int slot = rand.nextInt( NUMSLOTS );
          generateConstantBuffer( buffer );
          sd.put( slot, buffer );
        } else {
          int slot = rand.nextInt( NUMSLOTS );
          sd.get( slot, buffer );
          confirmConstantBuffer( slot, buffer );
        }
        if (((++numOps)%50)==0) {
          System.out.println( numOps+" operations" );
        }
      }
    }

    private void generateConstantBuffer( byte buffer[] ) {
      byte b = (byte)rand.nextInt( 256 );
      for (int i=0; i<buffer.length; ++i)
        buffer[i] = b;
    }

    private void confirmConstantBuffer( int slot, byte buffer[] ) {
      int b = buffer[0];
      for (int i=1; i<buffer.length; ++i) {
        if (b != buffer[i]) {
          throw new RuntimeException( "Corrupted slot "+slot );
        }
      }
    }
  }
}
```

❺ Flip a coin and either read or write data

● Fill a buffer with a single, repeated byte

● Check a buffer to see if it is filled with a single, repeated byte

```
static public void main( String args[] ) throws IOException {
  if (args.length != 1) {
    System.err.println( "Usage: java SimpleDatabase <filename>" );
    System.exit( 1 );
  }
  String filename = args[0];

  SimpleDatabase sd = new SimpleDatabase( filename );
  SimpleDatabaseTester sdt = new SimpleDatabaseTester( sd );
  sdt.test();
}
}
```

❶ If the file doesn't exist, it is created as a RandomAccessFile. If the file is read from before it is written to, it may or may not contain garbage, depending on the underlying operating system implementation. To ensure that the file contains homogeneous slots, we write the contents of a newly allocated array, which must contains zeros, to each slot in the file.

❷ getLock() is used by both get() and put() to lock a slot before reading from it or writing to it. Each slot is locked independently. A lock can be shared or exclusive; this is specified by the second parameter. Once a lock is acquired using this call, the caller is responsible for releasing it.

❸ The first line of this section acquires an exclusive lock by calling getLock(). The last line of this section releases the lock. In between, the data is written to the slot. You'll notice that the data is written in two pieces, and there is a call to Thread.yield() between these writes. This is to ensure that there is some chance that other threads and processes will get to run during this write.

   If you comment-out the first and last lines, you remove the protection this program has provided against data corruption—it becomes possible for two different threads or processes to write to the same slot at the same time. However, unless the data files are huge, the chances of this happening are very low. (We still need the locking. Saying a piece of software has a "very low chance" of data corruption is simply not sufficient.)

   In any case, writing the data in two steps, with a call to Thread.yield() between them, greatly increases the chances of file corruption—which allows you to experiment with this program and make a useful comparison between the safe and unsafe modes of operation.

   Note that we release the lock in a finally block—this is because we want to make sure that we release the lock *no matter what*. Regardless of any kind of exception that might be thrown inside the try block, we'll still release the lock.

❹ The get() method gets a shared lock instead of an exclusive lock because it is reading, not writing, the data. It is safe for multiple threads or processes to read the same slot at the same time.

❺ Flip a coin using Random.nextInt(). On the basis of that coin flip, either read a slot or write a slot. In both cases, pick the slot randomly.

1.4   Summary

The New I/O API likely is not a replacement for the stream-based java.io package. The stream metaphor is extremely elegant and flexible, and efficient enough for many purposes. The NIO package does, however, provide a lower level at which to write I/O code, for situations where efficiency is important. In the current release, the old system has been cleanly re-implemented on top of the new API, where appropriate.

The New I/O API provides a completely new paradigm for doing efficient I/O. By taking over the control not only of data sources and sinks (Channels), but also of buffers that hold the data (Buffers), the new API can provide tremendous speed improvements while also providing more powerful features, including simple datatype conversion, nonblocking I/O, multiplexed I/O, and integrated support for character set encodings (Charsets). These topics are discussed in depth in chapter 2, "Advanced NIO."

Advanced NIO
(New Input/Output)

This chapter covers

- Reading and writing data with MappedByteBuffers
- Optimizing network communication using nonblocking I/O
- Encoding and decoding with Charsets
- Discovering and using NetworkInterfaces

This chapter covers the more advanced features of the NIO (New Input/Output) system, such as multiplexed I/O and nonblocking I/O. All of these features make use of the channel and buffer objects from the `java.nio` package that are described in detail in chapter 1, "Basic NIO." It is not necessary to read chapter 1 in its entirety before attempting this chapter; however, a perusal of sections 1.1 and 1.2 of that chapter will provide the basics required to understand the topics discussed here.

The features discussed in this chapter rely on the new concepts and classes of the NIO system; they are some of the main features that motivated the development of the NIO system. In this chapter, you'll find out about techniques that can go a long way toward making your Java application ready for heavy, real-world use.

2.1   *Reading and writing with MappedByteBuffers*

A `MappedByteBuffer` allows you to map a portion of a file into a memory buffer. The contents of the file are presented to the program as `Buffer`, which can be read from and written to like any other buffer. Changes made to the buffer are automatically propagated to the file by the underlying implementation of `MappedByteBuffer`.

File mapping provides an I/O *metaphor* that's entirely different from the kinds traditionally used to read and write files. Instead of treating the file as a kind of random-access stream, the file is treated like a gigantic array. This can make certain operations much easier to perform, but the main advantage is *speed*—data is retained in buffers at the operating system (OS) level, rather than being copied into user-space memory for each `read()` and out of user-space memory for each `write()`.

Of course, reading an entire file into memory would serve the same purpose, but, in general, files can be too large to read into memory. Some applications take the trouble to read in only those portions that are needed, but this is more complicated. `MappedByteBuffers` have the same interface as regular `ByteBuffers`, and so are easy to use.

A `MappedByteBuffer` uses *loading-on-demand*—that is, it loads into memory only the data that is being accessed. Thus, it is possible to create a 100-MB `Mapped-ByteBuffer` that maps to a 100-MB file, and change an arbitrary byte in the file by using the `put()` method of the `MappedByteBuffer`. This will only cause the small portion around the changed byte to be loaded into memory. The blocks that aren't loaded don't take up any memory.

2.1.1 *Advantages of MappedByteBuffers*

The primary advantage of a memory-mapped file is *speed*. The underlying implementation is operating system–dependent, but under some implementations, a mapped byte buffer gives you direct access to the operating system–level buffers.

This means that it can be possible for you to access your file *without any copying*— the fastest access possible.

Because memory-mapped files are tied so directly to operating system details, the design of the operating system can influence the way that the mapped buffers operate. Generally speaking, for the sake of efficiency, file I/O is performed in units called *blocks*, rather than on a byte-by-byte basis. The size of the blocks varies but is usually in the range of a few kilobytes.

Memory that is demand-loaded is therefore loaded in blocks. The MappedByte-Buffer will only load those blocks containing a byte that has been read from, or written to. The operating system can also remove a block from memory—this generally happens only if the block hasn't been used in a while. In either case, the operating system maintains a set of blocks in memory that reflect a subset of the file data on disk.

Figure 2.1 shows what a MappedByteBuffer might look like after it has been in use for a while. In the MappedByte-Buffer, the gray blocks currently reside in memory, while the clear blocks do not.

Under some operating systems, files are always read by mapping their data into blocks of memory, and these

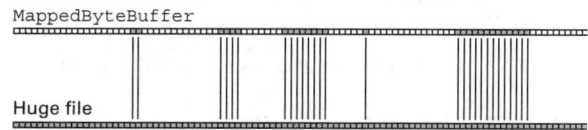

Figure 2.1 A MappedByteBuffer only loads the blocks that have been accessed. The gray blocks within the MappedByteBuffer have been loaded from the file, while the clear ones have not. The clear blocks do not take up any memory at all, which allows very large files to be handled without running out of RAM.

blocks are shared by all processes that access that file. An implementation of the MappedByteBuffer can take advantage of this by using these low-level blocks directly. One side effect of this technique is that changes made to the contents of the MappedByteBuffer are seen instantly by other programs that are reading the file. Likewise, changes made to the file by other programs are seen instantly within the content of the MappedByteBuffer.

WARNING   The propagation of changes between different programs accessing the same file is operating system–dependent. Changes made at one point in one program may or may not be seen at another point in another program. The only consistency guarantee provided by the New I/O API is that multiple instances of MappedByteBuffer in the same program will be consistent with each other.

2.1.2 *Disadvantages of MappedByteBuffers*

A `MappedByteBuffer` is not the most usual way to access a file—streams are used more often for day-to-day file I/O. However, memory-mapped I/O has become common on modern operating systems because it fits in so well with the underlying paging system, and it is used by the OS itself, as well as by high-performance applications like database engines.

Reading and writing data via a `MappedByteBuffer` takes some getting used to. Generally, when we modify an array, we know that the modified data won't be saved until we actually write it to a file. This is not the case for `MappedByteBuffers`—the changes are made *directly to the file itself* (but see the discussion of *copy-on-write* semantics in annotation 1 of listing 2.1). This means we must take great care when modifying the data in a `MappedByteBuffer` in order to avoid leaving the file in a corrupted state. We're used to modifying data structures such as arrays or buffers, and *then* writing them out when our modifications are done. With a `MappedByteBuffer`, each tiny change is instantly saved to the filesystem.

2.1.3 *Using MappedByteBuffers*

A few utility methods can help you make better use of `MappedByteBuffers`:

- `force()`—After calling this method, any changes made to any portion of this `MappedByteBuffer` will be flushed out to the underlying storage device, usually a disk. Generally, the operating system does this automatically, but not immediately, after any write. Instead of letting the operating system take care of this at its own discretion, you can call `force()` after every `write()` to ensure that the data is in fact safely stored on the hard drive, but this is much slower.

- `load()`—As mentioned previously, reading or writing any byte of a block will cause that block to be loaded into memory. You can also cause an explicit load of all the blocks in a `MappedByteBuffer` by calling `load()`.

- `isLoaded()`—Calling this method allows you to find out whether all the data in the `MappedByteBuffer` has been loaded into RAM. This is only a hint, not a guarantee, because the underlying operating system is free to page data in and out of virtual memory at any time.

WARNING   Calling `force()` on a `MappedByteBuffer` that corresponds to a remote storage device does *not* guarantee that all changes that have been made to the data have been flushed to that storage device. The consistency guarantee only applies to local storage devices.

2.1.4 *Example: checksumming*

FastChecksum (see listing 2.1) illustrates the technique of reading a file using a `MappedByteBuffer`. This program maps a portion of a file into memory and does a crude checksum on it (really, just a sum of all the bytes). Taking checksums of files is a quick way of comparing them. If the checksums differ, then the files differ; if the checksums are the same, then the files are probably, but not necessarily, the same.

Listing 2.1 FastChecksum.java

(see \Chapter2\FastChecksum.java)

```
import java.io.*;
import java.nio.*;
import java.nio.channels.*;

public class FastChecksum
{
  static public void main( String args[] ) throws Exception {
    if (args.length != 3) {
      System.err.println( "Usage: java FastChecksum "+
                          "<filename> <start pos> <# bytes>" );
      System.exit( 1 );
    }
    String filename = args[0];
    int start = Integer.parseInt( args[1] );
    int length = Integer.parseInt( args[2] );

    long fileLength = new File( filename ).length();

    if (length < start) {
      throw new IllegalArgumentException( "length < start" );
    }

    if (length < 0) {
      throw new IllegalArgumentException( "length < 0" );
    }

    if (start+length > fileLength) {
      throw new IllegalArgumentException( "start+length > fileLength" );
    }

    FileInputStream fin = new FileInputStream( filename );
    FileChannel finc = fin.getChannel();
    MappedByteBuffer mbb =
      finc.map( FileChannel.MapMode.READ_ONLY, start, length );

    long sum = 0;
    for (int i=0; i<length; ++i) {
      sum += mbb.get( i );
    }
```

❶ Map the requested portion of the file into memory

● Sum the bytes in this portion

```
      fin.close();

      System.out.println( "Sum: "+sum );
  }
}
```

❶ FileChannel.MapMode is a typesafe enumeration for the different modes of access allowed by the map() method. There are three modes available:

- READ_ONLY—The buffer can be read from, but not written to
- READ_WRITE—The buffer can be read from and written to
- PRIVATE—The buffer can be read from and written to, but writing is done using *copy-on-write* semantics. This means that any changes that are made to the buffer are made to a private copy; they are *never* propagated to the underlying file. Generally, in order to save memory, this private copy is made on demand, and is generally done in small pieces, rather than all at once

This program should run faster than its counterpart that uses traditional I/O. However, if the command-line arguments specify that the entire file should be check-summed, then the program will in fact have to load the entire file into memory.

WARNING There is no unmap method. If there were, the memory released by such a method could be reallocated to another MappedByteBuffer, at which point there would be two such buffers, both of which pointed to the same file data. This would introduce the possibility of data corruption.

As a result, the mapping only becomes invalidated when the MappedByte-Buffer object is garbage-collected.

2.2   *Nonblocking I/O*

One of the biggest complaints about the original java.io classes is that they don't support nonblocking I/O. The New I/O API has included full support, and it's one of the most important of the new features.

Nonblocking I/O is a method of carrying out read and write operations (as well as other, less-common operations) without *blocking* on the method calls that carry them out. To block on a method call means to be forced to wait until it is finished before returning. Thus, a nonblocking I/O operation is one that doesn't need to wait until the operation is finished before it returns. This can greatly decrease the overhead of managing many I/O connections, especially in a client/server environment.

This section will describe the new nonblocking I/O features in the New I/O API. We'll concentrate on using this feature to write client/server programs that can handle a great number of connections efficiently. Specifically, we'll look at two different implementations of a very simple chat system—one using *polling* and one using *multiplexing*. First, though, we'll explore some naive implementations—both single- and multithreaded. We'll be looking closely at the *server* side of this chat system. The client is rather trivial, and doesn't enlighten the discussions in this chapter—it can be downloaded from the book's web site.

2.2.1 *The multithreaded approach*

In the early days of Java, it was very easy to write a chat server, but it was hard to write a chat server that could handle many connections at once. This is because it was very common to create a thread for every connection. This meant that each client had its own thread on the server, so a server with many clients had many threads.

These early versions of Java could not handle a tremendous number of threads. There was a certain overhead for each thread, and even if few of the clients were chatting, the server would grind to a halt. These days, JVMs can handle more and more threads each year. But in many implementations, it's still the case that threading carries an undesirable overhead. It's hard enough dealing with a lot of I/O without having to deal with a lot of threads at the same time.

To really understand the multithreaded approach, and why it failed, it's important to understand why it was so desirable. Here's a hypothetical version of the server-side pseudocode that handled a single client:

```
while (true) {
  ChatMessage cm = client.rcvMessage();
  for (client2 in clients) {
    client2.sendMessage( cm );
  }
}
```

This code fragment reads a single message from a single client and then sends that message out to all the other clients in the system. Simple, right? That's the beauty of the multithreaded model: each client has its own thread, and inside that thread is a very simple read/write loop.

The call to `client.rcvMessage()` is a *blocking* call. This means that the call waits until a message comes in from the client. If the client is sending lots of data, this wait might be short. But sometimes a user gets up for a few minutes, or even goes to lunch. This call can take minutes, or hours, or more, before it returns. This is *another* reason why having one thread per client is so desirable—no matter how long this thread blocks on this call, the other clients are being handled by the other threads. No one client can bring the system to a halt.

This is the essence of blocking I/O—whatever operation you're doing, you can't be doing something else in the same thread. Whatever this thread is doing for one client, it's not doing anything for any other clients. Having one thread per client takes care of this problem, but it means having too many threads.

2.2.2 *The really bad single-threaded approach*

Given the problems of using too many threads, you might have briefly considered the option of using a single thread. Here's one way you can do this, expressed as pseudocode:

```
while (true) {
  for (client in clients) {
    ChatMessage cm = client.rcvMessage();
    for (client2 in clients) {
      client2.sendMessage( cm );
    }
  }
}
```

The idea here is to deal with each client in turn—you get a message from the first client and send it out to everyone. Then you get a message from the second client and send it out to everyone. And it all works inside a single thread!

Unfortunately, this is even worse. If the first client doesn't send any data for a while, the second client never gets any attention, even if it's sending lots of data. Even if the first client only delays a tiny bit, that delay is still time wasted—it's time spent waiting and doing *nothing else*. That's the worst thing you can have in a server.

There are refinements of this scheme—splitting the clients across, say, twenty threads, or sorting the clients based on how much time they spend not sending data, but all of these waste time, and all of them will eventually get bogged down.

There must be a better way.

2.2.3 *Polling*

One better way to do the I/O is through polling. Polling means checking each connection to see if it has any data. If it does, you deal with it, and if not, you don't waste any time waiting for it to have some. You poll all of the clients, deal with any data that has come in, and then wait a tenth of a second. Then you start the process over.

Polling isn't perfect, mainly because of that tenth of a second. That might not seem like a long time, but a high-powered server has to provide response times far smaller than that. The delay can be shortened to a twentieth of a second, or a fiftieth, or even less, but a smaller delay between polling rounds means greater overhead. You're spending so much time checking the clients that you don't have as much time to actually deal with the input as it comes in.

Polling, in fact, doesn't require the New I/O API because it's always been possible in Java, even using only the `java.io` package. However, the New I/O API has direct support for nonblocking I/O, which makes polling cleaner.

Since the nonblocking I/O method of polling uses the New I/O API, it therefore uses channels rather than streams. The following code does a *blocking* read from a network socket:

```
ByteBuffer buffer = ByteBuffer.allocate( bufferSize );
Socket newSocket = ss.accept();
SocketChannel sch = socket.getChannel();
buffer.clear();
sch.read( buffer );
```

According to the documentation, a socket channel that is in blocking mode will block on the call to `read()`. Specifically, it will wait until *at least one byte* has come in. The read might get lots of data, or it might only get one byte, but `buffer` will *never* be empty after this call.

Here's the nonblocking version:

```
ByteBuffer buffer = ByteBuffer.allocate( bufferSize );
Socket newSocket = ss.accept();
newSocket.configureBlocking( false );
SocketChannel sch = socket.getChannel();
buffer.clear();
sch.read( buffer );
```

This call to `read()` will return an empty buffer if there is nothing to read, because of the call to `configureBlocking()`, which sets the channel to be in nonblocking mode.

The server inner loop at the start of section 2.2.2 contained a call to another method called `rcvMessage()`. Using polling, this method can be rewritten to optionally return `null` when there's no input:

```
while (true) {
  for (client in clients) {
    ChatMessage cm = client2.rcvMessage();
    if (cm != null) {
      for (client2 in clients) {
        client2.sendMessage( cm );
      }
    }
  }
}
```

In this case, we only send the message out if we actually got one, and it all runs inside a single thread!

In the next section, we'll take a close look at a chat server that uses polling.

2.2.4 *Example: a polling chat server*

In this section, we'll take a look at a complete chat server program that uses polling to carry out all of its I/O operations in a single thread. Not only does it use polling to read data from clients, but it uses polling to actually accept new client connections. It has to do this; otherwise, the main thread would be blocked by the call to ServerSocket.accept().

The central loop of the PollingChatServer program can be represented by the following pseudocode:

```
while (true) {
  if (there are new connections to the server socket) {
    add those connections to the list of active sockets
  }

  for each socket in (the list of active sockets) {
    if (there is data coming into that socket) {
      echo that data back to all clients
    }
  }

  if (any sockets have been closed) {
    remove those sockets from the active list
  }
}
```

To start the server, you must select a port for it to listen on. 5555 is a good one to try:

```
java PollingChatServer 5555
```

To connect to the PollingChatServer, you can use the client applet contained in ChatClient.java and ChatClientApplet.java, using the HTML template contained in client.html. This can be done using the following command:

```
appletviewer ChatClientApplet
```

client.html must be modified to use the same port number that the server is listening on. Here are the complete contents of client.html:

```
<applet code="ChatClientApplet.class" width=500 height=300>
<param name="host" value="hostname">
<param name="port" value="5555">
</applet>
```

PollingChatServer itself is shown in listing 2.2.

Listing 2.2   PollingChatServer.java

(see \Chapter2\PollingChatServer.java)

```java
import java.io.*;
import java.net.*;
import java.nio.*;
import java.nio.channels.*;
import java.util.*;

public class PollingChatServer implements Runnable
{
  static private final int sleepTime = 100; //SLEEP_TIME
  private int port;
  private Vector sockets = new Vector();
  private Set closedSockets = new HashSet();

  public PollingChatServer( int port ) {
    this.port = port;
    Thread t = new Thread( this, "PollingChatServer" );
    t.start();
  }

  public void run() {
    try {
      ServerSocketChannel ssc = ServerSocketChannel.open();
      ssc.configureBlocking( false );
      ServerSocket ss = ssc.socket();
      InetSocketAddress isa = new InetSocketAddress( port );
      ss.bind( isa );

      ByteBuffer buffer = ByteBuffer.allocate( 4096 );

      System.out.println( "Listening on port "+port );

      while (true) {
        SocketChannel sc = ssc.accept();

        if (sc != null) {
          Socket newSocket = sc.socket();
          System.out.println( "Connection from "+newSocket );
          newSocket.getChannel().configureBlocking( false );
          sockets.addElement( newSocket );
        }

        for (Enumeration e = sockets.elements();
             e.hasMoreElements();) {
          Socket socket = null;
          try {
```

❶ Open a nonblocking server socket

❷ A new connection comes in on the server socket

```
          socket = (Socket)e.nextElement();
          SocketChannel sch = socket.getChannel();
          buffer.clear();
          sch.read( buffer );
          if (buffer.position() > 0) {
            buffer.flip();
            System.out.println( "Read "+buffer.limit()+
                              " bytes from "+sch.socket() );
            sendToAll( buffer );
          }
        } catch( IOException ie ) {
          closedSockets.add( socket );
        }
      }

      removeClosedSockets();

      try {
        Thread.sleep( sleepTime );
      } catch( InterruptedException ie ) {}
    }
  } catch( IOException ie ) {
    ie.printStackTrace();
  }
}

private void sendToAll( ByteBuffer bb ) {
  for (Enumeration e=sockets.elements();
        e.hasMoreElements();) {
    Socket socket = null;
    try {
      socket = (Socket)e.nextElement();
      SocketChannel sc = socket.getChannel();
      bb.rewind();
      while (bb.remaining()>0) {
        sc.write( bb );
      }
    } catch( IOException ie ) {
      closedSockets.add( socket );
    }
  }
}

private void removeClosedSockets() {
  for (Iterator it=closedSockets.iterator(); it.hasNext();) {
    Socket socket = (Socket)it.next();
    sockets.remove( socket );
    System.out.println( "Removed "+socket );
  }
  closedSockets.clear();
}
```

❸ Data is read on one of the client sockets

❹ Data is written to each of the client sockets

Dead sockets are removed in a ❺ separate phase

```
  static public void main( String args[] ) throws Exception {
    int port = Integer.parseInt( args[0] );
    new PollingChatServer( port );
  }
}
```

❶ Instead of using the normal method of calling `new ServerSocket( port )`, we create
a `ServerSocketChannel` and put it in nonblocking mode using `configureBlock-`
`ing()`. We call the `ServerSocketChannel`'s `socket()` method to get access to the
`ServerSocket` object. We bind the server socket to the user-specified port using the
`ServerSocket`'s `bind()` method.

The `ServerSocket` object and the `ServerSocketChannel` should be thought of as
two objects referring to the same underlying operating system resource. More precisely, the `ServerSocket` is built *on top* of the `ServerSocketChannel`.

❷ Here, we *poll* for any incoming connections to our server socket. Since it has been
placed in nonblocking mode, a call to `accept()` will return `null` if there are no
incoming connections. If there is an incoming connection, we place it in `sockets`,
the list of currently active sockets.

❸ We check each open socket to see if any data is coming in. The sockets are all in
nonblocking mode; this means that if a socket has no data coming in to it, we'll get
an empty buffer back. If we get a buffer that isn't empty, we send that data to all of
the clients using the `sendToAll()` method.

❹ `sendToAll()` sends the contents of a buffer to each of the currently open sockets. It
calls `rewind()` before each send to make sure the buffer's position value is pointing
to the beginning of the buffer, so that everything gets written.

❺ Any time a `write()` to a socket fails, we take that socket to be closed, and add it to
a list of dead sockets called `closedSockets`. The `removeClosedSockets()` method
takes all of the closed sockets and removes them from the main socket list, `sockets`.

This is done as a separate step because removing the dead sockets while we are
iterating through them is dangerous—the data structures can get confused, causing
some sockets to be skipped during the reading or writing process.

All things considered, polling isn't a bad method of doing lots of I/O in a single
thread. But the fact is that it does waste some CPU cycles, and it does cause small
but perceptible delays in throughput. To get the tightest response possible, you
need to use *multiplexed nonblocking I/O*. This will be discussed in the next section.

2.2.5 *Multiplexing with select()*

Polling isn't really the best way to do multiplexed I/O, although, for a long time, it
was the only way to do it in Java. JDK 1.4 brings us a better solution—the *selector*.

The Selector

Multiplexing centers around the use of an object called a `Selector`. This object watches a set of channels of various kinds and alerts you when one of them has received some input. Instead of having to check each of the channels periodically, like you do when you're polling, you can call a single method, `Selector.select()`, which will block until one or more of the channels is ready. You then deal with whatever information has come in, and then you call `select()` again. You can see how simple the main loop is in the following schematic listing:

```
while (true) {
  selector.select();

  // deal with new input ...
}
```

The advantage of using selectors is tremendous. If you'll recall from section 2.2.2, the naive approach was to wait for input from one of the clients, which meant we were ignoring all of the other clients while we were waiting. The beauty of `select()` is that you can wait for input from *all* of the clients at once.

    The `select()` method treats server sockets and regular sockets in the same way. Server sockets receive new connections, while regular sockets receive bytes. The `select()` call treats them both as a kind of *I/O event*.

    Note that `select()` only works with *selectable channels*—that is, `Channels` that implement the `SelectableChannel` interface. Both `Socket` and `ServerSocket` implement `SelectableChannel`. In the base implementation, only five classes are selectable: `DatagramChannel`, `Pipe.SinkChannel`, `Pipe.SourceChannel`, `Server-SocketChannel`, and `SocketChannel`.

    `select()` is very efficient. The Java version of `select()`, in fact, seems to be based on the Unix system call of the same name. The purpose of `select()` is to make available to the user the fundamentally asynchronous, multiplexed nature of I/O that you find at the operating system level. While the `select()` approach is slightly more complicated to understand than the elegant stream approach, the difficulties are justified by the increase in speed and flexibility.

Listening and reading with select()

In this section, we will re-implement the chat server of section 2.2.4 using `select()`. As before, our server will consist of a server socket that is listening for connections, and a set of client sockets, each of which is connected to a chat client at the other end. And, as in the polling version, we'll do everything in a single thread. Our new implementation, MultiplexingChatServer, will be much more efficient than PollingChatServer because it won't spend any time polling, or waiting between polls.

The first thing we need to do is create a `Selector`. This object is the center of the process: it is the object that alerts us to the presence of incoming input.

```
import java.nio.channels.*;

Selector selector = Selector.open();
```

The static `open()` call creates a new `Selector` object. Now that we have a selector, we can create some channels to register with it. These channels will be the channels that the selector watches for I/O activity.

Since this is a standard chat server, we'll create a server socket, just like we did in the PollingChatServer.

```
ServerSocketChannel ssc = ServerSocketChannel.open();
ssc.configureBlocking( false );
ServerSocket ss = ssc.socket();
InetSocketAddress isa = new InetSocketAddress( port );
ss.bind( isa );
```

Note that we create the server socket by creating a `ServerSocketChannel` first, and then calling its `socket()` method to get access to the `ServerSocket` object. We do this mainly because we need to configure it as a nonblocking socket by calling the `configureBlocking()` method of its channel.

NOTE   A `ServerSocket` will have a `ServerSocketChannel` if and only if the channel was created first using `ServerSocketChannel.open()`.

Normally, the first thing we'd do after creating a server socket would be to call its `accept()` method to listen for an incoming connection. Because we're multiplexing, we're not going to do that. Instead, we register the server socket by calling the `register()` method of the `ServerSocketChannel` object:

```
ssc.register( selector, SelectionKey.OP_ACCEPT );
```

The second argument to this method describes the set of *I/O operations* we would like to listen for. Although they are called *operations*, they really should be thought of as *events*. There are four kinds of I/O events that a `Selector` can listen for:

- `OP_READ`—This event is triggered when it becomes possible for the channel to have data read from it. In a networking context, if even a single byte comes in from the remote side of a connection, this event will be triggered. This event is valid for regular sockets, but not for server sockets.

- `OP_WRITE`—This event is triggered when it becomes possible to write to a channel. In a system without much I/O load, a socket will always be ready to have data written to it. However, socket buffers are finite, and a heavily loaded server will sometimes have a bottleneck at the outgoing socket buffers. In this case, it is possible that a simple write to a socket will block until the buffers have enough room for the data to be written. This event is valid for regular sockets, but not for server sockets.

- OP_CONNECT—This event is triggered when a regular socket is ready to complete its connection to a remote server. This event is valid for regular sockets, but not for server sockets.

- OP_ACCEPT—This event is triggered when one or more incoming connections have arrived at the server socket. This event is valid for server sockets, but not for regular sockets.

NOTE You can find out what selection operations are valid for a particular SelectableChannel by calling its validOps() method.

Table 2.1 shows which operations are valid with each kind of socket.

Table 2.1 Valid operations for each kind of socket. Each operation is only valid for one of the two kinds of socket.

Operation	Socket	ServerSocket
OP_READ	✔	
OP_WRITE	✔	
OP_CONNECT		✔
OP_ACCEPT		✔

These operations can be *or'ed* together, allowing you to specify more than one operation at a time. For example, to register a regular socket for reading and writing, you could use the following line of code:

```
sc.register( selector,
  SelectionKey.OP_READ   |
  SelectionKey.OP_WRITE );
```

Although we've been ignoring it so far, the call to register() returns an object called a SelectionKey. This object represents the registration of the channel and has a number of purposes. You can unregister a channel by calling the SelectionKey's cancel() method. Also, if a channel has been registered for a number of different events, and one is triggered, you can use the `SelectionKey` to find out which ones were triggered. You can get the selection key like this:

```
SelectionKey sk = sc.register( selector, ops );
```

Now that we've registered our server socket with our selector, we're ready to start waiting for incoming connections. In our main loop, we call `select()`:

```
int numKeys = selector.select();
```

We are now waiting for any of the registered channels to have some event come in. At some point, one or more clients will try to connect, and when this happens, `select()` will return. The value it returns is the number of events that have been triggered.

The selected set

When one or more events have been triggered on one or more channels, the selection keys corresponding to these channels are put into a set called the *selected set*. You can get access to this set by calling the selector's `selectedKeys()` method.

```
Set skeys = selector.selectedKeys();
```

Using this set, you can iterate through the selection keys and process each one:

```
Iterator it = skeys.iterator();
while (it.hasNext()) {
  SelectionKey rsk = (SelectionKey)it.next();
  // process selection key
}
```

In our chat server, we're listening for two kinds of events: incoming connections to the server socket, and incoming data to the regular sockets. Each selection key represents a channel that has had an event, so our first task is to find out what kind of channel it was, and what kind of event it received.

```
SelectionKey rsk = (SelectionKey)it.next();
int rskOps = rsk.readyOps();
// The following line checks to see if the 'SelectionKey.OP_ACCEPT'
// bit is set within 'rskOps'
if ((rskOps & SelectionKey.OP_ACCEPT) == SelectionKey.OP_ACCEPT) {
  // it's an incoming connection; add it to the list of connections
} else {
  // it's data arriving at a regular socket; process it
}
```

In the preceding code, we check the selection key to find out what kind of event (operation) was triggered. If it was an *accept* operation, then we know that this must be the server socket accepting a new connection. Otherwise, we know that it must be regular data arriving at a regular socket.

Note that the selector doesn't carry out the operation in question—it only tells us that the operation is ready to be carried out. If it's an accept operation, we need to perform the actual accept:

```
Socket socket = serverSocket.accept();
```

If, instead, we've just had some data coming in to a `SocketChannel`, we need to read the data and process it:

```
buffer.clear();
// The selection key contains a reference to its SocketChannel
SocketChannel ch = (SocketChannel)rsk.channel();
ch.read( buffer );
buffer.flip();
sendToAll( buffer );
```

If we've just gotten a new connection, we also have to add the new channel to the selector, so that the selector is listening for incoming data on it. We'll register this `SocketChannel` just like we registered the `ServerSocketChannel`, only we'll register it for `OP_READ` rather than for `OP_ACCEPT`.

```
SocketChannel sc = socket.getChannel();
sc.configureBlocking( false );
sc.register( selector, SelectionKey.OP_READ );
```

NOTE   The arrival of data isn't the only thing that will trigger an `OP_READ` event. This event will also be triggered if the connection is closed or if there is an error of some kind. This is true of all four types of events. The rationale behind this is that if you are waiting for data to arrive, you want to know when it arrives, but you also want to know when there is a fatal error preventing its arrival.

Once we've dealt with incoming data or new incoming connections, we're nearly done with our inner loop. Before we can go back to processing events, we have to make sure that we tell the selector that we've just processed a channel. We do this by removing the channel's `SelectionKey` from the selected set:

```
selector.selectedKeys().remove( selectionKey );
```

NOTE   Once a `SelectionKey` has been added to a selector's selected set, it must be removed explicitly. If you do not remove it from the selected set, it will still be in the selected set the next time an event comes in, making it seem like the event has been triggered again. Failure to remove a `SelectionKey` from the selected set can result in a bug in which an event seems to be triggered repeatedly.

The big view

Figure 2.2 gives an overview of the flow of events in the chat server's main thread:
The steps in figure 2.2 are described in more detail here:

1 A new `ServerSocketChannel` is created. This will be used to listen for new connections.

2 The `ServerSocketChannel` is registered with the `Selector`. We will be able to receive notice of I/O events for the `ServerSocketChannel` by calling this `Selector`'s `select()` method. The call to `register()` returns a `SelectionKey`.

3 `select()` waits until one or more registered channels have I/O events.

4 `selectedKeys()` is used to find out which channels have I/O events. Specifically, it returns a `Set` containing `SelectionKeys`. Each `SelectionKey` can be used to get access to the underlying `Channel`.

5 If a new connection has come in, `ServerSocketChannel.accept()` is called to get the new `SocketChannel`.

6 The new `SocketChannel` is registered with the `Selector`, just as the `ServerSocketChannel` was. Whereas the `ServerSocketChannel` is being watched for new incoming connections, the new `SocketChannel` is being watched for incoming chat data.

7 Incoming chat data is processed. In our simple chat system, this means it is sent out to all other connections.

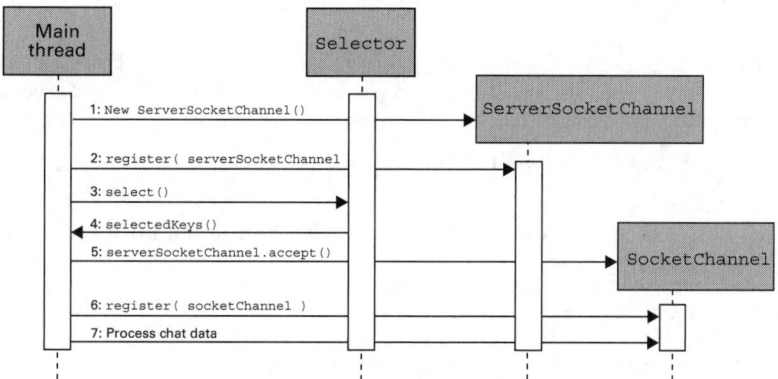

Figure 2.2   The flow of events in the main thread of the chat server

The source

In the preceding sections, we've gone through the essential elements of our chat server's inner loop. Listing 2.3 shows the complete program.

Listing 2.3 MultiplexingChatServer.java

(see \Chapter2\MultiplexingChatServer.java)

```java
import java.io.*;
import java.net.*;
import java.nio.*;
import java.nio.channels.*;
import java.util.*;
public class MultiplexingChatServer implements Runnable
{
  private int port;
  private Vector sockets = new Vector();
  private Set closedSockets = new HashSet();

  public MultiplexingChatServer( int port ) {
    this.port = port;
    Thread t = new Thread( this, "MultiplexingChatServer" );
    t.start();
  }

  public void run() {
    try {
      ServerSocketChannel ssc = ServerSocketChannel.open();
      ssc.configureBlocking( false );
      ServerSocket ss = ssc.socket();
      InetSocketAddress isa = new InetSocketAddress( port );
      ss.bind( isa );

      Selector selector = Selector.open();
      ssc.register( selector, SelectionKey.OP_ACCEPT );
      System.out.println( "Listening on port "+port );

      ByteBuffer buffer = ByteBuffer.allocate( 4096 );

      while (true) {
        int numKeys = selector.select();
        if (numKeys>0) {
          Set skeys = selector.selectedKeys();
          Iterator it = skeys.iterator();
          while (it.hasNext()) {
            SelectionKey rsk = (SelectionKey)it.next();
            int rskOps = rsk.readyOps();
            if ((rskOps & SelectionKey.OP_ACCEPT) ==
                SelectionKey.OP_ACCEPT) {
              Socket socket = ss.accept();
              System.out.println( "Connection from "+socket );
              sockets.addElement( socket );
```

Prepare a nonblocking ServerSocket

Add the ServerSocket to the selector

Wait for an I/O event

Deal with a new incoming connection

```
                SocketChannel sc = socket.getChannel();
                sc.configureBlocking( false );
                sc.register( selector, SelectionKey.OP_READ );
                selector.selectedKeys().remove( rsk );
              } else if ((rskOps & SelectionKey.OP_READ) ==
                       SelectionKey.OP_READ) {
                SocketChannel ch = (SocketChannel)rsk.channel();
                selector.selectedKeys().remove( rsk );
                buffer.clear();
                ch.read( buffer );
                buffer.flip();
                System.out.println( "Read "+buffer.limit()+
                                    " bytes from "+ch.socket() );
                if (buffer.limit()==0) {
                  System.out.println( "closing on 0 read" );
                  rsk.cancel();
                  Socket socket = ch.socket();
                  close( socket );
                } else {
                  sendToAll( buffer );
                }
              }
            }

            removeClosedSockets();
          }
        }
    } catch( IOException ie ) {
      ie.printStackTrace();
    }
  }

  // This method is identical to
  // PollingChatServer.sendToAll()
  private void sendToAll( ByteBuffer bb ) {
    for (Enumeration e=sockets.elements();
         e.hasMoreElements();) {
      Socket socket = null;
      try {
        socket = (Socket)e.nextElement();
        SocketChannel sc = socket.getChannel();
        bb.rewind();
        while (bb.remaining()>0) {
          sc.write( bb );
        }
      } catch( IOException ie ) {
        closedSockets.add( socket );
      }
    }
  }
}
```

● **Deal with the arrival of chat**

● **Send a buffer of data to all clients**

```
private void close( Socket socket ) {          ●  Put the socket
  closedSockets.add( socket );                     on the to-close list
}

// This method is identical to                     Remove dead sockets
// PollingChatServer.removeClosedSockets()          from active list
private void removeClosedSockets() {           ●
  for (Iterator it=closedSockets.iterator(); it.hasNext();) {
    Socket socket = (Socket)it.next();
    sockets.remove( socket );
    System.out.println( "Removed "+socket );
  }
  closedSockets.clear();
}

static public void main( String args[] ) throws Exception {
  int port = Integer.parseInt( args[0] );
  new MultiplexingChatServer( port );
}
}
```

Although the MultiplexingChatServer doesn't cover *every* valid use of selectors, it covers the ones you'll use in most of your servers—accepting new connections and processing the data coming from them.

Even though this technique can be done in a single thread, you'll probably want to use multiple threads in practice, to take advantage of any parallelism within the underlying operating system or hardware. Additionally, any time-consuming data processing should probably be moved to other threads, if only so that thread priorities can be used to fine-tune the amount of time spent on I/O and the amount of time spent on data processing.

2.3   *Encoding and decoding with Charsets*

Since its release, Java has used Unicode characters throughout. However, because most operating systems are not fully Unicode-compliant, most Java programs are still effectively using 8-bit characters. Although a great deal of support for transitioning between 8-bit ASCII and 16-bit Unicode has been available within the Java API, it is generally circumvented.

Charsets integrate Unicode characters with the New I/O API by providing methods for converting ByteBuffers to CharBuffers, and back again. Precisely defined, a Charset is a particular mapping between bytes and Unicode characters. There are many different ways of performing this mapping—some optimized for space, others optimized for completeness of encoding. The Charset facility within the New I/O API allows multiple mappings to coexist peacefully, since each Charset object can represent a different mapping, and each one can encode and decode characters separately.

2.3.1 *Decoding and encoding*

Converting bytes to chars is called decoding. This might seem backwards, but it makes sense. Before Unicode adoption, a char was considered to be nothing more than a byte with an interpretation attached. Java chars, however, are their own entities, and should not be considered equivalent to any particular byte-encoding. In particular, a char can be encoded by any number of bytes. As a result, there is no definitive mapping that turns a char into one or more bytes. Instead, there are multiple mappings. Each one can be represented by a different `Charset` object.

A `Charset` is created using the `Charset.forName()` method. The single argument to the method is a string providing the name of the `Charset`.

```
String charsetName = "ISO-8859-1";
Charset charset = Charset.forName( charsetName );
```

While the available `Charsets` differ from system to system, the ones listed in Table 2.2 are available in any Java installation.

Table 2.2 These `Charsets` are available in every Java installation. Other `Charsets` may also be available.

Name	Definition
US-ASCII	Traditional 7-bit ASCII
ISO-8859-1	ISO Latin alphabet 1; also known as ISO-LATIN-1
UTF-8	8-bit UCS Translation Format
UTF-16BE	16-bit UCS Transformation Format (big-endian)
UTF-16LE	16-bit UCS Transformation Format (little-endian)
UTF-16	16-bit UCS Transformation Format (byte order determined by optional byte-order mark)

2.3.2 *Finding available Charsets*

You can find out what `Charsets` are available on your system by using ListCharsets (see listing 2.4). It lists each `Charset`, followed by a sublist of the *aliases* of that `Charset`. An alias is another name for the same `Charset`.

Listing 2.4   ListCharsets.java

(see \Chapter2\ListCharsets.java)

```
import java.util.*;
import java.nio.charset.*;

public class ListCharsets
{
  static public void main( String args[] ) throws Exception {
    SortedMap charsets = Charset.availableCharsets();
    Set names = charsets.keySet();
    for (Iterator e=names.iterator(); e.hasNext();) {
      String name = (String)e.next();
      Charset charset = (Charset)charsets.get( name );
      System.out.println( charset );
      Set aliases = charset.aliases();
      for (Iterator ee=aliases.iterator(); ee.hasNext();) {
        System.out.println( "    "+ee.next() );
      }
    }
  }
}
```

Here is some sample output from this program, showing the variety of Charsets and their aliases:

```
ISO-8859-1
    latin1
    ISO8859-1
    IBM819
US-ASCII
    us
    ISO_646.irv:1991
UTF-16
    utf_16
UTF-16BE
    iso-10646-ucs-2
    utf_16be
UTF-16LE
    utf_16le
UTF-8
    UTF8
windows-1252
    Cp1252
```

This is only a partial listing. You'll notice that most Charsets have a large number of aliases.

2.3.3 *Using encoders and decoders*

Once you have acquired a `Charset` object, you can use it to convert a `ByteBuffer` to a `CharBuffer`, and vice versa. To do this, you must first create a `CharsetEncoder` or a `CharsetDecoder` using the `newEncoder()` and `newDecoder()` methods. When you have an instance of a `CharsetEncoder` or `CharsetDecoder`, you can carry out a conversion using either the `encode()` or `decode()` method, respectively.

The following code fragment demonstrates the process of converting a `Byte-Buffer` to a `CharBuffer` using a `Charset`:

```
Charset charset = Charset.forName( charsetName );
CharsetDecoder decoder = charset.newDecoder();
CharBuffer charBuffer = decoder.decode( byteBuffer );
```

Likewise, you can convert a `CharBuffer` to a `ByteBuffer` as follows:

```
Charset charset = Charset.forName( charsetName );
CharsetEncoder encoder = charset.newEncoder();
ByteBuffer byteBuffer = encoder.encode( charBuffer );
```

The decoding process involves reading bytes, one at a time, from the input `Byte-Buffer`. Many `Charset`s deal with characters that use more than one byte per character; in these cases, multiple bytes have to be read to produce a single character. Each time the decoder reads enough bytes to produce a character, this character is written to the `CharBuffer`. The decoder makes sure not to write more characters than can fit in the `CharBuffer`, or to read more bytes than are available in the `Byte-Buffer`. In the preceding example, the `CharBuffer` is created by the `CharsetDe-coder`, so it won't overrun; however, there are variants of `decode()` and `encode()` that take a destination buffer as an argument, and these buffers might not be large enough.

The encoding process can also generate more than one byte per character. It reads characters, one at a time, from the `CharBuffer`. For each character, it writes one or more bytes to the `ByteBuffer`. The capacities of the buffers are likewise respected.

The preceding description is accurate for most `CharsetDecoder`s, but it is by no means a requirement—a `CharsetDecoder` could, if it wanted to, process the characters in a strange order, or copy data into other buffers. However, it must preserve the ordering of the characters and properly maintain the buffers' limit and position values.

You can combine the previous code fragments to convert a piece of text from one encoding to another by converting it first to a `CharBuffer` using one `Charset`, and then converting it back to a `ByteBuffer` using another `Charset`.

```
Charset charsetA = Charset.forName( charsetName );
CharsetDecoder decoderA = charsetA.newDecoder();
Charset charsetB = Charset.forName( charsetName );
CharsetEncoder encoderB = charsetB.newEncoder();

CharBuffer charBuffer = decoderA.decode( byteBuffer );
ByteBuffer newByteBuffer = encoderB.encode( charBuffer );
```

The TranslateCharset program (see listing 2.5) can be used to convert a file from one encoding to another. You specify the source file and the destination file, along with the names of the old and new Charsets, on the command line. For example, the following command-line command would use TranslateCharset to convert the plaintext file old.txt to be the 16-bit Unicode file new.txt:

```
java TranslateCharset old.txt ISO-8859-1 new.txt UTF-16BE
```

Listing 2.5   TranslateCharset.java

(see \Chapter2\TranslateCharset.java)

```
import java.io.*;
import java.nio.*;
import java.nio.channels.*;
import java.nio.charset.*;

public class TranslateCharset
{
  static public void main( String args[] ) throws Exception {
    if (args.length != 4) {
      System.err.println(
        "Usage: java TranslateCharset <infile> <incharset> "+
        "<outfile> <outcharset>" );
      System.exit( 1 );
    }

    String inFilename = args[0];
    String inFileCharsetName = args[1];
    String outFilename = args[2];
    String outFileCharsetName = args[3];

    File infile = new File( inFilename );
    File outfile = new File( outFilename );

    RandomAccessFile inraf =
      new RandomAccessFile( infile, "r" );
    RandomAccessFile outraf =
      new RandomAccessFile( outfile, "rw" );

    FileChannel finc = inraf.getChannel();
    FileChannel foutc = outraf.getChannel();

    MappedByteBuffer inmbb =
      finc.map( FileChannel.MapMode.READ_ONLY, 0, (int)infile.length() );
```

```
    Charset inCharset = Charset.forName( inFileCharsetName );       ● Create
    Charset outCharset = Charset.forName( outFileCharsetName );        the
                                                                       encoder
    CharsetDecoder inDecoder = inCharset.newDecoder();                 and
    CharsetEncoder outEncoder = outCharset.newEncoder();               decoder

    CharBuffer cb = inDecoder.decode( inmbb );        ● Convert from one
    ByteBuffer outbb = outEncoder.encode( cb );          encoding to another

    foutc.write( outbb );

    inraf.close();
    outraf.close();
  }
}
```

For most applications, you won't have to worry about `Charsets`. Many of the simple text-processing facilities in Java (such as `System.out.println()`) will take care of the details for you, using reasonable defaults. However, if you intend to create an application that uses text in a substantial way, `Charsets` are an elegant and efficient way to deal with Unicode encodings.

2.4   *Network interfaces*

The new `NetworkInterface` object provides access to the operating system–level objects that represent the interfaces on which network communications can happen. Some high-end servers come equipped with multiple network cards, and there are several reasons why this might be done. For example, having multiple network cards can allow a machine to engage in network communications at a much higher rate. To the extent that network I/O is bound by the network interface cards, multiple cards can parallelize communications, increasing throughput.

Having multiple interface cards can also be a physical strategy for securing a machine. For example, access to certain services might be restricted to connections coming through a particular interface that only certain users have access to. A server could have one network interface card for connections originating within the same office, and another network interface card for connections coming from the wider Internet. Multiple cards also provide redundancy in the face of hardware failure.

Network interfaces don't necessarily have to be physical devices. Most machines have a *loopback interface* that allows the machine to connect to itself. While this does not require special hardware to implement, the interface nevertheless has status as a network interface.

Each `NetworkInterface` object represents one of the network interfaces on your machine. Each one of these objects can be used to gather information about that interface. You can also get a list of `InetAddress` objects from an interface, which allows you to create a `ServerSocket` that only listens on a particular address.

We'll be seeing example output from some programs and program fragments in this section. The output was generated by running the programs on two different systems—Windows 95 and a Linux/GNU system.

2.4.1 When to use a network interface

Generally, you don't need to think about network interfaces. In most configurations, a machine has a *default* interface that is used for all IP communications. This means that socket programming can be done without reference to the particular interface that is being used. If you don't know what a network interface is, then you probably don't need to use one.

However, as mentioned previously, there are times when you need to access a particular interface. Or, to put it another way, there are times when you need to override the default network interface. With the arrival of JDK 1.4, you can now do this using the `NetworkInterface` class.

2.4.2 Getting a list of NetworkInterfaces

`NetworkInterface` provides a static method called `getNetworkInterfaces()`. This method provides an `Enumeration` of the `NetworkInterface` objects available.

Here is an example of its use:

```
Enumeration interfaces = NetworkInterface.getNetworkInterfaces();
while (interfaces.hasMoreElements()) {
  NetworkInterface ni = (NetworkInterface)interfaces.nextElement();
  // ...
}
```

This fragment iterates through all of the network interfaces on the system.

2.4.3 Reporting on NetworkInterfaces

You can pass a `NetworkInterface` to `System.out.println` to see what information is available on your system (see listing 2.6).

Listing 2.6 from ListNetworkInterfaces.java

(see\Chapter2\ListNetworkInterfaces.java)

```
Enumeration interfaces = NetworkInterface.getNetworkInterfaces();
while (interfaces.hasMoreElements()) {
  NetworkInterface ni = (NetworkInterface)interfaces.nextElement();
  System.out.println( ni );
}
```

Under Linux, this results in the following output:

```
name:ppp0 (ppp0) index: 115 addresses:
/111.222.33.44;

name:eth0 (eth0) index: 2 addresses:
/192.168.0.1;

name:lo (lo) index: 1 addresses:
/127.0.0.1;
```

Under Windows, we get the following:

```
name:lo0 (localhost) index: 2 addresses:
/127.0.0.1;

name:lan0 (3Com EtherLink III ISA (3C509/3C509b) in ISA mode) index: 1
  addresses:
/192.168.0.2;
```

Each paragraph represents a different network interface. There are a number of pieces of information in each entry, as shown in figure 2.3.

- interface name—The short name of the network interface. On Unix systems, this string is used by the ifconfig command, which can be used to configure the system to use a particular IP address for a particular network interface.

- interface full name—A longer, more descriptive name for the network interface. This string is probably not used in any official capacity, but rather exists to provide a more user-friendly description of the interface. A program for selecting a network interface might display this string in the user interface.

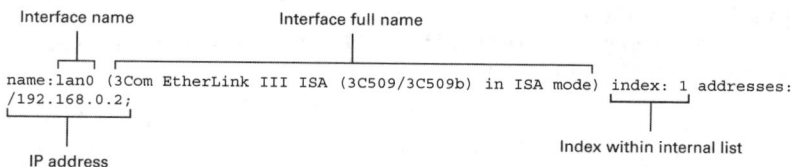

Figure 2.3 These are the parts of a NetworkInterface report. This report is generated by the toString() method of the NetworkInterface object.

- index—This is the index of this interface within an internal table.
- IP address—A list of all the Internet addresses bound to this interface.

2.4.4   *Getting a list of InetAddresses*

Although the output in section 2.4.3 provides a list of addresses, they are inconveniently imbedded within a block of text. However, it's easy to get a list of InetAddress objects belonging to a given interface by using the getInetAddresses() method.

```
NetworkInterface ni = ...;
Enumeration e = ni.getInetAddresses();
while (e.hasMoreElements()) {
  InetAddress ia = (InetAddress)e.nextElement();
  System.out.println( ia );
}
```

Most network interfaces have a single address; for the ones that don't, the preceding code will list the addresses.

2.4.5   *Getting a NetworkInterface by InetAddress*

Given that there may be several network interfaces on a given system, how do you pick one to use? One way is to pick the interface based on an address that is bound to it. NetworkInterface provides a static method called getByInetAddress(), which allows you to get the NetworkInterface object corresponding to a particular Inet-Address object.

ReportByAddress (see listing 2.7) looks up a network interface based on an address provided on the command line. It then prints out some information about this interface.

Listing 2.7   ReportByAddress.java

(see \Chapter2\ReportByAddress.java)
```
import java.net.*;

public class ReportByAddress
{
  static public void main( String args[] ) throws Exception {
    InetAddress ia = InetAddress.getByName( args[0] );
    NetworkInterface ni = NetworkInterface.getByInetAddress( ia );
    System.out.println( ni );
  }
}
```

Here's an example of this program in action under Windows:

```
java ReportByAddress 192.168.0.2

name:lan0 (3Com EtherLink III ISA (3C509/3C509b) in ISA mode) index: 1
    addresses:
/192.168.0.2;
```

Note that the address used to find this interface is listed in the `addresses:` section of the output.

2.4.6 Getting a NetworkInterface by name

You can also access a `NetworkInterface` given only its short device name, such as `lan0` or `ppp0`. This is done by using the `getByName()` method.

ReportByName (see listing 2.8) looks up a network interface based on a name provided on the command line. It then prints out some information about this interface.

Listing 2.8   ReportByName.java

(see \Chapter2\ReportByName.java)

```
import java.net.*;

public class ReportByName
{
  static public void main( String args[] ) throws Exception {
    NetworkInterface ni = NetworkInterface.getByName( args[0] );
    System.out.println( ni );
  }
}
```

Here's the output of this program under Linux:

```
java ReportByName eth0

name:eth0 (eth0) index: 2 addresses:
/192.168.0.1;
```

This program can be used to find the IP address corresponding to a particular interface name.

2.4.7 Listening on a particular address

As was mentioned at the beginning of this section, one practical reason why you'd need to use `NetworkInterface` objects is to create server sockets that only listen on a particular address. This can be useful if you are hosting multiple Internet addresses on the same machine.

In order to understand how this works, we need to understand a little bit more about what it means to listen on a socket.

Listening on the default address

If you've written socket code in Java before, you know that you don't need to think about network interfaces to listen on a socket. This is because most machines are configured to have a default address to listen on, if none is specified.

This default address is generally 0.0.0.0, which isn't really an address at all. It's more like a placeholder that says, "listening on this address means listening on all addresses at once." This means that if a connection comes in for the specified port, on any interface, then that is considered a connection.

To illustrate this, we'll try out some code. The following piece of code does the following:

- Listens for a connection on a particular port number
- Gets one incoming connection on that port
- Prints out information about that connection

```
int port = 5555;
ServerSocket ss = new ServerSocket( port );
Socket s = ss.accept();
System.out.println( s );
```

If you execute this program, it won't quit right away. It will sit there waiting for an incoming connection. By using the netstat command under Linux, we can see that the program is waiting on a connection. The output in figure 2.4 shows that something is listening on 0.0.0.0:5555, which means it's listening on port 5555, on all addresses.

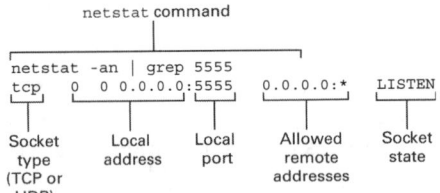

Figure 2.4
Output from the netstat command. netstat lists all open sockets, along with information about them. This listing shows the information for a socket listening for new connections on port 5555.

Getting the first address of an interface

Before we get into the mechanics of listening on particular interfaces, we need to define a helper method called getAddress().

A `NetworkInterface` object can have multiple addresses bound to it. However, it is often the case that each `NetworkInterface` in the system has only one address bound to it. For convenience's sake, we're going to assume that is the case.

The `NetworkInterface` class does *not* include a method called getInetAddress or getSingleInetAddress. It only provides `getInetAddresses()`, which returns an `Enumeration`. To simplify matters, we've created a helper function that grabs the first address in the `Enumeration` and returns it. It is also possible for a `NetworkInterface` to have *no* addresses; in this case, an empty `Enumeration` is returned.

```
static private InetAddress getAddress( NetworkInterface ni ) {
  Enumeration e = ni.getInetAddresses();
  if (!e.hasMoreElements())
    return null;
  InetAddress ia = (InetAddress)e.nextElement();
  return ia;
}
```

It is common to assume that the first address for an interface is sufficient; more sophisticated programs can provide a configuration interface to specify a different address.

Listening on an address

Listening for a connection on a particular address is a lot like accepting letters only if they are addressed to you personally. Listening on all addresses, then, is like accepting any letter that shows up at your door.

As mentioned previously, being particular about what address you listen on can let you multiplex the connections that are coming in. This is analogous to having roommates, each of whom receives letters at the same address. When the mail comes in, it is sorted by recipient before it is handed over.

NOTE Technically, a program listens on an *address*, not an *interface*. However, if an interface has a single address bound to it, then it is reasonable to say that a program listening on that *address* is also listening on that *interface*.

Now we're going to find out how to listen for connections on a particular interface. The Accept program will do this for us (see listing 2.9). Accept listens on an interface and listens for a single incoming connection. It won't do anything with this incoming connection—Accept just *listens*. We can examine the state of this listening process by running `netstat` at the same time. `netstat` shows the states of all ports that are being listened on—we can use it to get direct feedback about what ports, and what network interfaces, are being listened on.

Listing 2.9   Accept.java

(see \Chapter2\Accept.java)

```java
import java.net.*;
import java.util.*;

public class Accept
{
  static private InetAddress getAddress( NetworkInterface ni ) {
    Enumeration e = ni.getInetAddresses();
    InetAddress ia = (InetAddress)e.nextElement();
    return ia;
  }

  static public void main( String args[] ) throws Exception {
    int port = Integer.parseInt( args[0] );
    String interf = args.length > 1 ? args[1] : null;

    if (interf != null) {
      NetworkInterface ni = NetworkInterface.getByName( interf );
      InetAddress ia = getAddress( ni );
      ServerSocket ss = new ServerSocket( port, 20, ia );
      System.out.println( "Listening" );
      Socket s = ss.accept();
      System.out.println( s );
    } else {
      ServerSocket ss = new ServerSocket( port );
      System.out.println( "Listening" );
      Socket s = ss.accept();
      System.out.println( s );
    }
  }
}
```

> **Return the first address of a network interface**

The first argument to this program is the number of the port to listen on, and is required. The second argument is the name of the interface to listen on, and is optional. If it is omitted, then the program listens on 0.0.0.0; that is, it listens on all interfaces at once.

Let's now take a look at the results of running this program. In each case, we'll run the program and then use the Unix command netstat to find out what's going on.

First, we'll run Accept and listen on all sockets:

```
java Accept 5555
```

Note that we're using port 5555. This choice is arbitrary—you can use any port on your system that you have permission to use, and which isn't already being used by something else. Generally, a nonprivileged user has permission to use any port greater than 1023.

Now that we've run Accept, it is listening on port 5555. We can use `netstat` to verify this. The exact Unix command we are using is `netstat -an | grep 5555`, which can be translated as "list all network sockets in use, but only report those mentioning '5555'."

```
netstat -an | grep 5555
tcp   0  0 0.0.0.0:5555     0.0.0.0:*        LISTEN
```

The output tells us that someone is listening on port 5555 on address `0.0.0.0`, that is, on every address. This is just like our earlier example.

We can verify that this is working by trying to connect to this address. The simplest way to do this is with the telnet program, which is available under most operating systems, including Windows and Linux. Under Unix and most versions of Microsoft Windows, you can simply telnet at the command line:

```
telnet localhost 5555
```

Since there is a program listening on port 5555, this connection request will succeed, and you'll see something like this:

```
Trying 127.0.0.1...
Connected to localhost.localdomain.
Escape character is '^]'.
Connection closed by foreign host.
```

If there hadn't been a program listening on port 5555, then you would have seen something like this:

```
telnet localhost 5555

Trying 127.0.0.1...
telnet: Unable to connect to remote host: Connection refused
```

Now, we'll try listening on a particular interface. We learned earlier that our Linux system had three interfaces: `ppp0`, `eth0`, and `lo`. Let's run Accept again and try listening on `eth0`. Then we'll run `netstat` again:

```
java Accept 5555 eth0

netstat -an | grep 5555
tcp   0  0 192.168.0.1:5555 0.0.0.0:*        LISTEN
```

Note the change. Again, we see that there is a program listening on port 5555. However, this time it's not listening on the default address, `0.0.0.0`, but rather on `192.168.0.1`. This is the local IP address assigned to our Linux box on its LAN, so it makes sense that we'd see that address here.

If you use telnet to verify this, you'll find that the behavior is slightly different. In our previous example, we used telnet to connect to localhost:5555. localhost is actually an alias for the address 127.0.0.1, which is an address that generally refers to the local machine.

If you try to connect to this address now, you'll find that it doesn't work. That's because our listening program is only listening on 192.168.0.1. Previously, we were listening on all addresses, so localhost was valid, but now we are only listening on a single address, and if you want to connect, you have to use that address. If you use telnet to connect to 192.168.0.1, you'll find that it works.

We can try listening on the lo0 interface:

```
java Accept 5555 lo0

netstat -an | grep 5555
tcp   0   0 127.0.0.1:5555     0.0.0.0:*         LISTEN
```

You can see that the program is now listening on 127.0.0.1, also known as local-host. Telnetting to 192.168.0.1 fails, as we see here:

```
telnet 192.168.0.1 5555
Trying 192.168.0.1...
telnet: Unable to connect to remote host: Connection refused
```

Meanwhile, telnetting to 127.0.0.1 succeeds, as we see here:

```
telnet 127.0.0.1 5555
Trying 127.0.0.1...
Connected to 127.0.0.1.
Escape character is '^]'.
Connection closed by foreign host.
```

Just to verify that we can do it, let's try running several servers at once on different interfaces. This is what you would do if you were configuring a machine to serve multiple web sites by using a different network interface card for each site.

Before we try this experiment, we'll do the control test. We'll create a server listening on *all* interfaces, and then try to run another server listening on all interfaces. The first one works fine, but the second one throws an exception:

```
java Accept 5555
Exception in thread "main" java.net.BindException: Address already in use
      at java.net.PlainSocketImpl.socketBind(Native Method)
      at java.net.PlainSocketImpl.bind(PlainSocketImpl.java:322)
      at java.net.ServerSocket.bind(ServerSocket.java:311)
      at java.net.ServerSocket.bind(ServerSocket.java:269)
      at java.net.ServerSocket.<init>(ServerSocket.java:185)
      at java.net.ServerSocket.<init>(ServerSocket.java:97)
      at Accept.main(Accept.java:23)
```

This makes sense—you can't have two programs listening at the same time on the same port and address.

Now, let's see what happens when we try listening on two different addresses. First, in one window we use Accept to listen on one interface:

```
java Accept 5555 eth0
Listening
```

Then we run another listener on another interface:

```
java Accept 5555 lo
Listening
```

Since no exception was thrown, we can conclude that both programs are listening happily and have not come into conflict with each other. But, to be sure, let's check out `netstat` to see what's really going on:

```
netstat -an | grep 5555
tcp   0   0 127.0.0.1:5555      0.0.0.0:*        LISTEN
tcp   0   0 192.168.0.1:5555    0.0.0.0:*        LISTEN
```

As you can see, we've got both servers listening at the same time, each one on a different interface.

2.5   *Summary*

The New I/O API strives to provide Java APIs for a number of operating system features that have become standard in modern operating systems, such as file locking, nonblocking I/O, and multiplexed I/O. In these cases, the Java API provides a portion that is portable across all Java installations, and a portion that may not work in all installations but that can make use of the more advanced features found in some operating systems.

The advantages provided by these features are a large part of what motivated the NIO in the first place. Efficiency is a primary motivation, because while Java is an excellent language for developing server-side programs, it has never been able to compete with languages like C and C++ in terms of raw speed. The new features described in this chapter—and the operating system features they expose—go a long way toward remedying this.

Java2D 3

Java2D is described by Sun Microsystems as "a powerful, flexible framework for device- and resolution-independent 2D graphics." It was added to the main Java distribution in version 1.2, and version 1.4 adds a number of new features. The two most significant are the Print Service API, in the `javax.print` package (and its sub-packages), which allows for greater control over printing and spooling, and the Image I/O API, in the `javax.imageio` package, which is a simpler and more powerful library for saving and loading images in various formats.

3.1   *The Print Service API*

The Print Service API provides a comprehensive facility for discovering printers and print services based on their attributes, and for printing to these services. While facilities for printing existed prior to the Print Service API, the facilities for handling the actual print services themselves were minimal.

The Print Service API enables you to do the following:

- Discover all printers on a system
- Discover all printers with a certain set of attributes
- Discover the default printer
- Create printable document objects (called docs) based on in-memory data
- Create docs based on on-disk data
- Create multidocs—document objects containing multiple docs, often of differing types
- Create print jobs
- Track print jobs as they are processed
- Receive notification of print events such as job completion, job failure, job cancellation, and the need for user intervention
- Install new lookup services that provide print services to clients calling the Print Service lookup methods

This section will cover the highlights of the Print Service facility, and provide examples of working code for printing data.

3.1.1   *Print Service packages*

The Print Service API consists of the following packages:

- `javax.print`—Contains the main Print Service classes and interfaces for defining print jobs, discovering printers and print services, and creating document objects
- `javax.print.attribute`—Contains classes that allow for the definition of printer and print service attributes
- `javax.print.attribute.standard`—Contains classes for the specification of a wide variety of printer attributes, such as page size, printer speed, color capabilities, resolution, and so on
- `javax.print.event`—Contains event objects and listener interfaces that allow programs to track the progress of print jobs and listen for changes in the attributes of print jobs and print services

3.1.2 Document flavors

Since the concept of the *printable document* is a very general one, the `DocFlavor` class (and related classes and interfaces) are very general.

A document flavor is defined as a pair of items:

- A MIME type for the data
- The class of an object from which the data will be drawn

The implementation of each print service is capable of printing some kinds of data, and not other kinds. Additionally, an implementation is either willing or unwilling to draw the data from a particular data source.

For example, a document flavor might specify that it is formatted as plain text and comes from a `String` object. Another document flavor might specify that it is formatted as HTML and comes from a byte array. Yet another document type might be formatted as GIF data and come from an input stream.

When a document is printed to a particular print service, that service is queried to find out if the print service in question has the document's flavor—that is, if it contains data in a known format, and if it comes from an object that can be used by this print service. If not, an exception is thrown.

3.1.3 Printer discovery

Printer discovery is the process of acquiring a list of printers and print services available through a computer. These services include local printers and network printers—indeed, anything that the underlying operating system regards as a print service of some kind.

Printer discovery operates through the `PrintServiceLookup` class. This class provides a number of static methods that allow for printer discovery:

- `PrintService[] lookupPrintServices( DocFlavor, AttributeSet )`—Finds any print services that are capable of printing documents of the specified document flavor, and that have the attributes specified in the given attribute set

- `MultiDocPrintService[] lookupMultiDocPrintServices( DocFlavor[], AttributeSet )`—Finds any print services that are capable of printing documents of *every* flavor in the specified list of document flavors, and that have the attributes specified in the given attribute set

- `PrintService lookupDefaultPrintService()`—Finds the print service defined by the operating system (and the installed lookup services) as the *default* service

As an example of how these methods can be used, the ListPrintServices program demonstrates a search for print services that specifies no constraints (see listing 3.1). As a result, it should find every print service on the system. For each print service, it prints out some useful information about that service.

Listing 3.1   ListPrintServices.java

(see \Chapter3\ListPrintServices.java)

```
import javax.print.*;
import javax.print.attribute.*;
import javax.print.attribute.standard.*;

public class ListPrintServices
{
  public ListPrintServices() {
    PrintService pss[] =
      PrintServiceLookup.lookupPrintServices( null, null );

    for (int i=0; i<pss.length; ++i) {
      System.out.println( pss[i] );
      PrintService ps = pss[i];

      PrintServiceAttributeSet psas = ps.getAttributes();
      Attribute attributes[] = psas.toArray();
      for (int j=0; j<attributes.length; ++j) {
        Attribute attribute = attributes[j];
        System.out.println( "  attribute: "+attribute.getName() );

        if (attribute instanceof PrinterName) {
          PrinterName pn = (PrinterName)attribute;
          System.out.println( "    printer name: "+pn.getValue() );
        }
      }

      DocFlavor supportedFlavors[] = ps.getSupportedDocFlavors();
      for (int j=0; j<supportedFlavors.length; ++j) {
        System.out.println( "  flavor: "+supportedFlavors[j] );
```

```
      }
    }
  }

  static public void main( String args[] ) throws Exception {
    new ListPrintServices();
  }
}
```

Here's an example of the output from this ListPrintServices:

```
Win32 Printer : HP LaserJet 1100
  attribute: printer-is-accepting-jobs
  attribute: color-supported
  attribute: printer-name
    printer name: HP LaserJet 1100
  attribute: queued-job-count
  flavor: image/gif; class="[B"
  flavor: image/gif; class="java.io.InputStream"
  flavor: image/gif; class="java.net.URL"
  flavor: image/jpeg; class="[B"
  flavor: image/jpeg; class="java.io.InputStream"
  flavor: image/jpeg; class="java.net.URL"
  flavor: image/png; class="[B"
```

(more flavors omitted)

```
Win32 Printer : HP LaserJet 1100 real
  attribute: printer-is-accepting-jobs
  attribute: color-supported
  attribute: printer-name
    printer name: HP LaserJet 1100 real
  attribute: queued-job-count
  flavor: image/gif; class="[B"
  flavor: image/gif; class="java.io.InputStream"
  flavor: image/gif; class="java.net.URL"
  flavor: image/jpeg; class="[B"
  flavor: image/jpeg; class="java.io.InputStream"
  flavor: image/jpeg; class="java.net.URL"
  flavor: image/png; class="[B"
```

(more flavors omitted)

The preceding output shows the attribute and document flavors for two printers (which are actually the same printer).

3.1.4 *Printer attributes*

Each of the attributes in the output listing in the previous section is represented by a class in the javax.print.attribute.standard package. Every possible attribute is represented by a different class. New classes can be added to the system to support new printer types, and as part of the implementation of new lookup services. Table 3.1 describes this correspondence of attributes and classes.

Table 3.1   Each attribute has its own class in the `javax.print.attribute.standard` package. This allows new attributes to be added to the system without having to modify the original installed codebase.

Value of `attribute.getName()`	**Class of** `attribute`
`printer-is-accepting-jobs`	`javax.print.attribute.standard.PrinterIs-AcceptingJobs`
`color-supported`	`javax.print.attribute.standard.ColorSupported`
`printer-name`	`javax.print.attribute.standard.PrinterName`

Each of the attribute classes can have additional methods that provide more information. For example, the `printer-name` attribute, corresponding to the `PrinterName` class, has a `getValue()` method, because `PrinterName` implements the `javax.print.attribute.TextSyntax` interface. (See the documentation for each individual class to find out what informational methods it provides.) Here's how you get access to the print service's name:

```
Attribute attribute = attributes[index];
if (attribute instanceof PrinterName) {
  PrinterName pn = (PrinterName)attribute;
  System.out.println( "printer name: "+pn.getValue() );
}
```

Since each kind of attribute is a different class, each one can provide different information, and so each one can have a unique set of methods.

3.1.5 *The SimpleDoc class*

To print something, you must supply an object that implements the `Doc` interface. You can create this class yourself, but in many cases, you can use the `SimpleDoc` class to take care of this for you.

The constructor for `SimpleDoc` takes three arguments:

- A `DocFlavor` object specifying the MIME type and the data-source type
- An object from which the data will be drawn
- A `DocAttributeSet` object containing attributes describing how the document should be printed

The object from which the data will be drawn must match the type specified in the DocFlavor object. For example, if the DocFlavor object specifies that the data will be drawn from an InputStream, then the object passed to this constructor must be some kind of InputStream.

3.1.6 *The DocPrintJob interface*

To print to a print service, you must first ask the print service to provide a print-job object. The class of this object is implementation-specific, but it must implement the DocPrintJob interface. This interface specifies methods regarding the print job, including methods to do the following:

- Print a document
- Install an event listener that listens for events such as these:
  - Job completed
  - Job canceled
  - Job failed
  - Job requires human intervention

Once you have a DocPrintJob object, you must turn your data into a Doc object. This allows you to call the print() method on the DocPrintJob object:

```
DocPrintJob job = printService.createPrintJob();
FileInputStream fin = new FileInputStream( "image.gif" );
Doc doc = new SimpleDoc( fin, DocFlavor.INPUT_STREAM.GIF, null );
job.print( doc, null );
fin.close();
```

This prints the GIF file to the specified PrintService.

3.1.7 *Example: printing an image*

Listing 3.2 shows the PrintImage program, which prints an Image to a PrintService. The image name is specified on the command line. (Different systems support printing different formats, but most systems support JPEG and GIF images.)

Listing 3.2   PrintImage.java

(see \Chapter3\PrintImage.java)

```java
import java.io.*;
import javax.print.*;
import javax.print.attribute.*;
import javax.print.attribute.standard.*;

public class PrintImage
{
  public PrintImage( String filename ) {
    try {
      PrintRequestAttributeSet pras =
        new HashPrintRequestAttributeSet();
      pras.add( new Copies( 1 ) );

      PrintService pss[] =
        PrintServiceLookup.lookupPrintServices(
          DocFlavor.INPUT_STREAM.GIF, pras );

      if (pss.length==0)
        throw new RuntimeException(
          "No printer services available." );

      PrintService ps = pss[0];
      System.out.println( "Printing to "+ps );

      DocPrintJob job = ps.createPrintJob();

      FileInputStream fin = new FileInputStream( filename );
      Doc doc = new SimpleDoc( fin,
                        DocFlavor.INPUT_STREAM.GIF, null );

      job.print( doc, pras );

      fin.close();
    } catch( IOException ie ) {
      ie.printStackTrace();
    } catch( PrintException pe ) {
      pe.printStackTrace();
    }
  }

  static public void main( String args[] ) throws Exception {
    if (args.length < 1) {
      System.err.println( "Usage: java PrintImage <image name>" );
      System.exit( 1 );
    }

    new PrintImage( args[0] );
  }
}
```

● **Select a PrintService**

● **Create and print the job**

This program selects a `PrintService` based on a number of criteria, and then prints the specified image to that `PrintService`.

3.1.8 Example: a custom print dialog box

Now we'll look at a custom print dialog box, which will serve to tie together the things we've learned in previous sections about the Print Service API. Of course, you can get a standard print dialog box by using the `ServiceUI.printDialog()` static method, but we're going to create our own. This simple dialog box allows the user to select a printer to print a GIF image to. The image is displayed in the dialog box itself, next to a list of printers. Below the printers is a status window that displays the status of a print job (see figure 3.1).

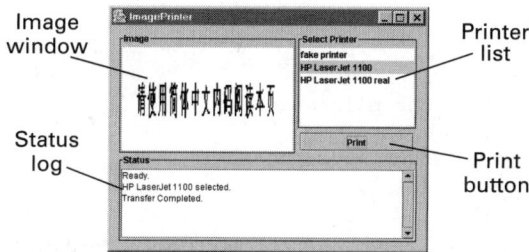

Figure 3.1 The dialog box generated by ImagePrinter. It allows you to select a printer from the printer list and print an image to it. The status log at the bottom displays the status of the print job.

ImagePrinter (see listing 3.3) installs a `PrintJobListener` object to track the status of a print job after the Print button is clicked. Each method of `PrintJobListener` corresponds to a different status update, and each one (except for `printJobNoMoreEvents()`) prints a message to the status window.

Listing 3.3 ImagePrinter.java

(See \Chapter3\ImagePrinter.java)

```java
import java.awt.*;
import java.awt.event.*;
import java.awt.image.*;
import java.io.*;
import javax.imageio.*;
import javax.print.*;
import javax.print.attribute.*;
import javax.print.attribute.standard.*;
import javax.print.event.*;
import javax.swing.*;
import javax.swing.event.*;
```

```
public class ImagePrinter extends JFrame
{
  private String filename;
  private BufferedImage image;
  private JTextArea statusTA;
  private PrintService printServices[];
  private PrintRequestAttributeSet attributeSet;

  public ImagePrinter( String filename ) throws IOException {
    super( "ImagePrinter" );
    this.filename = filename;

    setupAttributeSet();
    findPrinters();
    loadImage( filename );
    setupGUI();

    showStatus( "Ready." );
  }

  private void setupAttributeSet() {
    // The required attributes of the printer(s) we
    // will display in the printer list
    attributeSet = new HashPrintRequestAttributeSet();
    attributeSet.add( new Copies( 1 ) );
  }

  private void doPrint( int service ) {
    try {
      PrintService ps = printServices[service];

      DocPrintJob job = ps.createPrintJob();

      job.addPrintJobListener( new PrintJobListener() {
        public void printDataTransferCompleted(
            PrintJobEvent pje ) {
          showStatus( "Transfer Completed." );
        }
        public void printJobCanceled( PrintJobEvent pje ) {
          showStatus( "Print Job Canceled." );
        }
        public void printJobCompleted( PrintJobEvent pje ) {
          showStatus( "Print Job Completed." );
        }
        public void printJobFailed( PrintJobEvent pje ) {
          showStatus( "Print Job Failed." );
        }
        public void printJobNoMoreEvents( PrintJobEvent pje ) {
        }
        public void printJobRequiresAttention( PrintJobEvent pje ) {
          showStatus( "Print Job Requires Attention." );
        }
      } );
```

● **Print a document to the specified printer**

```
        FileInputStream fin = new FileInputStream( filename );
        Doc doc = new SimpleDoc( fin,
                            DocFlavor.INPUT_STREAM.GIF, null );

        job.print( doc, attributeSet );

        fin.close();
    } catch( IOException ie ) {
      ie.printStackTrace();
    } catch( PrintException pe ) {
      pe.printStackTrace();
    }
}

private void findPrinters() {
  printServices =
    PrintServiceLookup.lookupPrintServices(
      DocFlavor.INPUT_STREAM.GIF, attributeSet );

  if (printServices.length==0)
    throw new RuntimeException(
      "No printer services available." );
}

private void loadImage( String filename ) throws IOException {
  image = ImageIO.read( new File( filename ) );
}

private void setupGUI() {
  setBackground( Color.white );
  JPanel panel0 = new JPanel();
  panel0.setBorder(
    BorderFactory.createEmptyBorder( 10, 10, 10, 10 ) );
  panel0.setLayout( new BorderLayout() );

  JPanel printerPanel = new JPanel();
  printerPanel.setLayout( new BorderLayout() );
  printerPanel.setBorder(
    BorderFactory.createTitledBorder(
      BorderFactory.createLineBorder( Color.black ),
      "Select Printer" ) );

  String printServiceNames[] = new String[printServices.length];
  for (int i=0; i<printServices.length; ++i) {
    printServiceNames[i] = printServices[i].getName();
  }
  final JList printerList = new JList( printServiceNames );
  printerList.addListSelectionListener(
    new ListSelectionListener() {
      public void valueChanged( ListSelectionEvent lse ) {
        if (!lse.getValueIsAdjusting()) {
          int ind = printerList.getSelectedIndex();
          if (ind==-1) {
            showStatus( "No printer selected." );
```

❶ Select printers that can print GIF files and that match the specified attributes

● Set up the interface, including the printer list, image window, and status log

```
          } else {
            String printerName = printServices[ind].getName();
            showStatus( printerName+" selected." );
          }
        }
      }
    } );
  printerList.setSelectionMode(
    ListSelectionModel.SINGLE_SELECTION );
  printerList.setPreferredSize( new Dimension( 20, 80 ) );

  printerPanel.add( printerList, BorderLayout.CENTER );

  JButton printButton = new JButton( "Print" );
  JPanel buttonPanel = new JPanel();
  buttonPanel.setBorder(
    BorderFactory.createEmptyBorder( 5, 5, 5, 5 ) );
  buttonPanel.setLayout( new BorderLayout() );
  printButton.addActionListener( new ActionListener() {
    public void actionPerformed( ActionEvent ae ) {
      int ind = printerList.getSelectedIndex();
      if (ind==-1) {
        showStatus( "No printer selected." );
      } else {
        doPrint( ind );
      }
    }
  } );
  buttonPanel.add( printButton, BorderLayout.CENTER );

  JPanel rightPanel = new JPanel();
  rightPanel.setLayout( new BorderLayout() );
  rightPanel.add( printerPanel, BorderLayout.CENTER );
  rightPanel.add( buttonPanel, BorderLayout.SOUTH );

  JPanel imagePanel = new JPanel();
  imagePanel.setLayout( new BorderLayout() );
  imagePanel.setBorder(
    BorderFactory.createTitledBorder(
      BorderFactory.createLineBorder( Color.black ),
      "Image" ) );

  ImageCanvas imageCanvas = new ImageCanvas( image );
  imageCanvas.setPreferredSize( new Dimension( 140, 80 ) );
  imageCanvas.setMinimumSize( new Dimension( 140, 80 ) );
  imagePanel.add( imageCanvas, BorderLayout.CENTER );

  JPanel panel1 = new JPanel();
  panel1.setLayout( new BoxLayout( panel1, BoxLayout.X_AXIS ) );
  panel1.add( imagePanel );
  panel1.add( rightPanel );

  JPanel statusPanel = new JPanel();
  statusPanel.setLayout( new BorderLayout() );
```

```
      statusPanel.setBorder(
        BorderFactory.createTitledBorder(
          BorderFactory.createLineBorder( Color.black ),
          "Status" ) );

      statusTA = new JTextArea( 6, 80 );
      statusTA.setEditable( false );
      JScrollPane statusSP = new JScrollPane( statusTA,
        JScrollPane.VERTICAL_SCROLLBAR_ALWAYS,
        JScrollPane.HORIZONTAL_SCROLLBAR_NEVER );
      statusPanel.add( statusSP, BorderLayout.CENTER );
      panel0.add( statusPanel, BorderLayout.SOUTH );

      panel0.add( panel1, BorderLayout.CENTER );

      getContentPane().setBackground( Color.white );
      getContentPane().add( panel0, BorderLayout.CENTER );

      setSize( 450, 350 );

      addWindowListener( new WindowListener() {
        public void windowActivated( WindowEvent we ) {
        }
        public void windowClosed( WindowEvent we ) {
        }
        public void windowClosing( WindowEvent we ) {
          System.exit( 0 );
        }
        public void windowDeactivated( WindowEvent we ) {
        }
        public void windowDeiconified( WindowEvent we ) {
        }
        public void windowIconified( WindowEvent we ) {
        }
        public void windowOpened( WindowEvent we ) {
        }
      } );
    }
```

Print a message to the status log ●

```
    private void showStatus( String status ) {
      statusTA.setText( statusTA.getText()+status+"\n" );
    }
```

Display an image ●

```
    static class ImageCanvas extends JPanel
    {
      private BufferedImage image;
      public ImageCanvas( BufferedImage image ) {
        this.image = image;
      }
      public void paintComponent( Graphics g ) {
        int width = getWidth();
        int height = getHeight();
        g.drawImage( image, 0, 0, width, height, null );
      }
```

```
    }
    static public void main( String args[] ) throws IOException {
      if (args.length != 1) {
        System.err.println(
          "Usage: java ImagePrinter <image filename>" );
        System.exit( 1 );
      }
      String filename = args[0];
      if (!filename.toLowerCase().endsWith( ".gif" ))
        throw new RuntimeException(
          "Image must be a gif: "+filename );

      ImagePrinter ip = new ImagePrinter( filename );
      ip.setVisible( true );
    }
}
```

❶ This `AttributeSet` object is used for two purposes: to get a list of printers and to print the document. In the former case, it is used to select only those printers that support the attributes; in the latter case, it is used to request those attributes of the printer.

Note that the messages shown in the status window will differ from system to system, and on the structure of any network you might be printing over. In some cases, situations like a canceled print job do not trigger the appropriate method in the `PrintJobListener`.

3.2   *Reading and writing images with the Image I/O API*

One of the most irritating things about the original Abstract Windowing Toolkit (AWT) design was that its image implementation was unnecessarily web-specific. It assumed that images would be decoded via the web browser's built-in image-decoding facilities; that images would be loaded asynchronously by default; and that only a few browser-specific formats would be required. It did not provide straightforward support for loading images from disk or from in-memory arrays, and it provided even less support for encoding and writing images, forcing some programmers to make use of undocumented `sun.*` classes for this purpose.

The image-loading architecture was also burdened with a peculiar model of image downloading that was directly tied into the AWT, and that didn't require explicit use of multithreaded techniques. While this made it quite easy to display partial images while they were downloading, it made most other things more difficult.

The Image I/O (IIO) API—consisting of classes from the `javax.imageio` packages—seeks to remedy these inconsistencies and omissions. It provides a uniform way to read and write images regardless of execution context. It can read and write to arbitrary streams. It is written in pure Java, so its capabilities will not depend on the platform or execution context.

Image formats are handled by a pluggable architecture, which allows new decoders and encoders to be added to the system simply by adding the properly formatted JAR file to the classpath. Properly written software can make use of plug-ins added after the software was written, which means that software developers do not need to worry about the details of any particular format when writing their code. Nevertheless, support for format-specific information, including image metadata and thumbnail images, is provided.

These new methods of reading and writing images go hand-in-hand with the new *immediate image model* embodied in the `java.awt.BufferedImage` and `java.awt.Raster` classes. This model emerged with the introduction and integration of the Java2D packages. Unlike the original *push model*, the immediate model does not require the use of `ImageConsumer` and `ImageProducer` classes. (It doesn't even require you to pass `null` in for these parameters at every function call site!) All of this greatly reduces the conceptual overhead of using images in Java.

3.2.1 *The plug-in model*

The plug-in model of the Image I/O API allows it to be extensible to new image formats—even image formats that were created after the Image I/O API was created. Each new format is implemented for reading or writing by a set of classes installed somewhere in the runtime environment's classpath.

Each time an image is read or written, each plug-in is queried as to whether it can handle the given task. This decision can be based on the suffix of a filename, or it can be based on inspection of the actual data coming from some data source. (The first four bytes, often called the *magic number*, are enough to identify most image formats.)

The first plug-in that accepts the task is given the responsibility of finishing the operation. How a plug-in decides whether or not it can handle a particular task is up to that plug-in.

3.2.2 *Simple reading*

The following code fragment shows how easy it can be to load an image using the Image I/O API. The `ImageIO` class provides a static method called `read()`, which allows for easy image reading:

```
String filename = "image.jpg";
image = ImageIO.read( new File( filename ) );
```

The `read()` method can also take a stream as an argument:

```
image = ImageIO.read( someInputStream );
```

URLs are also supported, allowing this new API to do what the older APIs could easily do—load an image from a remote web server:

```
URL url = new URL( http://www.schaik.com/pngsuite/ccwn2c08.png );
image = ImageIO.read( url );
```

Reading images from URLs was already easy to accomplish using the older API, but it has been included in the new API for completeness.

3.2.3 *Simple writing*

In addition to the `read()` method, `ImageIO` supplies the complementary method called `write()` that allows for one-line writing of images:

```
String filename = "image.png";
ImageIO.write( image, "png", new File( filename ) );
```

Note that the second argument specifies the image format. In section 3.2.8 we'll see how this can be derived from the filename.

3.2.4 *The ImageIO class*

The `read()` and `write()` methods described in the preceding sections are both static methods of the `ImageIO` class. This class provides a number of static methods for the following purposes:

- Simplified reading and writing of images
- Configuring a memory or disk cache to use for aiding in reading and writing
- Getting information about what formats are supported for reading and writing

3.2.5 *Discovering available formats*

Since the Image I/O API is a pluggable API, it does not handle any image formats intrinsically. Each supported format comes in the form of a bundle of classes that are installed into the runtime system, either as part of the runtime environment or as part of a particular application. (The Image I/O API comes, by default, with a set of standard image types, but this set is not formally specified anywhere in the documentation—it seems to consist of the JPEG, GIF, and PNG image formats.) Since no particular formats are absolutely inherent in the Image I/O API, it is important to be able to find out at runtime what formats are available.

Each format is available either as a reader, a writer, or both. There are separate methods for discovering readers and writers, called `ImageIO.getReaderFormat-`

Names() and ImageIO.getWriterFormatNames(). Each of these methods returns an array of strings; each string represents an image format. The ShowImageIOInfo program illustrates their use (see listing 3.4).

Listing 3.4   ShowImageIOInfo.java

(see \Chapter3\ShowImageIOInfo.java)

```
import javax.imageio.*;

public class ShowImageIOInfo
{
  public ShowImageIOInfo() {
    String names[] = ImageIO.getReaderFormatNames();
    for (int i=0; i<names.length; ++i) {
      System.out.println( "reader "+names[i] );
    }

    names = ImageIO.getWriterFormatNames();
    for (int i=0; i<names.length; ++i) {
      System.out.println( "writer "+names[i] );
    }
  }
static public void main( String args[] ) throws Exception {
    new ShowImageIOInfo();
  }
}
```

Here's an example of the output of this program:

```
reader png
reader jpeg
reader JPEG
reader gif
reader jpg
reader JPG
writer PNG
writer png
writer jpeg
writer JPEG
writer jpg
writer JPG
```

You'll notice that some of the formats are entered multiple times. This is in recognition of the fact that some formats, such as JPEG, often have different extensions and are often written differently. The entries for "jpg", "JPG", "jpeg", and "JPEG" all map to the same plug-in.

You'll also notice that the GIF format does not support writing—presumably because the GIF format is surrounded by licensing issues.

3.2.6 *Example: reading and displaying an image*

The ShowImage program shows the use of the `ImageIO.read()` method in context (see listing 3.5). This program displays the image specified on the command line in a window.

Listing 3.5 from ShowImage.java

(see \Chapter3\ShowImage.java)

```java
private BufferedImage image;

public ShowImage( String filename ) {
  try {
    image = ImageIO.read( new File( filename ) );
  } catch( IOException ie ) {
    ie.printStackTrace();
  }
}

public void paint( Graphics g ) {
  g.drawImage( image, 0, 0, null );
}
```

Note that `ImageIO.read()` returns a `BufferedImage`. This is in keeping with the notion that the Image I/O API is strongly connected with the immediate image model, whose flagship class is `BufferedImage`. Since `BufferedImage` is, of course, a subclass of `Image`, you can use this object anywhere you use an `Image`; however, treating it as a `BufferedImage` allows you to make use of the powerful features in the Java2D library.

3.2.7 *Example: writing an image*

One of the very useful things that the Image I/O API can do is generate images. This can be very useful on the server side of a web application that needs to generate custom images for user-specific web pages. The WriteImageType program illustrates this technique (the relevant section of code is shown in listing 3.6). The graphics themselves are generated using standard Java2D drawing routines. The resulting image is then written to a file in a format specified on the command line. As mentioned in section 3.2.5, the API doesn't come, by default, with the ability to write GIF images.

Listing 3.6   from WriteImageType.java

(see \Chapter3\WriteImageType.java)

```
public WriteImageType( String filename, String type ) {
  try {
    int width = 200, height = 200;
    int x0 = 20, y0 = 20, x1 = width-20, y1 = width-20;

    // TYPE_INT_ARGB specifies the image format: 8-bit RGBA packed
    // into integer pixels
    BufferedImage bi = new BufferedImage( width, height,
      BufferedImage.TYPE_INT_ARGB );

    Graphics2D g2 = bi.createGraphics();

    // ... draw some stuff to the image

    ImageIO.write( bi, type, new File( filename ) );
  } catch( IOException ie ) {
    ie.printStackTrace();
  }
}
```

The drawing is done the same way it is for on-screen drawing: using a Graphics2D object. But this Graphics2D object belongs to the image, rather than to the on-screen window.

3.2.8 *The ImageReader class*

The ImageIO.read() and ImageIO.write() methods are really convenience methods. They handle the most common cases, namely reading or writing single images; ImageIO.read() derives the image type from the data itself. Using the ImageReader and ImageWriter classes directly allows you to have more control over the reading and writing processes.

An ImageReader is a source of images. By calling its read() method, you can load one or more images from a source of image data. This source may be a file, a URL defining an image on a remote machine, or a stream that supplies the image data (the stream being, perhaps, wrapped around an in-memory image source).

The ShowImageIR program (see listing 3.7) takes responsibility for finding and instantiating the correct kind of ImageReader for a particular file suffix. It also explicitly creates an InputImageStream, which is a wrapper around a regular input stream that allows the stream to be used by an ImageReader.

Because this approach makes it possible to read multiple images from a multi-image file format such as the GIF format, the program listed here also serves as a

simple animation player. It reads the entire set of images from a multi-image file
and animates them in a window.

Listing 3.7   ShowImageIR.java

(see \Chapter3\ShowImageIR.java)

```java
import java.awt.*;
import java.awt.image.*;
import java.awt.geom.*;
import java.awt.event.*;
import java.io.*;
import java.util.*;
import javax.imageio.*;
import javax.imageio.stream.*;
import javax.swing.*;

public class ShowImageIR extends Panel implements Runnable
{
  private BufferedImage images[];
  private int imageIndex=0;

  public ShowImageIR( String filename ) {
    try {
      FileInputStream fin = new FileInputStream( filename );
      String suffix =
        filename.substring( filename.lastIndexOf( '.' )+1 );
      System.out.println( "suf "+suffix );
      Iterator readers = ImageIO.getImageReadersBySuffix( suffix );
      ImageReader imageReader = (ImageReader)readers.next();
      ImageInputStream iis = ImageIO.createImageInputStream( fin );
      imageReader.setInput( iis, false );
      int num = imageReader.getNumImages( true );
      System.out.println( "Found "+num+" images" );
      images = new BufferedImage[num];
      for (int i=0; i<num; ++i) {
        images[i] = imageReader.read( i );
      }
      fin.close();
    } catch( IOException ie ) {
      ie.printStackTrace();
    }

    new Thread( this ).start();
  }

  public void paint( Graphics g ) {
    if (images==null)
      return;
    g.drawImage( images[imageIndex], 0, 0, null );
    imageIndex = (imageIndex+1)%images.length;
  }
```

*Read the
images*

```
public void run() {
  while (true) {
    try {
      Thread.sleep( 100 );
      repaint();
    } catch( InterruptedException ie ) {}
  }
}
```

● **Animate the images**

```
static public void main( String args[] ) throws Exception {
  JFrame frame = new JFrame( "ShowImageIR.java" );
  Panel panel = new ShowImageIR( args[0] );
  frame.getContentPane().add( panel );
  frame.setSize( 400, 400 );

  // Listener: quit on window close
  frame.addWindowListener( new WindowListener() {
    public void windowActivated( WindowEvent we ) {
    }
    public void windowClosed( WindowEvent we ) {
    }
    public void windowClosing( WindowEvent we ) {
      System.exit( 0 );
    }
    public void windowDeactivated( WindowEvent we ) {
    }
    public void windowDeiconified( WindowEvent we ) {
    }
    public void windowIconified( WindowEvent we ) {
    }
    public void windowOpened( WindowEvent we ) {
    }
  } );

  frame.setVisible( true );
  }
}
```

This program uses a background thread to animate the multiple images.

3.2.9 *The ImageWriter class*

Just as there is an ImageReader class, there is an ImageWriter class that allows you to have explicit control over the writing process. Using the ImageWriter class directly, you can select an ImageWriter for a particular format and explicitly assign an output data sink for the data to be written to.

The example shown in listing 3.8 duplicates the program in listing 3.6, but uses an `ImageWriter` explicitly rather than using `ImageIO.write()` to hide the details.

Listing 3.8   from WriteImageIW.java

(see \Chapter3\WriteImageIW.java)

```java
public WriteImageIW( String filename, String type ) {
  try {
    int width = 200, height = 200;
    int x0 = 20, y0 = 20, x1 = width-20, y1 = width-20;

    BufferedImage bi = new BufferedImage( width, height,
                                      BufferedImage.TYPE_INT_ARGB );

    Graphics2D ig2 = bi.createGraphics();

    GradientPaint paint =
      new GradientPaint( x0, y0, Color.white, x1, y1, Color.black );
    ig2.setPaint( paint );
    ig2.fillRect( 0, 0, width-1, height-1 );

    BasicStroke stroke = new BasicStroke( 10, BasicStroke.CAP_ROUND,
                                      BasicStroke.JOIN_ROUND );
    ig2.setPaint( Color.lightGray );
    ig2.setStroke( stroke );
    ig2.draw( new Ellipse2D.Double( x0, y0, x1-x0, y1-y0 ) );

    Font font = new Font( "TimesRoman", Font.BOLD, 20 );
    ig2.setFont( font );
    String message = "Java2D!";
    FontMetrics fontMetrics = ig2.getFontMetrics();
    int stringWidth = fontMetrics.stringWidth( message );
    int stringHeight = fontMetrics.getAscent();
    ig2.setPaint( Color.black );
    ig2.drawString( message, (width-stringWidth)/2,
                    height/2+stringHeight/4 );

    Iterator imageWriters =
      ImageIO.getImageWritersByFormatName( type );
    ImageWriter imageWriter = (ImageWriter)imageWriters.next();
    File file = new File( filename );
    ImageOutputStream ios =
      ImageIO.createImageOutputStream( file );
    imageWriter.setOutput( ios );
    imageWriter.write( bi );
  } catch( IOException ie ) {
    ie.printStackTrace();
  }
}
```

Because the file is being created, the type of the file must be specified on the command line.

3.2.10 *Customizing the reading process*

We've seen that using ImageReaders and ImageWriters allows for—and in fact requires—greater explicit control over the reading or writing process. So far, this has only resulted in more steps being taken to do the same thing. In this section, we'll see how we can exert more control over the reading process.

The CreateImageStrip program (see listing 3.9) takes a multi-frame file (such as an animated GIF) and loads the frames into a single image—an *image strip*. This could be easily done by loading each image separately and then copying the images into a separate strip image. But we're going to load the images directly into the strip by providing the ImageReader with a new destination image before each image is read. These destination images will be *subimages* of the strip image—one for each frame.

CreateImageStrip uses the ImageReadParam class. This class allows you to define settings for the loading process. In this example, we call its setDestination() method, which allows you to define where the pixels go when they are read.

Listing 3.9   CreateImageStrip.java

(see \Chapter3\CreateImageStrip.java)

```java
import java.awt.*;
import java.awt.image.*;
import java.awt.geom.*;
import java.awt.event.*;
import java.io.*;
import java.util.*;
import javax.imageio.*;
import javax.imageio.stream.*;
import javax.swing.*;

public class CreateImageStrip extends Panel
{
  private BufferedImage image;
  private int imageWidth, imageHeight;

  public CreateImageStrip( String filename ) {
    try {
      FileInputStream fin = new FileInputStream( filename );
      String suffix =
        filename.substring( filename.lastIndexOf( '.' )+1 );
```

```
Iterator readers = ImageIO.getImageReadersBySuffix( suffix );
ImageReader imageReader = (ImageReader)readers.next();
ImageInputStream iis = ImageIO.createImageInputStream( fin );
imageReader.setInput( iis, false );
int num = imageReader.getNumImages( true );
System.out.println( "Found "+num+" images" );
```

Prepare the Image-Reader

```
int totalHeight = 0;
int maxWidth = 0;
for (int i=0; i<num; ++i) {
  totalHeight += imageReader.getHeight( i );
  int w = imageReader.getWidth( i );
  if (w>maxWidth)
    maxWidth = w;
}
```

Find the total height and the maximum length

```
imageWidth = maxWidth;
imageHeight = totalHeight;

ImageTypeSpecifier its =
  (ImageTypeSpecifier)imageReader.getImageTypes( 0 ).next();
image = its.createBufferedImage( imageWidth, imageHeight );
```

```
int currentY = 0;
for (int i=0; i<num; ++i) {
  int wd = imageReader.getWidth( i );
  int ht = imageReader.getHeight( i );
  ImageReadParam irp = imageReader.getDefaultReadParam();
  BufferedImage subImage =
    image.getSubimage( 0, currentY, wd, ht );
  irp.setDestination( subImage );
  imageReader.read( i, irp );
  currentY += ht;
}
```

Read the images

```
    fin.close();
  } catch( IOException ie ) {
    ie.printStackTrace();
  }
}
public void paint( Graphics g ) {
  g.drawImage( image, 0, 0, null );
}

static public void main( String args[] ) throws Exception {
  // ... omitted
}
}
```

Each subimage is really a region of the larger strip image. Writing to each subimage, in turn, results in the images being drawn one-by-one down the length of the strip image.

3.2.11 *Listeners*

As mentioned previously, unlike the original image architecture in the AWT, the Image I/O API is not inherently asynchronous. This means, effectively, that when you load an image or a set of images, they are loaded then and there, in the current thread. Of course, this doesn't mean you can't write programs that load images in the background—it's just that you must explicitly create background threads to do so.

You can avoid having to create background threads in some instances by using *event listeners*. These allow you to install callbacks that are triggered when certain events happen. Five listeners are defined in the `javax.imageio.event` package:

- `IIOReadProgressListener`
- `IIOReadUpdateListener`
- `IIOReadWarningListener`
- `IIOWriteProgressListener`
- `IIOWriteWarningListener`

The progress listeners are used to listen for events that occur during normal reading and writing, including periodic updates as to how much of the data has been loaded. These can be used, for example, to update an on-screen progress bar. The warning listeners provide information on problems or glitches with the transmission that are not severe enough to cause an exception to be thrown, but that might be of interest to an application. The `IIOReadUpdateListener` is used to supply information about loading progressive images, or images with thumbnails, such as TIFF images. Within the loading process of such images, there are multiple points at which it would be reasonable to refresh the image in a graphical program, and this listener provides notification of these points.

The ChangeFormat program (see listing 3.10) demonstrates a listener that simply prints a report about each method that is called. The program itself is an image file-format conversion program. You give it two filenames on the command line—the first being the actual name of the file, and the second reflecting the desired format. It then converts the file from the current format to the desired format. For example, to convert a file called image.jpg to the PNG format, you would use this command:

```
java image.jpg image.png
```

The program installs an IIOReadProgressListener into the ImageReader before loading begins.

Listing 3.10   ChangeFormat.java

(see \Chapter3\ChangeFormat.java)

```java
import java.awt.*;
import java.awt.image.*;
import java.io.*;
import java.util.*;
import javax.imageio.*;
import javax.imageio.event.*;
import javax.imageio.stream.*;

public class ChangeFormat
{
  static public void main( String args[] ) throws Exception {
    if (args.length < 2) {
      System.err.println(
        "Usage: java PrintImage <infile> <outfile>" );
      System.exit( 1 );
    }
    String infile = args[0], outfile = args[1];

    FileInputStream fin = new FileInputStream( infile );
    String suffix = infile.substring( infile.lastIndexOf( '.' )+1 );
    Iterator readers = ImageIO.getImageReadersBySuffix( suffix );
    ImageReader imageReader = (ImageReader)readers.next();
    ImageInputStream iis = ImageIO.createImageInputStream( fin );
    imageReader.setInput( iis, false );

    imageReader.addIIOReadProgressListener(                    ● Install the listener
      new IIOReadProgressListener() {
        public void imageComplete( ImageReader source ) {
          System.out.println( "image complete "+source );
        }
        public void imageProgress( ImageReader source,
                                   float percentageDone ) {
          System.out.println( "image progress "+source+": "+
                              percentageDone+"%" );
        }
        public void imageStarted( ImageReader source,
                                  int imageIndex ) {
          System.out.println( "image #"+imageIndex+" started "+
                              source );
        }
        public void readAborted( ImageReader source ) {
          System.out.println( "read aborted "+source );
        }
        public void sequenceComplete( ImageReader source ) {
          System.out.println( "sequence complete "+source );
```

```
        }
        public void sequenceStarted( ImageReader source,
                                     int minIndex ) {
          System.out.println( "sequence started "+source+": "+
                              minIndex );
        }
        public void thumbnailComplete( ImageReader source ) {
          System.out.println( "thumbnail complete "+source );
        }
        public void thumbnailProgress( ImageReader source,
                                       float percentageDone ) {
          System.out.println( "thumbnail started "+source+": "+
                              percentageDone+"%" );
        }
        public void thumbnailStarted( ImageReader source,
                                      int imageIndex,
                                      int thumbnailIndex ) {
          System.out.println( "thumbnail progress "+source+", "+
                              thumbnailIndex+" of "+imageIndex );
        }
      } );

    BufferedImage image = imageReader.read( 0 );

    suffix = outfile.substring( outfile.lastIndexOf( '.' )+1 );
    Iterator imageWriters =
      ImageIO.getImageWritersBySuffix( suffix );
    ImageWriter imageWriter = (ImageWriter)imageWriters.next();
    File file = new File( outfile );
    ImageOutputStream ios = ImageIO.createImageOutputStream( file );
    imageWriter.setOutput( ios );
    imageWriter.write( image );
  }
}
```

**Read the image in
one format, and
write it in another**

Here's the output of the program:

```
image #0 started com.sun.imageio.plugins.gif.GIFImageReader@c39a2d
image progress com.sun.imageio.plugins.gif.GIFImageReader@c39a2d: 2.0%
image progress com.sun.imageio.plugins.gif.GIFImageReader@c39a2d: 4.0%
image progress com.sun.imageio.plugins.gif.GIFImageReader@c39a2d: 6.0%
image progress com.sun.imageio.plugins.gif.GIFImageReader@c39a2d: 8.0%
[... omitted ...]
image progress com.sun.imageio.plugins.gif.GIFImageReader@c39a2d: 94.0%
image progress com.sun.imageio.plugins.gif.GIFImageReader@c39a2d: 96.0%
image progress com.sun.imageio.plugins.gif.GIFImageReader@c39a2d: 98.0%
image progress com.sun.imageio.plugins.gif.GIFImageReader@c39a2d: 100.0%
image complete com.sun.imageio.plugins.gif.GIFImageReader@c39a2d
```

Note that the relatively simply GIF format only triggers three of the methods in this interface: `imageStarted()`, `imageProgress()`, and `imageComplete()`.

3.2.12 *Example: generating a graph*

Let's put the techniques of the previous sections to a real-world test. Listing 3.11 shows a class called `Graph`, which allows you to generate a simple graph for some month-by-month data, such as log data from a web server (see figure 3.2).

The data is supplied to the `Graph` class in the form of an array of doubles—one value for each month. The line is rendered using anti-aliasing to make it look as smooth as possible.

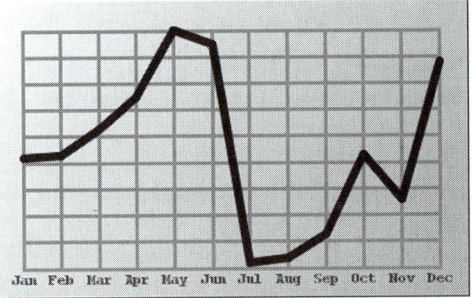 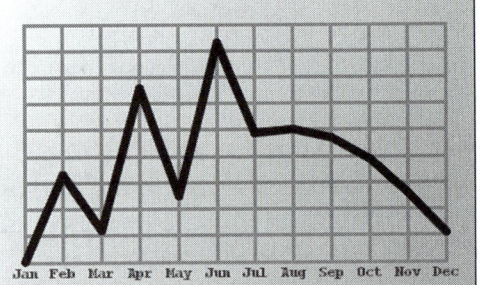

Figure 3.2   Graphs generated by Graph.java

Listing 3.11   Graph.java

(See \Chapter3\Graph.java)

```java
import java.awt.*;
import java.awt.image.*;
import java.io.*;
import java.util.*;
import javax.imageio.*;
import javax.imageio.stream.*;

public class Graph
{
  // A blank border around the graph
  static private final int border = 25;

  private BufferedImage image;

  // The graph data
  private double data[];
```

```java
private int width, height;

// The background grid
static private final int gridWidth=12, gridHeight=10;

static private final String months[] = {
  "Jan", "Feb", "Mar", "Apr", "May", "Jun", "Jul", "Aug", "Sep",
  "Oct", "Nov", "Dec" };

public Graph( double data[], int width, int height ) {
  this.data = data;
  this.width = width;
  this.height = height;
}

private void generateImage() {
  image = new BufferedImage( width, height,
                             BufferedImage.TYPE_INT_ARGB );
  Graphics2D g2 = image.createGraphics();
  g2.setRenderingHint(RenderingHints.KEY_ANTIALIASING,
      RenderingHints.VALUE_ANTIALIAS_ON);

  GradientPaint paint =
    new GradientPaint( 0, 0, Color.white, width, height,
                       Color.lightGray );
  g2.setPaint( paint );
  g2.fillRect( 0, 0, width-1, height-1 );

  g2.setPaint( Color.black );

  BasicStroke veryThin = new BasicStroke( 1,
                                BasicStroke.CAP_ROUND,
                                BasicStroke.JOIN_ROUND );
  BasicStroke thin = new BasicStroke( 3, BasicStroke.CAP_ROUND,
                                BasicStroke.JOIN_ROUND );
  BasicStroke thick = new BasicStroke( 7, BasicStroke.CAP_ROUND,
                                BasicStroke.JOIN_ROUND );
  g2.setStroke( thin );
  g2.setPaint( new Color( 155, 155, 155 ) );

  for (int i=0; i<gridWidth; ++i) {
    int x = border+(i*(width-2*border))/(gridWidth-1);
    g2.drawLine( x, border, x, height-border );
  }
  for (int i=0; i<gridHeight; ++i) {
    int y = border+(i*(height-2*border))/(gridHeight-1);
    g2.drawLine( border, y, width-border, y );
  }

  g2.setStroke( thick );
  g2.setPaint( Color.black );

  for (int i=1; i<data.length; ++i) {
    int x0 = border+
      (int)(((width-2*border)*(i-1))/(gridWidth-1));
```

Generate the image from the raw data using Graphics2D drawing methods

Draw the background

Draw the grid

Draw the data

```
      int y0 = border+
         (int)(((height-2*border)*data[i-1])/(gridHeight-1));
      int x1 = border+
         (int)(((width-2*border)*i)/(gridWidth-1));
      int y1 = border+
         (int)(((height-2*border)*data[i])/(gridHeight-1));
      y0 = height-1-y0;
      y1 = height-1-y1;

      g2.drawLine( x0, y0, x1, y1 );
    }

  g2.setStroke( veryThin );
  g2.setPaint( Color.darkGray );

 Font font = new Font( "Courier", Font.BOLD, 12 );
  g2.setFont( font );
  for (int i=0; i<12; ++i) {
    String month = months[i];
    FontMetrics fontMetrics = g2.getFontMetrics();
    int stringWidth = fontMetrics.stringWidth( month );
    int stringHeight = fontMetrics.getAscent();
    int x = border+
       (int)(((width-2*border)*(i))/(gridWidth-1)) - stringWidth/2;
    int y = height-border+stringHeight;
    g2.drawString( month, x, y );
  }
}
public void write( String filename ) throws IOException {
  // Generate the image if we haven't already
  if (image == null)
    generateImage();

  // Find an ImageWriter that can write the file type
  // specified by the filename
  String suffix =
    filename.substring( filename.lastIndexOf( '.' )+1 );
  Iterator imageWriters =
    ImageIO.getImageWritersBySuffix( suffix );
  ImageWriter imageWriter = (ImageWriter)imageWriters.next();
  if (imageWriter==null)
    throw new RuntimeException( "Format for "+filename+
                                " not supported" );

  File file = new File( filename );
  ImageOutputStream ios =
    ImageIO.createImageOutputStream( file );
  imageWriter.setOutput( ios );
  imageWriter.write( image );
}
```

● Draw
the data

● Draw the
month names

● Write the
image to
the file

```
static public void main( String args[] ) throws IOException {
    // Some sample data
    double data0[] = { 4.2, 4.3, 5.3, 6.5, 9.0, 8.5, 0.2, 0.4,
                       1.3, 4.3, 2.6, 7.8 };
    Graph graph0 = new Graph( data0, 400, 250 );
    graph0.write( "graph0.png" );

    // Some more sample data
    double data1[] = { 0, 3.3, 1.2, 6.6, 2.5, 8.3, 4.9, 5,
                       4.7, 3.9, 2.6, 1.1 };
    Graph graph1 = new Graph( data1, 400, 250 );
    graph1.write( "graph1.png" );
  }
}
```

Code like this could very easily be built into a servlet, allowing a site to generate custom log graphs for its administrators without having to worry about calling external graphing software. You can generate the images on the fly for each request, or cache them in the filesystem to save processing power.

3.3   Summary

This chapter has surveyed the two most important new features that JDK 1.4 adds to the Java2D package: the new Print Service API and the new Image I/O API. Both of these features supplement an existing facility by adding new features, and, in the case of the ImageIO framework, making easy what was once unnecessarily difficult.

The original printing API provided a minimal amount of control over printing and printer jobs. The Print Service API is designed to meet the standards of printing interfaces that have been established by common desktop operating systems. Thus, it supports the full range of printer options and allows for the addition of new options as needed. It also adds full control over the printing, canceling, and querying of print jobs, so that a Java application can make itself responsible for all aspects of printing. This is a major step toward making Java a viable platform for applications development.

The Image I/O API also increases Java's status as an excellent application language by providing support for reading and writing standard image formats. Unlike the previous API, which was specialized for browsers, this API does not favor any particular image format or image delivery mechanism. It allows the full power of the stream classes in the java.io package to be leveraged, meaning that any data source or sink that can be exposed as a stream can be used to save and load images. It's also a great deal more convenient.

Java Web Start (JAWS)

4

This chapter covers
- The Java Web Start execution model
- Server-side configuration
- The JNLP configuration file
- Using or bypassing the JAWS sandbox
- Accessing the local disk

Java Web Start (JAWS) is a new application deployment system. It allows you to install software with a single click within a web browser that has been enhanced with the Java Web Start plug-in. It transparently handles complex installation procedures, and it caches software on the local hard drive so that successive executions of the program are as fast as possible. It can even use different versions of the JDK for different applications, and will download new versions if that is required by the applications.

Java Web Start does not require that any special modifications be made to an application before it can be used within the system. JAWS does, however, execute applications within a *sandbox*, for security reasons. This security barrier can be bypassed by *trusted* applications—that is, applications that have been digitally signed by a trusted party. Untrusted applications are provided with limited system access via the `javax.jnlp` package.

JAWS is based on the Java Network Launching Protocol & API—or JNLP. JNLP is the underlying technology that defines the underlying abstractions; JAWS is the reference implementation.

This chapter will provide an overview of JAWS, and will illustrate the process of creating and deploying a JAWS program with a simple but complete drawing application called PicoDraw.

4.1 Understanding the JAWS execution model

An application does not need to be modified to be run within JAWS. Although applications will generally want to make use of the `javax.jnlp` package for getting access to the local system, this is not a requirement. A JAWS application is a set of Java classes, along with any necessary data, just like a regular application. And, just like a regular application, a JAWS application starts from its `main()` method.

The application files—data and Java classes—are placed on the web server along with a special *launch file*, also called a JNLP file after the *Java Network Launching Protocol & API*, which is the technology on which Java Web Start is based. This file is described in section 4.2.2.

When a JAWS application is launched, it is downloaded from the web server, unless it has already been downloaded. The exact way the user initiates the application depends on the operating system, but for all platforms, there is a central client program called the Application Manager. This program displays a list of JAWS applications that it knows about, including those that were first launched via a link in a web browser.

JAWS applications can also be run in *offline mode*. If a JAWS application is fully downloaded and does not itself require network access, then it can be run without access to the server from which it was downloaded.

4.1.1 Client, server, and application

Like an applet, a JAWS application is downloaded from a remote web server. Unlike an applet, a JAWS application is always cached on the local machine, and the cache is continuously updated by the JAWS runtime system. Before a JAWS application is launched, the JAWS environment compares the cache against the software stored on the server and downloads anything that is new.

If the application contains any data files, these data files are downloaded to the local machine along with the class files. The JAWS application has access to these files, but they are not treated as regular files. A JAWS application may or may not have access to the local filesystem, but it always has access to any data that was downloaded along with the classes.

This data isn't really *server-side* data because it is never accessed directly from the server. It also isn't exactly *client-side* data, since the JAWS application may or may not have access to the files of the client. Instead, we must make a third category: *application-side*. This third "side" consists of the application data that has been downloaded into the local cache.

The JAWS model is illustrated in figure 4.1.

As we will see in section 4.3.1, application-side data is accessed via the Class-Loader.getResource() methods. Thus, the local cache is not visible to the application via the traditional File, InputStream, and OutputStream classes. However,

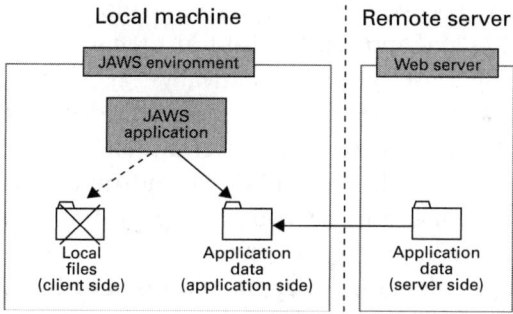

Figure 4.1   The JAWS model adds a third term to the client/server paradigm, called here the *application side.* **Application-side data is automatically copied into the local cache by the JAWS environment and can always be accessed by the application, even if local filesystem access is prohibited.**

some control over the caching process is available through the `javax.jnlp.Down-loadService` class.

4.1.2 *The sandbox*

JAWS applications, like applets, do not have the run of the local machine the way regular applications do. Instead, they are run within a *sandbox*, which is a security wrapper that controls which system resources can be used and which can't. The sandbox can be bypassed by a trusted application—this is described in section 4.4.

Despite these limitations, a JAWS application can make *restricted* use of some system resources through the `javax.jnlp` package. This package provides a number of *services* that can be offered by the client system. These services provide controlled access to system resources. For example, a JAWS application can write to a file, but the saving process always uses a dialog box; this means that the user must authorize each write.

Thus, Java Web Start provides two separate mechanisms for access to the local system: *sandbox* and *direct*. Sandbox access uses the `javax.jnlp` package for restricted access, while direct access uses digital code signing for unrestricted access. Sandbox access will be described in detail in section 4.3, and code signing will be outlined in section 4.4.

4.1.3 *Consider the possibilities*

Think about how the JAWS architecture fits into the scheme of things. It represents a bridge between applets and full-fledged applications, combining, as much as possible, the best features of both. It might make possible an application or deployment that you've considered in the past, but rejected either because it was too small to warrant a complex installation process, or too large to download on demand.

The difference between applets and applications isn't just technical—it's also *psychological*. An applet is something a user gets automatically—and without hassle—on a web page, while an application is something that a user does, or does not, choose to include on her system. Application-side caching changes many of the rules about applets, breaking down old file-size and download-time barriers. Would you like to place a complicated application on your web page and treat it like an applet? If the initial download is small, maybe you can.

Java Web Start also presents challenges. An application is usually a single bundle, installed by an installer program, but a JAWS application can come in pieces—and it should, if you don't want your users waiting through long downloads. This might mean refactoring your code, adding interface boundaries so that unused components don't need to be downloaded. The same thing goes for data. And because JAWS applications don't have an interactive installation step, there may be configuration issues you need to address within the application itself, rather than at installation time.

In the next section, we'll look in detail at the process of deploying a JAWS application.

4.2 Building and deploying a JAWS application

JAWS applications are deployed from a web server. JAWS does not require a special web server, or any kind of server-side module. The only required change is that the web server must be made to understand the `application/x-java-jnlp-file` MIME type.

Remember that the client web browser must have the Java Web Start plug-in installed.

4.2.1 JAR files

All application code and data must be packaged as JAR files. These files can be created with the jar tool provided with the JDK 1.4 distribution. Here's an example of its use:

```
jar cvf program.jar Program*.class data.txt images/image*.gif
```

You can package your program as a single JAR file, or break it up into multiple JAR files. The advantage of using multiple JAR files is that it means that the JAWS runtime doesn't have to download the entire application before it starts executing.

By default, all JAR files are downloaded, but you can set particular JAR files to be *lazy*, which means they aren't downloaded until they are needed. You can also use the `DownloadService` from the JNLP API to request that particular JAR files be downloaded.

4.2.2 The JNLP file

The JNLP is the starting point for the execution of a JAWS application. When the user clicks on a link pointing to a JNLP file, the browser downloads the JNLP file. This file instructs the JAWS system to download and launch the application.

The main function of the JNLP is to list the JAR file resources that make up the program. The first time a JAWS application is run, these JAR files are downloaded, and before each successive run, the JAWS environment downloads any JAR files that have changed on the server. Thus, the application is kept as up-to-date as possible on the local machine.

The easiest way to create a JNLP file is to copy an existing one and modify it for your application. Listing 4.1 shows a JNLP file containing most of the tags you need for regular operation.

Listing 4.1   PicoDraw.jnlp

(See \Chapter4\PicoDraw.jnlp)

```
<?xml version="1.0" encoding="utf-8"?>
<jnlp                                           ● The outermost tag, containing
                                                   the entire specification

  <!-- The JNLP version this file is compatible with -->
  spec="1.0+"

  <!-- The codebase of the application.  Each relative
       URL in this file is relative to this URL -->
  codebase="http://server/PicoDraw/"

  <!-- The relative URL of this file -->
  href="PicoDraw.jnlp">

  <information>                               ● Provide information about the program

    <!-- The title of the application -->
    <title>PicoDraw</title>

    <!-- The vendor of the application -->
    <vendor>Manning Publications</vendor>

    <!-- A web page containing more information about the
         application.  This URL will be displayed in
         the JAWS Application Manager -->
    <homepage href="http://www.manning.com/"/>

    <!-- Description elements are displayed in various places
         in the Application Manager -->
    <description>PicoDraw</description>
    <description kind="short">
      A *very* tiny draw program</description>

    <!-- A URL pointing at a GIF or JPG icon file -->
    <icon href="images/picodraw.jpg"/>

    <!-- Declares that the application can run without
         access to the server it was downloaded from -->
    <offline-allowed/>

  </information>

  <security>                              ❶ Request access to the local machine
      <!-- Request that the application be given full
           access to the local (executing) machine,
           as if it were a regular Java application.
           Requires that all JAR files be signed
           by a trusted party -->
```

```
        <all-permissions/>

    </security>

    <resources>                              ● Declare the application's server-side JAR files

      <!-- Specify the versions of the Java Runtime Environment
           (JRE) that are supported by the application.
           Multiple entries of this kind are allowed, in which
           case they are considered to be in order of preference -->
      <j2se version="1.4"/>

      <!-- Specify the relative URL of a JAR file containing
           code or data.  Specifying lazy tells the JAWS system
           that the file does not need to be downloaded before
           the application can be run -->
      <jar href="lib/classes.jar"/>
      <jar href="lib/backgrounds.jar"/>

    </resources>
                                                      Declare the class
    <application-desc main-class="PicoDraw"/>   ●  containing main()
  </jnlp>
```

❶ If you do leave out all-permissions, you are stating that the application is *untrusted*, which means that it will have restricted access to the local machine on which it executes. Including this declares that it is *trusted*, and thus will have access to the local machine. However, declaring it trusted is not enough—the applet must also be digitally signed by a trusted party.

4.2.3 Configuring the web server

As mentioned previously, Java Web Start does not require a special web server. The only requirement is that the web server recognize the application/x-java-jnlp-file MIME type. When the web server is asked for a JNLP file, it must send the file *as this type*.

See your web server documentation (or your system administrator) for instructions on adding a MIME type to your web server installation.

4.3 Using the sandbox: services

The sandbox offers the JAWS application restricted access to system resources via the javax.jnlp package. For example, it is possible for the application to read and write files, but each time a file is opened for reading or writing, the user must explicitly approve this through a Load or Save dialog box. This feature is intended to allow applications to load or save documents, rather than to allow free access to any files on the system.

Each form of access is represented by a different *service class*. The following services are provided by Java Web Start:

- `BasicService`—Interacts with the browser in online mode
- `ClipboardService`—Enables clipboard objects to be passed to and from the system clipboard, allowing cutting and pasting between a JAWS application and other applications
- `DownloadService`—Provides control over the application-side file cache
- `FileOpenService`—Allows user-authorized file reads
- `FileSaveService`—Allows user-authorized file writes
- `PersistenceService`—Provides a cookie-like persistence mechanism for storing small pieces of data
- `PrintService`—Enables printing

Using a service requires that you acquire a server object from the `ServiceManager` class, via the `lookup()` method:

```
try {
  PrintService ps =
    (PrintService)
    ServiceManager.lookup( "javax.jnlp.PrintService" );
} catch( UnavailableServiceException use ) {
  use.printStackTrace();
}
```

Each individual service class has its own API, described in the documentation included with the Java Web Start system (and thus with JDK 1.4).

To compile a program that uses the `javax.jnlp` package, you must explicitly add the JNLP JAR file to the classpath:

```
javac -classpath [path to JNLP jarfile] *.java
```

The PicoDraw example program in section 4.5 will illustrate the use of `ClipboardService`, `FileOpenService`, `FileSaveService`, `PrintService`, and `BasicService`.

4.3.1 *Using the sandbox: resources*

One of the most important services offered by the sandbox is the ability to access application data. The JAWS sandbox allows an application to load resources via its `ClassLoader`. This method does not use the `javax.jnlp` package—the JAWS runtime environment makes use of a special `ClassLoader` object that redirects resource requests to the application-side file cache. Specifically, the `ClassLoader.getResource()` method returns a URL pointing directly to a file within the cache. You can also use `ClassLoader.getResourceAsStream()` to open this URL as an `InputStream`.

Here's what the process looks like for loading an image:

```
ClassLoader cl = getClass().getClassLoader();
URL imageURL = cl.getResource( backgroundDirectory+"/"+name );

ImageIcon icon = new ImageIcon( imageURL );
drawCanvas.setBackgroundImage( icon.getImage() );
```

This process will be described in greater detail in section 4.5.

4.4   Bypassing the sandbox

It is possible to bypass the sandbox entirely. While the security measures offered by the sandbox are crucial for casual use of JAWS programs from untrusted sources, deployment of fully functional applications can be hindered by the restrictions.

You can use *digital code signing* to verify the authenticity of your application's JAR files. Once a user has verified that an application comes from a trusted source, she can instruct the application to run with full privileges. While the full details of digital code signing and the use of authentication servers is beyond the scope of this chapter, we'll cover the basics of code signing here. We'll create a self-signed test certificate, which is fine for testing and for deployment within an enterprise, where the server and client machines trust each other. (For public configurations, where the client and server do not trust each other, a third-party trust source, such as Veri-Sign, can be used to sign the application's JAR files.)

The keytool program allows for the generation of an authentication key:

```
keytool -genkey -keystore myKeystore -alias myself
```

This program will prompt you for information about the key, and the information will then be provided to end users when they are considering whether or not to trust your application. The key is stored in the file myKeyStore, under the alias `myself`.

Once you have a key safely tucked away in a keystore, you can use it to sign a JAR file with the jarsigner program. The following command signs test.jar—that is, it replaces test.jar with a signed version of itself:

```
jarsigner -keystore myKeystore test.jar myself
```

Place this signed version of test.jar on your web server in place of the unsigned version.

Finally, you must modify the JNLP to request full access to the local machine by adding a `security` tag as a child of the `jnlp` tag:

```
<?xml version="1.0" encoding="utf-8"?>
<jnlp
  spec="1.0+"
  codebase="http://server/PicoDraw/"
  href="PicoDraw.jnlp">
  <information>
  <!-- ... -->
  </information>
  <security>
      <all-permissions/>
  </security>
  <resources>
  <!-- ... -->
  </resources>
  <application-desc main-class="PicoDraw"/>
</jnlp>
```

When users execute this program by clicking on the JNLP link, they will be presented with a dialog box, as shown in figure 4.2.

The Details button allows the user to inspect the security certificate in detail before executing the program.

Figure 4.2   The JAWS environment asks the user's permission before the signed application is allowed to execute.

4.5   Example: a simple drawing program

This section contains a detailed example application that runs within the JAWS environment. It is a simple drawing program called PicoDraw. It is, in fact, *very* simple—all you can do, drawing-wise, is draw lines with the mouse, as shown in figure 4.3. (You can't even erase them.)

Despite the program's simplicity, in addition to drawing, you can save and load, print, load application-side data, bring up a web page in a browser window, and copy the drawing to the system clipboard. PicoDraw attempts to access the local disk directly; if it is not digitally signed, this will fail, and it will use the `FileOpen-Service` and `FileSaveService` services to perform loading and saving. Table 4.1 describes the features of PicoDraw, along with the services these features use.

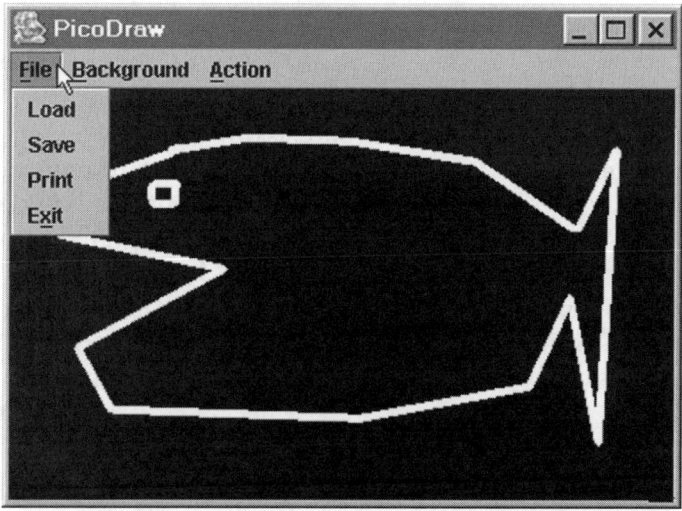

Figure 4.3   PicoDraw—a simple drawing program. This program demonstrates how a JAWS application interacts with the local machine for saving, loading, printing, and the like.

Table 4.1 PicoDraw demonstrates a number of different services from the javax.jnlp package. The different menu items each use a different service.

Menu	Menu item	Service	What it does
File	Load	`FileOpenService`	Load a drawing from the local disk
File	Save	`FileSaveService`	Save a drawing to the local disk
File	Print	`PrintService`	Print the drawing to a printer
Background	bg<n>.gif	(Doesn't use a service—loads image data through the `ClassLoader`)	Load image file bg<n>.gif
Action	Image to Clipboard	`ClipboardService`	Copy drawing, as an image, to the system clipboard
Action	Show Instructions	`BasicService`	Instruct the browser to show a remote web page

The following sections describe the three classes: `PicoDraw.java`, `DrawCanvas.java`, and `TransferableImage.java`. The bulk of the interesting code is in the first class, `PicoDraw.java`. This is a rather large example, but that is necessary, since this program demonstrates how the full application is integrated into the JAWS runtime system.

The server-side files for this example are contained in \Chapter4\server-signed.zip and \Chapter4\server-unsigned.zip. The `buildsignedjars.sh` and `buildunsignedjars.sh` scripts can be used to build (and possibly sign) the JAR files.

4.5.1 *PicoDraw.java*

`PicoDraw`, shown in listing 4.2, is the main class of the PicoDraw program. It handles the basic user interface and deals with things like saving, loading, and printing. It does not, however, handle the actual drawing—that's done in `DrawCanvas`.

Listing 4.2 PicoDraw.javatt

(See \Chapter4\PicoDraw.java)

```
import java.awt.*;
import java.awt.datatransfer.*;
import java.awt.event.*;
import java.awt.geom.*;
import java.awt.image.*;
import java.awt.print.*;
import java.io.*;
```

```java
import java.net.*;
import java.util.*;
import javax.swing.*;
import javax.jnlp.*;

public class PicoDraw extends JFrame
{
  // Application directory containing images
  static private final String backgroundDirectory = "backgrounds";

  // Application file containing list of background images
  static private final String backgroundList = "backgrounds.txt";

  // Local default directory for saving files
  static private final String savefileDirectory = "c:\\";

  // URL for web page showing instructions.  Change
  // this to point to the instructions file on your server
  static private final String instructionsURL =
    "http://serverhostname/jaws/PicoDraw/instructions.html";

  // Drawing field
  private DrawCanvas drawCanvas;

  // The last file we saved to
  private String lastFilename;

  // The last directory we saved to
  private File choosingDirectory;

  // Are we running inside a JAWS sandbox?
  private boolean useSandbox = false;

  /**
   * Constructor: set up the user interface
   */
  public PicoDraw() {
    super( "PicoDraw" );

    setupGUI();
    addListeners();
  }

  /**
   * Set up the user interface
   */
  private void setupGUI() {
    Container cp = getContentPane();

    JMenuBar mb = new JMenuBar();
    setJMenuBar( mb );

    JMenu fileMenu = new JMenu( "File" );
    fileMenu.setMnemonic( KeyEvent.VK_F );
    mb.add( fileMenu );
```

❶ **Build the user interface in the constructor**

```
JMenuItem loadMI = new JMenuItem( "Load", KeyEvent.VK_X );
loadMI.addActionListener( new ActionListener() {
    public void actionPerformed( ActionEvent ae ) {
      load();
    }
  } );
fileMenu.add( loadMI );

JMenuItem saveMI = new JMenuItem( "Save", KeyEvent.VK_X );
saveMI.addActionListener( new ActionListener() {
    public void actionPerformed( ActionEvent ae ) {
      save();
    }
  } );
fileMenu.add( saveMI );

JMenuItem printMI = new JMenuItem( "Print", KeyEvent.VK_X );
printMI.addActionListener( new ActionListener() {
    public void actionPerformed( ActionEvent ae ) {
      print();
    }
  } );
fileMenu.add( printMI );

JMenuItem exitMI = new JMenuItem( "Exit", KeyEvent.VK_X );
exitMI.addActionListener( new ActionListener() {
    public void actionPerformed( ActionEvent ae ) {
      exit();
    }
  } );
fileMenu.add( exitMI );

JMenu backgroundMenu = new JMenu( "Background" );
backgroundMenu.setMnemonic( KeyEvent.VK_B );
mb.add( backgroundMenu );
String backgrounds[] = getBackgrounds();
for (int i=0; i<backgrounds.length; ++i) {
  final String bgname = backgrounds[i];
  JMenuItem mi = new JMenuItem( bgname );
  mi.addActionListener( new ActionListener() {
    public void actionPerformed( ActionEvent ae ) {
      loadBackground( bgname );
    }
  } );
  backgroundMenu.add( mi );
}

JMenu actionMenu = new JMenu( "Action" );
actionMenu.setMnemonic( KeyEvent.VK_A );
mb.add( actionMenu );

JMenuItem toClipboardMI = new JMenuItem( "Image to Clipboard" );
toClipboardMI.addActionListener( new ActionListener() {
```

② Add a menu item for each background image

```java
      public void actionPerformed( ActionEvent ae ) {
        imageToClipboard();
      }
    } );
    actionMenu.add( toClipboardMI );

    JMenuItem instructionsMI = new JMenuItem( "Show Instructions" );
    instructionsMI.addActionListener( new ActionListener() {
      public void actionPerformed( ActionEvent ae ) {
        showInstructions();
      }
    } );
    actionMenu.add( instructionsMI );

    cp.setLayout( new BorderLayout() );
    drawCanvas = new DrawCanvas();
    cp.add( drawCanvas, BorderLayout.CENTER );

    setSize( 400, 300 );
    setLocation( 40, 40 );
    setVisible( true );
  }
  /**
   * Exit cleanly if window is closed
   */
  private void addListeners() {
    addWindowListener( new WindowListener() {
      public void windowActivated( WindowEvent we ) {
      }
      public void windowClosed( WindowEvent we ) {
      }
      public void windowClosing( WindowEvent we ) {
        exit();
      }
      public void windowDeactivated( WindowEvent we ) {
      }
      public void windowDeiconified( WindowEvent we ) {
      }
      public void windowIconified( WindowEvent we ) {
      }
      public void windowOpened( WindowEvent we ) {
      }
    } );
  }

  /**
   * Load a list of backgrounds from a list within the application
   */
  private String[] getBackgrounds() {
    try {
      // List of backgrounds
      Vector vec = new Vector();
```

```
      // Read file from resource
      ClassLoader cl = getClass().getClassLoader();
      InputStream in = cl.getResourceAsStream( backgroundList );
      InputStreamReader isr = new InputStreamReader( in );
      BufferedReader br = new BufferedReader( isr );

      while (true) {
        String line = br.readLine();
        // null line means end of stream
        if (line==null)
          break;

        vec.addElement( line );
      }
      in.close();

      // Turn Vector into array of Strings
      String dummy[] = new String[0];
      return (String[])vec.toArray( dummy );

    } catch( IOException ie ) {

      System.err.println( "Failed to load background list." );
      ie.printStackTrace();

      // Return empty background list
      return new String[0];
    }
  }

  /**
   * Exit cleanly
   */
  private void exit() {
    setVisible( false );

    // Dispose of JFrame resources
    dispose();

    System.exit( 0 );
  }

  /**
   * Write to an output stream: wrap a DataOutputStream
   * around it
   */
  private void write( OutputStream out ) throws IOException {
    write( new DataOutputStream( out ) );
  }

  /**
   * Write document to DataOutputStream
   */
  private void write( DataOutputStream dout ) throws IOException {
    Vector lines = drawCanvas.lines();
```

Read a list of background filenames from the application-side pool ❸

Write the document to a DataOutputStream ❹

```
  // Write # of lines
  int nlines = lines.size();
  dout.writeInt( nlines );

  // Write endpoints of each line
  for (int i=0; i<nlines; ++i) {
    Line2D line = (Line2D)lines.elementAt( i );
    dout.writeDouble( line.getX1() );
    dout.writeDouble( line.getY1() );
    dout.writeDouble( line.getX2() );
    dout.writeDouble( line.getY2() );
  }
}

/**
 * Read from an input stream: wrap a DataInputStream
 * around it
 */
private void read( InputStream in ) throws IOException {
  read( new DataInputStream( in ) );
}

/**
 * Read document from a DataInputStream
 */
private void read( DataInputStream din ) throws IOException {
  Vector lines = drawCanvas.lines();

  // Remove all existing lines -- loading a document
  // means erasing the existing document, if any
  lines.removeAllElements();

  // Read the # of lines
  int nlines = din.readInt();

  // Read the endpoints of each line
  for (int i=0; i<nlines; ++i) {
    double x1 = din.readDouble();
    double y1 = din.readDouble();
    double x2 = din.readDouble();
    double y2 = din.readDouble();
    Line2D.Double line = new Line2D.Double( x1, y1, x2, y2 );
    lines.addElement( line );
  }
}

/**
 * Load, either directly or via the sandbox method
 */
private void load() {
  if (useSandbox) {
```

Read the document from a DataInputStream ❺

6 Loading and saving is either direct, or via the sandbox method

```
      loadSandbox();
   } else {
      loadDirect();
   }
}

/**
 * Save, either directly or via the sandbox method
 */
private void save() {
   if (useSandbox) {
      saveSandbox();
   } else {
      saveDirect();
   }
}

/**
 * Load directly from the filesystem.  If it fails,
 * switch to sandbox mode and try again
 */
private void loadDirect() {
   try {
      // Let the user pick a file
      File file = chooseFile( this, false );

      FileInputStream fin = new FileInputStream( file );
      read( fin );
      fin.close();
   } catch( SecurityException se ) {
      System.err.println( "Failed to do direct read; "+
                          "using sandbox method...." );

      // Switch to sandbox mode and try again
      useSandbox = true;
      load();
   } catch( IOException ie ) {
      ie.printStackTrace();
   }
}

/**
 * Save directly to the filesystem.  If it fails,
 * switch to sandbox mode and try again
 */
private void saveDirect() {
   try {
      // Let the user pick a file
      File file = chooseFile( this, true );

      FileOutputStream fout = new FileOutputStream( file );
      write( fout );
      fout.close();
```

6 Loading and saving is either direct, or via the sandbox method

6 Loading and saving is either direct, or via the sandbox method

7 Load a file directly from the filesystem

8 Save a file directly to the filesystem

```
    } catch( SecurityException se ) {
      System.err.println( "Failed to do direct write; "+
                          "using sandbox method...." );

      // Switch to sandbox mode and try again
      useSandbox = true;
      save();
    } catch( IOException ie ) {
      ie.printStackTrace();
    }
  }

  /**
   * Load via the sandbox method
   */
  private void loadSandbox() {
    try {
      FileOpenService fos =
        (FileOpenService)ServiceManager.lookup(
          "javax.jnlp.FileOpenService" );

      FileContents fc = fos.openFileDialog( null, null );

      if (fc!=null) {
        InputStream in = fc.getInputStream();
        read( in );

        // Remember what name we used
        lastFilename = fc.getName();
      } else {
        System.err.println( "Open aborted" );
      }

      // We've loaded new data -- draw it
      repaint();
    } catch( UnavailableServiceException use ) {
      use.printStackTrace();
    } catch( IOException ie ) {
      ie.printStackTrace();
    }
  }

  /**
   * Save via the sandbox method.  Use background thread to
   * write to one end of a pipe; the FileSaveService reads
   * from the other end
   */
  private void saveSandbox() {
    try {
      FileSaveService fss =
        (FileSaveService)ServiceManager.lookup(
          "javax.jnlp.FileSaveService" );
```

❾ Load a file using the sandbox method

❿ Save a file using the sandbox method

● Get a FileSaveService object from the ServiceManager

```
      // Use the filename we last loaded from
      String filename = lastFilename;
      if (lastFilename==null)
        lastFilename = "data.pd";

      PipedInputStream pin = new PipedInputStream();
      final PipedOutputStream pout = new PipedOutputStream( pin );

      Thread writeThread = new Thread( new Runnable() {
        public void run() {
          try {
            write( pout );
            System.out.println( "Background write done." );
          } catch( IOException ie ) {
            System.err.println( "Background write failed!" );
            ie.printStackTrace();
          } finally {
            try {
              pout.close();
            } catch( IOException ie ) {
              System.err.println(
                "Background write failed to close!" );
              ie.printStackTrace();
            }
          }
        }
      } );
      writeThread.start();

      FileContents fc = fss.saveFileDialog( savefileDirectory,
                                    null, pin, filename );

      // Remember what name we used
      if (fc != null)
        lastFilename = fc.getName();
    } catch( UnavailableServiceException use ) {
      use.printStackTrace();
    } catch( IOException ie ) {
      ie.printStackTrace();
    }
  }

  /**
   * Show a generic file chooser for saving and loading.
   */
  public File chooseFile( Component comp, boolean savep ) {
    if (choosingDirectory == null) {
      choosingDirectory =
        new File( System.getProperty( "user.dir" ) );
    }
```

Create a pipe

Background thread writes to pipe

FileSaveService reads from pipe

```
      JFileChooser jfc = new JFileChooser( choosingDirectory );

      int ret = savep ? jfc.showSaveDialog( comp )
                      : jfc.showOpenDialog( comp );
      if (ret == JFileChooser.APPROVE_OPTION) {
        File file = jfc.getSelectedFile();
        String name = file.getPath();
        choosingDirectory = jfc.getCurrentDirectory();
        file = new File( name );
        return file;
      }
      return null;
  }

  /**
   * Load a background, given its application-side filename
   */
  private void loadBackground( String name ) {
    // Read image from resource
    ClassLoader cl = getClass().getClassLoader();
    URL imageURL = cl.getResource( backgroundDirectory+"/"+name );

    ImageIcon icon = new ImageIcon( imageURL );
    drawCanvas.setBackgroundImage( icon.getImage() );
  }

  /**
   * Print drawing to a printer
   */
  private void print() {
    try {
      PrintService ps =
        (PrintService)ServiceManager.lookup(
          "javax.jnlp.PrintService" );

      boolean ok = ps.print( drawCanvas );

      if (!ok)
        System.err.println( "Unable to print!" );
    } catch( UnavailableServiceException use ) {
      use.printStackTrace();
    }
  }

  /**
   * Bring up instructions in the web browser
   */
  private void showInstructions() {
    boolean ok = true;
    Exception exception = null;

    try {
      BasicService bs = (BasicService)
        ServiceManager.lookup( "javax.jnlp.BasicService" );
```

● **Read a background image from the application-side pool**

⑪ **Print the drawing to a printer**

⑫ **PrintService.print() prints a document; drawCanvas implements Printable**

⑬ **Display a web page in the web**

```
        URL url = new URL( instructionsURL );

        ok = bs.showDocument( url );
      } catch( UnavailableServiceException use ) {
        exception = use;
        ok = false;
      } catch( MalformedURLException mue ) {
        exception = mue;
        ok = false;
      }

      // Handle either Exception here
      if (!ok) {
        System.err.println( "Couldn't show instructions.\n"+
                            "Please direct your browser to "+
                            instructionsURL+"." );
        if (exception != null)
          exception.printStackTrace();
      }
    }

    /**
     * Copy image to system clipboard
     */
    private void imageToClipboard() {
      Image image = drawCanvas.getImage();
      TransferableImage ti = new TransferableImage( image );

      try {
        ClipboardService cs =
          (ClipboardService)ServiceManager.lookup(
            "javax.jnlp.ClipboardService" );

        cs.setContents( ti );

      } catch( UnavailableServiceException use ) {
        System.err.println( "Can't get access to clipboard" );
        use.printStackTrace();
      }
    }

    static public void main( String args[] ) {
      new PicoDraw();
    }
  }
```

⑭ Copy the drawing to the system clipboard

❶ The constructor builds the user interface and sets up any necessary event listeners. The PicoDraw object itself is a JFrame—it must create, and make visible, its own window. In both of these ways, a JAWS program is more like a regular Java application than an applet.

❷ The Background menu contains one entry for each background image that is available to the program. This list is read from the application-side data via the `getBackgrounds()` method.

❸ The file backgrounds.txt contains a list of filenames—each one corresponds to one of the background images in the application-side backgrounds/ directory.

To read this application-side file, we use the `ClassLoader` resource facility. This facility allows each custom `ClassLoader` to provide data resources in its own way. The JAWS `ClassLoader` provides access to the application side stored within the JAWS cache.

The code here calls `ClassLoader.getResourceAsStream()`, but if you were to call `ClassLoader.getResource()`, you'd get a URL pointing to a file in the cache. The URL would look something like this:

```
jar:file:./C:/PROGRAM FILES/JAVA WEB START/.javaws/cache/http/
    D192.168.0.1/P80/DMjaws/DMPicoDraw/DMlib/RMPicoDraw.jar!/
    backgrounds.txt
```

Each application-side resource can be identified by a unique URL of this kind, and these URLs are used by the `ClassLoader` resource facility to offer application-side data to the application.

❹ ❺ As we see in the comment for **❻**, there are two different ways that our application can gain access to the local hard drive in order to save and load documents. However, both methods require that we write our data to, and read it from, a stream.

The code in these two sections takes care of reading and writing our custom document savefile format. We use `DataInputStream` and `DataOutputStream` objects so that we have a fully portable format.

❻ JAWS applications run inside a sandbox. This means that we don't have free access to the local filesystem as we would in a regular Java application. However, as we saw in sections 4.3 and 4.4, there are two secure methods for accessing the local filesystem—direct and sandbox. In `PicoDraw`, we attempt to use the direct method, and if it fails, we try the sandbox method. This applies to both loading and saving.

For this particular application, there actually isn't much point in providing two methods—the sandbox method suffices, and it is always available. However, in general, applications may strongly prefer to use the direct method, since it allows for uninhibited filesystem access, while the sandbox method only allows access to files selected directly by the user within a file-selection dialog box.

The best thing to do, then, is to use the direct method when possible, and to use the sandbox method if the direct method doesn't work. The sandbox method may require a reduction in program functionality; if so, this should be made very clear to the user.

In PicoDraw, we keep a boolean called useSandbox. This is set whenever we discover that we cannot use the direct method of filesystem access. Once it is set, we never try the direct method again, because it will not succeed. (In the current implementation, the availability of direct access is not going to change while the application is running.)

❼ ❽ Using the direct method, we ask the user to select a file using a regular JFileChooser. We read from, or write to, this file using the read() and write() methods described previously.

❾ Using the sandbox methods, we gain access to files only through dialog boxes that let the user explicitly pick a file. We acquire a FileOpenService object from the ServiceManager; this service allows us to open a dialog box to ask the user to select a file. This file is provided to the application in the form of a FileContents object, which can be read from or written to via its getInputStream() and getOutputStream() methods.

Once we've acquired an InputStream, we can pass it to read() (described previously) to load our document.

❿ Saving via the sandbox method requires certain formalities, just as loading via the sandbox did. We gain access to the filesystem by creating a FileSaveService object, and using it to write the file.

However, it is more complicated in this case. FileSaveService.saveFileDialog() takes an InputStream object. It reads the data from this InputStream and writes it to the file selected by the user. *The writing process takes its data from a stream.**

The best way to do this is to use a pipe—a PipedInputStream/PipedOutputStream pair. Our application writes to one end of the pipe, using the write() method, and FileSaveService reads the data from the other end, and writes it to the local file.

In order to write the data to this pipe, we need to use a background thread to do the write. It's tempting to write the data in the main thread, but this could be a terrible mistake. We have no idea how much data there might be, and the internal buffer used by a pipe has a finite capacity. If this buffer were to fill, the write would block the main thread; the save would never happen.

A finite buffer is also why we don't want to write to an internal buffer using ByteArrayOutputStream/ByteArrayInputStream. Using a pipe means that the writing process can write arbitrary amounts of data, and take arbitrarily long to write it—just as you would if you were writing directly to the filesystem.

---

*In theory, one should be able to write to a file using the FileOpenService; however, that did not work on the system used to develop the code for this book.

⑪ ⑫ The `javax.jnlp.PrintService` allows a JAWS application to print to a printer. Any object that implements the `java.awt.print.Printable` interface (or the `java.awt.print.Pageable` interface) can be passed to `PrintService.print()`.

⑬ The `javax.jnlp.BasicService` class allows a JAWS application to cause the host browser to bring up a particular web page. `BasicService.isWebBrowserSupported()` can be used to determine whether or not `BasicService` is capable of bringing up a web page in a browser.

⑭ Here, we wrap the image in a `TransferableImage`, which implements the `java.awt.datatransfer.Transferable` interface. This allows the data to be transferred to the system clipboard. The system clipboard is the clipboard, if any, that can be used by other programs, whether they are written in Java or not.

4.5.2 DrawCanvas.java

The `DrawCanvas` class (shown in listing 4.3) handles the actual drawing of the program. As mentioned previously, there's only one thing you can do: draw lines with the mouse. `DrawCanvas` also deals with rendering the drawing as an `Image` object, and it deals with printing by implementing the `java.awt.print.Printable` interface.

Listing 4.3 DrawCanvas.java

(See \Chapter4\DrawCanvas.java)

```java
import java.awt.*;
import java.awt.event.*;
import java.awt.image.*;
import java.awt.geom.*;
import java.awt.print.*;
import java.util.*;
import javax.swing.*;

/**
 * A Canvas you can draw lines in.  Also knows how to
 * print itself, via the Printable interface
 */
public class DrawCanvas extends JPanel implements Printable
{
    // A list of java.awt.geom.Line2D that have been drawn
    private Vector lines = new Vector();

    // Background image
    private Image backgroundImage;

    // The index of the line that is currently being drawn
    private int newLine = -1;

    // Draw a thick line
    private BasicStroke stroke =
```

DrawCanvas is the program's drawing surface

❶

```
      new BasicStroke( 5, BasicStroke.CAP_ROUND,
                       BasicStroke.JOIN_ROUND );

  /**
   * Constructor: add listeners
   */
  public DrawCanvas() {
    addListeners();
  }

  /**
   * Return the list of lines
   */
  public Vector lines() {
    return lines;
  }

  /**
   * Install a background image
   */
  public void setBackgroundImage( Image backgroundImage ) {
    this.backgroundImage = backgroundImage;
    repaint();
  }

  /**
   * Draw the lines and background
   */
  public void paintComponent( Graphics g ) {
    Graphics2D g2 = (Graphics2D)g;

    g2.setStroke( stroke );

    int width = getWidth();
    int height = getHeight();

    // Draw the background
    if (backgroundImage!=null) {
      // Draw a background image
      g2.drawImage( backgroundImage, 0, 0, width, height, null );
    } else {
      // Draw a blank rectangle
      g2.setColor( Color.black );
      g2.fillRect( 0, 0, width-1, height-1 );
    }

    // Draw the lines
    g2.setColor( Color.white );
    for (Enumeration e = lines.elements(); e.hasMoreElements();) {
      Line2D line = (Line2D)e.nextElement();
      g2.draw( line );
    }
  }
}
```

● **paintComponent() is for screen rendering, printing, and offscreen image rendering**

```
/**
 * Add a new line to the list
 */
private void startDrawingLine( int x, int y ) {
  Line2D line = new Line2D.Double( x, y, x, y );
  lines.addElement( line );

  // Remember the index, within the list,
  //  of the new line
  newLine = lines.size()-1;

  repaint();
}

/**
 * We're still drawing the line: endpoint of the line
 * tracks the mouse cursor
 */
private void updateDrawingLine( int x, int y ) {
  // We must be in the middle of drawing the new line
  if (newLine==-1)
    return;

  Line2D line = (Line2D)lines.elementAt( newLine );
  line.setLine( line.getX1(), line.getY1(), x, y );
  repaint();
}

/**
 * Done drawing the line
 */
private void endDrawingLine() {
  newLine = -1;
}

/**
 * Render the document as an Image
 */
public Image getImage() {
  int width = getWidth();
  int height = getHeight();
  BufferedImage bi = new BufferedImage( width, height,
    BufferedImage.TYPE_INT_ARGB );
  Graphics2D g2 = (Graphics2D)bi.getGraphics();
  paintComponent( g2 );
  return bi;
}

/**
 * Event listeners for drawing lines
 */
private void addListeners() {
  addMouseListener( new MouseListener() {
    public void mousePressed( MouseEvent me ) {
```

● **getImage() renders the drawing as an Image object**

```
      startDrawingLine( me.getX(), me.getY() );
    }
    public void mouseEntered( MouseEvent me ) {
    }
    public void mouseExited( MouseEvent me ) {
    }
    public void mouseReleased( MouseEvent me ) {
      endDrawingLine();
    }
    public void mouseClicked( MouseEvent me ) {
    }
  } );

  addMouseMotionListener( new MouseMotionListener() {
    public void mouseDragged( MouseEvent me ) {
      updateDrawingLine( me.getX(), me.getY() );
    }
    public void mouseMoved( MouseEvent me ) {
    }
  } );
}
/**
 * Render printable image
 */
public int print( Graphics graphics, PageFormat pageFormat,
                  int pageIndex ) throws PrinterException {
  paintComponent( graphics );
  return Printable.PAGE_EXISTS;
}
}
```

**print() lets
DrawCanvas
implement the**

❶ DrawCanvas is the program's drawing surface. The user clicks and drags within this Component to draw lines.

Like any on-screen Component, DrawCanvas has a paintComponent() method, which is used to render it to the screen. However, this method is also used for printing and for rendering the drawing as an Image object.

Printing is possible because DrawCanvas implements the java.awt.print.Printable interface. Specifically, the DrawCanvas.print() method implements the Printable.print() method. paint() calls paintComponent() on the supplied Graphics object.

DrawCanvas can also render its contents as an Image object. This Image can be stored in the system clipboard, allowing the drawing to be pasted into other programs.

4.5.3 *TransferableImage.java*

The `TransferableImage` class (see listing 4.4) is used to wrap an `Image` of the user's drawing so that it can be copied into the system clipboard. It does this by implementing the `java.awt.datatransfer.Transferable` interface. Each kind of data that can be transferred to the system clipboard corresponds to a different instance of `DataFlavor`; in this case, we use `DataFlavor.imageFlavor`.

We pass this `Transferable` to the clipboard system via the `ClipboardService.setContents()` method; the clipboard system then calls `getTransferData()`, which responds by returning the `Image` object wrapped inside the `Transferable`.

Listing 4.4   TransferableImage.java

(See \Chapter4\TransferableImage.java)

```java
import java.awt.*;
import java.awt.datatransfer.*;

/**
 * Wrapper class for copying image to system clipboard
 */
public class TransferableImage implements Transferable
{
  private Image image;

  public TransferableImage( Image image ) {
    this.image = image;
  }

  public DataFlavor[] getTransferDataFlavors() {
    return new DataFlavor[] { DataFlavor.imageFlavor };
  }

  public boolean isDataFlavorSupported( DataFlavor flavor ) {
    return DataFlavor.imageFlavor.equals( flavor );
  }

  public Object getTransferData( DataFlavor flavor )
      throws UnsupportedFlavorException {
    if (!isDataFlavorSupported( flavor ))
      throw new UnsupportedFlavorException( flavor );

    return image;
  }
}
```

This Transferable object only supports the imageFlavor flavor

Return the Image when the system requests it

See the documentation for the `java.awt.Transferable` package for more information on using `Transferable` objects.

4.6   *Summary*

Java Web Start solves a number of problems that have plagued Java and kept it from being recognized as a language for real-world application development. Deploying software using JAWS is just as easy—if not easier—than deploying native applications. Software updates are made transparent and trivial. An enterprise can use Java Web Start to deploy an entire suite of custom and prepackaged applications with a minimum of intervention on the part of the IT support staff. Once the JAWS client is installed, everything else can be handled from a central location; updates are automatic.

Java Web Start also solves the security dilemma posed by the Web, which demands that we choose between security and functionality. JAWS solves this by allowing both: applications are run inside a sandbox, which protects the local host; applications can also be authenticated through a trusted party, and then allowed to access the resources of the machine with the freedom of a locally installed application.

The most important feature of Java Web Start is the convenience for end users: once the JAWS client is installed, a single click brings them a complete application. The only real drawback is the initial installation—JAWS is about a megabyte and requires an explicit installation step.

JAWS is an excellent solution for enterprise-wide software deployment. Explicit installation and upgrades can become a thing of the past because JAWS deals with keeping track of code versions, automatically downloading necessary resources. JAWS can even use multiple installed JDKs, and download new ones as they are required.

Logging

5

This chapter covers

- Logging methods
- Configuring logging
- Custom handlers
- Custom filters
- Custom formatters
- Logging efficiency

Over the years that Java has been in widespread commercial use, a number of logging solutions have been created. Smaller projects sometimes use freely available libraries, while larger projects have been known to have their own built-in logging systems.

The Logging API within JDK 1.4, in the `java.util.logging` package, provides a flexible and powerful system for logging messages, and—just as important—for turning these messages on and off, without the need for recompiling. This means that logging messages can be turned on by the end user, long after the software has shipped.

This is perhaps the greatest benefit, since it means that even post-release software can provide detailed debugging information in the event of a problem. This doesn't just mean being able to find bugs in the software—logging messages can help debug problems with other software, or problems caused by unforeseen interactions between software. For example, a DSL dial-up system written in Java might be able to help debug problems with DSL hardware—the logging messages can contain detailed information about the dial-up process, which in turn can help pinpoint where the hardware fails.

The Logging API uses a system-wide configuration file to define default settings, and additional configuration files can be used to provide greater control. Programmatic control is also available—you can configure the logging system directly from your program.

The structure of the logging system is outlined in section 5.1, and configuration is described in section 5.2. The logging system is demonstrated in a program in section 5.3. Section 5.4 describes the implementation of a custom log `Handler`, and section 5.5 demonstrates a custom log `Formatter`.

5.1   *Logging overview*

The simplest way to log a message is as follows:

```
Logger.global.info( "hi" );
```

This results, under the default JDK configuration, in the following output:

```
Dec 19, 2001 2:41:13 PM MyProgram main
INFO: hi
```

The object `Logger.global` is a global `Logger` object; however, `Logger.global` is only for casual use of the logging system. Here's the right way to do it:

```
Logger logger = Logger.getLogger( "current.package" );
logger.info( "hi" );
```

As we'll see in section 5.1.3, the argument to `getLogger()`—the logger's name—is generally, but not always, a package name.

5.1.1 Log message format

Although the format used by the logging system is variable and customizable, it does have a default format, as detailed in figure 5.1.

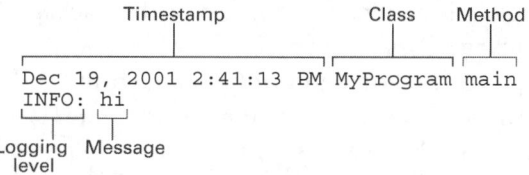

Figure 5.1   **The default format used by the Logging API. Each log message takes up two lines. The first line shows the date and time, as well as the class and method from which the log was posted. The second line shows the logging level and the log message itself.**

5.1.2 Logging levels

A logging level is a measure of severity for a message. The logging system can be tuned to only display messages of a certain severity, or higher. The info() method shown in the previous section corresponds to the INFO logging level, which is the default level in the standard configuration.

The following logging levels are available:

- SEVERE—Used for catastrophic errors—conditions from which the program may not recover, and which, in any case, require immediate attention.

- WARNING—Used for serious problems that may or may not be catastrophic. These do not necessarily require immediate attention, but they should definitely be noted.

- INFO—Used for run-of-the-mill messages. The INFO level is the default, and so messages logged at the INFO level are seen during normal runs.

- CONFIG—Used for logging configuration settings, generally at startup.

- FINE, FINER, FINEST—Used for detailed logging. This information is generally logged for debugging. The finer the level, the more information is logged at that level. This makes a great deal of information available, but the user doesn't need to wade through it unless she wants to.

5.1.3 *Logger names and the logger hierarchy*

To log a message, you need a Logger object, and Logger objects are provided by the Logger.getLogger() factory methods. getLogger() either creates a new Logger or returns an existing one.

The argument to getLogger() is generally the name of the package from which it is called. This way, each package uses its own Logger object, which allows each package to have its log messages turned on and off independently.

It is not a requirement, however, that the argument to getLogger() be a package name—it can, in fact, be any string. You can use this freedom to partition logging messages in different ways; for example, you might subdivide the my.package logger name into my.package.io and my.package.net, allowing you to control I/O-related log messages and network-related log messages separately. Generally, however, it is best to follow the package hierarchy, since that is what the end user will expect.

A logger's name places it within a hierarchy analogous to the package hierarchy, as shown in figure 5.2.

You'll notice that the root of the hierarchy tree is a logger called the *root logger*, which has the empty string as its name.

The parent-child relationship is more than just cosmetic—a Logger inherits the following properties from its parents:

- Level—If a logger does not have its logging level explicitly set, or if it is set to null, it uses the logging level of its parent
- Handlers—If a logger chooses to publish a log message to its own handlers, it will also be published to its parent's handlers

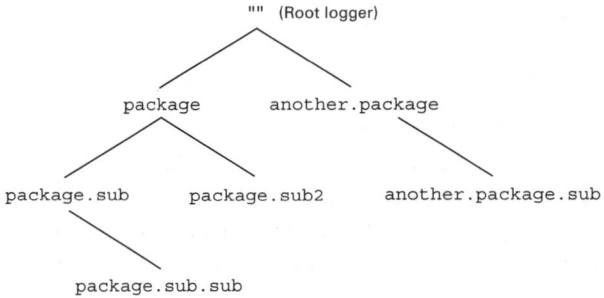

Figure 5.2 Each logger is placed within a hierarchical namespace based on its name. The names are generally, but not necessarily, package names. Setting the logging level of a logger also sets the logging level of its children. At the root of the tree is a logger whose name is the empty string—this is the *root logger*.

- ResourceBundles—If a logger does not have its own ResourceBundle (for use in localizing logging messages), then it will inherit its parent's ResourceBundle

5.1.4 Logging methods

Each logger has a number of methods used for logging. The most general methods allow you to specify the logging level, the message string, a list of *argument* objects, the source class, the source method, and even a Throwable. Other methods take fewer arguments, and are thus more convenient, if less general.

The methods can be divided into four categories:

- log()—Allows you to specify a log level, a message string, and either a Throwable or a list of argument objects.
- logp()—Like log(), but also allows you to specify the source class and source method. Short for "log precise."
- logrb()—Like logp(), but also allows you to specify a ResourceBundle to be used for localizing the raw message string. Short for "log with resource bundle."
- severe(), info(), warning(), fine(), etc.—These convenience methods take only a message string; the logging level is implicit in the name of the method.

5.1.5 The LogRecord class

A LogRecord object encapsulates a message sent to the logging system. Most of the Logger.log() methods take a String as an argument, but this string is encapsulated by the logger within a LogRecord.

A LogRecord contains the following elements:

- The raw message string
- A logging level
- The logger's name
- A timestamp
- Optional argument objects
- An optional ResourceBundle
- The source class and method
- A unique sequence number
- An optional Throwable
- The thread ID of the Thread that generated the LogRecord

5.1.6 *Handlers*

Each logger is assigned one or more `Handlers`. A logger is assigned a handler by using its `addHandler()` method. A handler takes a `LogRecord` and sends it somewhere—the destination depends on the handler (see figure 5.2). Each logger can have any number of handlers installed. Remember, also, that after a logger passes a `LogRecord` to its handlers, the logger then hands the `LogRecord` off to its parent so that the parent can send the `LogRecord` to *its* handlers. (This action can be enabled and disabled using the logger's `setUseParentHandlers()` method.) Additionally, there is a set of *global handlers* that are used for any `LogRecords` logged by the root handler.

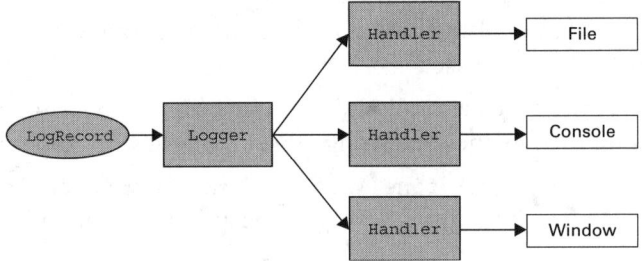

Figure 5.3   Each `Logger` can have multiple `Handlers` installed. Each `Handler` sends the `LogRecords` it receives to a different destination.

The following five handlers are included in the `java.util.logging` package:

- `FileHandler`—Writes log messages to a particular file
- `ConsoleHandler`—Writes log messages to the console (or command-line shell)
- `MemoryHandler`—Writes log messages to a circular buffer; can dump recent messages, on command, to another handler
- `SocketHandler`—Writes log messages to a server listening on a particular host and port
- `StreamHandler`—Writes log messages to a particular stream

We'll learn how to build a custom handler in section 5.4.

It is possible that a handler will have some kind of internal problem. Since these errors are not interesting or relevant to the main application code, the `Logger.log()` methods do not throw exceptions. Instead, errors in handler code should be passed to `Handler.reportError()`, which in turn will pass them to an object called an `ErrorManager`. An `ErrorManager` has a single method, `error()`, which looks like this:

```
public void error( String msg, Exception ex, int code );
```

The default `ErrorManager` only reports the *first* error that occurs; all others are silently ignored. You can change this policy by installing your own `ErrorManager`: simply subclass `ErrorManager` and replace the implementation of `error()` with your own.

5.1.7 *Filters*

Setting the logging level of a logger provides some measure of control over what is logged; filters provide even more control. `Filter` is an interface containing a single method:

```
public boolean isLoggable( LogRecord record );
```

A `Filter` can make a decision about each individual log message that passes through the logger it is installed on. These decisions can be based on anything you like—some information contained in the message, the class or method the message was generated from, the `Thread` it was created in, and so on. This can greatly reduce the number of messages, which is useful if you have a lot coming out of your code; it can also help hone the information, making it easier to read and therefore more useful for debugging.

Filters can be assigned to both loggers and handlers via their respective `set-Filter()` methods. Before a logger passes a `LogRecord` on to its handlers, it calls the `isLoggable()` method of its `Filter` (if any is assigned), and only passes the `LogRecord` on if `isLoggable()` returns `true`. Likewise, a handler uses its `Filter`'s `isLoggable()` method to determine whether or not it should send the message to its destination.

5.1.8 *Formatters*

A `Formatter` is used by a `Handler` to turn a `LogRecord` into a `String` so that it can be displayed or stored in some way. There are two `Formatters` in the `java.util.log-ging` package:

- `SimpleFormatter`—Produces the default format seen in section 5.1.1
- `XMLFormatter`—Transforms a `LogRecord` into a standard XML format

The bulk of the `Formatter`'s work is done by the `format()` method:

```
public abstract String format( LogRecord record );
```

This method turns a `LogRecord` into a `String`. Subclasses of `Formatter` override this method.

`format()` generally calls `formatMessage()` to turn the raw `LogRecord` message into a `String`. `formatMessage()` takes care of the details of localization and generally does not need to be overridden.

5.1.9 *Logging efficiency*

Although logging can be useful, it can also use up a substantial portion of a machine's CPU power, especially if a module's logging level is set very low. There are times when copious logging, caused by a low logging level setting, can even make a bug temporarily disappear. This is particularly frustrating when the bug in question is the reason you turned the logging level down in the first place.

You should also note that each call to a log method takes some CPU power, even if the method in question returns immediately without logging anything. Also, watch out for the arguments that you pass into the log method—if you're building strings, or, worse, calling methods, to create these arguments, then this code is being run every time, even if the log messages are being thrown away.

As with all optimization, you should be most concerned about this in tight inner loops. In the tightest of inner loops, it might make sense to put an extra conditional around the calls to the logger—only use the logger if a verbosity flag is set, which should only be under special development conditions. Unfortunately, this verbosity flag won't be under the control of the logging configuration file, so these log messages won't be available to end users.*

5.1.10 *The philosophy of logging*

Log messages are created during development, but they must serve the software throughout its lifetime. It's important to keep this in mind when choosing what to log and what to leave out. Logging is more than just a debug mode that ends when the software is shipped—or even when the software is made obsolete by a new version. Logging lives and dies with the software itself.

The logging messages created during development are the only way an application can communicate with the outside world beyond its regular functioning. If technical support isn't readily available, log messages are the last resort of the systems integrator. Keep these things in mind when writing your code. *Plan* your logging. Use it to report information that might help someone fix a bug, correct an

---

* It's possible that some future JVM or JIT will have the capability to remove `Logger` calls, which could solve this problem.

installation, debug a configuration, and so on. The problem may not be in your software, but it may involve your software, and your log messages may well go a long way toward fixing a bug in something else.

5.2 Configuring the Logging system

The Logging API allows for sophisticated and flexible configuration. All loggers are defined within the context of a `LogManager`. While it is possible to override the default `LogManager`, this is rarely done—most customization can be done by creating custom handlers and formatters.

The default `LogManager` reads its configuration from jre/lib/logging.properties, formatted as a properties file, within the JDK installation directory. The `java.util.logging.config.file` system property allows a different file to be specified, while the `java.util.logging.config.class` system property allows another class to be used to carry out the configuration process. The `LogManager.readConfiguration()` methods tell the `LogManager` to read or reread the standard configuration file, or to read configuration data from a supplied `InputStream`.

5.2.1 Configuring handlers

The configuration file allows properties of each handler to be set, as the following examples show:

```
java.util.logging.FileHandler.pattern = %h/java%u.log
java.util.logging.FileHandler.limit = 50000
java.util.logging.FileHandler.count = 1
java.util.logging.FileHandler.formatter = java.util.logging.XMLFormatter
```

Let's take a look at the parts of one of these configuration lines—see figure 5.4.

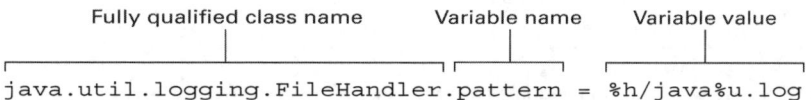

Figure 5.4 The format of a handler configuration line from the logging.properties file. Each variable is qualified by the package and class names of the handler being configured; this means that each handler can have its own set of configuration values.

The handler values set in the configuration file are available through the `LogManager.getProperty()` method. These values are identical across all instantiations of a particular `Handler` class.

In section 5.4, we'll take a look at a custom handler whose fully qualified class name is `org.jdk14tut.logging.WindowHandler`. It has two properties, `width` and `height`, which are set in the configuration file like this:

```
org.jdk14tut.logging.WindowHandler.width=800
org.jdk14tut.logging.WindowHandler.height=100
```

5.2.2 *Configuration values for standard handlers*

As mentioned previously in section 5.1.6, there are five standard handlers included in the `java.util.logging` package. Each can be configured separately; some variables are recognized by all five, while others are used only by specific handlers:

- The `level` and `filter` variables (described in table 5.1) are common to all five handlers.
- The `formatter` and `encoding` variables (described in table 5.2) are used in all handlers except for `MemoryHandler`. `MemoryHandler` doesn't actually turn `LogRecords` into text output, so it doesn't need those variables.
- `FileHandler` has configuration variables relating to output filenames and log rotation (see table 5.3).

Note that a handler's `Formatter` and `Filter` can be set using the handler's `setFormatter()` and `setFilter()` methods, respectively.

Table 5.1   These configuration variables are available for all five standard handlers.

Variable	What it is	Default value
level	The logging level	`Level.INFO` or `Level.ALL`, depending on the handler
filter	An optional `Filter` to filter log messages	No filter

Table 5.2   These configuration variables are available for `ConsoleHandler`, `FileHandler`, `StreamHandler`, and `SocketHandler`—that is, all of the standard handlers except for `MemoryHandler`.

Variable	What it is	Default value
formatter	A `Formatter` object to format `LogRecords` before output.	`java.util.logging.SimpleFormatter` or `java.util.logging.XMLFormatter`, depending on the handler
encoding	The character set encoding to use	The default platform encoding

Table 5.3   These configuration variables are available for `FileHandler`.

Variable	What it is	Default value
limit	The maximum number of bytes to write to any one file, or zero for no limit	No limit
count	The number of output files to cycle through for log rotation	1
pattern	A pattern specifying the format of the log filename	%h/java%u.log
append	Whether the logger should append to the file (as opposed to overwriting)	false

The `pattern` variable merits special attention. This string is used to construct the filename used when writing log messages to disk. Each of the %-constructs is replaced at runtime with the appropriate value—the `pattern` value is a kind of filename template. For example, the string %h/java%u.log uses the %h construct, which denotes the value of the user.home system property, and the %u construct, which resolves to a unique number. If the user.home property is /home/mito and the unique number is 12345, the resulting filename would be /home/mito/java12345.log. All of the constructs begin with a % character, except for the single-character construct /, which denotes the pathname separator character for the local platform. Table 5.4 shows the constructs that can be used for the `pattern` value.

Table 5.4   These constructs are used in the value of the `pattern` configuration variable for `FileHandler`. They are replaced at runtime with the value described in the right-hand column.

Construct	Meaning
/	The pathname separator character for the local platform.
%t	The system temporary directory.
%h	The value of the user.home system property.
%g	The generation number to distinguish rotated logs. Each time a log is rotated, the generation number is increased by one so that the new log does not overwrite the old log. This value reaches a maximum of count-1 before it cycles back to 0.
%u	A unique number generated to distinguish the file from files already in use on disk.
%%	Represents a single % sign.

As mentioned previously, `MemoryHandler` maintains a circular buffer of recent messages; when triggered, the `MemoryHandler` will *push* the most recent messages to another handler, such as a `FileHandler`. The variables listed in table 5.5 are available.

Table 5.5 The following configuration variables are available for `MemoryHandler`.

Variable	What it is	Default value
size	The size of the memory buffer, measured in number of log messages.	1000
push	The push level. An incoming message of this level, or greater, will trigger a push.	Level.SEVERE
target	The class name of a handler for this Memory-Handler to push to.	(no default)

A `SocketHandler` writes messages to a remote server. By default, it uses the XML-Formatter. It has the configuration variables listed in table 5.6.

Table 5.6 These configuration variables are available for `SocketHandler`.

Variable	What it is	Default value
host	The hostname of the server to connect to	(no default)
port	The port number to connect to on the host	(no default)

5.2.3 *Configuring loggers*

In addition to containing the handler configuration values described in the previous section, the configuration file permits the log level of a particular `Logger` to be set. Since a `Logger` corresponds to a package within the larger application, this allows you to configure your application's logging on a package-by-package basis.

The following line sets the logging level for the package com.xyz.myapp:

```
com.xyz.myapp.level = SEVERE
```

This value is inherited by any subpackages of the main package, so if our application had two subpackages called `io` and `net`, these would inherit the value of SEVERE. However, these logging levels can also be configured separately:

```
com.xyz.myapp.level = SEVERE
com.xyz.myapp.io.level = INFO
com.xyz.myapp.net.level = WARNING
```

A logger's level can be set at runtime using the `Logger.setLevel()` method.

You also can provide a default setting for all loggers, by using the empty string as the package name, as follows:

```
.level= ALL
```

5.2.4 Global handlers

The default configuration in the JDK sends logging messages only to the console (also known as the command line). This is defined by the following line in the logging.properties file:

```
handlers= java.util.logging.ConsoleHandler
```

This line specifies that a `ConsoleHandler` will be created on startup, and that all loggers will send to this handler by default.

The logging.properties that comes with the JDK also contains a line, commented out with a #, which, when uncommented, will also send messages to a log file in the user's home directory:

```
#handlers= java.util.logging.FileHandler, java.util.logging.ConsoleHandler
```

5.3 Using logging in a program

To show logging in action, we'll take a program we already saw in chapter 2—the MultiplexingChatServer (refer to listing 5.3). The most important thing about this example is noticing what information is logged at what logging levels. Properly choosing logging levels is crucial for making logging usable.

The following logging levels are used in the revised MultiplexingChatServer (see listing 5.1), from highest priority to lowest priority:

- SEVERE—Used for all errors. The SEVERE level is likely to be included in any log file or console, and we want to make sure that any unintended situation is seen in every log.

- INFO—Used for information we want to see as a matter of course. INFO is the default level for loggers and handlers, so information logged at this level will be seen during a normal run.

- CONFIG—Used for configuration information, usually shown at startup. This logging level is generally used to show what the program intends to do, and how it will do it, rather than what it is actually doing.

- FINE—Used for information we only want if we need a lot of detail—for example, during debugging.

■ FINER—Used for very detailed information. Generally, there is so much of this stuff that we don't log it unless it's absolutely necessary—say, for debugging a particularly thorny problem.

Note that the version of `MultiplexingChatServer` shown in listing 5.1 has been modified to be placed in package `org.jdk14tut.chat`, which has been created just for this example. This package also contains the corresponding `ChatClient` and `ChatClientApplet` classes, and a `client.html` file for use with `appletviewer`.

In listing 5.1, each line that logs data to the logger is marked in boldface.

Listing 5.1   MultiplexingChatServer.java

(See \Chapter5\org\jdk14tut\chat\MultiplexingChatServer.java)
(See also \Chapter5\org\jdk14tut\chat\MultiplexingChatClient.java,
\Chapter5\org\jdk14tut\chat\MultiplexingChatClientApplet.java
\Chapter5\client.html)

```java
package org.jdk14tut.chat;

import java.io.*;
import java.net.*;
import java.nio.*;
import java.nio.channels.*;
import java.util.*;
import java.util.logging.*;
import org.jdk14tut.logging.*;

public class MultiplexingChatServer implements Runnable
{
  private int port;
  private Vector sockets = new Vector();
  private Set closedSockets = new HashSet();
  static private Logger logger;

  static {
    logger = Logger.getLogger( "org.jdk14tut.chat" );   ❶   Create the logger
    //logger.setLevel( Level.ALL );    ❷    Set the log level
  }

  public MultiplexingChatServer( int port ) {
    new LoggerGUI();

    this.port = port;                                         CONFIG level is used to
    logger.config( "Will listen on port "+port );   ❸    show settings

    Thread t = new Thread( this, "MultiplexingChatServer" );
    t.start();                                                Log the creation of
    logger.fine( "Started background I/O thread" );  ❹    background thread at
  }                                                          level FINE
```

```
public void run() {
  logger.fine( "Background thread started" );
  try {
    ServerSocketChannel ssc = ServerSocketChannel.open();
    logger.finer( "Opened server socket channel" );
    ssc.configureBlocking( false );
    ServerSocket ss = ssc.socket();
    InetSocketAddress isa = new InetSocketAddress( port );
    ss.bind( isa );
    logger.finer( "server socket channel bound to "+isa );

    Selector selector = Selector.open();
    ssc.register( selector, SelectionKey.OP_ACCEPT );
    logger.finer( "Registered "+ssc+" with selector" );

    logger.info( "Listening on port "+port );

    ByteBuffer buffer = ByteBuffer.allocate( 4096 );
    logger.finer( "Allocated buffer, "+
                  "capacity="+buffer.capacity() );

    while (true) {
      logger.finer( "Going into select()" );
      int numKeys = selector.select();
      logger.finer( "Returned from select()" );
      if (numKeys>0) {
        Set skeys = selector.selectedKeys();
        logger.finer( "select() returned with "+skeys.size()+
                      " keys in selected set" );
        Iterator it = skeys.iterator();
        while (it.hasNext()) {
          SelectionKey rsk = (SelectionKey)it.next();
          logger.finer( "Selection key: "+rsk );
          int rskOps = rsk.readyOps();
          if ((rskOps & SelectionKey.OP_ACCEPT) ==
              SelectionKey.OP_ACCEPT) {
            logger.finer( "Selection key is ACCEPT type" );
            Socket socket = ss.accept();
            logger.info( "Connection from "+socket );
            sockets.addElement( socket );
            SocketChannel sc = socket.getChannel();
            sc.configureBlocking( false );
            sc.register( selector, SelectionKey.OP_READ );
            logger.finer( "Registered "+sc+" with selector" );
            selector.selectedKeys().remove( rsk );
          } else if ((rskOps & SelectionKey.OP_READ) ==
                     SelectionKey.OP_READ) {
            logger.finer( "Selection key is READ type" );
            SocketChannel ch = (SocketChannel)rsk.channel();
            selector.selectedKeys().remove( rsk );
            buffer.clear();
```

⑤ Log the start of the background thread at level FINE

⑥ FINER and FINEST levels are used for even more detailed messages about inner workings

⑦ Log the port we're listening on, at level INFO

⑧ Log each incoming connection

```
                ch.read( buffer );
                buffer.flip();
                logger.finer( "Read "+buffer.limit()+
                                " bytes from "+ch.socket() );
                if (buffer.limit()==0) {
                  logger.info( "closing on 0 read" );
                  rsk.cancel();
                  Socket socket = ch.socket();
                  close( socket );
                } else {
                  sendToAll( buffer );
                }
              }
            }

          removeClosedSockets();
          }
        }
    } catch( IOException ie ) {
      logger.info( "Error in main I/o loop: "+ie );
    }
}

private void sendToAll( ByteBuffer bb ) {
  logger.finer( "Sending buffer, "+bb.limit()+" bytes" );
  for (Enumeration e=sockets.elements();
        e.hasMoreElements();) {
    Socket socket = null;
    try {
      socket = (Socket)e.nextElement();
      logger.fine( "Sending to "+socket );
      SocketChannel sc = socket.getChannel();
      logger.finer( "Starting write to "+socket );
      bb.rewind();
      while (bb.remaining()>0) {
        sc.write( bb );
      }
      logger.finer( "Finished write to "+socket );
    } catch( IOException ie ) {
      logger.info( "closing on write exception" );
      closedSockets.add( socket );
    }
  }
}

private void close( Socket socket ) {
  closedSockets.add( socket );
}

private void removeClosedSockets() {
  for (Iterator it=closedSockets.iterator(); it.hasNext();) {
    Socket socket = (Socket)it.next();
```

Log all reads and writes at level FINER ⑨

⑩ **Log each close**

● **Log all reads and writes at level FINER**

● **Log each close**

```
      sockets.remove( socket );
      logger.fine( "Removed closed socket "+socket );
    }
    closedSockets.clear();
  }

  static public void main( String args[] ) throws Exception {
    int port = Integer.parseInt( args[0] );
    new MultiplexingChatServer( port );
  }
}
```

❶ The rule of thumb is to use the package name as the logger name, and that's what we're doing here. Any other classes in this package should also use this logger name.

❷ This line is commented out because it generates a great deal of logging output—turn it on to see all messages.

Note also that the logging configuration file generally assigns a default level of INFO to all loggers and handlers; uncommenting this line of code will not necessarily produce any more messages unless the configuration file is also modified to set the default handlers to level ALL.

❸ The CONFIG level is generally used to show the values of configuration settings. Thus, we use it to display the port we intend to listen on. When we actually set out to begin listening on the port, we'll log that too, but that will be at level INFO.

❹ The FINE, FINER, and FINEST levels are used to log information about the inner workings of the program. Three levels are provided to allow greater control over the amount of data being logged.

Here, we've logged the creation of a background thread for doing the multi-plexed I/O. While the existence of the background thread is crucial to the internal workings of the program, it is meant to be forgotten about when the code is working properly. During debugging, however, we'd like to know about it.

❺ We log the start of the background thread at the FINE level for the same reason we log its creation. There are some subtle portability bugs caused by race conditions involving thread startup; to find such bugs, it is useful to know when every thread starts and stops.

❻ The FINER and FINEST levels should be used for messages that you might want to turn off, even if you are interested in some detailed messages.

In this program, the FINER level is used to log actions that generally work perfectly, so we usually don't need to worry about them happening.

❼ The INFO level is good for messages we would like to have printed out in most situations. The configuration file sets the default level for both loggers and global handlers to INFO, so such messages will show up in the console.

❽ ❿ We log connections and disconnections at level INFO, because we generally want to see these—they give an indication of the basic behavior of the program, and, in this case, the usage of the program by its clients. This is the kind of information we want to see in most circumstances.

❾ We log individual data reads and writes at the FINER level because we don't want to see them, even if we have turned on FINE logging. For a deployed chat server, these messages would be so numerous they would drown out all other logging, and may in fact degrade the performance of the server significantly. However, they are available if we really need them.

Listing 5.2 shows the output of the logging messages in this logging-enabled version of MultiplexingChatServer.

Listing 5.2   chatoutput.txt

(See \Chapter5\org\jdk14tut\chat\chatoutput.txt)

Initialize

```
Jan 3, 2002 4:30:50 PM org.jdk14tut.chat.MultiplexingChatServer ....
CONFIG: Will listen on port 5555
Jan 3, 2002 4:30:50 PM org.jdk14tut.chat.MultiplexingChatServer ....
FINE: Started background I/O thread
Jan 3, 2002 4:30:50 PM org.jdk14tut.chat.MultiplexingChatServer run
FINE: Background thread started
Jan 3, 2002 4:30:50 PM org.jdk14tut.chat.MultiplexingChatServer run
FINER: Opened server socket channel
Jan 3, 2002 4:30:50 PM org.jdk14tut.chat.MultiplexingChatServer run
FINER: server socket channel bound to 0.0.0.0/0.0.0.0:5555
Jan 3, 2002 4:30:50 PM org.jdk14tut.chat.MultiplexingChatServer run
FINER: Registered sun.nio.ch.ServerSocketChannelImpl[/0.0.0.0:50....
```

Accept an incomming connection

```
Jan 3, 2002 4:30:50 PM org.jdk14tut.chat.MultiplexingChatServer run
INFO: Listening on port 5555
Jan 3, 2002 4:30:50 PM org.jdk14tut.chat.MultiplexingChatServer run
FINER: Allocated buffer, capacity=4096
Jan 3, 2002 4:30:50 PM org.jdk14tut.chat.MultiplexingChatServer run
FINER: Going into select()
Jan 3, 2002 4:31:37 PM org.jdk14tut.chat.MultiplexingChatServer run
FINER: Returned from select()
Jan 3, 2002 4:31:37 PM org.jdk14tut.chat.MultiplexingChatServer run
FINER: select() returned with 1 keys in selected set
```

```
Jan 3, 2002 4:31:37 PM org.jdk14tut.chat.MultiplexingChatServer run
FINER: Selection key: sun.nio.ch.SelectionKeyImpl@72e449
Jan 3, 2002 4:31:37 PM org.jdk14tut.chat.MultiplexingChatServer run
FINER: Selection key is ACCEPT type
Jan 3, 2002 4:31:37 PM org.jdk14tut.chat.MultiplexingChatServer run
INFO: Connection from Socket[addr=/192.168.0.2,port=3795,localpo....
Jan 3, 2002 4:31:37 PM org.jdk14tut.chat.MultiplexingChatServer run
FINER: Registered java.nio.channels.SocketChannel[connected loca....
```

**Read a chat message
from a client**

```
Jan 3, 2002 4:31:37 PM org.jdk14tut.chat.MultiplexingChatServer run
FINER: Going into select()
Jan 3, 2002 4:31:40 PM org.jdk14tut.chat.MultiplexingChatServer run
FINER: Returned from select()
Jan 3, 2002 4:31:40 PM org.jdk14tut.chat.MultiplexingChatServer run
FINER: select() returned with 1 keys in selected set
Jan 3, 2002 4:31:40 PM org.jdk14tut.chat.MultiplexingChatServer run
FINER: Selection key: sun.nio.ch.SelectionKeyImpl@1d332b
Jan 3, 2002 4:31:40 PM org.jdk14tut.chat.MultiplexingChatServer run
FINER: Selection key is READ type
Jan 3, 2002 4:31:40 PM org.jdk14tut.chat.MultiplexingChatServer run
FINER: Read 4 bytes from Socket[addr=/192.168.0.2,port=3795,loca....
```

**Send the chat
message to the client**

```
Jan 3, 2002 4:31:40 PM org.jdk14tut.chat.MultiplexingChatServer ....
FINER: Sending buffer, 4 bytes
Jan 3, 2002 4:31:40 PM org.jdk14tut.chat.MultiplexingChatServer ....
FINE: Sending to Socket[addr=/192.168.0.2,port=3795,localport=5555]
Jan 3, 2002 4:31:40 PM org.jdk14tut.chat.MultiplexingChatServer ....
FINER: Starting write to Socket[addr=/192.168.0.2,port=3795,loca....
Jan 3, 2002 4:31:40 PM org.jdk14tut.chat.MultiplexingChatServer ....
FINER: Finished write to Socket[addr=/192.168.0.2,port=3795,loca....
```

By building this logging version of MultiplexingChatServer, you can see what the log messages look like on your system, and modify the logging configuration file to control which log messages you see. In the next section, we'll take a look at another way to view the output of a logger.

5.4   *Writing a custom handler*

In this section, we'll examine another way to view log messages. We'll create a class called LoggerGUI, which allows the user to view log messages in a window. The main window displays a list of loggers that are currently instantiated within the Logging system (see figure 5.5).

Selecting one of the loggers listed in the main window and clicking the show button will bring up a logging window that displays the messages sent to that logger (see figure 5.6).

Using this system, it is possible to open several windows, each showing the output of a different package within your program. This can help control the amount of information you have to wade through.

Implementing LoggerGUI

The LoggerGUI system is implemented via a *custom* handler called WindowHandler. This handler is installed the same way that a ConsoleHandler or FileHandler is installed, but instead of sending data to the console or a file, it sends data to a window.

The system actually consists of a number of classes:

- LoggerGUI—The main window for the system (see listing 5.3). Clicking on a logger listed in this window opens a new WindowHandler for that logger.
- WindowHandler—A handler that displays log information in a window (see listing 5.4). This handler uses a StreamWindow to display the information.
- StreamWindow—A window that has an OutputStream (see listing 5.5). Any data written to this OutputStream is appended to the text in the window.

Using this system in a program is very simple:

```
new LoggerGUI();
```

Figure 5.5   The main window of LoggerGUI. This window shows a list of the loggers currently instantiated within the logging system. Selecting one of them and clicking show brings up a logging window for that logger.

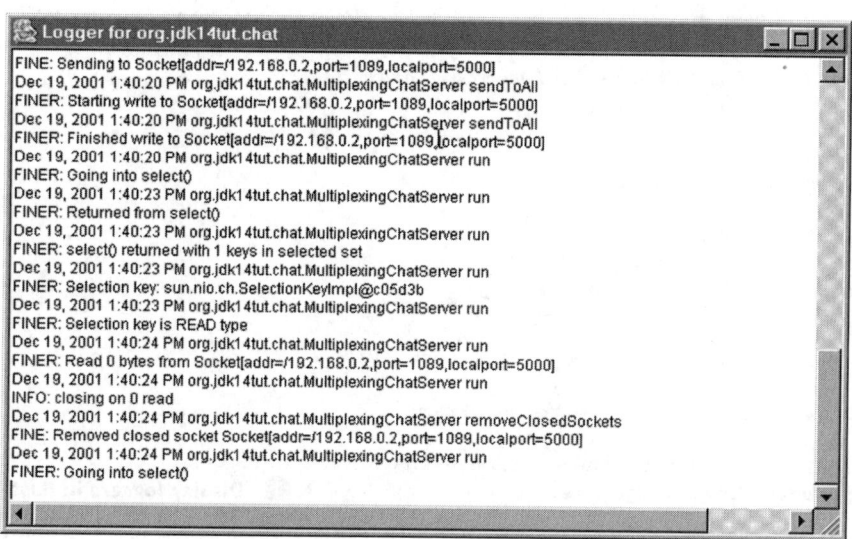

Figure 5.6 **This logging window from LoggerGUI shows the information logged to a single logger.**

This will create a main window listing the loggers that are currently instantiated within the logging system. The size of this window can be configured through settings in the logging.properties file, like this:

```
org.jdk14tut.logging.WindowHandler.width=800
org.jdk14tut.logging.WindowHandler.height=100
```

To show this custom handler off, we can use LoggerGUI within our log-enabled MultiplexingChatServer. Here's the constructor:

```
public MultiplexingChatServer( int port ) {
  new LoggerGUI();

  this.port = port;
  logger.config( "Will listen on port "+port );

  Thread t = new Thread( this, "MultiplexingChatServer" );
  t.start();
  logger.fine( "Started background I/O thread" );
}
```

Note that this should be done late, after you've created all your loggers. That way, the LoggerGUI window will list all the loggers you've created—it won't show loggers that were created after it was created.

Listing 5.3 LoggerGUI.java

(See \Chapter5\org\jdk14tut\chat\LoggerGUI.java)

```java
package org.jdk14tut.logging;

import java.awt.*;
import java.awt.event.*;
import javax.swing.*;
import java.io.*;
import java.util.*;
import java.util.logging.*;

/**
 * Main GUI window for logging-window system
 */
public class LoggerGUI extends JFrame
{
  // List displaying the currently-instantiated loggers
  private JList loggerList;

  /**
   * Set up the interface and make visible
   */
  public LoggerGUI() {
    super( "Logging" );

    setupGUI();
    addListeners();
    populateList();

    setVisible( true );
  }

  /**
   * Set up the interface
   */
  private void setupGUI() {
    Container cp = getContentPane();

    loggerList = new JList();
    loggerList.setSelectionMode(
      ListSelectionModel.SINGLE_SELECTION );

    cp.setLayout( new BorderLayout() );
    cp.add( loggerList, BorderLayout.CENTER );

    JButton showButton = new JButton( "show" );
    cp.add( showButton, BorderLayout.SOUTH );
    showButton.addActionListener( new ActionListener() {
      public void actionPerformed( ActionEvent ae ) {
        String name = (String)loggerList.getSelectedValue();
        if (name != null && !name.equals( "" )) {
          openWindow( name );
        }
```

❶ **Display loggers in JList**

```
      }
    } );

    setLocation( 40, 40 );
    setSize( 200, 200 );
  }

  /**
   * List the currently-instantiated Loggers
   */
  private void populateList() {
    // Get the names of the currently-instantiated loggers
    LogManager logManager = LogManager.getLogManager();
    Enumeration e = logManager.getLoggerNames();

    // Build a Vector of the names
    Vector names = new Vector();
    while (e.hasMoreElements()) {
      String name = (String)e.nextElement();
      names.addElement( name );
    }

    // Display the names in the JList
    loggerList.setListData( names );
  }

  /**
   * Add listener to properly close window when
   * close-button is pressed
   */
  private void addListeners() {
    addWindowListener( new WindowListener() {
      public void windowActivated( WindowEvent we ) {
      }
      public void windowClosed( WindowEvent we ) {
      }
      public void windowClosing( WindowEvent we ) {
        // Remove window if the close-button is pressed
        closeWindow();
      }
      public void windowDeactivated( WindowEvent we ) {
      }
      public void windowDeiconified( WindowEvent we ) {
      }
      public void windowIconified( WindowEvent we ) {
      }
      public void windowOpened( WindowEvent we ) {
      }
    } );
  }

  /**
   * Open a Logger Window for a given Logger
```

Find out what loggers exist and show them

```
  */
  private void openWindow( String loggerName ) {
    Logger logger = Logger.getLogger( loggerName );

    // Create a WindowHandler
    WindowHandler windowHandler = new WindowHandler( loggerName );

    // Install it as a handler for the logger
    logger.addHandler( windowHandler );
  }

  /**
   * Hide and dispose of the window
   */
  private void closeWindow() {
    setVisible( false );
    dispose();
  }
}
```

❷ **Create a WindowHandler for a given logger**

❶ At any given moment, there are a number of loggers that have been instantiated and installed in the system. Generally, these correspond to packages, although they don't have to. Each one has a name, which is usually the package name. We list these names in a JList.

❷ When the show button is clicked, a WindowHandler is created for the selected logger. This WindowHandler displays everything logged to that logger.

> **Listing 5.4   WindowHandler.java**

(See \Chapter5\org\jdk14tut\chat\WindowHandler.java)

```
package org.jdk14tut.logging;

import java.awt.*;
import java.awt.event.*;
import java.io.*;
import java.util.logging.*;

/**
 * Log Handler that sends its output to a window
 */
public class WindowHandler extends StreamHandler
{
  // The default width and height for a logging window;
  // these can be overridden in the logging.properties file
  static private final int defaultWidth = 400;
  static private final int defaultHeight = 500;

  // The logger being displayed in this window
  private Logger logger;
```

```
/**
 * Set up the connection between the stream
 * handler and the stream window: log data
 * written to the handler goes to the window
 */
public WindowHandler( String loggerName ) {
  logger = Logger.getLogger( loggerName );

  // Get the output stream that feeds the window
  // and install it in the Stream handler
  WindowHandlerWindow whw =
    new WindowHandlerWindow( loggerName );
  OutputStream out = whw.getOutputStream();
  setOutputStream( out );

  setLevel( Level.ALL );
}

/**
 * Log a LogRecord.  We flush after every log
 * because we want to see log messages as soon as
 * they arrive
 */
public void publish( LogRecord lr ) {
  // Check any filter, and possibly other criteria,
  // before publishing
  if (!isLoggable( lr ))
    return;

  super.publish( lr );
  flush();
}
/**
 * De-install this Handler from its Logger
 */
private void removeHandler() {
  logger.removeHandler( this );
}

/**
 * Inner class: WindowHandlerWindow is a StreamWindow.
 * We need to override closeWindow() so that we
 * can de-install the handler when the window is
 * closed
 */
class WindowHandlerWindow extends StreamWindow
{
  public WindowHandlerWindow( String name ) {
    super( "Logger for "+name );

    // Assume the defaults, initially
    int width = defaultWidth;
    int height = defaultHeight;
```

❶ Connect the StreamWindow to the StreamHandler

❷ Check Filter (and other criteria) first

❸ Flush after every log

● This is called on window close

Get window width and height values from the logging.properties file ●

```
          LogManager manager = LogManager.getLogManager();

          // We need the fully-qualified class name to access
          // the properties
          String className = WindowHandler.class.getName();

          String widthString = manager.getProperty( className+".width" );
          if (widthString != null) {
            width = Integer.parseInt( widthString );
          }

          String heightString = manager.getProperty( className+".height" );
          if (heightString != null) {
            height = Integer.parseInt( heightString );
          }

          setSize( width, height );
        }
      protected void closeWindow() {
        removeHandler();
        super.closeWindow();
      }
    }
  }
}
```

Get window width and height values from the logging.properties file

❶ The `StreamWindow` displays anything written to its stream. The `StreamHandler` is a log handler that writes log data to a stream. Connecting these two, we get a `WindowHandler`—a log handler that writes its data to a window.

❷ Before we publish a `LogRecord`, we want to check to make sure that our `Filter`, if we have one installed, approves. The default implementation of `Handler.isLoggable()` calls `filter.isLoggable()`, if a `Filter` is installed. Additionally, subclasses of `Handler` may add other checks to this method by overriding it; however, overridden versions of `Handler.isLoggable()` are obliged to call `super.isLoggable()` to ensure that any checks inherited from superclasses are carried out.

❸ When logging to a file, we generally want to use buffering so that we can efficiently handle lots of log data. However, when logging to a window, we generally want to see the data as soon as it comes in, so we override the buffering by calling `flush()` after every log.

Listing 5.5   StreamWindow.java

(See \Chapter5\org\jdk14tut\chat\StreamWindow.java)

```
package org.jdk14tut.logging;

import java.io.*;
import java.awt.*;
```

```java
import java.awt.event.*;
import javax.swing.*;

public class StreamWindow extends JFrame
{
  // The text area in which we display incoming text
  private TextArea textArea;

  // Data written to this stream is appended to the
  // text area
  private StreamWindowStream out;

  /**
   * Create a new StreamWindow -- set up the interface
   * and install listeners.  Make the window visible
   * after everything else is done
   */
  public StreamWindow( String name ) {
    super( name );

    out = new StreamWindowStream();

    setupGUI();
    addListeners();

    setVisible( true );
  }

  /**
   * Add the text area to the window, and set the window
   * size
   */
  private void setupGUI() {
    Container cp = getContentPane();

    textArea = new TextArea();

    cp.setLayout( new BorderLayout() );
    cp.add( textArea, BorderLayout.CENTER );

    setLocation( 100, 100 );
    setSize( 100, 100 );
  }

  /**
   * Close the window properly if the close-button is
   * pressed
   */
  private void addListeners() {
    addWindowListener( new WindowListener() {
      public void windowActivated( WindowEvent we ) {
      }
      public void windowClosed( WindowEvent we ) {
      }
      public void windowClosing( WindowEvent we ) {
```

❶ **Each StreamWindow has a single OutputStream**

```
        // Remove window if the close-button is pressed
        closeWindow();
      }
      public void windowDeactivated( WindowEvent we ) {
      }
      public void windowDeiconified( WindowEvent we ) {
      }
      public void windowIconified( WindowEvent we ) {
      }
      public void windowOpened( WindowEvent we ) {
      }
    } );
}

/**
 * Return the output stream that is connected
 * to this window
 */
public OutputStream getOutputStream() {
  return out;
}

/**
 * Close the window, and dispose of it
 */
protected void closeWindow() {
  setVisible( false );
  dispose();
}

/**
 * Add text to the end of the text showing in the
 * text area
 */
private void appendText( String string ) {
  textArea.append( string );
}

/**
 * Inner class: an output stream.  Writing to
 * this stream sends the data to the window
 */
class StreamWindowStream extends OutputStream
{
  // This is used to write a single byte.  We
  // pre-allocate it to save time
  private byte tinyBuffer[] = new byte[1];

  /**
   * Closing the stream closes the window
   */
  public void close() throws IOException {
    closeWindow();
```

❷ Inner class: connected to a window

```
    }
    /**
     * Write a single byte
     */
    public void write( int b ) throws IOException {
      // Store the single byte in the array and
      // write the array
      tinyBuffer[0] = (byte)b;
      write( tinyBuffer );
    }

    /**
     * Write an array of bytes
     */
    public void write( byte b[] ) throws IOException {
      // Convert the bytes to a string and append
      String s = new String( b );
      appendText( s );
    }

    /**
     * Write a sub-array of bytes
     */
    public void write( byte b[], int off, int len )
        throws IOException {
      // Convert the bytes to a string and append
      String s = new String( b, off, len );
      appendText( s );
    }
  }
}
```

❶ Data written to this stream is appended to the text in the window.

❷ StreamWindowStream is an inner class of the StreamWindow because it needs access to the StreamWindow in order to write text to the window, and to close the window when the stream is closed.

5.5 *Writing a custom formatter*

It's hard to keep track of log data as it is sent to a WindowHandler window. In this section, we'll create a custom Formatter called BriefFormatter, which uses a considerably briefer format for logging LogRecords. The regular, long format is good for log files and the console, but BriefFormatter is ideal for the LoggerGUI system.

Using BriefFormatter is simple—just install it into your handler using Handler.setFormatter(). Here's the constructor for WindowHandler, modified to use BriefFormatter:

```
public WindowHandler( String loggerName ) {
  logger = Logger.getLogger( loggerName );

  // Get the output stream that feeds the window
  // and install it in the Stream handler
  WindowHandlerWindow whw =
    new WindowHandlerWindow( loggerName );
  OutputStream out = whw.getOutputStream();
  setOutputStream( out );

  // Use a BriefFormatter to format data
  setFormatter( new BriefFormatter() );

  setLevel( Level.ALL );
}
```

`BriefFormatter` is similar to `SimpleFormatter`, which is the default `Formatter` used by the logging system. `SimpleFormatter` displays the full date and time, followed by the class and method. On the next line, it displays the logging level and the log message itself:

```
Dec 19, 2001 1:40:23 PM org.jdk14tut.chat.MultiplexingChatServer run
FINER: Returned from select()
```

`BriefFormatter`, in contrast, displays only the time and log message, on a single line, which makes it much more appropriate for display in a window, as shown in figure 5.7.

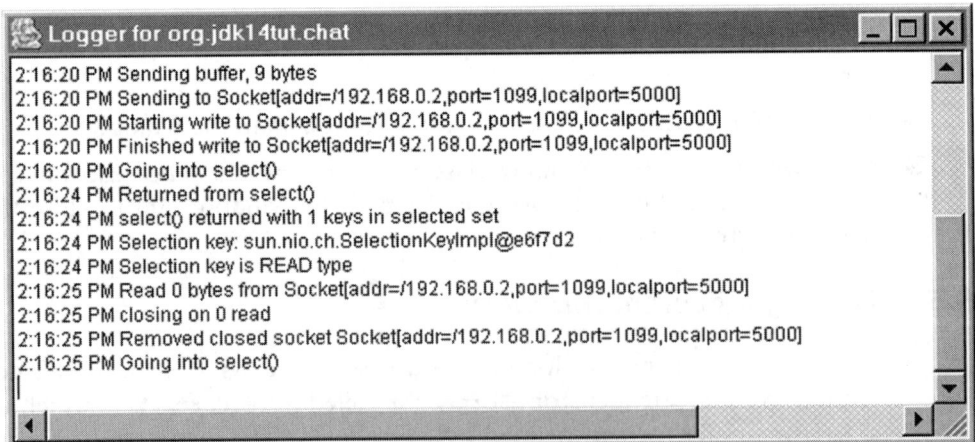

Figure 5.7 Logger window using `BriefFormatter` instead of the default `SimpleFormatter`. `BriefFormatter` displays less information and only uses a single line, which makes it more appropriate for a window.

Implementing a `Formatter` means subclassing the `Formatter` class. You generally only need to override the `format()` method. Optionally, you can override the `formatMessage()` method, which is called by `format()`, and which is responsible for formatting and localizing the message contained within the `LogRecord`; however, the default implementation suffices for most applications, so you don't generally need to override `formatMessage()`. That is what we do in listing 5.6.

Listing 5.6   BriefFormatter.java

(See \Chapter5\org\jdk14tut\chat\BriefFormatter.java)

```
package org.jdk14tut.logging;

import java.text.*;
import java.util.Date;
import java.util.logging.*;

public class BriefFormatter extends Formatter
{
  // Buffer for formatting a LogRecord
  private StringBuffer stringBuffer = new StringBuffer();

  // Buffer for formatting the time
  private StringBuffer dateBuffer = new StringBuffer();

  // Pre-allocate these to save time
  private Date date = new Date();
  Object args[] = { date };

  // MessageFormat for formatting the time like this:
  // 4:51:13 PM
  static private final String FORMATSTRING = "{0,time,medium}";
  private MessageFormat format = new MessageFormat( FORMATSTRING );

  // The character that is used to separate lines.
  // It's best to use this value instead of assuming that \n is
  // the line separator
  private String lineSeparator =
    (String)java.security.AccessController.doPrivileged(
    new sun.security.action.GetPropertyAction( "line.separator" ) );

  // Synchronized because the StringBuffers are shared
  synchronized public String format( LogRecord record ) {
    // Initialize the buffers
    stringBuffer.setLength( 0 );
    dateBuffer.setLength( 0 );

    // Format the time into dateBuffer
    date.setTime( record.getMillis() );
    format.format( args, dateBuffer, null );

    // Append the date
```

① Preallocate StringBuffers to save time

② Preallocate date stuff to save time

● Format a LogRecord

● Re-initialize the StringBuffers

● Format the record by appending to stringBuffer

```
        stringBuffer.append( dateBuffer );

        // Append a space
        stringBuffer.append( " " );

        // Append the log message -- call formatMessage()
        // to format the message itself
        String message = formatMessage( record );
        stringBuffer.append( message );

        // Add a newline
        stringBuffer.append( lineSeparator );

        return stringBuffer.toString();
    }
}
```

Format the record by appending to stringBuffer

formatMessage() formats the log message itself

❶ When building up a formatted string, it's faster to use a `StringBuffer` than it is to use a `String`. However, we can save even more time by preallocating `StringBuffers` and using them for formatting. This requires that we make `format()` synchronized, since each call to `format()` uses the same pair of `StringBuffers`.

❷ When formatting the date, we can save time by preallocating a `Date` object, and the single-element array used to hold the `Date` when it is passed to `MessageFormat.format()` (not to be confused with `BriefFormatter.format()`, which does our log message formatting).

You'll notice in the listing that some care has been taken, wherever possible, to avoid allocating objects inside `format()`. Logging is something that needs to be optimized to some degree. Most of the time, loggers are set to a relatively high level, and there isn't too much log data. However, during debugging, it is common to generate a lot more log data by lowering the logging level. In some cases, an incredible amount of logging data can be generated. This logging can easily take up a substantial portion of the processing power allocated to the program, which can alter its behavior—sometimes enough to make a bug go away, which is very frustrating. This is why it is important to take some care that the `format()` routine isn't wasting memory or CPU power.

5.6   *Summary*

Logging isn't as simple as it seems. The larger a program is, the more data is logged, and sifting through that data can become impossible. Logging systems provide methods to turn log messages on and off, individually and in groups, but this generally introduces complexity to the system.

The complexity of a logging system is a drawback in two ways—it drains resources that would otherwise be used by the program, and it inhibits programmers from using it wherever it is useful and necessary.

The Logging API in JDK 1.4 strikes a balance between these competing requirements. It allows for a swift implementation, and yet provides a hierarchy of verbosity levels. Logging is compartmentalized by package, which allows you to turn logging on and off for individual packages. Proper use of configuration files makes detailed control very easy.

All of these contribute to a system that can allow you to enhance even the largest, most complex programs with an enormous amount of self-description, which can greatly aid maintenance down the line.

Assertion facility

6

This chapter covers

- Using assertions
- Controlling assertions from the command line
- Controlling assertions from code
- Knowing when to use assertions

171

The assertion facility provides a mechanism for adding optional "sanity checks" to your code. These checks are used during the development and testing phases, but are turned off when the software is deployed. This allows the programmer to insert debugging checks that might be too slow or memory-intensive to use in a real context, but that help during development. In a sense, assertions are a lot like error checks, except that they are turned off for deployment.

Assertions generally are implemented in such a way that they can be compiled out; in languages like C and C++, this means using the preprocessor. Since Java doesn't have macro facilities, features that otherwise might be created by the programmer must be built into the language themselves. As a result, assertions have not been used widely in Java. The 1.4 release of the JDK corrects this.

One of the most important features of this facility is that these checks can be turned on and off at runtime, which means that you don't have to decide during development whether or not these checks should remain in the code or be removed before deployment.

6.1 Assertion basics

An *assertion* is a conditional expression that should evaluate to `true` if and only if your code is working correctly. If the expression evaluates to `false`, an error is signaled.

Here is an example of an assertion (shown in bold):

```
public class aClass {
  public void aMethod( int argument ) {
    Foo foo = null;

    // ... somehow get a Foo object

    // Now check to make sure we've managed to get one:
    assert foo != null;
  }
}
```

This asserts that `foo` is not `null`. If `foo` is in fact `null`, an `AssertionError` is thrown. Any code that executes after this line can safely assume that `foo` is not `null`.

Assertions are very simple, but we'll be looking at their usage in detail because assertions are very important in the quest for robust code. In this chapter, we'll learn not only how to use assertions, but when and where to use them.

6.1.1 Why use assertions?

It is widely acknowledged in programming circles that software isn't stable enough. We all know we're not doing enough error-checking. It is also acknowledged that error-handling comprises a substantial amount of programming effort and a substantial portion of the resulting code. Error-handling code is also relatively dull to write, especially compared with the main algorithm whose errors are being handled.

Furthermore, dealing with errors can sometimes force you to consider design questions that you may be trying to avoid. In such situations, programmers generally just ignore the possibility of error, mostly because they don't want to lose their train of thought.

As programmers, we need to do more error-checking, and assertions are an important step in this direction. Assertions can be used to catch conditions that we don't expect to happen. This may sound paradoxical, but given that we rarely check for enough errors, it makes a certain sense. For every error we think of while programming, there are a whole bunch more that never occur to us. It's not possible to eliminate all errors, but we can plan ahead for the unexpected.

6.1.2 *Assertions vs. other error code*

The programmer's decision to use an assertion instead of other error-handling code is often based on a general rule of programming psychology: the less likely a programmer thinks an error is, the less code she will write to deal with it. An assertion is easier to write than a `RuntimeException`; a `RuntimeException` is easier to write than a regular `Exception`. Since assertions are easy and quick to use, getting into the habit of using them means you will catch more errors before they cause you trouble.

The choice between these different methods of dealing with an exceptional case really depends on how "exceptional" the exception really is. Is it something that should *never* happen? Something that should only happen due to the error of another programmer? Of the end user? Of the system administrator who configured the server? Of the person who configured the client machine? Is it something that will never happen after the software is released? Is it something that can be tolerated in the field? What damage can result if this exceptional case happens even *once* in a real-life situation?

All of these questions are relevant. A good rule of thumb is that you should use an assertion for exceptional cases that you would like to forget about. An assertion is the quickest way to deal with, and forget, a condition or state that you don't expect to have to deal with. For example, an application might have a hidden configuration file that it never deletes. Since it's *possible, but unlikely,* that the user will ever delete this hidden configuration file, it might be a good idea, after trying to open the file, to assert that the open worked. It almost certainly will, but it's a good idea to check.

Just about any computer programmer—or any computer user—can tell you that software isn't stable enough. Some software bugs are routine, and most of them come without a hint of explanation. You have likely encountered some, if not all, of these problems:

- Printer drivers not printing, and not giving a warning
- Files not showing up on an FTP site after upload
- Web servers returning empty pages
- Hardware devices not being recognized
- System configuration differing after each reboot
- Programs crashing because of corrupted input
- Programs simply not running, or failing unexpectedly

Buried under each of these bugs, many levels down the chain of inter-program communication, is an exceptional condition that some programmer, somewhere, forgot to handle. Handling these errors gracefully is the best possible approach, but it's not possible to handle everything in a complete fashion. Think of an assertion as the smallest (and easiest) way to handle an exceptional case.

6.1.3 *Designing by contract*

If you are familiar with the *design-by-contract* programming methodology, then you can think of assertions as a good way of ensuring *preconditions, postconditions,* and *invariants.* Preconditions are contractual guarantees that must be true at the start of a method, and postconditions are the same, except they are in effect at the end of a method. Assertions can be good for ensuring preconditions if, and only if, the method is not a public method. (Public methods should make an explicit check and throw an exception—see section 6.4.2 for more on this.) Assertions are always good for postconditions.

Invariants, broadly defined, are conditions that should always be true. They are often checked before and after a computation. Since they should always be true, assertions are an excellent way to implement them.

6.2 *Working with assertions*

An assertion is a convenient syntax for checking for an error. In a sense, it's really just a shorthand for a full error check. In this section, we'll examine the syntax used for assertions and look at the equivalent expression from pre-assertion Java. We'll also examine the command-line and programmatic interfaces that can be used to enable and disable assertions at runtime.

6.2.1 *Assertion syntax*

An assertion is a conditional error; operationally, assertions are very simple. There are two distinct flavors of assertion: simple and complex.

Flavor 1 (simple)

Using the simpler syntax, an assertion consists of the keyword `assert`, followed by an expression:

```
assert expression;
```

This should be read as, "if expression isn't true, that's very bad, so throw an error immediately."

Here is the assertion example from section 6.1. This uses the simple syntax:

```
public class aClass {
  public void aMethod( int argument ) {
    Foo foo = null;

    // ... somehow get a Foo object

    // Now check to make sure we've managed to get one:
    assert foo != null;
  }
}
```

Again, operationally, this is roughly equivalent to the following:

```
public class aClass {
  public void aMethod( int argument ) {
    Foo foo = null;

    // ... somehow get a Foo object

    // Now check to make sure we've managed to get one:
    if (!(foo != null)) {
      throw new AssertionError();
    }
  }
}
```

Flavor 2 (complex)

The more complex syntax goes as follows:

```
assert expression_1 : expression_2;
```

This should be read as, "if expression_1 isn't true, throw an error containing the value of expression_2."

NOTE The second expression must be a valid argument to the constructor of the
AssertionError object.

Here's the example from the previous section, but this time using the complex syntax:

```
public class aClass {
  public void aMethod( int argument ) {
    Foo foo = null;

    // ... somehow get a Foo object

    // Now check to make sure we've managed to get one:
    assert foo != null : "Can't get a Foo, argument="+argument;
  }
}
```

This is roughly equivalent to the following:

```
public class aClass {
  public void aMethod( int argument ) {
    Foo foo = null;

    // ... somehow get a Foo object

    // Now check to make sure we've managed to get one:
    if (!(foo != null)) {
      throw new AssertionError(
        "Can't get a Foo, argument="+argument );
    }
  }
}
```

As mentioned in the previous note, the second expression in the complex version of
assert must be a valid argument to the constructor of the AssertionError object.
AssertionError has constructors that take any of the following types:

- object
- boolean
- char
- int
- long
- float
- double

This allows the second expression of an assertion to have any kind of data type as an argument, making assertions as easy to use as System.out and System.err. This is intended to encourage the use of assertions over print statements.

Choosing a flavor

The choice of whether to use the simple syntax or the complex syntax comes down to how much information you want to provide the person running the program. In some cases, it's enough to tell the person where the error occurred; in others, it's important to print out certain values so that the bug can be repaired. If you can't decide, a good rule of thumb is to use the simple syntax. If, at some later point, you want the assertion to provide more information, you can easily change it to use the complex syntax.

6.2.2 *Compiling with assertions*

Assertions require a change to Java's *syntax*, so there is a slight issue with backward-compatibility. Once assert is a keyword, it can no longer be a variable or method name, and code like this is not compatible with the new syntax:

```
public void method() {
   int assert = getAssert();
}
```

Because of the dangerous possibility of breaking seven years' worth of Java code, the JDK 1.4 from Sun Microsystems allows you to select whether you want the new syntax or not.

To use the old syntax, and thus allow the word "assert" to be used as a keyword, you must execute the compiler using the −source 1.3 option. At the command line, you would type this:

```
javac -source 1.3
```

To use the new syntax, and thus enable assertions, you would use this command on the command line:

```
javac -source 1.4
```

If unspecified, -source 1.3 is assumed, so that existing code will compile normally even if it uses assert as a regular identifier. It is expected that all code will eventually compile under the new syntax; the older syntax is provided for those cases where the keyword assert was used as a variable or class name.

If you use assertions in your code, it will be incompatible with versions of the JRE prior to 1.4 because assertions need methods and fields from the Class and

`ClassLoader` classes. This is true even if you don't use the programmatic enable and disable methods mentioned in section 6.2.4.

This shouldn't be cause for alarm—using any new feature of a new release of Java will make the resulting class files incompatible with earlier versions of the JRE. Note that this incompatibility is purely a *library* incompatibility—there is no compatibility problem at the JVM level.

6.2.3 *Controlling assertions from the command line*

One of the most useful features of assertions is that they can be turned off during normal usage, so that they don't incur any speed penalty. By the same token, they need to be turned on when a problem arises. Assertions are off by default.

Although the assertion specification does not require a particular technique for enabling or disabling assertions, it does strongly recommend that such a technique exist for any implementation of the Java language. The implementation described here is that of the release of JDK 1.4 from Sun Microsystems. It is likely that most other implementations will closely follow this model.

Assertions are enabled on the command line via the `-ea` switch, which is an abbreviation for the `-enableassertions` switch. The following two commands are equivalent:

```
java -ea myPackage.myProgram
java -enableassertions myPackage.myProgram
```

Assertions are similarly disabled with either the `-da` or `-disableassertions` commands:

```
java -da myPackage.myProgram
java -disableassertions myPackage.myProgram
```

Assertions can be enabled or disabled for specific packages or classes. To specify a class, use the class name. To specify a package, use the package name followed by "`...`":

```
java -ea:<class> myPackage.myProgram
java -da:<package>... myPackage.myProgram
```

Note that each enable or disable modifies the one before it, so that you can, for example, enable assertions in general, but disable them in a particular package.

```
java -ea -da:<package>... myPackage.myProgram
```

Finally, you can enable or disable assertions in the unnamed root package (the one in the current directory) using the following commands:

```
java -ea:... myPackage.myProgram
java -da:... myPackage.myProgram
```

Note that assertions within system classes that come installed with your JVM can be enabled and disabled separately using the -esa and -dsa switches, which are abbreviations for -enablesystemassertions and -disablesystemassertions, respectively. The various command-line switches for using assertions are listed in table 6.1.

Table 6.1 Command-line switches for enabling and disabling assertions. These options are taken from JDK 1.4 from Sun Microsystems; other implementations may have other techniques for turning assertions on and off.

Switch	Example	Meaning
-ea	Java -ea	Enable assertions by default
-da	Java -da	Disable assertions by default
-ea:<classname>	Java -ea:AssertPackageTest	Enable assertions in class AssertPackageTest
-da:<classname>	Java -da:AssertPackageTest	Disable assertions in class AssertPackageTest
-ea:<packagename>...	Java -ea:pkg0...	Enable assertions in package pkg0
-da:<packagename>...	Java -da:pkg0...	Disable assertions in package pkg0
-esa	Java -esa	Enable assertions in system classes
-dsa	Java -dsa	Disable assertions in system classes

Command-line examples

Let's take a look at some examples of these options in action. In these examples, we have an application called AssertPackageTest that creates an instance of each of three classes, each one in a different package. These instances will print a message if assertions are turned on for them:

```
import pkg0.Class0;
import pkg0.subpkg0.Class2;
import pkg1.Class1;

public class AssertPackageTest
{
  static public void main( String args[] ) {
    new Class0();
    new Class1();
    new Class2();
```

```
    }
}
```

The following examples of running `AssertPackageTest` first state what is being done, and then show the command that runs the program and the output it produces (if any).

Leave assertions off by default:
```
java AssertPackageTest
```
(No output)

Turn assertions on for all non-system classes:
```
java -ea AssertPackageTest
Assertions enabled in AssertPackageTest
Assertions enabled in pkg0.Class0
Assertions enabled in pkg1.Class1
Assertions enabled in pkg0.subpkg0.Class2
```

Turn assertions on for a single package:
```
java -ea:pkg0... AssertPackageTest
Assertions enabled in pkg0.Class0
Assertions enabled in pkg0.subpkg0.Class2
```

Forget the "..." after a package name:
```
java -ea:pkg0 AssertPackageTest
```
(No output)

Turn assertions on for a single class:
```
java -ea:pkg0.Class0 AssertPackageTest
Assertions enabled in pkg0.Class0
```

Turn assertions on for a different class:
```
java -ea:pkg0.subpkg0.Class2 AssertPackageTest
Assertions enabled in pkg0.subpkg0.Class2
```

Turn assertions on for a subpackage:
```
java -ea:pkg0.subpkg0... AssertPackageTest
Assertions enabled in pkg0.subpkg0.Class2
```

Turn assertions on in general, but off for a package:
```
java -ea -da:pkg1... AssertPackageTest
Assertions enabled in AssertPackageTest
Assertions enabled in pkg0.Class0
Assertions enabled in pkg0.subpkg0.Class2
```

Turn assertions on for a package, but off for a subpackage of that package:
```
java -ea:pkg0... -da:pkg0.subpkg0... AssertPackageTest
Assertions enabled in pkg0.Class0
```

Turn assertions on only in the unnamed default package:
```
java -ea:... -da:pkg0... -da:pgk1... AssertPackageTest
```

```
Assertions enabled in AssertPackageTest
```

Turn assertions on in general, but off in the unnamed default package:

```
java -ea -da:... AssertPackageTest
Assertions enabled in pkg0.Class0
Assertions enabled in pkg1.Class1
Assertions enabled in pkg0.subpkg0.Class2
```

6.2.4 *Controlling assertions programmatically*

It is also possible to enable or disable assertions from the program itself. In general, this is something you won't need to do unless you are writing a debugger or some other kind of program whose purpose is to manage a Java program running in the same JVM.

Each class contains an "assertion status" flag that tells the system whether assertions are enabled for that class. Each time an assert line is reached, the containing class is checked for the value of this flag, to see if the assertion should be processed or skipped.

This flag can be set via the class's ClassLoader, using the following approach:

```
public void setClassAssertionStatus(String className,
                                    boolean enabled);
```

The arguments are as follows:

- className—The name of the class whose assertion status is to be set
- enabled—Whether assertions should be on or off

This flag can also be turned on for an entire package using another method of ClassLoader:

```
public void setPackageAssertionStatus(String packageName,
                                      boolean enabled);
```

The arguments are as follows:

- packageName—The name of the package whose classes are to have their assertion status set
- enabled—Whether assertions should be on or off

Note that this method applies not just to the specified package, but to all subpackages within it.

A ClassLoader also has a default assertion status that is passed to any class loaded through it. The default can be set with the following method of ClassLoader:

```
public void setDefaultAssertionStatus(boolean enabled);
```

The argument is as follows:

- enabled—Whether assertions should be on or off by default

Finally, ClassLoader has a method that lets you clear all the assertion settings that have gone before. This not only clears the default assertion status (thus turning assertions off by default), it also removes any per-class and per-package settings that have been made against this ClassLoader:

```
public void clearAssertionStatus();
```

Another method, Class.desiredAssertionStatus(), will be discussed in section 6.2.8.

NOTE   The assertion status flags set by these methods do not affect classes already loaded and initialized by the ClassLoader—they only affect classes that are loaded and initialized subsequently. Remember to set these flags before loading the classes that you want to be affected by them.

6.2.5 *Removing assertions completely*

Even if you run your code with assertions disabled, they are still in the class files. Although this depends completely on the particular implementation of the Java platform you are using, it is quite likely that the assertions will be taking up some space, as well as some time, in your running program.

If this is a problem, you can apply the standard technique for removing code without actually removing it:

```
static final boolean doAsserts = false;

public void method() {
  if (doAsserts) assert expression;
}
```

Because doAsserts is final, the Java compiler is required to remove this line of code from the execution, resulting in savings in both time and space.

WARNING   Removing assertions is strongly discouraged unless there is good reason, such as the need to run with a very small memory footprint. Assertions are most useful if they can be turned on at any time, even long after the release of the software.

6.2.6 *Determining if assertions are enabled*

There are times when you might need to determine whether assertions are enabled. For example, your assertions might need to do extra calculations in order to properly check your code, and you might want to avoid doing those calculations if assertions are disabled.

The following fragment of code tests to see whether assertions are enabled or not:

```
public void method() {
  boolean assertionsAreEnabled = false;

  assert (assertionsAreEnabled = true);

  if (assertionsAreEnabled) {
    System.out.println( "Assertions are enabled!" );
  } else {
    System.out.println( "Assertions are disabled!" );
  }
}
```

Note the trickiness here—that's a *single* equals sign inside the assertion expression, so it's an assignment rather than a comparison. Instead of checking whether assertionsAreEnabled is true, it actually sets assertionsAreEnabled to be true.

It is, in general, a bad idea to put any kind of side effects inside an assert expression, because you don't know if the expression will even get executed—that depends on whether assertions are enabled. This case is an exception, though—not only is the side effect localized to this fragment, but it is in fact the *point* of the construction. We allow the assertion status to have a side effect because we want to know if assertions are enabled.

One thing you might want to do in very critical applications is to refuse to run without assertions. This is somewhat nonstandard, since assertions, by their very nature, are supposed to be enabled at the whim of the person running the program, rather than at the whim of the programmer. However, if it is important to ensure that they are on, the following can be done:

```
public void method() {
  boolean assertionsAreEnabled = false;

  assert (assertionsAreEnabled = true);

  if (!assertionsAreEnabled) {
    throw new RuntimeException( "Assertions must be enabled!" );
  }
}
```

Be careful not to fall into the trap of using an assertion to do this check. The following code won't work if assertions are turned off, and thus misses the whole point:

```
public void method() {
  boolean assertionsAreEnabled = false;

  assert (assertionsAreEnabled = true);

  assert assertionsAreEnabled;
}
```

6.2.7 *Catching an assertion failure*

Since assertions fail by throwing an error, it's possible to catch an assertion failure. Under normal circumstances, you should rethrow the error, because it is crucial that assertion failures come to the attention of the operator of the program as soon as possible.

However, there are times when you might want to catch an `AssertionError`, do something, and then rethrow the error. If your application has a network console, you might want to send the assertion failure across the network to the console before quitting.

If you do catch an assertion failure, make sure to rethrow it! It's okay to catch an exception, because exceptions are *designed* to be caught. But an assertion failure generally implies a really unexpected failure—something that deserves immediate attention.

In the example in listing 6.1, we trap the `AssertionError` in order to get stack trace information. We then rethrow the `AssertionError` from within the `catch` block.

Listing 6.1

```
public void method() {
    AssertionError ae = null;

    try {

      int a = anotherMethod();

      // ...

      assert i==10;        ●   The assertion

      // ...

    } catch( AssertionError ae2 ) {     ●   Trapping the assertion failure

      ae = ae2;·

      StackTraceElement stes[] = ae.getStackTrace();
```

```
      if (stes.length>0) {
        StackTraceElement first = stes[0];
        System.out.println( "NOTE: Assertion failure in "+
          first.getFileName()+" at line "+first.getLineNumber() );
      } else {
        System.out.println( "NOTE: No info available." );
      }

      throw ae;        ●   Rethrowing the assertion failure
    }
}
```

6.2.8 *Assertions and class initialization*

According to the assertion specifications, whether or not assertions are turned on for a class is determined during the initialization process. In most circumstances, a class cannot be used before it has been initialized. But there are some cases in which this is not true, which presents an ambiguity: if a class is not yet initialized, are assertions on or off?

Listing 6.2 presents an example of how code in a class can be run before it is finished initializing. It makes use of a certain paradoxical relationship between two classes, CircularA and CircularB.

Listing 6.2

```
public class CircularA
{
  static {
    CircularB.report();
  }
}

public class CircularB extends CircularA
{
  static public void report() {
    boolean assertionsOn = false;
    assert assertionsOn=true;
    System.out.println( "Assertions are "+
      (assertionsOn?"on":"off") );
  }

  static public void main( String args[] ) {
    report();
  }
}
```

Here's the problem: CircularB must be initialized before its main() method can run, and CircularB is a subclass of CircularA, so CircularA must be initialized before CircularB can be initialized. However, CircularA has a static initializer that makes a call to CircularB, so CircularB.report() gets called before CircularB is fully initialized.

By running CircularA with assertions fully disabled, you can see that assertions are nevertheless enabled during initialization:

```
java -da -dsa CircularB
Assertions are on
Assertions are off
```

The assertion specification requires that assertions be enabled within a class during its initialization period, regardless of any other command-line settings or Class-Loader settings that have been (or will be) put into effect. This is the reason that the first call to report() states that assertions are on. Because of this, if a class checks, using the usual methods, to see if assertions are on, it will get a false positive during the initialization process.

The following method allows you to find out whether assertions will be enabled or not after initialization is complete. This is a method of Class.

```
public boolean desiredAssertionStatus();
```

In the few cases where you might validly make an execution decision based on whether assertions are enabled or not, this method can help you find this out during the initialization process.

Let's take a look at CircularA again. It was shown originally in listing 6.2, but in listing 6.3 it has been modified to check the real assertion status using desiredAssertionStatus():

Listing 6.3

```
public class CircularA
{
  static {
    CircularB.report();
  }
}

public class CircularB extends CircularA
{
  static public void report() {
    boolean assertionsOn = false;
    assert assertionsOn=true;
    boolean assertionsWillBeOn =
      new CircularA().getClass().desiredAssertionStatus();
```

```
    System.out.println(
      "Assertions in CircularA: current="+assertionsOn+
      " desired="+assertionsWillBeOn );
  }

  static public void main( String args[] ) {
    report();
  }
}
```

Here's the output:

```
java -da -dsa CircularB
Assertions in CircularA: current=true desired=false
Assertions in CircularA: current=false desired=false
```

As you can see, the desired assertion status is always `false`, even though assertions are temporarily on during initialization.

6.3   Assertion examples

This section presents examples of the kinds of conditions you might check for inside an assertion. We'll use both flavors of assertions so that you get a feel for each one.

6.3.1   Avoiding inconsistent states

The most common application of assertions is to ensure that the program remains in a consistent state.

JARGON   A *consistent state* is any configuration of your program that makes sense according to the logic you've defined for it. An *inconsistent state* is any configuration that should never be reached.

Here's an example that checks for an inconsistent state. Let's say your program makes use of a `PipedInputStream`/`PipedOutputStream` pair.

```
import java.io.*;

public class Example
{
  private PipedInputStream pin;
  private PipedOutputStream pout;

  private void initializePipe() throws IOException {
    pin = new PipedInputStream();
    pout = new PipedOutputStream( pin );
  }
}
```

When the program starts, it has not yet created these objects, so it is in the state shown in table 6.2. Although the pipe cannot be used (because it is not there), this is nevertheless a *consistent state*, because it is intentional: before we've created our pipe, these variables must necessarily be null.

Table 6.2   Before the pipe is created, the variables must be null.

Variable	Value
pin	null
pout	null

Later on, we create the pipe by calling initializePipe(), at which point the state of our variables has changed, as shown in table 6.3. We're still in a consistent state, because here we define consistency to mean a state in which we have both ends of the pipe available to us.

Table 6.3   After the pipe is created, the state of the variables changes.

Variable	Value
pin	java.io.PipedInputStream@3fbdb0
pout	java.io.PipedOutputStream@3e86d0

Still later, our program closes the pipe and sets both variables to null, as shown in table 6.4. This is again a consistent state, representing the fact that we're done with the pipe.

Table 6.4   When the pipe is closed, the state of the variables is set to null.

Variable	Value
pin	null
pout	null

When our code has become much more complicated, however, we find that we have a bug in which, for some complicated reason, pin was set to null while pout was still pointing to an object (see table 6.5). This is an inconsistent state. As the designers of the code, we know that this state should never be entered. It represents no *conceptual* state that we could name. It does not represent the state in which we haven't started using the pipe, nor the state in which we are in the middle of using the pipe.

Table 6.5   A bug causes one variable to be non-`null`.

Variable	Value
pin	null
pout	java.io.PipedOutputStream@3e86d0

Realizing this, we decide to add assertions in various places to check for this inconsistent state. We want to make sure that both objects are `null` at the same time.

```
public void someMethod() {
  assert (pin==null) == (pout==null) :
    "Warning: pipe is inconsistent" );
}
```

We can sprinkle this assertion all over the code, as necessary.

6.3.2 *Narrowing the range of states*

There are times when we need to restrict the set of states that our program can be in, but we wouldn't really call it an issue of *consistency.* Generally this is as simple as trying to ensure that a particular variable contains a value within a certain subrange of possible values.

Let's say that our program is a little physics simulation, and our math should ensure that the velocities of our objects don't get out of control. Let's make sure:

```
public void runSimulation() {
  // ...

  assert
    Math.abs( velocity ) < 2000 :
    "Object way too fast! velocity="+velocity;
}
```

This example ensures that `velocity` never gets to be 2,000 or greater.

6.3.3 *Ensuring consistency between container objects and contained objects*

We'll use a somewhat more complex program to give a sense of what it means for a program to be in an inconsistent state and demonstrate the use of assertions. Our example will be an excerpt from a hypothetical chat server.

The `ChatServer` object maintains two lists of `Connection` objects. Each `Connection` object represents the connection to a `Client` and can be in one of two states: active or suspended. A suspended `Client` is one whose user has left his computer for a while.

The ChatServer object also has two methods for sending out messages to connected clients:

- sendMessage() sends a message to a particular connection
- sendMessageToAll() iterates through all of the active connections and calls sendMessage() on each one to send it a message

The problem is to make sure that the active list only contains active clients, and that the suspended list only contains suspended clients. To this end, we create a couple of methods, setActive() and setSuspended(). These set the state of a connection and also move it to the correct list:

```java
import java.io.*;
import java.net.*;

public class ChatServer
{
  private List activeConnections;
  private List suspendedConnections;

  // ...

  synchronized void setActive( Connection connection ) {
    connection.setActive();
    suspendedConnections.remove( connection );
    activeConnections.add( connection );
  }

  synchronized void setSuspended( Connection connection ) {
    connection.setSuspended();
    passiveConnections.remove( connection );
    suspendedConnections.add( connection );
  }

  synchronized private void sendMessageToAll( Message message ) {
    for (Iterator iter=activeConnections.iterator();
                  iter.hasNext();) {
      Connection connection = (Connection)iter.next();
      sendMessage( connection, message );
    }
  }

  synchronized private void sendMessage( Connection connection,
                                         Message message ) {
    // ... send the message out to a particular connection
  }
}
```

Creating methods to perform list maintenance doesn't solve the problem entirely. Other code in our class, not seen here, might modify the activeConnections and suspendedConnections lists. Sometimes this happens on behalf of code we don't have control over (or even have source code for). Even when we do control the code entirely, we still might make a mistake and fail to maintain the lists properly.

This is a perfect job for assertions:

```
import java.io.*;
import java.net.*;

public class ChatServer
{
  private List activeConnections;
  private List suspendedConnections;

  // ...

  synchronized void setActive( Connection connection ) {
    connection.setActive();
    suspendedConnections.remove( connection );
    activeConnections.add( connection );
  }

  synchronized void setSuspended( Connection connection ) {
    connection.setSuspended();
    passiveConnections.remove( connection );
    suspendedConnections.add( connection );
  }

  synchronized private void sendMessageToAll( Message message ) {
    for (Iterator iter=activeConnections.iterator();
               iter.hasNext();) {
      Connection connection = (Connection)iter.next();
      assert connection.isActive();
      sendMessage( connection, message );
    }
  }

  synchronized private void sendMessage( Connection connection,
                                   Message message ) {
    assert activeConnections.contains( connection );
    // ... send the message out to a particular connection
  }
}
```

You might have noticed that there is some redundancy to the assertions. sendMessageToAll() iterates through the connections, and then calls sendMessage() for each connection. Both methods use assertions to make sure messages are never sent to a suspended connection. We're really getting two assertions per connection, which isn't necessary unless we suspect that the status of a connection can be changing at any time, and it probably can't because we're using proper synchronization.

If the preceding code were the only code in the class, we might consider taking out the second assertion, because it isn't necessary. But we might have other places in our code that call `sendMessage()` directly, so we want to make sure we have an assertion happening in that case.

TIP   We don't need to worry so much about the efficiency of assertions, because, in real usage, the assertions don't even get run. They only get run in a developmental context, where we don't mind wasting a few CPU cycles if it means our code is more stable.

6.3.4 *More complicated consistency checks*

Sometimes, there are consistency checks that are just too complicated to easily fit inside a single expression on a single line. In such cases, we can make a helper method that does the consistency check, and use an assertion to call it.

For example, suppose we have a class called `EmployeeDatabase` that contains a number of interlocking maps, lists, and sets. If you're not careful, it's easy to get some of the relationships between these objects into an inconsistent state.

At the same time, checking for consistency involves traversing the lists, keeping track of which things are on which lists, comparing sets of membership states, and so on. Often, consistency checking for such data structures involves building up a subset of the relationship from scratch while making sure it is consistent.

Since an assertion is an assertion of a single expression, it can be awkward, or even impossible, to put a complicated calculation right inside the `assert` expression, so we move it out to a helper method:

```
public class EmployeeDatabase()
{
  private Set employees;
  private Map employeeGroups;
  private SortedMap employeeTitles;
  private Set groups;
  private Map groupMemberships;
  private Set projects;
  private List groupDeadlines;

  public void doSomething() {

    // ...
    assert isConsistent() : "Error: inconsistent state!";
  }

  private boolean isConsistent() {

    // check lots and lots of stuff here
    // ...
  }
}
```

Setting things up this way can make code a lot easier to read, since the safety checks are all in one place. It also helps avoid having multiple copies of the safety checks in several places in the code, thus reducing code size and eliminating redundancy.

6.4   *Knowing when to use assertions*

The trickiest thing about assertions isn't knowing how to use them—it's knowing *when* and *where* to use them. This section outlines a number of guidelines, summarized in table 6.6, which should help you understand what assertions are appropriate for, and what they are not appropriate for.

Table 6.6   Assertions are often confused with regular conditionals. Follow these rules to distinguish what your particular situation calls for.

Assertion do's	Assertion don'ts
Do use to enforce internal assumptions about aspects of data structures	Don't use to enforce command-line usage
Do use to enforce constraints on arguments to private methods	Don't use to enforce constraints on arguments to public methods
Do use to check conditions at the end of any kind of method	Don't use to enforce public usage patterns or protocols
Do use to check for conditional cases that should never happen	Don't use to enforce a property of a piece of user-supplied information
Do use to check for conditional cases that should never happen, even if you're really sure they can never happen	Don't use as a shorthand for `if (something) error();`
Do use to check related conditions at the start of any method	Don't use as an externally controllable conditional
Do use to check things in the middle of a long-lived loop	Don't use as a check on the correctness of your compiler, operating system, or hardware, unless you have a specific reason to believe there is something wrong with it and are in the process of debugging it
Do use in lieu of nothing	

6.4.1 *Rules of use*

An assertion is not just a concise way to say `if (expression) then`. Rather, it is the basis of a discipline for making programs more robust.

It is very important to distinguish between situations where an assertion is needed and situations where a regular conditional is needed. The following rules should give you an idea of when assertions are appropriate, and when they are not.

Rule: do not use assertions to enforce command-line usage

Programs that use command-line arguments should always check the validity of the arguments, but this should be done with a regular conditional. The following example is an inappropriate use of an assertion:

```
public class Application
{
  static public void main( String args[] ) {
    // BAD!!
    assert args.length == 3;

    int a = Integer.parseInt( args[0] );
    int b = Integer.parseInt( args[1] );
    int c = Integer.parseInt( args[2] );
  }
}
```

It may be true that your program simply cannot run unless it is supplied with three arguments on the command line, but in this case it would be better to throw a proper RuntimeException:

```
public class App
{
  static public void main( String args[] ) {
    if (args.length != 3)
      throw new RuntimeException( "Usage: <progname> a b c" );

    int a = Integer.parseInt( args[0] );
    int b = Integer.parseInt( args[1] );
    int c = Integer.parseInt( args[2] );
  }
}
```

Assertions are meant to require that the program be consistent with itself, not that the user be consistent with the program.

Rule: use assertions to enforce constraints on arguments to private methods

The following private method takes two arguments; one is required, and one is optional:

```
private void method( Object required, Object optional ) {
  assert( required != null ) : "method(): required=null";
}
```

In general, `private` methods are probably being called by code we have control over, and which we expect are written correctly and consistently. As a result, we would like to think that all calls to our method are correct. We enforce this assumption with an assertion.

The same reasoning may apply to `protected` and `package-protected` methods.

Rule: do not use assertions to enforce constraints on arguments to public methods

The following public method takes two arguments: a source and a sink that are connected. Before disconnecting them, we'd like to ensure that they are connected to begin with:

```
public void disconnect( Source source, sink sink ) {
  // BAD!!
  assert source.isConnected( sink ) :
    "disconnect(): not connected "+source+","+sink;
}
```

In this example, `disconnect()` can only remove a connection between a `Source` and a `Sink` if they are in fact connected. However, because this method is `public`, the code that calls it might not be under your control.

More importantly, a `public` method guarantees that it will enforce the requirements of its specified interface in all situations. Assertions, on the other hand, are not guaranteed to run—they will only enforce their constraints if assertions are enabled in the runtime environment. This violates the promises made by the `public` method.

In this case, you should assume that the calling code might be in error, and throw a proper exception:

```
public void disconnect( Source source, sink sink ) throws IOException
{
  if (!source.isConnected( sink )) {
    throw new IOException(
      "disconnect(): not connected "+source+","+sink );
  }
}
```

This exception will be thrown regardless of whether assertions are on or off.

Rule: do not use assertions to enforce public usage patterns or protocols

The following `public` class can be in one of two states: open or closed. It is an error to open a `Connection` that is already open, or to close one that is already closed. However, we would not use an assertion to ensure that these mistakes are not made:

```
public class Connection
{
  private boolean isOpen = false;

  public void open() {
    // ...
    isOpen = true;
  }

  public void close() {
    // BAD!!
    assert isOpen : "Cannot close a connection that is not open!";
    // ...
  }
}
```

The programmer has attempted to enforce the requirement that a Connection can only be closed if it is already open.

This usage is valid *if and only if* the Connection class were a private class, or were otherwise guaranteed to be invisible to the outside, *and* if we were willing to ensure and assume that any code that uses this class is written correctly. In this case, it would be legitimate to enforce this assumption with an assertion.

However, if the Connection class is used publicly, it would not be surprising to find a bug in which someone tried to close a Connection that wasn't open in the first place. In this case, a regular exception would be better:

```
public class Connection
{
  private boolean isOpen = false;

  public void open() {
    // ...
    isOpen = true;
  }

  public void close() throws ConnectionException {
    if (!isOpen) {
      throw new ConnectionException(
        "Cannot close a connection that is not open!" );
    }
    // ...
  }
}
```

If you go the other route, and attempt to ensure that this code is only called from call sites you control, think twice. Any code you write now may be used or reused later in a different configuration. Anything can happen after the initial revision, so it's best to be on the safe side. Using an explicit exception provides the most information to a frustrated programmer down the line.

Rule: do not use assertions to enforce a property of a piece of user-supplied information

In the following code fragment, the programmer has used an assertion to make sure that a ZIP code has either five or nine digits:

```java
public void processZipCode( String zipCode ) {
  if (zipCode.length() == 5) {
    // ...
  } else if (zipCode.length() == 9) {
    // ...
  } else {
    // BAD!!
    assert false : "Only 5- and 9-digit zip codes supported";
  }
}
```

Assertions should be used to enforce internal consistency, not correct input. The preceding code would be better served by using an explicit exception:

```java
public void processZipCode( String zipCode )
    throws ZipCodeException {
  if (zipCode.length() == 5) {
    // ...
  } else if (zipCode.length() == 9) {
    // ...
  } else {
    throw new ZipCodeException(
      "Only 5- and 9-digit zip codes supported" );
  }
}
```

6.4.2 *What to check for*

Once you know where assertions should be used, you have to decide what to check and what not to check. Assertions are often used to check for things that are usually neglected, so keep the following rules in mind when you are deciding where to use assertions.

Rule: use assertions to enforce internal assumptions about aspects of data structures

The following private method takes an array of three integers. We use an assertion to make sure that the array is of the correct length:

```java
private void showDate( int array[] ) {
  assert( array.length==3 );
}
```

We expect calls to this code to be written properly, and thus to only supply arrays of length three. This assertion merely enforces this assumption.

Java does have bounds-checked arrays, which means that this assertion isn't quite as crucial as it would be in a language like C or C++. However, this does not mean that using an assertion here isn't a good idea.

Rule: use assertions to check conditions at the end of any kind of method

Let's enhance the previous example with a few *postconditions*—that is, conditions checked after the body of a method, just before returning:

```java
public class Connection
{
  private boolean isOpen = false;

  public void open() {
    // ...

    isOpen = true;

    // ...

    assert isOpen;
  }
  public void close() throws ConnectionException {
    if (!isOpen) {
      throw new ConnectionException(
        "Cannot close a connection that is not open!" );
    }
    // ...

    isOpen = false;

    // ...

    assert !isOpen;
  }
}
```

These assertions might seem redundant, but there's no telling what might come between the line where isOpen is set to true, and the line where isOpen is asserted to be true.

The assignment might eventually be put inside a conditional, removing the direct redundancy. Someone might forget to throw an exception, causing the assertion to be reached when it should have been skipped. The method might grow to be much larger, and get factored into several methods for readability. There's no telling what might happen to your code.

Rule: use assertions to check for conditional cases that should never happen

In the following code, the assertion checks for a conditional case that can't happen:

```
private int getValue() {
  if (/* something */) {
    return 0;
  } else if (/* something else */) {
    return 1;
  } else {
    return 2;
  }
}

public void method() {
  int a = getValue(); // returns 0, 1, or 2

  if (a==0) {
    // deal with 0 ...
  } else if (a==1) {
    // deal with 1 ...
  } else if (a==2) {
    // deal with 2 ...
  } else {
    assert false : "Impossible: a is out of range";
  }
}
```

In this example, we are receiving a value that we believe can only be in a certain range. It is valid in this case to use an assertion because method() makes no promises about handling values other than 0, 1, or 2.

Here is another way to write the code for method():

```
public void method() {
  int a = getValue(); // returns 0, 1, or 2

  if (a==0) {
    // deal with 0 ...
  } else if (a==1) {
    // deal with 1 ...
  } else {
    assert a==2 : "Impossible: a is out of range";
    // deal with 2 ...
  }
}
```

This code is semantically equivalent to the original version.

Here is yet another equivalent implementation of the same method:

```
public void method() {
  int a = getValue(); // returns 0, 1, or 2

  switch( a ) {
    case 0:
      // deal with 0 ...
      break;
    case 1:
      // deal with 1 ...
      break;
    case 2:
      // deal with 2 ...
      break;
    default:
      assert false : "Impossible: a is out of range";
      break;
  }
}
```

Rule: use assertions to check for conditional cases that should never happen, even if you're really sure they can never happen

This next example might seem overly cautious:

```
public void method() {
  int a = getValue(); // returns 0, 1, or 2

  assert a>=0 && a<=2 : "Impossible: a is out of range";

  // ...

  if (a==0) {
    // deal with 0 ...
  } else if (a==1) {
    // deal with 1 ...
  } else {
    assert a==2;
    // deal with 2 ...
  }
}
```

In the preceding code fragment, it looks like we've checked twice for the same exact condition. As written, the assertions are redundant, because the value doesn't change between the first and second assertions. But let's take a look at the same code two releases later:

```
public void method() {
  int a = getValue(); // returns 0, 1, or 2
```

```
assert a>=0 && a<=2 : "Impossible: a is out of range";

// ...

boolean shouldPromote = shouldPromote( b, c, d );
if (shouldPromote && somethingElse)
  a++;
a = modifyMaybe( a );

// ...

if (a==0) {
  // deal with 0 ...
} else if (a==1) {
  // deal with 1 ...
} else {
  assert a==2;
  // deal with 2 ...
}
}
```

See? Without intending to complicate the invariants of your code, you or someone else has made the situation rather more complicated. Someone has inserted code between the first assertion and the second assertion that changes the value of the variable being checked. The second assertion is no longer redundant.

TIP   It is good programming discipline to always have a final `else {}` case for any conditional. If you add one, but you know that it should never be reached, add an `assert false;`.

Rule: use assertions to check related conditions at the start of any method

In this example, the method `processZipCode()` wants to make sure that the program has already loaded a valid ZIP code map before it can process a ZIP code:

```
public void processZipCode( String zipCode ) {
  assert zipCodeMapIsValid();

  // ...
}
```

It is a fine idea to check related data structures in select locations, just in case. The idea here is to catch bugs early and often.

Rule: use assertions to check things in the middle of a long-lived loop

The `Server` class shown in listing 6.4 contains an inner loop that listens for network connections. This code might run for hours or days.

```
Listing 6.4
public class Server
{
  private ServerSocket serverSocket;

  public void acceptConnections() {
    while (true) {
      Socket socket = serverSocket.accept();        ● Long pause here

      assert socketListIsValid();        ● It's good to check some stuff

      // deal with new connection ...
    }
  }
}
```

A check placed in the middle of the long-lived loop ensures that assumptions that
were made at the start of the loop continue to hold after time has passed.

6.4.3 *Miscellaneous rules*

This section highlights a few rules that don't fit into either of the previous two categories. Many of them serve to prevent the use of assertions where a stronger form
of error-checking is preferable.

Rule: do not use an assertion as a shorthand for "if (something) error();"

Here, we incorrectly use an assertion to make sure that a port number is 1024 or
greater:

```
public class Server
{
  private int port;

  public void listen() {
    // BAD!!
    assert port >= 1024 : "No permission to listen on port "+port;

    // ...
  }
}
```

In the preceding code, the programmer has been a little bit lazy, using an assertion
for a valid, exceptional condition. Apparently he has forgotten that assertions generally do not run outside the development process. This should be an exception:

```
public class Server
{
  private int port;
```

```
  public void listen() {
    if (port < 1024) {
      throw new RuntimeException(
        "No permission to listen on port "+port );
    }
    // ...
  }
}
```

This version of the code ensures that the port number will be checked even when assertions are not enabled.

Rule: do not use an assertion as an externally controllable conditional

Here's a clever trick you might be tempted to do:

```
public class Application
{
  static private boolean turnLoggingOn() {
    // Turn logging on
    // ...

    return true;
  }

  static public void main( String args[] ) throws Exception {
    // ...

    // BAD!!
    assert turnLoggingOn();
  }
}
```

```
java -da Application
```

```
java -ea Application
```

As we saw in section 6.2.3, you can enable or disable assertions from the command line. You could use this ability to enable or disable something else by invoking that something else from within an assertion.

As clever as this is, it's bad idea, because it changes the semantics of the -ea and -da switches, and hijacks this facility for another purpose. End users should be able to enable or disable assertions purely on the basis of how vigilant they want the software to be during its execution; they should not have to worry about otherwise changing the semantics of the program.

WARNING Assertions should never have side effects, because the semantics of your program would be subject to whether assertions are enabled are not.

Rule: do not use assertions to check the correctness of your compiler, operating system, or hardware, unless you are debugging it

This code is clearly redundant:

```
public void method() {
  int a = 10;

  // REDUNDANT!!
  assert a==10;
}
```

As written, this assertion cannot possibly be triggered without a serious problem with your system at some level. A compiler bug might cause this assertion to trigger, and if you suspect that your compiler has a bug, this is a perfectly valid thing to do. However, putting such things in your code as a matter of course can confuse someone who might read it down the line, causing them to spend a good deal of time trying to figure out why the assertion was added in the first place.

Final rule: any assertion is better than nothing

As we saw at the beginning of the chapter, assertions are meant, above all, to be convenient enough to be added as an afterthought. Any time you suspect that you might be making an assumption that might not be true, and it makes you at all nervous, add an assertion. An assertion that is never triggered is far better than one that would have been triggered but isn't there.

6.5 Summary

In the computer science community, assertions are widely understood to be a powerful and flexible way to allow code to check itself for errors. It is designed to be as convenient as possible so that programmers can use it during development without distracting themselves from the task at hand.

In this sense, assertions have a *psychological* design as much as they have a technological design. Assertions are relatively cheap to implement, and while the implementation can differ from platform to platform, it is safe to assume that assertions can be used freely without a loss of program speed. The result will be better, more reliable code.

Exceptions

JDK 1.4 includes a couple of new features related to exceptions. One is a mechanism called chained exceptions. When a piece of code catches one exception, only to throw another exception, the first exception can be thought of as the cause of the second one. The chained exception feature provides a formal recognition of this programming pattern.

Additionally, JDK 1.4 has provided a new Exceptions API which adds a programmatic interface to the stack trace contained within an exception. This allows you to create your own thread dumps, or to otherwise examine the stack corresponding to the creation point of an `Exception` (or other `Throwable`).

7.1 *Chained exceptions*

It is a common programming practice to catch one exception only to throw another one. This is generally done in a context where an exception of one type must be converted to another type in order to satisfy the `throws` clause of the method, which requires that the method only throw certain exceptions.

The following example is taken from a hypothetical implementation of an output stream:

```
public void write( byte b[] ) throws IOException {
  // ...
  try {
    // ...
  } catch( SomeInternalException e ) {
    throw new IOException( e.toString() );
  }
}
```

The code inside the `try` block potentially throws a `SomeInternalException`, but the `write()` method can only throw an `IOException` (or a subclass thereof). Thus, we throw a new `IOException`, passing into its constructor the string representation of the old `SomeInternalException`. When this exception is printed out, it shows the types of both of the exceptions:

```
java.io.IOException: SomeInternalException: message
        at MyOutputStream.write(MyOutputStream.java:43);
```

This has a couple of disadvantages. The original exception is not retrievable, so any specialized code (such as is found in a debugger or runtime analyzer) that might want to examine the exception will not be able to get access to the original exception. Also, there is no consistent convention for how such an exception should be formatted. We used the return value of the `toString()` method of the old exception as an argument to the constructor for the new exception, but this is by no means the only way to do it.

In order to formalize this technique and achieve consistency in the way that these things are handled and displayed, every `Throwable` now officially has a *cause*, which itself is another `Throwable`.

The value of a `Throwable`'s cause can be set in its constructor:

```
new Exception( "message", oldException );
```

Or it can be set using its `initCause()` method:

```
Exception e = new Exception( "message" );
e.initCause( oldException );
```

Actually, you can only use the constructor form if the class actually provides such a constructor, as do some of the basic ones, including `Exception`, `RuntimeException`, `Error`, and `Throwable`.

You can get the cause of an exception by calling its `getCause()` method:

```
Throwable originalException = exception.getCause();
System.out.println( "Original Exception:\n"+originalException );
```

Listing 7.1 shows a program, TraverseExceptionChain, that will print out an entire cause chain.

Listing 7.1   TraverseExceptionChain.java

(See \Chapter7\TraverseExceptionChain.java)
```
public class TraverseExceptionChain
{
  /**
   * Traverse a chain of exceptions and print each one out
   */
  static public void traverseExceptionChain( Throwable t ) {
    while (t != null) {
      System.out.println( t );            ● Traverse by repeatedly
      t = t.getCause();                      calling getCause()
    }
  }

  /**
   * Test routine: synthesize a nice chain of exceptions
   * and traverse it
   */
  static public void main( String args[] ) {
    int array[] = new int[10];
    try {
      // out-of-bounds access
      array[500] = 1;
    } catch( Exception e ) {
      Exception e2 = new Exception( "Two", e );     ❶ Add a couple of links
      Exception e3 = new Exception( "Three", e2 );     to the chain
```

```
    traverseExceptionChain( e3 );
  }
 }
}
```

❶ The first exception was an `ArrayIndexOutOfBoundsException`. These lines add a couple more links to the exception chain just to give `traverseExceptionChain()` something substantial to work with.

The output looks like this:

```
java.lang.Exception: Three
java.lang.Exception: Two
java.lang.ArrayIndexOutOfBoundsException
```

The exceptions in the chain run from newest to oldest; the original exception is the last in the chain.

7.2   *StackTraceElements*

Prior to JDK 1.4, the only way you could get a stack trace was by printing it to an output stream. This produced a textual, human-readable dump of the stack trace. While very useful for programmers, this wasn't easily usable by programs themselves. If a program wanted access to stack trace information, it would have to parse the stack data. Most programmers chose to avoid the issue entirely.

With the new release, however, you get easy access to the stack trace through the new Exception API. You can use this in a number of ways. In some situations, you might decide how to handle an exception based on where it was thrown from, and you can find this out from the stack trace. You can even use this mechanism to provide your own method for dumping the stack trace in a human-readable form. We'll see an example of this in section 7.2.3, where we'll augment a traditional stack trace with snippets of the source code it pertains to.

7.2.1   *What is a stack trace?*

The call stack is the set of methods that are currently in progress in a given thread— the one currently executing, the method that called it, the method that called *that*, and so on. A *stack trace* is a description of the state of the call stack at a given moment in time (see figure 7.1). Each method that calls another method adds another line to the call stack, describing the exact point at which the call was made.

DEFINITION   A *stack frame* is a single line of the call stack, and it refers to the point at which one method called another.

NOTE Stack frames are numbered from least recent to most recent, but are generally listed in reverse order. Thus, the last stack frame of the stack trace, which corresponds to the most-recently called method, is listed first, followed by the second-to-last, and so on, until the first stack frame is reached.

It's easy to get a stack trace, because there is one contained in every exception. You can create an exception just to see what the stack trace is:

```
public void bar()
{
  // do stuff ...
  throw new RuntimeException( "hi" );
  // do more stuff ...
}
```

NOTE Although it's rarely done, you don't *have* to throw an exception—you can just create it, inspect it, and then discard it.

In the example shown in figure 7.1, we have a main() method that creates a new object and calls its foo() method, which calls bar(), which throws an exception.

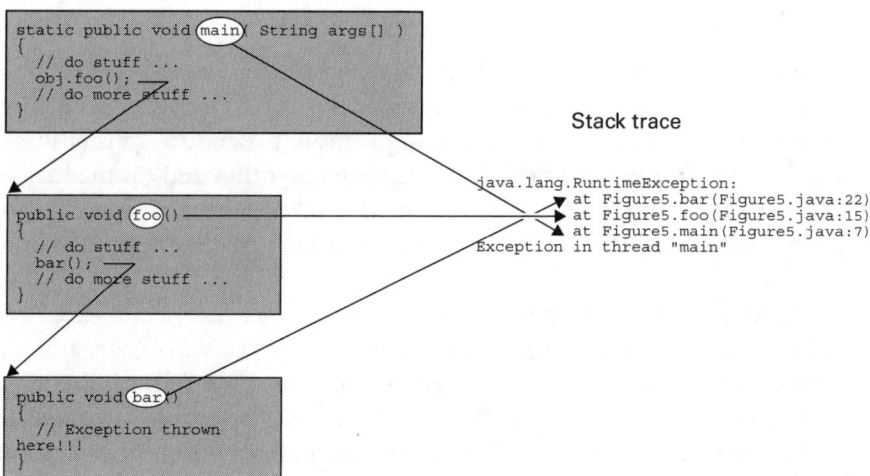

Figure 7.1 A stack trace shows each method in the call stack, which is the list of methods currently executing within this thread. Each method that calls another method adds another line to the call stack describing the exact point at which the call was made.

Note that each line of the exception corresponds to a different point in the execution. Each line of the stack trace, except for the first one, shows the name of a class and a method. It also shows the name of a source code filename and a line number within that file—this helps the programmer fix the bug by allowing her to seek out this location in the code.

Each of these pieces of information—the filename, the method name, and so on—is available from the StackTraceElement class, as we'll see in the next section.

7.2.2 Using StackTraceElements

Each Exception—each Throwable, in fact—now has a method called getStack-Trace(). This method returns an array of StackTraceElements:

```
public StackTraceElement[] getStackTrace()
```

Each StackTraceElement allows you to get the following pieces of information about it:

- Method name
- Class name
- Source code filename
- Line number within the source code file
- Whether or not the method is native code

It is also possible to *set* the stack frame using the setStackTrace() method. This is only done in exceptional circumstances—for example, exceptions that are thrown on a remote server while using remote procedure calls (RPCs) are often brought over to the local side. An exception is synthesized on the local side at the site of the local call, and it is filled out with the stack trace information from the remote side, using the setStackTrace() method. See section 7.2.4 for an example of this.

Note that there is *no public constructor* for StackTraceElement. According to the source code for the StackTraceElement class, these objects are created only by the JVM. This prevents the creation of false stack frames, but it does allow StackFrameElement objects from another thread (or even from another program entirely, such as an RPC server) to be inserted into a different exception.

7.2.3 Writing a custom stack trace dumper

Java is a fairly introspective language, and it makes sense that it would allow the inspection of stack traces. Stack traces are a basic part of the language, and explicit stack information is already a part of the language. Providing explicit access to this information doesn't slow down the implementation at all, or use any more memory. It was an excellent call on the part of the designers.

In this section, we'll build a better stack trace dumper. Each line of our stack trace will show a bit of the source code corresponding to that point in the code. This augmented stack trace will be generated by a class called ContextStack-Dump—named thus because it shows the *source code context* of each line in the stack dump.

A ContextStackDump object is created from an Exception (or, really, any Throwable). Once it's created, you can call its printStackTrace() method just as you would call that method directly on the exception. That is, you would replace this:

```
try {
  // ...
} catch( SomeException se ) {
  se.printStackTrace();
}
```

with this:

```
try {
  // ...
} catch( SomeException se ) {
  ContextStackDump csd = new ContextStackDump( se );
  csd.printStackTrace();
}
```

The code for ContextStackDump is shown in listing 7.2.

Listing 7.2   ContextStackDump.java

(see \Chapter7\ContextStackDump.java)
```
import java.io.*;

public class ContextStackDump
{
  static private final int numContextLines = 2;
  private Throwable throwable;

  public ContextStackDump( Throwable throwable ) {      ●  Takes a Throwable in
    this.throwable = throwable;                             the constructor
  }

  public void printStackTrace() {
    System.err.print( getDump() );
  }

  public String getDump() {
    return generateDump( throwable );
```

Generate the text in memory so it can be returned as a String

```
    }

    private String generateDump( Throwable e ) {
      ByteArrayOutputStream baos = new ByteArrayOutputStream();
      OutputStreamWriter osw = new OutputStreamWriter( baos );
      PrintWriter out = new PrintWriter( osw );

      out.println( e );

      StackTraceElement stes[] = e.getStackTrace();
      for (int i=0; i<stes.length; ++i) {
        StackTraceElement ste = stes[i];
        String filename = ste.getFileName();
        int lineNumber = ste.getLineNumber();
        out.println( "\t"+ste );
        try {
          out.println( getContext( filename, lineNumber ) );
        } catch( IOException ie ) {
          out.println( "\t   (No source information available)" );
        }
      }
      out.flush();

      String dump = new String( baos.toByteArray() );
      Throwable cause = e.getCause();
      if (cause != null) {
        dump += "Caused by: ";
        dump += generateDump( cause );
      }
      return dump;
    }

    private String getContext( String filename, int line )
      throws IOException {
      int start = line-numContextLines;
      int end = line+numContextLines+1;
      String context = "";

      FileInputStream fin = new FileInputStream( filename );
      InputStreamReader isr = new InputStreamReader( fin );
      LineNumberReader lnr = new LineNumberReader( isr );
      for (int i=1; i<start; ++i) {
        lnr.readLine();
      }
      for (int i=start; i<end; ++i) {
        String lineText = lnr.readLine();
        lineText = "\t   "+i+":"+
          (i==line?"->":"   ")+lineText;
        context += lineText;
        if (i!=end-1)
          context += "\n";
      }
      fin.close();
```

Generate information for each StackTraceElement

If there is a cause exception, dump it too

Load the source context

```
        return context;
    }
}
```

This implementation of ContextStackDump doesn't try very hard to find source files—it only looks in the current directory. It won't find files elsewhere in your classpath. It won't even find files in a subdirectory of the current directory, which means it won't find files in package directories.

Ideally, this program would search the entire classpath—or a *source path* specified in some other way—and search it, carefully using fully qualified class names and making sure to look inside JAR files.

As mentioned previously, you can use ContextStackDump by creating an instance and calling its printStackTrace() method. You can also automate this somewhat: listing 7.3 shows a specialized subclass of Thread called CSDThread. Any exception thrown inside this thread—if it isn't caught—will be dumped to System.err as a ContextStackDump, rather than in the normal format.

The CSDThread object catches all uncaught exceptions and prints out a Context-StackDump before quitting. Since dumping and quitting is the default behavior for uncaught exceptions, this thread provides the default behavior, but augmented with a better kind of stack dump.

If you find that you like this kind of dump, you can use CSDThreads wherever you use regular Threads.

NOTE   You can't directly change your main thread to be a CSDThread, but you can spawn a new CSDThread and have it call your main() routine. However, make sure your main thread knows not to repeat this process and create *another* CSDThread—avoid getting into an infinite loop!

Listing 7.3   CSDThread.java

(see \Chapter7\CSDThread.java)

```java
import java.io.*;

public class CSDThread extends Thread
{
  public CSDThread( Runnable runnable ) {
    super( runnable );
  }

  public void run() {
    try {
      super.run();
    } catch( Throwable e ) {
      ContextStackDump csd = new ContextStackDump( e );
      csd.printStackTrace();
      System.exit( 1 );
    }
  }

  static class CSDTest implements Runnable
  {
    public CSDTest() {
      Thread thread = new CSDThread( this );
      thread.start();
    }

    public void run() {
      run0();
    }

    public void run0() {
      run1();
    }

    public void run1() {
      throw new RuntimeException( "Bang!" );
    }
  }

  static public void main( String args[] ) {
    new CSDTest();
  }
}
```

Catch uncaught exceptions and print a ContextStackDump

Test program

Throw an exception

Note that you shouldn't subclass CSDThread because your subclass's run() method will override the run() method of CSDThread. Since CSDThread.run() is where the action is, this will cause the CSDThread to cease to function. Instead of subclassing CSDThread, create a Runnable and pass it to the constructor of CSDThread.

Listing 7.4 shows the output of running the test inside CSDThread.

Listing 7.4 Output of CSDThread.java

```
java.lang.RuntimeException: Bang!   |#0.1
        CSDThread$CSDTest.run1(CSDThread.java:35)
         33:
         34:        public void run1() {
         35:->           throw new RuntimeException( "Bang!" );
         36:        }
         37:    }
        CSDThread$CSDTest.run0(CSDThread.java:31)
         29:
         30:        public void run0() {
         31:->           run1();
         32:        }
         33:
        CSDThread$CSDTest.run(CSDThread.java:27)
         25:
         26:        public void run() {
         27:->           run0();
         28:        }
         29:
        java.lang.Thread.run(Thread.java:539)
          (No source information available)
        CSDThread.run(CSDThread.java:11)
          9:        public void run() {
         10:            try {
         11:->             super.run();
         12:            } catch( Throwable e ) {
         13:                ContextStackDump csd = new ContextStackDump( e );
```

1 The last stack frame of the stack trace

The source for this class wasn't found

The first stack frame of the stack trace

1 The exception occurred on line 35 of CSDThread.java, so the beginning of this line of code is marked with a "->" in the output. Two lines of context are shown before and after this line.

In this expanded stack dump, each stack frame is shown, followed by a short snippet of source code showing the location in the source that the stack frame corresponds to. The exact line in the source itself is marked with an arrow (->), and two lines before and after the line are also shown, to provide some context. Line numbers are included at the left to help the reader in looking through the source code.

7.2.4 Synthesizing a stack trace

The new Exception API also allows you to *set* the values of a stack trace, using the Throwable.setStackTrace() method. This permits you to synthesize a stack trace to better inform the user. For the most part, you don't want to mess with stack traces, because the accuracy of a stack trace is crucial to debugging. A stack trace that doesn't faithfully reflect the status of the actual stack can make debugging *much* harder.

NOTE　　Since `StackTraceElement` doesn't have any public constructors, you can't actually create one.* So you can't just make a stack trace up from scratch, which is probably good. Creating entirely fictional stack traces isn't useful.

Reasons for synthesizing

Synthesizing a stack trace is justified when it is done to include stack trace information that might otherwise be out of reach. The `setStackTrace()` documentation states that the method is intended for use in remote procedure call (RPC) and related systems. (Java's remote method invocation (RMI) facility uses exception chaining rather than exception synthesis; however, exception synthesis would be a reasonable alternative.)

Since an RPC method call executes on a remote system, any exceptions that are thrown are thrown on the remote system, not the local system. The local system, thus, does not have direct access to the exception, as shown in figure 7.2.

A simple way of dealing with this would be to simply throw another exception on the local side, but this exception wouldn't have all the stack trace information from the remote exception, as shown in figure 7.3. The information in the remote process is lost—the stack trace of the remote exception is completely different from the stack trace of the local exception.

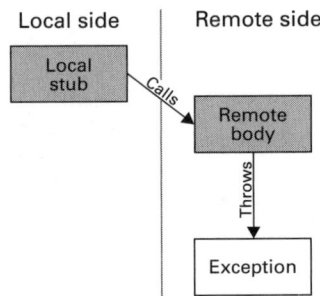

Figure 7.2　An exception thrown on the remote side of an RPC is not accessible to the local program.

A task system

In this section, we'll take a look at—and solve—a problem similar to the RMI problem discussed in the previous section. Suppose we have an object called a `Task` that represents a piece of computation to perform. When a `Task` is executed, it is executed in a worker thread taken from a special *thread pool* instead of in the main threads of the program. Using a fixed-sized pool of worker threads lets us control the amount of processing power that is spent on a particular category of

---

* You can't create one without resorting to unpalatable serialization trickery, that is.

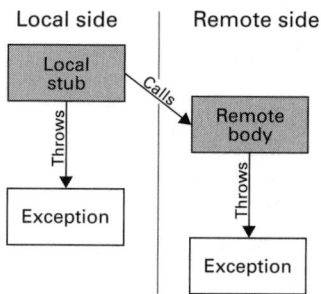

Local side

Remote side

Local stub

Calls

Remote body

Throws

Throws

Exception

Exception

Figure 7.3
One way of dealing with the inaccessibility of the remote
exception is to create a new exception on the local side.
However, this local exception lacks the stack trace information
of the remote exception.

computation, but it also frees us from having to worry about how many threads we use for the main processing.

Let's assume that our application has approximately 100 main threads going at one time, and that each of these threads, from time to time, carries out a particular CPU-intensive task. We're worried that the CPU will be overloaded, so we decide to make sure that only five threads are carrying out this task at any given time. To do so, we create a pool of five worker threads. The CPU-intensive task is turned into a `Task` object, and when a main thread executes a `Task`, the `Task` is handed off to one of the five worker threads.

We know that, at most, five threads will be carrying out this particular computation at any given time. Even if the number of main threads later grows to become 200, the number of worker threads is still set to be five, so the number of threads carrying out this computation is still fixed at five, keeping the situation under control.

Additionally, the worker threads in this pool can be given a priority appropriate to the tasks being executed in it. Thus, different pieces of the computation can be given different priorities even though, semantically, they seem to be running the same main threads.

Main threads and worker threads

Each `Task` object has a `run()` method, which contains the computation to be done. It also has a `carryOut()` method, which instructs the task system to execute the `run()` method in a separate worker thread. Calling `carryOut()` in the main thread causes the `Task`'s `run()` method to be executed in a worker thread, as shown in figure 7.4.

`carryOut()` is the method used by the calling code to actually carry out the work of the `Task`. Semantically, we are hiding the fact that `run()` executes in a different thread. Thus, the implementation of this `carryOut()` is semantically, but not actually, equivalent to this:

```
public void carryOut() {
  run();
}
```

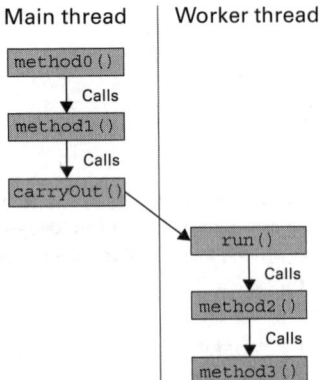

Figure 7.4
The main thread of the program calls on the Task's carryOut()
method. This causes the Task's run() **method to be executed in**
a worker thread.

Secretly, the work is moved over to a worker thread. This method blocks until the work is done.

The sequence diagram in figure 7.5 demonstrates the flow of control between the call to carryOut() and the call to run(). Threading is represented in this diagram using different shades of gray on the activation bars—the main thread is represented by a white bar, while the worker thread is represented by a gray bar.

The classes used in this system are shown in figure 7.6 and are listed here:

- Task—A unit of work; its run() method is executed in a worker thread.
- TaskQueue—Stores a list of Tasks to be executed; worker threads get Tasks to carry out from here.
- TaskManager—Handles the TaskQueue and the set of worker threads. This is not actually a separate class, but rather is implemented as static methods within the Task class.
- TaskThread—A worker thread.

This Task example is similar to the RPC system, because a piece of computation is being executed *on behalf of the main thread by another thread*. Unlike RPC, however, this thread is inside the same process space.

Nevertheless, we have the same problem. Since the task executes in one thread, but the code that created the task executes in another thread, the entire process is spread across two threads. If an exception should be thrown in the worker thread, this exception will only include stack information from the worker thread. Likewise, if we choose to create an exception inside the main thread, this exception will only contain information from within the main thread.

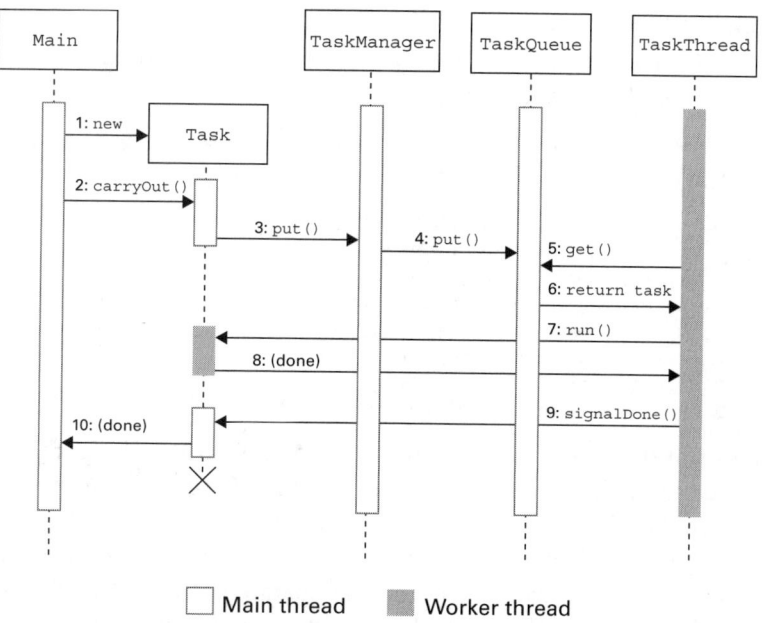

Figure 7.5 Sequence diagram of the process of carrying out a `Task`. The process is spread between the main and worker threads, represented by white and gray bars, respectively.

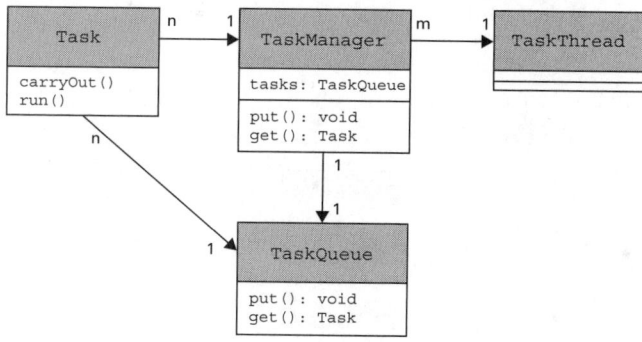

Figure 7.6 Classes used in the `Task` system. A `Task` is a unit of work that gets exectued by the worker thread on behalf of the main thread. `Tasks` are placed on a `TaskQueue` by the `TaskManager`; `TaskThreads`, which are the worker threads, get `Tasks` from the `TaskManager` and execute them.

Chained exceptions for tasks

We could use *chained exceptions* to connect these two threads together. The resulting stack dump might look like this:

```
java.lang.RuntimeException: Exception while sleeping for 2
        at Task.carryOut(Task.java:38)
        at TaskTest.method1(TaskTest.java:47)
        at TaskTest.method0(TaskTest.java:43)
        at TaskTest.run(TaskTest.java:38)
        at java.lang.Thread.run(Thread.java:539)
Caused by: java.lang.RuntimeException: Exception while sleeping for 2
        at TaskTest$1.method3(TaskTest.java:32)
        at TaskTest$1.method2(TaskTest.java:21)
        at TaskTest$1.run(TaskTest.java:17)
        at Task$TaskThread.run(Task.java:86)
```

This stack dump shows two exceptions—the top half comes from the main thread, while the bottom half comes from the worker thread, as shown in figure 7.7.

To solve this problem, we're going to use `setStackTrace()` to *synthesize* an exception that unifies these two sets of `StackFrameElements`. In doing so, we'll strive to hide the fact that `Tasks` are run in a separate thread. This allows the `Task` to seem like it is being run in the main thread, which helps give the `Task` object single-

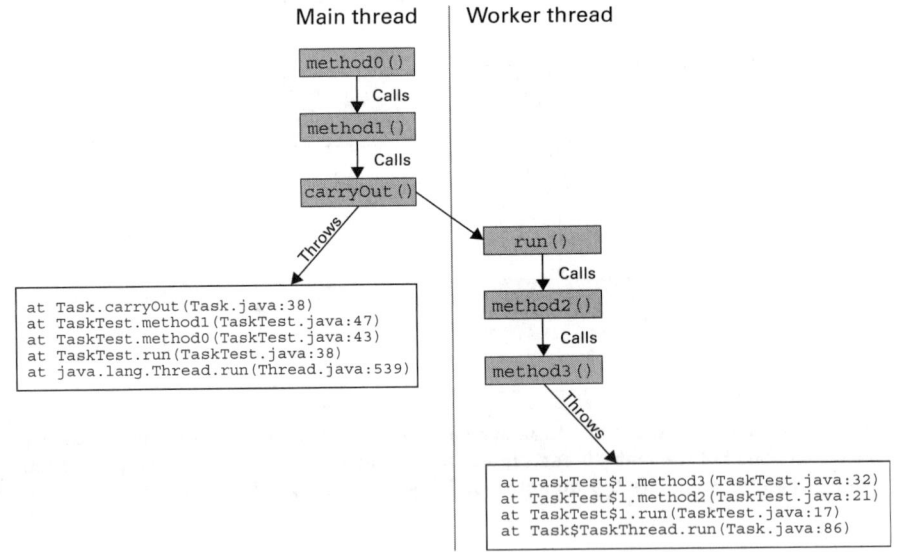

Figure 7.7 If an exception is thrown in the worker thread, this exception only knows about stack frames in the worker thread. Likewise, the exception thrown in the main thread only knows about stack frames in the main thread.

thread semantics. We want to hide the use of background threads—they are only there to help control CPU usage and task priorities, not to provide multithreaded semantics. (In debugging, especially debugging the Task system itself, it is useful to turn off the exception synthesis so that you can really see what is going on. This can be done by changing the value of the static boolean Task.synthesizing.)

All of the logic that handles the background threads and exception synthesis is contained within the code for Task, presented in listing 7.5.

Listing 7.5 Task.java

(see \Chapter7\Task.java)

```java
import java.util.*;

abstract public class Task
{
  static private TaskQueue tasks = new TaskQueue();
  static private final int numTaskThreads = 5;
  static private boolean initialized = false;
  private Exception exception;

  // Set this to false to turn off synthesizing, for
  // debugging the Task system
  static private final boolean synthesizing = true;

  /**
   * Accessor method for exception
   */
  Exception exception() {
    return exception;
  }

  /**
   * Accessor method for exception
   */
  void exception( Exception exception ) {
    this.exception = exception;
  }

  /**
   * Start up the background task threads
   */
  synchronized static private void init() {
    if (initialized)
      return;
    for (int i=0; i<numTaskThreads; ++i) {
      TaskThread tt = new TaskThread( "task thread "+i );
      tt.start();
    }
    initialized = true;
```

❶ Get and set methods for Task's exception

❷ Create the background worker threads

```
  }
  /**
   * Initiate the execution of a task by putting it in
   * the task queue
   */
  public void carryOut() throws Exception {
    try {
      init();
      // synchronize on 'this' so that we don't get our
      // done-signal before we start waiting for it
      synchronized( this ) {
        // Note that "tasks" has class scope
        tasks.put( this );
        waitTilDone();
      }
    } catch( Exception e ) {
      if (synthesizing)
        throw synthesizeException( e );
      else
        throw e;
    }
  }

  /**
   * Synthesize an exception that combines info from a task's
   * main thread and the worker thread in which the Task
   * was running
   */
  private Exception synthesizeException( Exception remote ) {
    Exception local = new Exception();
    StackTraceElement remoteSTEs[] = remote.getStackTrace();
    int remoteLen = remoteSTEs.length;
    StackTraceElement localSTEs[] = local.getStackTrace();
    int localLen = localSTEs.length;
    StackTraceElement synthSTEs[] =
      new StackTraceElement[remoteLen+localLen-2];
    for (int i=0; i<remoteLen-1; ++i)
      synthSTEs[i] = remoteSTEs[i];
    for (int i=1; i<localLen; ++i)
      synthSTEs[i+remoteLen-2] = localSTEs[i];
    Exception synth = new Exception( remote.getMessage() );
    synth.setStackTrace( synthSTEs );
    return synth;
  }

  /**
   * Main thread calls this to wait for the worker
   * thread to finish executing the Task
   */
  private void waitTilDone() throws Exception {
    synchronized( this ) {
```

❸ Trigger background processing

❹ Synthesize an exception

❺ carryOut() calls this to wait

```
        try {
          wait();
        } catch( InterruptedException ie ) {}
        if (exception!=null) {
          Exception exception2 = exception;
          exception = null;
          throw exception2;
        }
      }
    }
  }

  /**
   * Worker thread calls this to signal the main thread
   * that it is done executing the Task
   * synchronize on 'this' so that we don't get our
   * done-signal before we start waiting for it
   */
  void signalDone() {
    synchronized( this ) {
      notify();
    }
  }

  /**
   * Override this with the code that the Task will
   * run in the worker thread
   */
  abstract public void run() throws Exception ;

  /**
   * Worker thread calls this to get the next Task from the
   * queue
   */
  static Task getNextTask() {
    return tasks.get();
  }
}

/**
 * Worker thread
 */
class TaskThread extends Thread {
  public TaskThread( String name ) {
    super( name );
    setDaemon( true );
  }

  public void run() {
    while (true) {
      Task task = Task.getNextTask();
      try {
        task.run();
      } catch( Exception e ) {
```

6 Worker thread calls this to signal main thread

7 Stub for subclasses

8 Queue for Task objects

9 A TaskThread is a worker thread

10 Get a Task, run it, repeat

```
                 task.exception( e );
            }
            task.signalDone();
        }
      }
  }
}
/**
 * Queue for holding tasks until it's time to
 * execute them
 */
class TaskQueue
{
   private Vector vec = new Vector();

   synchronized public void put( Task task ) {
     vec.addElement( task );
     notifyAll();
   }

   synchronized public Task get() {
     while (true) {
       if (vec.size()>0) {
         Task task = (Task)vec.elementAt( 0 );
         vec.removeElementAt( 0 );
         return task;
       } else {
         try { wait(); } catch( InterruptedException ie ) {}
       }
     }
   }
}
```

⑩ **Get a Task, run it, repeat**

❶ The processing of a Task may throw an exception inside the worker thread. If it does, this exception is "passed" to the main thread by putting it in the variable exception.

❷ The background worker threads take over for the calling threads at the point at which Task.run() is called. The number of worker threads in this pool determines the portion of processing power that is allocated to the execution of Tasks; likewise, the priority of these threads determines the priority with which these Tasks will be executed.

❸ The main thread calls carryOut(), which places the Task on a queue. Once the main thread has done this, it has to wait until the Task is completed by a worker thread. It performs this wait by calling waitTilDone().

When an exception is thrown in the worker thread, it is used to synthesize a new exception that seems to have occurred in the main thread.

4 synthesizeException() takes an Exception as an argument. This Exception was thrown in another thread, but we want it to seem as if it came from here, running in the main thread. To do this, we create a new Exception in the main thread.

The exception from the worker thread looks something like this:

```
java.lang.RuntimeException: Exception while sleeping for 2
        at TaskTest$1.method3(TaskTest.java:32)
        at TaskTest$1.method2(TaskTest.java:21)
        at TaskTest$1.run(TaskTest.java:17)
        at Task$TaskThread.run(Task.java:86)
```

The exception created here in the worker thread, inside synthesizeException(), looks like this:

```
java.lang.RuntimeException
        at Task.synthesizeException(Task.java:42)
        at Task.carryOut(Task.java:37)
        at TaskTest.method1(TaskTest.java:47)
        at TaskTest.method0(TaskTest.java:43)
        at TaskTest.run(TaskTest.java:38)
        at java.lang.Thread.run(Thread.java:539)
```

The synthesized exception merges the two and removes the lines for Task$Task-Thread.run and Task.synthesizeException. The call stacks of the two exceptions are sutured together between the two boldfaced lines in the following code:

```
java.lang.RuntimeException: Exception while sleeping for 2
        at TaskTest$1.method3(TaskTest.java:32)
        at TaskTest$1.method2(TaskTest.java:21)
        at TaskTest$1.run(TaskTest.java:17)
        at Task.carryOut(Task.java:37)
        at TaskTest.method1(TaskTest.java:47)
        at TaskTest.method0(TaskTest.java:43)
        at TaskTest.run(TaskTest.java:38)
        at java.lang.Thread.run(Thread.java:539)
```

5 All the carryOut() method does is place the Task into a queue. Once carryOut() does this, it needs to go to sleep until the worker threads run the Task. It does this here in waitTilDone(). If an exception was thrown in the worker thread, it will be waiting for us in rte, so we throw it if it's there.

6 Once a worker thread has finished running a Task, it calls signalDone() to tell the main thread that the task is finished.

7 The calling code makes a subclass of Task and provides an implementation of the run() method. This is where the actual work of the Task is placed.

8 This class is a simple blocking queue specialized to return Task objects.

9 TaskThread is a `Thread`, and not a `Runnable`, because we want to use its implementation of `run()`.

10 The duty of the `TaskThread` is simple: get a `Task` object from the queue and call its `run()` method. When this is done, get another one and do it again. And so on.

Now that we've created `Task`, we need a program to test this system, and we have one: `TaskTest.java` (see listing 7.6), which produced the synthesized stack dump listing seen in the preceding note #4. `TaskTest` starts up 20 main threads, and each main thread creates a `Task` that consists of pausing for a brief period. Once this task is completed, it creates another `Task`, and the cycle continues. In order to demonstrate the synthesized exceptions, each thread has a chance of throwing an exception after each pause.

Listing 7.6 TaskTest.java

(see \Chapter7\TaskTest.java)

```java
import java.util.*;

public class TaskTest implements Runnable
{
  static private Random rand = new Random();

  /**
   * Start background thread
   */
  public TaskTest() {
    Thread t = new Thread( this );
    t.start();
  }

  /**
   * Holds the work to be done by the Task.
   * TaskTestTask just sleeps for a little while
   */
  public void run() {
    while (true) {
      try {
        final int delay = rand.nextInt( 5 );

        TaskTestTask ttt = new TaskTestTask( delay );

        method0( ttt );
      } catch( Exception e ) {
        e.printStackTrace();
      }
    }
  }
```

1 Each thread pauses over and over

2 A new Task is created each time through the loop

```
/**
 * Dummy method to make the stack trace longer
 */
private void method0( Task task ) throws Exception {
  method1( task );
}

/**
 * Dummy method to make the stack trace longer
 */
private void method1( Task task ) throws Exception {
  task.carryOut();
}

/**
 * Start up a bunch of testers
 */
static public void main( String args[] ) {
  for (int i=0; i<20; ++i) {
    new TaskTest();
  }
}
}
```

● **The main() routine starts up 20 main threads**

```
/**
 * A Task to test the Task system with.
 * TaskTestTask just sleeps for a little while
 */
class TaskTestTask extends Task
{
  private int delay;
  static private Random rand = new Random();

  public TaskTestTask( int delay ) {
    this.delay = delay;
  }

  public void run() throws Exception {
    method2();
  }

  private void method2() {
    method3();
  }

  private void method3() {
    Thread workerThread = Thread.currentThread();
    try {
      Thread.sleep( delay * 1000 );
      System.out.println( "Slept for "+delay );
    } catch( InterruptedException ie ) {}
```

```
    if (rand.nextInt( 100 )<50) {
       throw new RuntimeException(
          "Exception while sleeping for "+delay );
    }
  }
}
```

> Sometimes, randomly, an exception is thrown

❶ Each background thread runs indefinitely. It creates a pausing Task, carries out the task, creates another pausing Task, carries it out, and so on.

❷ The Task's run() method does not call Thread.sleep() directly; it calls an intermediate method method2(), which calls method3(), which then calls Thread.sleep(). All these calls are necessary to provide a deep stack trace to better illustrate stack trace synthesis.

When TaskTest is run, the 20 main threads compete for the "attention" of the 5 worker threads. The 20 main threads place their Tasks on the task queue, and the 5 worker threads take Tasks from this queue and execute them. Most of the time, all 20 main threads are blocked inside the carryout() method of their current Tasks; meanwhile, 5 of them are actually being executed by the worker threads. With proper prioritization of the threads within the pool, this allows for flexible control over the use of the CPU.

7.3 *Summary*

The new exceptions features of JDK 1.4 make it a lot easier to do things that were previously possible, but which hadn't been standardized. Many programmers had created their own exception chaining facility, but JDK 1.4 standardizes this and integrates into the JVM in such a way that exception chains are displayed in the regular stack traces.

The new release also allows for programmatic inspection—and modification—of stack traces. These are features that are likely to be used by debuggers or low-level execution subsystems, such as RPC, as well as having useful day-to-day applications, as we saw in sections 7.2.3 and 7.2.4. All in all, there aren't a whole lot of reasons to mess with stack traces, but if you need to do so, the functionality is there.

8

Collections

The release of JDK 1.4 adds a few minor features to the Collections Framework in the `java.util` package. A number of utility methods have been added to the `Collections` class; each of these deals with `Lists` in some way.

There are three new classes discussed in this chapter: `LinkedHashMap`, `LinkedHashSet`, and `IdentityHashMap`. The first two are variations on the `HashMap` and `HashSet` classes (respectively), and they preserve the order in which objects are added to them. The third, `IdentityHashMap`, is a `Map` that overrides the `hashCode()` methods of its keys, allowing objects to be differentiated based on identity rather than on content.

There is also a new marker interface*, `RandomAccess`, which allows a class to declare that it is suitable for fast random access. More precisely, this means that it has efficient implementations of the `get()` and `set()` methods.

8.1 Utilities

A number of utility methods have been added as static methods in the `Collections` class. These utilities provide a number of simple but commonly used routines. If you've used the Collections Framework a lot, you've probably written some of these utilities yourself; now they are available as part of the library.

For some of these, the documentation claims that the implementation is faster than "the naive implementation." Being part of the Collections Framework probably helps these methods use private information to make themselves faster. As a result, these routines should be preferred over hand-rolled implementations.

8.1.1 Rotating list elements

The `Collections.rotate()` method rotates the elements of a list, which means that it advances each element a certain number of steps. Elements that are advanced off the end of the list are wrapped around to the beginning of the list, which is why this is called `rotate()` and not `shift()`. Rotation can go in the negative direction as well, which means that each element can be moved backward, and elements that fall off the front of the list are wrapped around to the end.

This is the type signature of the `rotate()` method:

```
Collections.rotate( List list, int distance );
```

The `distance` value specifies the number of steps to rotate. This value can be negative.

---

*A *marker interface* is an interface that doesn't contain any methods; a class implements such an interface merely to signal that it has a certain property.

Figure 8.1 shows a rotation of 1. Each element in the list is moved forward by one step, as shown by the arrows on top. The element at the end cannot be moved forward, so it wraps around to the front of the list, occupying the first slot in the list.

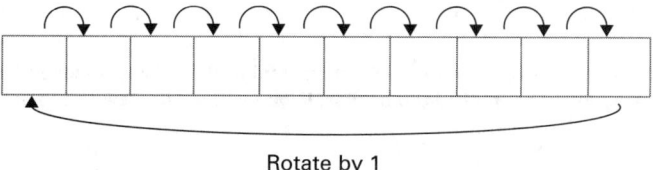

Rotate by 1

Figure 8.1 A rotation by 1. Each element is moved forward by one step. The last element of the list must wrap around to the beginning of the list.

It is also possible to rotate a sublist of a larger list. The elements of the sublist are *aliases* for the elements of the containing list, which means that changes made to the sublist are reflected in the containing list. Thus, a rotation of the elements of a sublist affects the selected elements of the containing list. This can be very useful, since it allows you to rotate an arbitrary contiguous portion of a list.

As an example, we'll use a list of 10 elements, and we'll choose from that list a sublist of five elements, ranging from element two to element six, inclusive. This sublist is taken from the larger list using the subList() method (see figure 8.2).

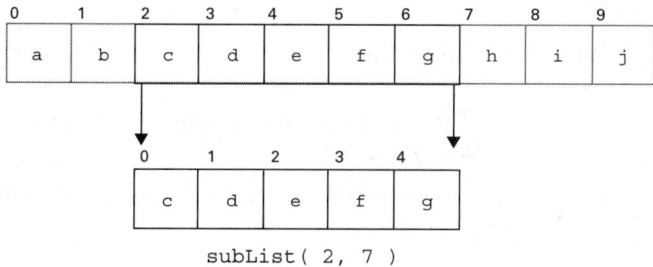

subList(2, 7)

Figure 8.2 A sublist of a larger list. This sublist is created by a call to the subList() method. The elements of this sublist are aliases for the elements of the containing list, so any modifications that we make to the sublist are reflected in the containing list.

By calling rotate() on this sublist, we rotate the elements of the sublist as if the sublist were its own list. Elements that are in the larger list, but are outside the sublist, are not affected (see figure 8.3).

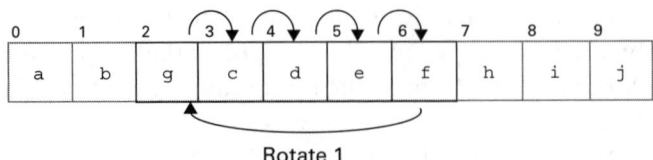

Rotate 1

Figure 8.3   A rotation of the elements of a sublist. Each element in the sublist is moved forward by one; the final element wraps around to the front of the sublist. If we confine our view to the sublist, this is a normal rotation.

8.1.2 *Replacing list elements*

The Collections.replaceAll() method replaces each occurrence of a particular element with another element. The signature of this method looks like this:

```
Collections.replaceAll( List list, Object oldVal, Object newVal );
```

Each occurrence of the value oldVal within the list, list, is replaced with newVal.

8.1.3 *Finding sublists within lists*

The Collections.indexOfSubList() method finds the first occurrence of a particular sublist within a containing list. It's rather like the indexOf() method, but it takes a List, rather than an Object, as the target to look for:

```
int Collections.indexOfSubList( List source, List target );
```

The value returned is the index, within the containing array, of the first element of the target list.

For example, let's look for the list { 1, 2 } within a larger list of random-looking digits. This list might occur multiple times, but indexOfSubList() only returns the first occurrence (see figure 8.4). In this example, the sublist { 1, 2 } occurs three

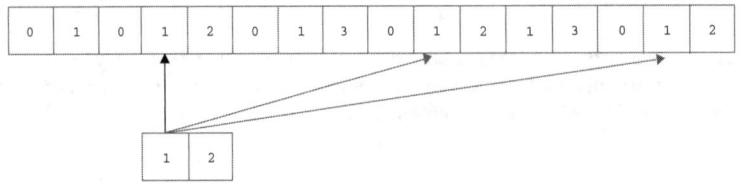

**Figure 8.4   A sublist might be found multiple times within the containing list. indexOfSubList()
returns the *first* of these occurrences.**

times within the containing list, at offsets 3, 9, and 14, but `indexOfSubList()` only returns the value 3.

Collections.lastIndexOfSubList()` finds the *last* occurrence of the target list within the containing list (see figure 8.5). In this example, `lastIndexOfSubList()` would return 14.

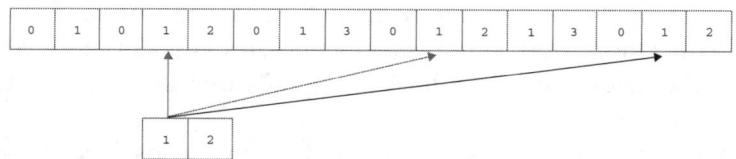

Figure 8.5 `lastIndexOfSubList()` **returns the index of the** *last* **occurrence of the sublist within the containing list.**

Both methods return `-1` if the target list is not found within the containing list.

8.1.4 *Swapping list elements*

The `Collections.swap()` utility method swaps two elements of a list. These elements are specified by two integers, which serve as indices into the list. Figure 8.6 shows a swap of elements c and g within a 10-element list:

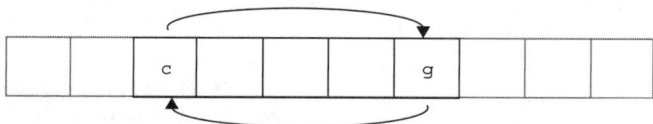

Figure 8.6 `swap()` **swaps the position of elements** c **and** g **within a 10-element list.**

In code, it looks like this:

```
Collections.swap( list, 2, 6 );
```

8.1.5 *Converting enumerations to lists*

The `Collections.list()` method converts an `Enumeration` to a `List`. The signature of this method is as follows:

```
Collections.list( Enumeration e );
```

`list()` achieves this conversion by running through all the elements of the `Enumeration` and adding them onto a list. The following is the equivalent of this method:

```
Enumeration e;

List list = new ArrayList();
while (e.hasMoreElements()) {
  list.add( e.nextElement() );
}
```

Most Enumerations are created from arrays or lists that are contained entirely within RAM. However, it is possible to create an Enumeration that "contains" more objects than could possibly fit in RAM. This is possible because it is not required that all of the elements of an Enumeration be in RAM at the same time—only that they be available, one at a time.

It's even possible to create an Enumeration that never ends. The Enumeration in listing 8.1 returns the prime numbers in order, starting at 2.

Listing 8.1   EndlessEnumeration.java

(See \Chapter8\EndlessEnumeration.java)

```java
import java.util.*;

public class EndlessEnumeration implements Enumeration
{
  // The last prime we returned
  // initialize it to be before the first prime
  private int lastPrime = 1;

  // There are always more primes
  public boolean hasMoreElements() {
    return true;
  }

  public Object nextElement() {
    // Start searching from after the last one we found
    int n = lastPrime+1;
    while (true) {
      if (isPrime( n )) {
        lastPrime = n;
        return new Integer( n );
      } else {
        n++;
      }
    }
  }

  private boolean isPrime( int n ) {
    // 2 is the lowest possible factor
    // n/2 is the highest possible factor
    for (int i=2; i<=n/2; ++i) {
      // If n is divisible by i, then it's not prime
      if ((n%i)==0) {
```

● **Check each integer until we find the next prime**

● **Divide by every possible factor to find out if it's prime**

```
          return false;
        }
      }
      return true;
    }

  static public void main( String args[] ) throws Exception {
    Enumeration e = new EndlessEnumeration();
    for (int i=0; i<20; ++i)
      System.out.println( e.nextElement() );
  }
}
```

The `hasMoreElements()` method always returns `true`, because this `Enumeration` always has more elements. If you pass an object of this class to `Collections.list()`, it will just run and run and run, generating primes endlessly, never returning from the call to `Collections.list()`. (Since the prime generation algorithm is pretty slow, the machine will probably fail before it runs out of memory to store the primes.)

8.2 LinkedHashMap and LinkedHashSet

The `LinkedHashMap` and `LinkedHashSet` classes are much like their unlinked counterparts, `HashMap` and `HashSet`, respectively. They differ in that each of these classes remembers the order in which entries were inserted. Iterating over the elements of these collections will produce the elements in the same order in which they were inserted.

8.2.1 Using LinkedHashMap

As an example, we'll create a `LinkedHashMap` as shown in figure 8.7 using the following code:

```
LinkedHashMap lhm = new LinkedHashMap();
lhm.put( "a", "Albert" );
lhm.put( "b", "Barbara" );
lhm.put( "c", "Chuck" );
```

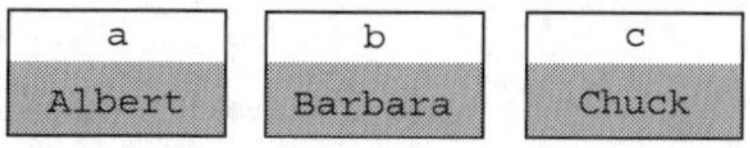

Figure 8.7   A mapping from single-character strings to names

We can iterate through the entries of this mapping as follows:

```
for (Iterator it = lhm.entrySet().iterator(); it.hasNext();) {
  Map.Entry me = (Map.Entry)it.next();
  System.out.println( me.getKey()+" --> "+me.getValue() );
}
```

The preceding code produces the following output:

```
a --> Albert
b --> Barbara
c --> Chuck
```

Since we used a `LinkedHashMap`, the entries of the map come out in the same order in which they were inserted. This is because a set of links are maintained inside the `LinkedHashMap` that form a kind of hidden linked list (as shown in figure 8.8).*

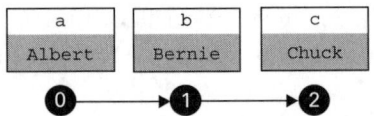

Figure 8.8   The mapping is augmented by a hidden linked list, which specifies an order of the entries.

Inserting vs. updating

Note that the `LinkedHashMap` maintains the order in which the entries were *inserted*. If the entry is *updated*, the ordering doesn't change. (In this context, we define an *update* as a call to `put()`, which uses a key that already exists in the mapping.) For example, we'll overwrite the value `Barbara` with the value `Bernie`:

```
LinkedHashMap lhm = new LinkedHashMap();
lhm.put( "a", "Albert" );
lhm.put( "b", "Barbara" );
lhm.put( "c", "Chuck" );
lhm.put( "b", "Bernie" );
```

The output of the preceding code shows that the value of the second entry has changed, but the order is the same as it was before:

```
a --> Albert
b --> Bernie
c --> Chuck
```

---

* Actually, it is a doubly linked list, which allows traversal to proceed in either direction.

Once an entry has been inserted into the hidden linked list, it is not moved, as shown in figure 8.9.

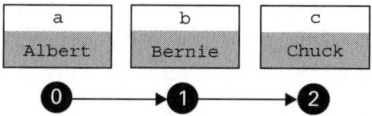

Figure 8.9 Putting a new value into a slot that already exists doesn't change the ordering of the entries. Here, the value of Barbara has been replaced with `Bernie`, but the ordering is the same.

Reinserting

In a `LinkedHashMap`, removing an old value and inserting a new value in its place has a different effect on the ordering than simply overwriting the old value with the new value. If you remove the value in question before reinserting it, as we do in the following code fragment, the ordering is changed:

```
LinkedHashMap lhm = new LinkedHashMap();
lhm.put( "a", "Albert" );
lhm.put( "b", "Barbara" );
lhm.put( "c", "Chuck" );
lhm.remove( "b" );
lhm.put( "b", "Bernie" );
```

The output shows that the ordering *has* changed this time:

```
a --> Albert
c --> Chuck
b --> Bernie
```

What is different about this case? The removal doesn't just remove the entry from the mapping; it removes it from the hidden linked list. The removed entry had a fixed position within the ordering defined by the hidden linked list, but that position is lost when the entry is removed (see figure 8.10). Adding the entry back into the `LinkedHashMap` (albeit with a different value) causes it to be put at the end of

Figure 8.10 Removing an entry from the `LinkedHashMap` also removes it from the hidden linked list. Whatever position the removed entry may have had in the ordering of the entries is lost.

the hidden linked list. In this sense, it is as if the entry has been added for the first time (see figure 8.11).

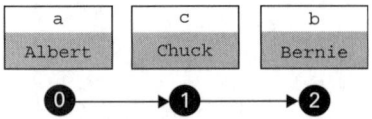

Figure 8.11   Putting the entry back in after removing it causes it to be put at the end of the hidden linked list.

Removing any element from the LinkedHashMap removes any information about its position within the insertion order.

8.2.2   Using LinkedHashSet

A LinkedHashSet is rather like a LinkedHashMap, except that it is a Set rather than a Map. Like a LinkedHashMap, a LinkedHashSet remembers the order in which objects are inserted. When you iterate over the objects, the elements of the set are produced in the same order in which they were inserted.

The following code illustrates this:

```
LinkedHashSet lhs = new LinkedHashSet();
lhs.add( "Albert" );
lhs.add( "Barbara" );
lhs.add( "Chuck" );
```

Iterating over the elements goes like this:

```
for (Iterator it = lhs.iterator(); it.hasNext();) {
  System.out.println( it.next() );
}
```

The preceding code produces the following output:

```
Albert
Barbara
Chuck
```

The insertion order is maintained using a linked list, as shown in figure 8.12.

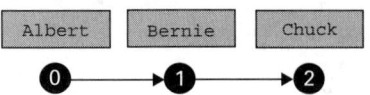

Figure 8.12   The set is augmented by a hidden linked list that specifies an order of the entries.

Adding a value more than once doesn't change the set, and it doesn't change the ordering either:

```
LinkedHashSet lhs = new LinkedHashSet();
lhs.add( "Albert" );
lhs.add( "Barbara" );
lhs.add( "Chuck" );
lhs.add( "Barbara" );
lhs.add( "Albert" );
```

The preceding code produces identical output to the earlier code, with the elements in the same order as before:

```
Albert
Barbara
Chuck
```

However, like the `LinkedHashMap`, removing and reinserting an element does change the order:

```
LinkedHashSet lhs = new LinkedHashSet();
lhs.add( "Albert" );
lhs.add( "Barbara" );
lhs.add( "Chuck" );
lhs.remove( "Barbara" );
lhs.add( "Barbara" );
```

Because `Barbara` was removed and reinserted in the preceding code, it moves to the end of the list:

```
Albert
Chuck
Barbara
```

This is because insertion-order information isn't maintained for elements that have been removed (see figure 8.13).

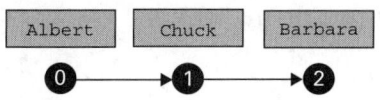

Figure 8.13   After removing `Barbara` and putting it back, it is put at the end of the hidden linked list. Ordering information is not maintained for removed elements.

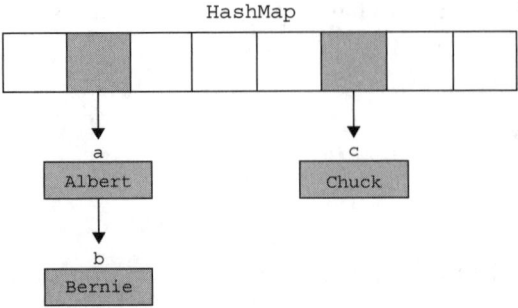

Figure 8.14 **HashMap** and **LinkedHashMap** are both implemented as an array of linked lists. Individual elements are stored in the linked lists; the head of each list occupies one of the slots of the array. The arrays are *sparse*, meaning that a significant number of the slots are empty.

8.2.3 *Efficiency of LinkedHashMap and LinkedHashSet*

LinkedHashMaps and LinkedHashSets have an efficiency roughly equal to that of HashMaps and HashSets, respectively. The operation of adding or removing an element is slightly slower, since the hidden linked lists must be maintained.

Strangely enough, however, iterating over the elements of a LinkedHashMap or LinkedHashSet is *faster* than it is for the unlinked varieties. To understand this, it is necessary to understand the way these classes are implemented. Since LinkedHashSet is implemented using a LinkedHashMap, we will not need to discuss it separately.

LinkedHashMap and HashMap are both implemented as an array of linked lists. Each array slot corresponds to a *hash bin*. A full discussion of hashing and hashing techniques is beyond the scope of this chapter; suffice it to say that, internally, these two classes are represented as an array of linked lists (see figure 8.14).

The arrays are *sparse*, which means that a significant number of the slots are empty. (The average, based on the default settings, is one-quarter empty.) Traversing this array, then, incurs a certain waste of time, since the traversal must visit each slot in the array whether it is empty or not (see figure 8.15).

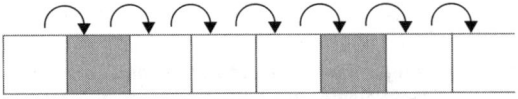

Figure 8.15 Traversing the elements of a **HashMap** requires traversing the entire array, which includes a significant number of elements that are empty.

A `LinkedHashMap`, on the other hand, has the added benefit of another linked list forming yet another chain through the elements. Traversing this list doesn't require traversing empty slots, because there are no empty slots in the linked list (see figure 8.16).

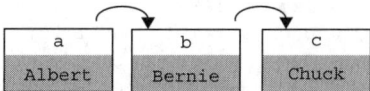

Figure 8.16 Traversing the elements of a `LinkedHashMap` only requires traversing the elements themselves. There are no empty slots in the linked list to waste time on.

It's important to understand that this extra efficiency doesn't come for free. It's the very act of maintaining the linked list that provides this speed boost during iteration, and this maintenance adds a bit of overhead to every operation that adds or removes an entry. A `LinkedHashMap` (or `LinkedHashSet`) might be faster for your application, but it might not—it all depends on how much time is spent building and modifying the hash table, and how much time is spent traversing it. A `LinkedHashMap` entry also uses a bit more memory.

8.2.4 *Example: searching a file path*

A file path—such as the Java classpath—is a perfect example of an ordered collection. It consists of a list of directories with a fixed order. To look for a file in a path means to look for a file in that collection of directories, respecting the order of the directories in the path.

As an example, we'll create a `Path` object that represents such a file path. You build a `Path` object by adding a series of directories to it, and then call its `find-File()` method to locate a file somewhere in the path.

This `Path` object also allows you to make a directory inactive in path—and make it active again—using the `setActive()` method. To this end, each directory in the `Path` has a *name* that can be used as a handle for making that directory active or inactive. This can be very useful if you are developing multiple projects with multiple tools. You might need to use different versions of a compiler for different projects (or for different parts of the same project!). Using a path-generation system can be a lot easier than editing configuration scripts and restarting your shell over and over.

The `Path` class also includes a `formatAsPath()` method, which formats the path in traditional classpath format.

The following is the listing of a test program that uses the Path class. It assumes the existence of two directories, "a" and "b", each of which contains a file called Test.java as well as some other .java files:

```
0 drwxr-xr-x   4 mito     100          0 Dec  3 16:38 .
0 drwxr-xr-x   2 mito     100          0 Dec  3 16:39 ./a
1 -rw-r--r--   1 mito     100         10 Dec  3 16:39 ./a/Test.java
1 -rw-r--r--   1 mito     100         10 Dec  3 16:51 ./a/Foo.java
0 drwxr-xr-x   2 mito     100          0 Dec  3 16:39 ./b
1 -rw-r--r--   1 mito     100         10 Dec  3 16:39 ./b/Test.java
1 -rw-r--r--   1 mito     100         10 Dec  3 16:51 ./b/Bar.java
```

We will create Path objects to search for instances of Test.java in these directories. The program is shown in listing 8.2, and it is interleaved with the output it produces, shown in bold italic.

Listing 8.2   PathTest.java

(See \Chapter8\PathTest.java)
```java
public class PathTest
{
  static public void main( String args[] ) {
    Path path = null;

    path = new Path();
    path.add( "a", ".\\pathtest\\a\\" );
    path.add( "b", ".\\pathtest\\b\\" );
    System.out.println( path.formatAsPath() );
```

// .\pathtest\a;.\pathtest\b   ❶ **Directory "a" followed by directory "b"**

```java
    path = new Path();
    path.add( "b", ".\\pathtest\\b\\" );
    path.add( "a", ".\\pathtest\\a\\" );
    System.out.println( path.formatAsPath() );
```

// .\pathtest\b;.\pathtest\a   ❷ **Directory "b" followed by directory "a"**

```java
    path = new Path();
    path.add( "a", ".\\pathtest\\a\\" );
    path.add( "b", ".\\pathtest\\b\\" );
    System.out.println( path.findFile( "Test.java" ) );
```

// .\pathtest\a\Test.java   ❸ **Test.java found in directory "a"**

```java
    path.setActive( "a", false );
    System.out.println( path.findFile( "Test.java" ) );
```

// .\pathtest\b\Test.java   ❹ **Test.java found in directory "b" because directory "a" was made inactive**

```java
  }
}
```

❶ ❷ Note that the order of the directories of a path matches precisely the order in which the directories were added to the Path object.

❸ Both "a" and "b" contain a file called Test.java. Since the search looks in "a" before "b", it finds the a\Test.java file first.

❹ The same path was searched as in #3, except that, this time, directory "a" was deactivated. As a result, b\Test.java is found.

The source for Path is shown in listing 8.3.

Listing 8.3   Path.java

(See \Chapter8\Path.java)

```java
import java.io.*;
import java.util.*;
import java.util.regex.*;

public class Path
{
  private LinkedHashMap directories = new LinkedHashMap();         ❶ Store the
                                                                     ordered set of
                                                                     directories
  public Path() {
  }

  public void add( String name, String directory ) {
    add( name, new File( directory ) );
  }
                                                                   ❷ Add a new
                                                                     directory to
  public void add( String name, File directory ) {                   the path
    Entry entry = new Entry( directory );
    directories.put( name, entry );
  }

  public void remove( String name ) {
    directories.remove( name );
  }

  public void setActive( String name, boolean active ) {           ❸ Activate or
    Entry entry = (Entry)directories.get( name );                    deactivate a
    if (entry == null)                                               directory
      throw new NoSuchElementException(
        "No element "+name+" in "+this );
    entry.active( active );
  }
                                                                   Find a file somewhere
  public File findFile( String target ) {                          ❹ in the path
    final File targetFile = new File( target );
    FileFilter filter = new FileFilter() {
      public boolean accept( File pathname ) {
        // This filter accepts files matching the target file
        return targetFile.getName().equals( pathname.getName() );
```

```
      }
    }; // end of anonymous inner class

    // Check each directory of the path in turn
    for (Iterator it=directories.keySet().iterator();
         it.hasNext();) {
      String name =  (String)it.next();
      Entry entry = (Entry)directories.get( name );

      // If this directory has been de-activated,
      // don't look in it
      if (!entry.active())
        continue;

// Search the directory with the filter
      File dir = entry.directory();
      File files[] = dir.listFiles( filter );

      if (files != null && files.length>0) {
        // listFiles() should only return one file
        return files[0];
      }
    }
    return null;
  }

  public String formatAsPath() {
    String s = "";
    for (Iterator it=directories.keySet().iterator();
         it.hasNext();) {
      String name =  (String)it.next();
      Entry entry = (Entry)directories.get( name );
      File dir = entry.directory();
      s += dir;
      if (it.hasNext()) {
        s += File.pathSeparator;
      }
    }
    return s;
  }
}

class Entry
{
  private File directory;
  private boolean active;

  public Entry( String name ) {
    this( new File( name ) );
  }

  public Entry( File directory ) {
    this.directory = directory;
    active = true;
```

```
  }
  public boolean active() {
    return active;
  }
  public void active( boolean active ) {
    this.active = active;
  }
  public File directory() {
    return directory;
  }
}
```

❶ LinkedHashMap has two axes of organization: the hash axis, on which we map directory names to directories; and the order axis, on which we store the ordering of the elements. The ordering matches the order in which the elements were added to the Path.

❷ add() and remove() simply call the respective add() and remove() methods of the directories LinkedHashMap, and so the order in which directories are added is preserved.

❸ setActive() lets you selectively turn various directories of the path on and off. This is easier than adding and removing them, because adding and removing have the side effect of changing the order of the directories. setActive() can disable a directory without changing its location in the overall order.

❹ findFile() traverses the list of directories in order, looking in each one to see if the file in question is there. It uses a FileFilter object to search each directory. If findFile() finds a file in a directory, it returns it immediately.

Note that we needed a LinkedHashMap for this program because the Path object needed to satisfy the following requirements:

- Sequential access—The directories must be traversed in a particular order
- Random access—It must be possible to activate and deactivate the directories individually

If we only had the first requirement, a List would have been sufficient. If we only had the second requirement, a HashMap would have been sufficient. However, to satisfy both, we need a LinkedHashMap.

8.3 *IdentityHashMap*

A regular `HashMap` considers two objects to be equal if

```
object0.equals( object 1 )
```

An `IdentityHashMap`, on the other hand, doesn't use the `equals()` method. It only considers two objects to be equal if

```
object0 == object1
```

This alteration in the behavior of the hashing method has subtle but important effects on the way `IdentityHashMap` behaves.

8.3.1 *Object equality*

Every Java object has a method called `equals()`, which is used to compare objects. The default implementation from `Object` compares objects using their identities, which means that two objects are equal if and only if they have the same reference. `Object.equals()` is implemented as follows:

```
public boolean equals( Object obj ) {
  return (this == obj);
}
```

Many objects override the `equals()` method because they wish to have a definition of equality that is based on the semantics of the object rather than its reference. For example, two separate `Integer` object references are equal if they have the same value, even if they are separate objects:

```
Integer i0 = new Integer( 40 );
Integer i1 = new Integer( 40 );
System.out.println( "i0 == i1: "+(i0==i1) );
System.out.println( "i0.equals( i1 ): "+i0.equals( i1 ) );
```

The preceding code results in the following output:

```
i0 == i1: false
i0.equals( i1 ): true
```

Clearly, these are separate objects, since they are created separately by two different calls to `new Integer()` and thus have different references. This is reflected in the fact that the `==` operator returns `false`. However, the `equals()` method returns `true` because it overrides the implementation in `Object` with another version that only returns `true` if the two `Integer` objects have the same value, regardless of whether they are the same object or not.

8.3.2 Hashing and equality

The exact implementation of equality is very important to the behavior of a hash table. When a key/value pair is inserted for a key that already exists in the table, the new value replaces the old value. Hash tables use the `equals()` method to determine if the key is already in the table.

Continuing to use `Integer` as an example, let's take a look at what happens when we insert two pairs that use the same exact `Integer` object:

```
Integer i0 = new Integer( 40 );

HashMap hm = new HashMap();
hm.put( i0, "first" );
hm.put( i0, "second" );

for (Iterator it = hm.entrySet().iterator(); it.hasNext();) {
  Map.Entry me = (Map.Entry)it.next();
  System.out.println( me.getKey()+" --> "+me.getValue() );
}
```

In this example, a key is used for two different values. Because the exact same object is used, the second value overwrites the first value, and so there is only a single value in the `HashMap` afterwards:

```
40 --> second
```

`IdentityHashMap` can help you avoid this overwriting. It treats two distinct `Integer` objects as different objects, even if they both contain the same integer value.

In table 8.1, we've used both `HashMap` and `IdentityHashMap` to try this out. For each class, we've tried two variations: one where we use the same `Integer` object as the key for both values, and one where we use two different `Integer` objects as keys. As you can see from the results in table 8.1, the only case in which the keys are treated as different objects is the last one, where we used an `IdentityHashMap`, and where we used two different `Integer` objects as keys.

Don't be fooled by the fact that these keys *look* identical. It's not possible for a `HashMap` to contain two different pairs with the same key. These two keys are `Integers` that have the same value and that have the same printed representation (as generated by their `toString()` methods), but they are separate objects and are treated as such by the `IdentityHashMap`.

8.3.3 Example: using the IdentityHashMap

Technically speaking, the `IdentityHashMap` violates one of the general principles of the `Map` interface, which is that `equals()` is always used to compare objects. `IdentityHashMap` should not be used frivolously, but there are situations when it is definitely called for.

Table 8.1 Comparison of `HashMap` and `IdentityHashMap`. They behave differently when given two separate `Integer` objects that have the same value—`IdentityHashMap` treats them as separate objects, while `HashMap` does not.

Hash table	Code	Results

HashMap	`Integer i0 = new Integer( 40 );`
	`hm.put( i0, "first" );`
	`hm.put( i0, "second" );`
		`40 --> second`

HashMap	`Integer i0 = new Integer( 40 );`
	`Integer i1 = new Integer( 40 );`
	`hm.put( i0, "first" );`
	`hm.put( i1, "second" );`
		`40 --> second`

IdentityHashMap	`Integer i0 = new Integer( 40 );`
	`Integer i1 = new Integer( 40 );`
	`ihm.put( i0, "first" );`
	`ihm.put( i0, "second" );`
		`40 --> second`

IdentityHashMap	`Integer i0 = new Integer( 40 );`
	`Integer i1 = new Integer( 40 );`
	`ihm.put( i0, "first" );`
	`ihm.put( i1, "second" );`
		`40 --> first`
		`40 --> second`

The following program, `DumpableGraph` (see listing 8.4), contains a simple implementation of a graph. It contains an inner class called `Node`. Each node has a *content string* that can be thought of as the name of the node, and each node also has a set of children. A node has a value and zero or more children. If a node has no children, it's a leaf; otherwise, it's a branch. A graph is one or more nodes connected to each other by the parent-child relation. (We would call it a tree, but it's really a graph because we are permitting back-references and cycles.)

`DumpableGraph` is dumpable because it has a method called `dump()`, which traverses the graph, printing out its contents. In this implementation, it is possible for a node to be its own ancestor, and so it is possible that the graph will contain a cycle. As a result, the `dump()` method has to be careful not to get caught in a loop as it traverses the graph; to do this, it uses a `Map` to keep track of the nodes that it has already dumped, thus avoiding an infinite loop.

Initially, we'll use a regular `HashMap` to keep track of the nodes, and we'll find that it doesn't work correctly. The bug is caused by the fact that our graph can have distinct nodes with the same content string. Once we've visited a node with the string "a", we won't visit any other nodes that also have the string "a", because we'll assume that these are the same node, even though they might not be. As we'll see, the solution is to use an `IdentityHashMap` instead of a regular `HashMap`.

But first, the flawed implementation is shown in listing 8.4.

Listing 8.4   DumpableGraph.java

(see \Chapter8\DumpableGraph.java)

```java
import java.io.*;
import java.util.*;

public class DumpableGraph
{
  public static class Node {                      ● Inner class Node
    private Object obj;
    private List children = new ArrayList();

    public Node( Object obj ) {
      this.obj = obj;
    }

    public void addChild( Node node ) {
      children.add( node );
    }

    public boolean equals( Object node ) {        ● Implement custom
      return obj.equals( ((Node)node).obj );        equality/hashing
    }

    public int hashCode() {
      return obj.hashCode();
    }

    public String toString() {
      return obj.toString();
    }

    public void dump() {
      // Start the dumping process with an empty
      // seen-set
      dump( "", new HashMap() );                  ● Use a regular Map
    }

    private void dump( String prefix, Map seen ) {    ● dump() traverses
      // Print out information about this node          the node graph...
      System.out.println( prefix+"Node: "+obj+
                      " ["+System.identityHashCode( obj )+"/"+
                      obj.hashCode()+"]" );
      if (children.size()==0) {

        // If there are no children, we've reached a leaf,
        // so we're done
        System.out.println( prefix+"  (no children)" );
      } else {

        // We only visit the children of this node if we
        // haven't already done so -- if we're not in the
```

```
        // seen-set                                          ...taking care not to
        if (!seen.containsKey( this )) {             ●      visit a node twice

            // Remember that we've processed this node by
            // putting it in the seen-set
            seen.put( this, null );

            // Dump all the children of this node
            for (Iterator it=children.iterator(); it.hasNext();) {
              Node node = (Node)it.next();

                // Indent the prefix by two spaces
                node.dump( prefix+"  ", seen );
            }
        } else {
          System.out.println( prefix+"  (loop)" );
        }
      }
    }
  }
}

static public void main( String args[] ) {   ●   Build the graph
  Node a = new Node( "a" );
  Node b = new Node( "b" );
  Node c = new Node( "c" );
  Node d = new Node( "d" );
  Node a2 = new Node( "a" );
  Node b2 = new Node( "b" );
  Node e = new Node( "e" );
  a.addChild( b );
  a.addChild( c );
  c.addChild( d );
  c.addChild( a );
  c.addChild( a2 );
  a2.addChild( b2 );
  a2.addChild( e );
  a.dump();
  }
}
```

Let's take a look at the program in action. Figure 8.17 shows an example graph. Each node is represented by a letter in a black circle, and the arrows point from parents to their children. The variable from the main() method in Listing 8.4 that holds the Node object is next to the black circle. Note that there are two nodes that have the same content string—nodes "a" and "a2" both have the content string "a".

When we run DumpableGraph, the output shows that we have a problem:

```
Node: a [9751148/97]
  Node: b [7947172/98]
    (no children)
```

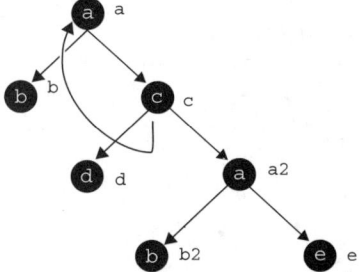

Figure 8.17 A graph composed of `DumpableGraph.Node` objects. Each node has a *content string*, shown inside the circle. The variable names next to the circles show the variables from listing 8.4 that contain the nodes. Note that node "c" has two children that are completely different `Node` objects, but which have the same content string of "a".

```
Node: c [4719703/99]
  Node: d [1375836/100]
    (no children)
  Node: a [9751148/97]
    (loop)
  Node: a [9751148/97]
    (loop)
```

The first boldfaced line shows that the top node "a" is a child of node "c". This corresponds to the curved arrow in figure 8.17. The dump() routine stops here because we don't want to get caught in a loop. But the second boldfaced line shows that there's another node called "a" that is a child of "c"—this is the node marked "a2" in the figure. This node has not yet been visited, and yet our dump() routine gives up and refuses to follow the arrow to that node.

The problem here is that we have two nodes with the content string "a". What's more, our dump() routine uses a regular old HashMap to keep track of the nodes we've already seen. As far as HashMap is concerned, these two nodes with the same content string *are the same node*. The equals() method would say that they are the same, and the hashCode() method would return the same value for both of them.

This is definitely a job for IdentityHashMap, which would be able to distinguish between the two nodes with the same content string. Let's update our code to use IdentityHashMap instead of HashMap:

```
public void dump() {
  dump( "", new IdentityHashMap() );
}
```

Because `IdentityHashMap` treats these two nodes as separate nodes, it actually dumps the last node out instead of mistaking it for the other node with the same content string. Here's the output from the updated program:

```
Node: a [7704795/97]
  Node: b [1375836/98]
    (no children)
  Node: c [4687246/99]
    Node: d [2866566/100]
      (no children)
    Node: a [7704795/97]
      (loop)
    Node: a [7704795/97]
      Node: b [1375836/98]
        (no children)
      Node: e [15805518/101]
        (no children)
```

This is one of the rare times when you need an `IdentityHashMap` instead of a regular `HashMap`. Generally speaking, you'll use an `IdentityHashMap` when you are dealing with objects as abstract `Objects` rather than as the things they are intended to be. In this example, the `Node` objects could be used for just about anything—parsing the code of a programming language, representing computers in a network, and so on. In that capacity, two `Node` objects containing the string "a" might be the same. But as pure `Objects` they are definitely different objects, and our `dump()` routine must treat them as such.

Before the arrival of JDK 1.4 and `IdentityHashMap`, you could have solved this by changing your definition of `Node.equals()` to distinguish between nodes with the same content string. (You'll note that the constructor `Node` actually takes a content `Object` as its argument, rather than requiring that it be a `String`. This object can be anything you wish to put inside a graph, and it can have any implementation of `equals()` and `hashCode()` that you want.)

However, you might have good reasons for using your particular implementation of `equals()`, and you may not want to change it. In this case, `System.identityHashCode()` can be used to distinguish between two separate objects that have the same hash code, and `==` can be used instead of `equals()`. In fact, we're doing this very thing, indirectly, when we use `IdentityHashMap`, because `IdentityHashMap` uses `System.identifyHashCode()` to distinguish between objects.

8.4   *The RandomAccess interface*

The `RandomAccess` interface is a *marker interface*, which means that it exists only to mark a class as having a certain property. As such, it is an *empty* interface—it has no methods. A class implements such an interface merely to advertise that it has a certain property. In this case, a `List` implementing `RandomAccess` advertises that the list supports efficient random access.

Here, random access means the use of `get()` and `set()` methods, in contrast to using the list's `Iterator`. In general, an `Iterator` is supposed to iterate through a list using the fastest possible method, while the `get()` and `set()` methods may or may not be efficient. If they are efficient, then the list should implement `RandomAccess`.

Code that does list processing and that would benefit from the list supporting fast random access should check the list first to see if it does in fact implement the `RandomAccess` interface:

```
if (!(list instanceof RandomAccess)) {
}
```

If the list does *not* implement `RandomAccess`, the code may have to use an alternative algorithm to process the list.

Here's an example of this in action. In listing 8.5, the `ListTransform` interface specifies a generic list-transforming routine that rearranges the elements within a list. `RandomTransform` is an example class that implements `ListTransform`; what it does is take a list and randomly swap its elements in order to randomize it (much like the `shuffle()` method in the `Collections` class). This is just a simple example transform—all that matters is that the transform require random access to be efficient.

The `RandomAccessifier` class simply applies a `ListTransform` to a `List`—but with an added bit of cleverness. If the `List` doesn't implement `RandomAccess`, it is first copied into a `List` that does. The transform is then applied, and the data is then copied back into the original list. If the `List` does implement `RandomAccess`, then the list is transformed in-place.

Listing 8.5   RandomAccessifier.java

(see \Chapter8\RandomAccessifier.java)

```
import java.util.*;

public class RandomAccessifier
{
  interface ListTransform                                      ●──  Interface for a
  {                                                                 list-transformer
    public void transform( List list );
  }

  static class RandomTransform implements ListTransform       ●  ListTransform
  {                                                              randomly rearranges
    private int count;                                           elements
    private Random rand = new Random();
```

```
    public RandomTransform( int count ) {
      this.count = count;
    }

    public void transform( List list ) {
      for (int i=0; i<count; ++i) {
        int ai = rand.nextInt( list.size() );
        int bi = rand.nextInt( list.size() );
        Collections.swap( list, ai, bi );
      }
    }
  }

  public static void transform( List list,
                                ListTransform transform ) {
    List origList = list;
    boolean ra = (list instanceof RandomAccess);
    if (!ra) {
      System.out.println( "Converting to RA" );
      list = new ArrayList( origList.size() );
      for (Iterator it=origList.iterator(); it.hasNext();) {
        list.add( it.next() );
      }
    }
    transform.transform( list );
    if (!ra) {
     origList.clear();
      int size = list.size();
      for (Iterator it=list.iterator(); it.hasNext();) {
        origList.add( it.next() );
      }
    }
  }

  static public void main( String args[] ) {
    List list = new LinkedList();
    for (int i=0; i<100; ++i) {
      list.add( new Integer( i ) );
    }

    RandomTransform rt = new RandomTransform( 10000000 );
    transform( list, rt );

    for (Iterator it=list.iterator(); it.hasNext();) {
      System.out.print( it.next()+" " );
    }
    System.out.println( "" );
  }
}
```

Move the elements into a RandomAccess list ❶

Copy into an ArrayList ❷

Move the elements back into the original list ❸

❶ ❸ Note that we avoid using the get() and set() methods when copying out of the original array, and when copying back into it. This is for the very same reason we are doing the copy in the first place: these methods aren't very efficient.

Instead, we use an Iterator to copy the elements out of the array. To copy the elements back in, we actually empty the array with the clear() method, and then add() the elements back in one-by-one.

❷ ArrayList is one of the two classes in JDK 1.4 that implements the RandomAccess interface, the other being Vector. It can safely be assumed that future releases of the JDK will take care to follow the convention of implementing the RandomAccess interface in classes for which it is appropriate.

The main() routine in the preceding example applies the RandomTransform to a LinkedList, which does *not* implement the RandomAccess interface. Using the RandomAccessifier to speed things up results in a significant speed improvement.

8.5   Summary

There's not a whole lot going on in the Collections Framework in this release, mostly because the Collections Framework is already so powerful. The new features added in this release could probably be written by applications programmers themselves, but having the implementations built into the core release standardizes their properties and allows for extra optimizations.

The addition of the RandomAccess marker interfaces heralds the addition of similar markers in the future—markers such as these will permit customization and specialization of standard collection operations that will allow for incremental increases in efficiency even as the core contracts of the Collections Framework classes are maintained.

Regular Expressions

This chapter covers

- Basic regular expression techniques
- The Java implementation of regular expressions
- Java equivalents of common Perl idioms
- Capturing groups
- Finding and replacing

257

Regular expressions (regexes) are a powerful tool for parsing strings and have been around for a long time. They have gained popularity in recent years, most particularly because of the rise of Perl as a language for systems programming and web development. Unix uses text files internally for much of its configuration and housekeeping, and web development in general is text-based, since it uses a human-readable data format (HTML). XML also promises to make text-based data increasingly common.

Since JDK 1.4, Java now includes regexes as part of the core platform, in the `java.util.regex` package. This chapter will provide a brief overview of regular expressions, and then consider the details of the Java implementation in the `java.util.regex` package. Section 9.3 compares some common Perl idioms to their Java equivalents, which should be useful for readers well-versed in Perl regular expressions.

9.1 Overview of regular expressions

A regular expression, or *regex*, is an expression that defines a subset of the space of all possible text strings. A regex is said to *match* a string if the string is within that subset. Thus, a regular expression is a criterion that can be applied to any string—it can match, or not match, the string.

A regex can be used to define a syntax for textual material, although regular expressions are not as powerful as full grammars, such as those used to define programming languages.* Regexes can be used to distinguish correct input from incorrect input, or to look for particular kinds of text within a larger body of text.

The most precise definition of regexes requires that we define our character space. While Java provides Unicode support in its regex implementation, this section will examine regexes using the familiar ASCII character set.

In the next few subsections, we'll take a look at different components of regular expressions and see what they do. In considering each regex, we'll answer the question, *what, within the example string, does this regex match?* We're only concerned with what it matches within the example string shown in the middle column of the example tables.

---

* Regular expressions correspond to the lowest level in what's known as the *Chomsky Hierarchy of Languages*, the next three levels being *context-free grammars, context-sensitive grammars*, and finally, *all formal grammars (Turing machine)*. A regular expression can recognize, for example, three "a" characters followed by three "b" characters, but it cannot recognize *n* "a" characters followed by *n* "b" characters. To match such a string, you would need to remember the number of "a" characters long enough to compare it with the number of "b" characters, which requires the recording of *state*. A regular expression cannot do this—you would need a context-free grammar.

WARNING In each of these examples, unless otherwise specified, we are assuming that matching is happening from left to right. That is, we find the first match that occurs in the string and ignore any other substrings that might match.

9.1.1 Literals

A *literal* is any character from the character set that doesn't have a special meaning within a regex. A literal in a regular expression matches only itself.

Table 9.1 Literal characters match themselves.

Regular expression	Example string	What, within the example string, does it match?
a	a	a (the entire string)
b	b	b (the entire string)
a	b	nothing
a	ab	only the a

Note that the regex does not necessarily have to match the entirety of a string.

9.1.2 The . wildcard

The . character matches *any* single character, except newline. Newlines are also recognized if the DOTALL flag is specified.

Table 9.2 The . character matches any single character of the input.

Regular expression	Example string	What, within the example string, does it match?
.	a	a
.	ab	a (or b if parsing happens from right to left)
. .	abcd	ab (or cd if parsing happens from right to left)

9.1.3 Quantifiers: * and +

The + character, when placed after a regular expression, matches one or more copies of that expression. The * character is like the + character, except that it can also match *no* instances of the expression—that is, it can match the empty string. These characters are called *quantifiers*.

Table 9.3 Quantifiers allow you to specify a repeated pattern.

Regular expression	Example string	What, within the example string, does it match?
a*	aaa	aaa
a*b*	aaabb	aaabb
.*	m	m
.*	"" *(empty string)*	"" *(empty string)*
.*	mnopq	mnopq
.+	mnopq	mnopq

9.1.4 Grouping with ()

Parentheses can be placed around any regular expression in order to treat it as a unit. This does not change what it matches, but it does allow modifiers (such as the quantifiers, above) to affect an entire expression, rather than a single character (see table 9.4). So, for example, just as g* means zero or more occurrences of g, (gh)* means zero or more occurrences of gh.

Table 9.4 Parentheses *group* characters, allowing them to be treated as a unit by other regex characters.

Regular expression	Example string	What, within the example string, does it match?
(gh)*	ghghghgh	ghghghgh
(a(bc)*)*	abcbcabcbc	abcbcabcbc

9.1.5 Character classes

A character class defines a set of individual characters. For example, the regex [abc] matches an a, a b, or a c; the regex [abc]+ matches one or more characters, each of which is an a, b, or c. You can also use the notation a-z to specify, in this case, all the characters between a and z.

Table 9.5 A character class specifies a set of characters and matches any character from that set.

Regular expression	Example string	What, within the example string, does it match?
`[abc]`	`a`	`a`
`[a-d]*`	`abcdef`	`abcd`
`[a-zA-Z_][a-zA-Z0-9_]*`	`aJavaIdentifier20`	`aJavaIdentifier20`

The last example in table 9.5 deserves mention. The first part of the regex, `[a-zA-Z_]`, matches any alphabetic character, or the underscore (_) character. The second part, `[a-zA-Z0-9_]*`, matches a sequence of alphabetic, numerical, or underscore characters. This is the syntactical definition of a Java identifier: it must be made of alphanumeric characters, and must not start with a number.

Putting a caret (^) at the start of such an expression *negates* the category, which means the expression matches only characters that are *not* in the set. Thus, the regex `[^abc]` matches any character which is not an a, b, or c.

Table 9.6 A caret (^) at the start of a character class *negates* the class. The expression only matches characters that are *not* in the class.

Regular expression	Example string	What, within the example string, does it match?
`[a-d]*`	`abcdefgh`	`abcd`
`[^a-d]*`	`abcdefgh`	`efgh`

9.1.6 *Predefined character classes*

There are shorthand expressions for certain character classes. \d, for example, matches any digit, while \D matches any non-digit. \d is thus a shorthand for `[0-9]`, while \D is a shorthand for `[^0-9]`. Likewise, \s matches any white space, while \S matches any non-white space.

Table 9.7 Some character classes are given shorthand expressions. You can use one of these characters instead of writing out the full definition of the class.

Regular expression	Example string	What, within the example string, does it match?
\d	0	0
\d\D\d	0A0	0A0
A\sA	A A	A A
\S\s\S	A A	A A

Table 9.8 lists all of the predefined character classes.

Table 9.8 Predefined character classes. These are one- or two-character shorthand expressions for some common character classes.

Predefined character class	What it matches	Equivalent expression
.	Any character	none
\d	Any decimal digit	[0-9]
\D	Any character *except* a decimal digit	[^0-9]
\s	Any white space character	[\t\n\x0B\f\r]
\S	Any character *except* a white space character	[^ \t\n\x0B\f\r]
\w	Any word character	[a-zA-Z_0-9]
\W	Any character *except* a word character	[^a-zA-Z_0-9]

There is also a set of *POSIX character classes.* These are like predefined character classes, but they are taken from the POSIX specification for regular expressions. Table 9.9 shows a couple of them; see the documentation for the rest.

Table 9.9 Some POSIX character classes. These are like predefined character classes, but they are taken from the POSIX specification for regular expressions.

Predefined character class	What it matches	Equivalent expression
\p{Lower}	Any lowercase letter	[a-z]
\p{Digit}	Any decimal digit	[0-9]

9.1.7 Sequencing and alternation

Concatenating two regular expressions creates a compound expression. To match this compound expression, the string must match the first expression, and then immediately the second expression, with no intervening characters.

Table 9.10 If two regular expressions match two strings, respectively, then the concatenation of the two regular expressions matches the concatenation of the two strings.

Regular expression	Example string	What, within the example string, does it match?
(ab)*	abab	abab
(cd)*	cdcd	cdcd
(ab)*(cd)*	ababcdcd	ababcdcd

You can also *or* two subexpressions together with the | symbol. To match, a string must match either of the subexpressions.

Table 9.11 A compound expression using the | character matches either the expression before the | or the expression after the |.

Regular expression	Example string	What, within the example string, does it match?
((ab)|(cd))*	abcdabcdcdab	abcdabcdcdab

Using the | character is also called *alternation*; the different expressions that are or'ed together are called *alternatives*.

9.1.8 Boundary matchers

The special symbols ^ and $ do not match particular characters—they match *positions* in relation to the line of text being considered. ^ matches the start of a line. Thus, while abc matches the central three characters in the string yyyabcyyy, ^abc does not, because ^abc requires that the string occur at the *start* of a line. Likewise, the $ matches the end of a line.

Table 9.12 includes some of the boundary matchers supported by the Pattern class.

Table 9.12   **Boundary matchers. These special symbols do not match particular characters—they match positions in relation to the line of text being considered.**

Regular expression	What it matches
^	The start of a the line
$	The end of the line
\b	A word boundary
\B	A non-word boundary
\z	The end of the input

Note that the definition of *line* depends on the definition of the *newline* character(s), which in turn is affected by the UNIX_LINES option (see section 9.2.3).

9.1.9 *Reluctant (non-greedy) matching*

All of the expressions we've looked at so far have been *greedy*—that is, they match as much as they can, going from left to right. For example, a* matches as many a characters as it can. (Many expressions, such as asdf, only match a single string, but these can be thought of as being greedy in a degenerate sense.) By default, each subexpression within a regular expression will match as long a string as it can, as long as such a match does not cause the entire expression to fail.

It is also possible to specify that certain quantifiers are to operate in a *non-greedy*, or *reluctant*, mode. This means that they will match the *shortest* possible string.

Here's an example. The regular expression (a+)(.+) separates a string into two parts—a sequence of a characters, matched by (a+), followed by a sequence of characters of any kind, matched by (.+). (See section 9.2.1 for details about using the () characters to extract parts of a matched string.)

Our input string is aaaabbbb. If we use our regex as-is, the match works out as shown in figure 9.1. However, if we change the first + to be +?, it becomes *reluctant*, in which case it matches as few a characters as possible, as shown in figure 9.2.

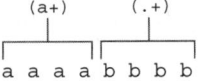

Figure 9.1   **+ is a regular greedy quantifier. The sub-regex (a+) matches as many a characters as possible—in this case, four of them.**

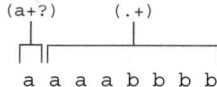

Figure 9.2 `+?` is a *reluctant* quantifier. The sub-regex `(a+?)` matches as few a characters as possible—in this case, just one. The second half of the regex, `(.+)`, matches the rest.

Of course, the regex shown in figure 9.2 could be simpler. We could do the same thing with the regex `(a)(.+)` and it would match in exactly the same way—the `(a+?)` acts just like `(a)` in this instance, only matching the initial a. But if we change the `(.+)` to be `(b+)`, we find that `(a+?)` matches aaaa (see figure 9.3).

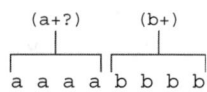

Figure 9.3 Even though `(a+?)` is reluctant, rather than greedy, it must match aaaa in order for the entire expression to match. That is, even though it wants to match as few characters as possible, it is willing to match more, so it matches all four in order for the entire match to succeed.

Both greedy and reluctant quantifiers want the entire match to succeed. A greedy quantifier will match as many characters as it can, as long as this doesn't cause the entire match to fail. Likewise, a reluctant quantifier will match as few as it can, as long as this doesn't cause the entire match to fail.

Putting a ? character after any quantifier makes it reluctant.

9.1.10 Other features

We've only looked at a few of the elements of regular expressions—there are a great deal more. Different implementations, in different languages, support different regular expression features. The Java implementation is very close to the Perl 5.0 implementation—see the documentation for `java.util.regex.Pattern` for a complete listing of valid regular expression elements.

9.2 Pattern and Matcher

The regex facility in `java.util.regex` is defined by only three classes:

- `Pattern`—Represents a regular expression
- `Matcher`—Matches a `Pattern` against a string
- `PatternSyntaxExpression`—Exception thrown while attempting to compile a regular expression

As in Perl, regexes are *compiled* before they are used. What this means is implementation dependent, but, generally speaking, it means that work is done on the regular expression to make matching faster.

Because regex compilation is slow, it is generally done only once. Java allows for explicit control over this, because it separates the compilation process from the matching process by having the two classes, `Pattern` and `Matcher`. Creating a `Pattern` object compiles the regex, while the `Matcher` object does the actual matching.

Creating a `Pattern` object is simple:

```
Pattern pattern = Pattern.compile( "\\S+\\s+\\S+" );
```

This regex matches two words (made of any non-white space characters) separated by some white space.

Once you have a `Pattern` object, you create a `Matcher` object for a particular input string:

```
Matcher matcher = pattern.matcher( "hey there" );
```

Note that the argument to `Pattern.matcher()` does not have to be a `String`—it has to be an object that implements the `java.lang.CharSequence` interface. The following classes implement `CharSequence`:

- `java.lang.String`
- `java.lang.StringBuffer`
- `java.nio.CharBuffer`

However, in the following text, we'll refer to the input to a `Matcher` as the input *string*, for the sake of simplicity.

`Matcher.matches()` will tell you if the entire string is matched by the regex:

```
if (matcher.matches()) {
  // ...
}
```

You can also use `Matcher` to find substrings of the input string. `Matcher.lookingAt()` is like `matches()`, except that the matched portion doesn't have to cover the entire string—it only has to start at the beginning of the string.

The `find()` method will tell the `Matcher` to look for the first substring that matches the regex. Each successive call looks for another match after the previous match.

For all three methods (`matches()`, `lookingAt()`, and `find()`), you can find out what substring of the input string was matched, using the `start()` and `end()` methods:

```
Pattern pattern = Pattern.compile( "\\S+\\s+\\S+" );
String inputString = "well, hey there feller";
Matcher matcher = pattern.matcher( inputString );
if (matcher.find()) {
  int start = matcher.start();
  int end = matcher.end();
```

```
   String matched = inputString.substring( start, end );
   System.out.println( matched );
}
```

This produces the following output:

```
well, hey
```

`Matcher` also provides a convenience method called `group()`, which performs the same actions as the previous boldfaced section:

```
Pattern pattern = Pattern.compile( "\\S+\\s+\\S+" );
String inputString = "well, hey there feller";
Matcher matcher = pattern.matcher( inputString );
if (matcher.find()) {
   String matched = matcher.group();
   System.out.println( matched );
}
```

9.2.1 *Capturing groups*

`Pattern` and `Matcher` also provide for *capturing groups*. A capturing group is a subexpression within a larger regular expression, enclosed in parentheses, as shown in figure 9.4. Just as you can get the start and end points of the substring matched by the regular expression, you can also get the start and end points matched by the capturing group. You can use the `start()` and `end()` methods, this time passing in a capturing group index, to find the endpoints of the specified capturing group.

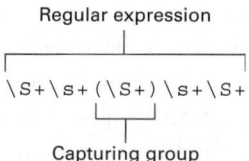

Figure 9.4 A capturing group is a subexpression within a regular expression. It is possible to find the start and end points of the substring matched by the capturing group, just as it is possible to find the start and end points of the string matched by the entire regular expression.

The regex in figure 9.4 matches a three-word sequence; the following code fragment will print out the middle word:

```
Pattern pattern = Pattern.compile( "\\S+\\s+(\\S+)\\s+\\S+" );
String inputString = "well hello again";
Matcher matcher = pattern.matcher( inputString );
if (matcher.find()) {
   int start = matcher.start( 1 );
   int end = matcher.end( 1 );
```

```
   String middleWord = inputString.substring( start, end );
   System.out.println( middleWord );
}
```

The following code fragment does the same thing, but uses the group() method to extract the string:

```
Pattern pattern = Pattern.compile( "\\S+\\s+(\\S+)\\s+\\S+" );
String inputString = "well hello again";
Matcher matcher = pattern.matcher( inputString );
if (matcher.find()) {
   String middleWord = matcher.group( 1 );
   System.out.println( middleWord );
}
```

9.2.2 *Find and replace*

The Matcher class also provides a couple of ways to do find-and-replace. The easiest way is with the replaceAll() method:

```
Pattern pattern = Pattern.compile( "\\S+" );
String inputString = "well hello again";
Matcher matcher = pattern.matcher( inputString );
String newString = matcher.replaceAll( "word" );
System.out.println( newString );
```

The output of this program is the string word word word. Each substring of the input string that matches the regex \S+ is replaced with word.

Another, more sophisticated, method uses appendReplacement() and appendTail(). After each find() within a string, appendReplacement() replaces the found string with the replacement string, and appends the replacement string to a StringBuffer. The characters *between* the matches aren't ignored—they are also copied to the StringBuffer, placed properly between the replacement strings. appendTail() is used at the end to copy any non-matched characters at the end of the string.*

One of the advantages of this method is that you can refer back to capturing groups from within the replacement string. In the following example, we will replace parentheses with square brackets. The characters between the parentheses are matched by a capturing group:

```
Pattern pattern = Pattern.compile( "\\((.*)\\)" );
```

The string $1 refers to the first capturing group. If we replace it with the string [$1], the contents of the capturing group are inserted between the square brackets.

---

* For a more precise definition of this process, see the documentation for Matcher.

(You can think of this as a kind of *context-sensitive* find-and-replace.) Here's the full listing:

```
Pattern pattern = Pattern.compile( "\\((.*)\\)" );
String inputString = "These should be (square brackets).";
StringBuffer sb = new StringBuffer();
Matcher matcher = pattern.matcher( inputString );
while (true) {
  if (!matcher.find())
    break;

  matcher.appendReplacement( sb, "[$1]" );
}
matcher.appendTail( sb );

String newString = sb.toString();

System.out.println( newString );
```

This produces the following output:

```
These should be [square brackets].
```

Because this process uses a `StringBuffer` for each step, it can be a very efficient way to process a lot of text, while still giving you the flexibility to make decisions at each step of the process.

9.2.3 *Flags*

The constructor for `Pattern` can take a second parameter, which is a set of *flags* that have been or'ed together. These flags modify the way that the regular expression matches. Table 9.13 lists the flags that are supported.

Table 9.13 These flags are supported by the Java regex package.

Flag	Meaning
Pattern.UNIX_LINES	Only the \n character is recognized as a newline character. Affects ., ^, and $
Pattern.CASE_INSENSITIVE	Uppercase and lowercase characters are considered the same— for the US-ASCII character set *only*
Pattern.UNICODE_CASE	Uppercase and lowercase characters are considered the same— as specified by the Unicode standard
Pattern.COMMENTS	White space is ignored; comments starting with a # and going to the end of the line are ignored
Pattern.MULTILINE	^ and $ characters match line terminators within a line, rather than only matching the start and end of the entire input

Table 9.13 These flags are supported by the Java regex package. *(continued)*

Flag	Meaning
`Pattern.DOTALL`	. matches line terminators as well
`Pattern.CANON_EQ`	Specifies that two characters match only if their canonical decompositions match

These flags, and their Perl equivalents, are used in the examples in the next section.

9.3   *Transitioning from Perl to Java*

Regular expressions have been around for a long time, but they came into truly widespread use with the emergence of Perl as one of the main languages of the web. While many languages support regexes through libraries, Perl integrates them fully into the syntax of the language. This fact might well be the strongest reason for the popularity of Perl.

Java supports regexes through a library rather than a specialized syntax, which is a feature or a bug, depending on who you talk to. Other than this, however, Java's regex support is quite strong.

In this section, we'll consider four simple Perl programs that use regexes, and we'll translate them into Java. In doing so, we'll note crucial differences in usage and syntax that may trip up the unwary Perl programmer. Each of the four programs is of the "read the input and parse each line as you go" variety; we'll look at some more sophisticated uses of regexes in later sections.

9.3.1   *Finding the longest word in a line*

`longestword.pl` (see listing 9.1) scans a series of colon-delimited lines and prints out the longest word from each line.

Listing 9.1   longestword.input.pl

(See \Chapter9\longestword.input.pl)
```
what:is:the:longest
whitespace : is : ignored
this:one : is : supercalifragilistically:easy
```

Listing 9.2 shows the output of the program. Running either the Java version or the Perl version of this program should produce the same output. The output of these programs should be the same, since the programs were written to do the exact same things. However, due to differences in the way that certain operating systems deal with newline characters (and due to differences in the ways that Perl and Java cope with these differences), your output may be different from what is shown here. However, the differences should *only* consist of differences in the representations of newlines.

Listing 9.2   longestword.output.pl

(See \Chapter9\longestword.output.pl)
```
longest
whitespace
supercalifragilistically
```

The Perl code for this program is shown in listing 9.3.

Listing 9.3   longestword.pl

(See \Chapter9\longestword.pl)
```
#!perl -w

while( <> ) {          ❶ Perl idiom for iterating through
  chop;                  all the lines of the input

    @words = split( /\s*:\s*/ );   ❷ Break the line into words using a regex, and
                                     assign the list of words to array "words"

# -1 means we haven't found a word yet
  my $longest = -1;
  my $longestLength = 0;
  for ($i=0; $i<@words; ++$i) {         Find the longest
    my $length = length $words[$i];     word in the line
    if ($length > $longestLength) {
      $longest = $i;
      $longestLength = $length;
    }
  }

  print "$words[$longest]\n";
}
```

---

❶ while(<>) is the Perl idiom for reading from standard input (as well as from any files listed on the command line). chop is used to remove the trailing newline at the end of the line.

❷ The regex here is \s*:\s*. If all we wanted to do was split the line by colons, we could use the regex :. However, we also want to ignore any white space around the colon, so we allow for this by adding \s* before and after the colon. \s* means "zero or more white space characters."

split returns an array value, which is assigned to the variables words.

The corresponding Java code is shown in listing 9.4.

Listing 9.4 LongestWord.java

(See \Chapter9\LongestWord.java)

```java
import java.io.*;
import java.util.regex.*;

public class LongestWord
{
  static public void main( String args[] ) throws IOException {
    // BufferedReader lets us read line-by-line
    Reader r = new InputStreamReader( System.in );
    BufferedReader br = new BufferedReader( r );

    Pattern pattern = Pattern.compile( "\\s*:\\s*" );

    while (true) {
      String line = br.readLine();

      // Null line means input is exhausted
      if (line==null)
        break;

      String words[] = pattern.split( line );

      // -1 means we haven't found a word yet
      int longest=-1;
      int longestLength=0;
      for (int i=0; i<words.length; ++i) {
        if (words[i].length() > longestLength) {
          longest = i;
          longestLength = words[i].length();
        }
      }

      System.out.println( words[longest] );
    }
  }
}
```

❶ Java construct for iterating through all the lines of the input

❷ Break the line into words using a regex. Assign the list of words to array "words"

● Find the longest word in the line

❶ In Java, the best way to read the input as text, a line at a time, is to use a Buffered-Reader, which features the readLine() method.

❷ In Java, the regex is identical to what it was in Perl—this is because the regex language is really a separate language from the language that uses it. Java uses a regular String to encode the regex, and so the normal escaping rules apply. In this case, we need to escape each \ character with another \ character—that is, to encode a \, we need to use \\. `Pattern.split()` returns an array reference, which we can assign to the array variable `words`.

The most important thing to take away from this example—aside from the obvious fact that Perl is more concise, if a bit more cryptic—is that certain characters in regexes need to be *escaped* in Java source code. Java, like most languages that support regexes in some way, encodes regexes as strings. Some characters inside double quotes, such as \ and single and double quotes, need to be escaped. In Perl, regexes fall into their own syntactic category, and the miraculous Perl parser is able to treat them separately, requiring little in the way of escape sequences. The parser in the Java compiler, however, requires that regex string constants must follow all the same escaping rules as regular strings—there is no special parsing for regexes.

9.3.2 *Parsing a tab-delimited file*

The tab-delimited file is a kind of cheap, lowest-common-denominator database. Spreadsheet programs and database engines often allow for exporting their data as tab-delimited files.

A tab-delimited file encodes each database record (or spreadsheet row) as a single line. Each field is stored as text, and the fields are separated by tab (\t) characters. For the purposes of this section, we'll add the stipulation that a tab character preceded by a backslash is considered part of the enclosing field, rather than as a field separator.

In this section, we'll consider the problem of reading a tab-delimited file into memory. When working with tab-delimited files, this is often the first thing you do. Admittedly, huge files shouldn't be read entirely into memory before processing starts, but the programs listed here can easily be modified to process their data while they are reading, rather than after reading everything.

Listing 9.5 shows the sample input we'll be using—an excerpt from a telephone database. Visually, tabs are indistinguishable from spaces, but in listing 9.5, there are *only* tabs, no spaces of any kind. Any white space you see inside a line is a tab character. (Grab the file from the web site if you want a better look.)

Listing 9.5   tabdelimited.input.txt

(See\Chapter9\tabdelimited.input.txt)

```
212-555-1212    information    6:30    15:30
818-222-3333    thingy         12:00   1:00
917-999-8888    cell\   phone  1:00    9:00
```

Note especially the sequence between cell and phone—this is an *escaped tab*—that is, a tab character immediately preceded by a backslash. This tells the reader code to treat this tab as part of the field cell phone, rather than as a field separator.

Listing 9.6 shows the output.

Listing 9.6   tabdelimited.output.txt

(See\Chapter9\tabdelimited.output.txt)

```
Record 0
  212-555-1212
  information
  6:30
  15:30
Record 1
  818-222-3333
  thingy
  12:00
  1:00
Record 2
  917-999-8888
  cell\       phone      ❶  Escaped tab
  1:00                       included in field
  9:00
```

Listing 9.7 shows the program in Perl.

Listing 9.7   tabdelimited.pl

(See\Chapter9\tabdelimited.pl)

```perl
#!perl -w

my @vec = ();

while( <> ) {                          Split on tabs, except
  chop;                                those that are escaped

  @words = split( /(?<!\\)\t/ );    ❶

  push @vec, [ @words ];            ❷  Put the data into a
}                                        two-dimensional array
my $i=0;
foreach $words (@vec) {
  print "Record $i\n";
  $i++;
  foreach $word (@$words) {
    print "  $word\n";
  }
}
```

❶ If we only wanted to split on tabs, the regex would be simple: \t. However, we also want to skip escaped tabs. You might think that it would be enough to use the regex [^\\]\t, which is translated as "match a non-backslash followed by a tab," but this isn't quite what we want. For example, when scanning the first field separator on the first line of the input file, it would match 2\t, which would remove the trailing 2 from the previous field, leaving it as 212-555-121.

Instead, we use something called a *zero-width negative lookbehind*, which allows us to specify a preceding backslash without including it in the match. A zero-width negative lookbehind looks like (?<!X), where X is the regular expression in question. Thus, we use (?<!\\)\t, which can be translated as "match a tab, but only if the tab doesn't have a backslash before it; in either case, don't include the preceding character in the match."

❷ Since a tab-delimited file is, in a sense, a representation of a grid of data, we need to store the information in a two-dimensional array—or in what passes for a two-dimensional array in Perl, namely an array of array references.

Listing 9.8 shows the translation into Java.

> **Listing 9.8   TabDelimited.java**

(See \Chapter9\ TabDelimited.java)

```
import java.io.*;
import java.util.regex.*;
import java.util.*;

public class TabDelimited
{
  static public void main( String args[] ) throws IOException {
    // BufferedReader lets us read line-by-line
    Reader r = new InputStreamReader( System.in );
    BufferedReader br = new BufferedReader( r );

    // We'll store the data in a vector of arrays
    Vector vec = new Vector();

    Pattern pattern = Pattern.compile( "(?<!\\\\)\\t" );   |#1

    while (true) {
      String line = br.readLine();
      if (line==null)
        break;

      String words[] = pattern.split( line );

      vec.addElement( words.clone() );
    }
    int ri=0;
    for (Enumeration e=vec.elements(); e.hasMoreElements();) {
```

❶ Split on tabs, except those that are escaped

● Put the data into a vector of arrays

```
    String words[] = (String[])e.nextElement();
    System.out.println( "Record "+ri );
    ri++;
    for (int i=0; i<words.length; ++i) {
      System.out.println( "   "+words[i] );
    }
  }
 }
}
```

❶ Again, we see that the regex is the same in Java as it is in Perl but for the need to escape the \ characters as \\.

This program uses a lookbehind construct, which is a rather more obscure regex feature than is used in most applications. It's important to carefully study the documentation for both Perl and Java regexes to see which of the more complex and unusual features are supported. Both implementations support many of the more esoteric constructs, but the two implementations are by no means identical. However, for 95% of day-to-day applications, they are the same.

9.3.3 *A command-line processor*

This section describes implementations of a simple command-line processor. This program takes a series of commands—either from the command line or from a file—and treats it like a command. The first word on each line is considered to be the command keyword itself, and the following words are treated like arguments to the command. A large conditional statement then executes the command, depending on which command it was.

As an example, we'll consider a hypothetical drawing language with commands like "moveto" and "setbounds". Listing 9.9 shows the example input file—this can be considered a simple *script*.

Listing 9.9   commandprocessor.input.txt

(See \Chapter9\commandprocessor.input.txt)

```
setname horace
moveto 10 10
moveto 20 20
setbounds 10 10 50 50
moveto 10 10
```

The last line of listing 9.9, shown in boldface, contains the command `moveto` followed by two arguments, `10` and `10`.

Naturally, we aren't interested in the implementation of the hypothetical drawing language, so in our implementation each command just prints itself out—the command name, followed by the arguments. Listing 9.10 shows the output produced from the input in listing 9.9.

Listing 9.10   commandprocessor.output.txt

(See \Chapter9\ commandprocessor.output.txt)

```
- setName horace
- moveTo 10 10
- moveTo 20 20
- setBounds 10 10 50 50
- moveTo 10 10
```

The output looks rather like the input, since each line shows the command and its arguments.

Listing 9.11 shows the Perl that implements this.

Listing 9.11   commandprocessor.pl

(See \Chapter9\ commandprocessor.pl)

```perl
#!perl -w

my @vec = ();

while( <> ) {
  chop;

  @words = split( /\s+/ );              ● Split on white space

  if ($words[0] eq "moveto") {          ● Select command based on first word
    # Grab the arguments from the word list
    my $x = $words[1];
    my $y = $words[2];

    # Call the routine that implements the command
    &moveTo( $x, $y );
  } elsif ($words[0] eq "setname") {
    # Grab the arguments from the word list
    my $name = $words[1];

    # Call the routine that implements the command
    &setName( $name );                           ❶ Process the
  } elsif ($words[0] eq "setbounds") {              command
    # Grab the arguments from the word list
    my $x = $words[1];
    my $y = $words[2];
    my $w = $words[3];
    my $h = $words[4];
```

```perl
      # Call the routine that implements the command
      &setBounds( $x, $y, $w, $h );
    } else {
      # Any unknown command, and we quit
      die "Error: $_";
    }
  }
}

sub moveTo {
  my ($x, $y) = @_;
  print "- moveTo $x $y\n";

}

sub setName {
  my ($name) = @_;
  print "- setName $name\n";
}

sub setBounds {
  my ($x, $y, $w, $h) = @_;
  print "- setBounds $x $y $w $h\n";
}
```

❶ **Process the command**

● **Implement each command**

❶ To process each command, we need to first extract the arguments. Extracting each one into a well-named variable is good practice because it's easier to read. We could check the values to make sure they are the correct type, but since it's Perl, we won't bother.

Listing 9.12 shows the Java version.

Listing 9.12   CommandProcessor.java

(See \Chapter9\ CommandProcessor.java)

```java
import java.io.*;
import java.util.regex.*;
import java.util.*;
public class CommandProcessor
{
  public CommandProcessor() {
  }
  public void processCommands( InputStream in ) throws IOException {
    // BufferedReader lets us read line-by-line
    Reader r = new InputStreamReader( System.in );
    BufferedReader br = new BufferedReader( r );
    Pattern pattern = Pattern.compile( "\\s+" );   ● Split on white space
    while (true) {
      String line = br.readLine();
      if (line==null)
```

```
        break;
      String words[] = pattern.split( line );
      if (words[0].equals( "moveto" )) {
        int x = Integer.parseInt( words[1] );
        int y = Integer.parseInt( words[2] );
        moveTo( x, y );
      } else if (words[0].equals( "setname" )) {
        String name = words[1];
        setName( name );
      } else if (words[0].equals( "setbounds" )) {
        int x = Integer.parseInt( words[1] );
        int y = Integer.parseInt( words[2] );
        int w = Integer.parseInt( words[3] );
        int h = Integer.parseInt( words[4] );
        setBounds( x, y, w, h );
      } else {
        System.out.println( "Error: "+line );
      }
    }
  }
  public void moveTo( int x, int y ) {
    System.out.println( "- moveTo "+x+" "+y );
  }

  public void setName( String name ) {
    System.out.println( "- setName "+name );
  }

  public void setBounds( int x, int y, int w, int h ) {
    System.out.println( "- setBounds "+x+" "+y+" "+w+" "+h );
  }
  static public void main( String args[] ) throws IOException {
    CommandProcessor cp = new CommandProcessor();
    cp.processCommands( System.in );
  }
}
```

Select command based on first word

❶ **Process the command**

● **Implement each command**

❶ We extract the arguments here like we did in the Perl version, but it's convenient to check the types of the values. This check is implicit in the attempt to convert, in this example, the string to an integer.

The three examples we've seen so far use the split construct. In our next example, we'll take a look at some more sophisticated matching.

9.3.4 *Parsing and modifying names*

This example is a bit more complicated. We'll write a program that parses a list of names. Each name is checked to make sure that it is well formed, using a very narrow definition of name—it must have a title (Ms., Mr., or Mrs.), a first name, and a last name. We'll also use the find-and-replace features of the Pattern object to convert Mrs. to Ms., contrasting this feature with the Perl s/// construct.

Listing 9.13 shows our input file, and listing 9.14 shows the output we desire. You'll notice that the names with a first name and a last name are parsed properly, but that names with just a single name (Mr. Wiggles) or with three names (Joe Don Baker) are rejected. You'll also notice, in the boldfaced output line, that we've converted Mrs. to Ms.

Listing 9.13   parsename.input.txt

(See \Chapter9\parsename.input.txt)

```
mr. Greg Travis
Ms. Susan Beal
Mr. Chiaki Sugai
Mr. Wiggles
Mrs. Joan Allen
mrs. Hawiggins
Mr. Joe Don Baker
```

Listing 9.14   parsename.output.txt

(See \Chapter9\parsename.output.txt)

```
mr. Greg Travis
  Title: mr.
  First Name: Greg
  Last Name: Travis
Ms. Susan Beal
  Title: Ms.
  First Name: Susan
  Last Name: Beal
Mr. Chiaki Sugai
  Title: Mr.
  First Name: Chiaki
  Last Name: Sugai
Mr. Wiggles
  (Doesn't match!)
Mrs. Joan Allen
  Title: Mrs.
  First Name: Joan
  Last Name: Allen
  Modernized: Ms. Joan Allen
```

```
mrs. Hawiggins
   (Doesn't match!)
Mr. Joe Don Baker
   (Doesn't match!)
```

More complicated regexes

To parse these names, we're going to make use of a few new features.

To begin with, our regular expression is going to be rather more complicated than some of the expressions we've been using in previous sections. Expressed the regular way, it looks like this:

```
/^\s*(M(s|r|rs)\.)\s+(\S+)\s+(\S+)\s*$/i
```

Regexes can get pretty nasty, as you can see. Fortunately, both Java and Perl allow you to put white space and comments into your regexes, to make them easier to read:

```
/^\s*        # Ignore any whitespace at
             # the start of the line
(M(s|r|rs)\.) # Match Ms., Mrs., and Mr. (titles)
\s+          # Space between title and first name
(\S+)        # First name
\s+          # Space between first name and last name
(\S+)        # Last name
\s*$         # Allow whitespace, but nothing else,
             # after name
/ix
```

To ensure that adding comments and white space doesn't change the semantics of your regex, you have to *tell* Java and Perl that you want to use them, and that they should be ignored. You'll see how this is done in listings 9.15 and 9.16.

We're also going to make use of capturing groups to divide each name into its component parts: title, first name, and last name.

Finally, we're going to use find-and-replace features of the two languages to replace Mrs. with Ms.

Listing 9.15 shows the code in Perl.

Listing 9.15   parsename.pl

(See\Chapter9\parsename.pl)

```perl
#!perl -w

while( <> ) {
  print;
  chop;

  # Save this for later
  my $line = $_;

  if (/^\s*          # Ignore any whitespace at
                     # the start of the line
      (M(s|r|rs)\.)  # Match Ms., Mrs., and Mr. (titles)
      \s+            # Space between title and first name
      (\S+)          # First name
      \s+            # Space between first name and last name
      (\S+)          # Last name
      \s*$           # Allow whitespace, but nothing else,
                     # after name
      /ix) {

    my $title = $1;
    my $firstName = $3;
    my $lastName = $4;

    print "  Title: $title\n";
    print "  First Name: $firstName\n";
    print "  Last Name: $lastName\n";

    my $modernLine = &modernize( $line );
    if ($modernLine ne $line) {
      print "  Modernized: $modernLine\n";
    }
  } else {
    print "  (Doesn't match!)\n";
  }
}

sub modernize {
  my ($line) = @_;

  $line =~ s/(?<=m)rs\./s./i;

  return $line;
}
```

Regex to parse the name, with comments and white space ❶

Conditional: did it match? ❷

Capturing groups ❸

'x' flag to allow comments and white space, 'i' flag for case-insensitivity ❹

Get the substrings matched by the capturing groups

Modernize the name, if possible

Regex to replace Mrs. with Ms. ❺

❶ This regex has been annotated with comments, and white space has been added to make the formatting clearer. This feature requires the x flag at the end of the regular expression, as we see at #4.

❷ Not every match succeeds; the /<regex>/ construct returns a boolean telling whether it did or not, and we can use this to determine whether to proceed or to signal an error.

❸ The title, first name, and last name are each matched by a regex in a capturing group. This allows us to pull these substrings out of the matched string.

❹ In Perl, regex options such as "allow comments and whitespace" are single characters placed at the end of the regex, after the closing / character. This particular option uses the x character.

❺ Here, we use the s/// construct, which performs find-and-replace, rather than the // construct, which only performs find. We are using the i option for this match, which specifies that it should be case-insensitive.

Note that although we want to find occurrences of Mrs., we only want to replace the rs. part of any such occurrences—we want to respect the case of the M, so we don't want to replace it. To this end, we again use the zero-width positive lookbehind construct, ?<=, which requires that there be an M before the rs., but which doesn't include the M in the match. (Contrast this with the zero-width *negative* lookbehind construct, ?<!, which requires that a particular regex *not* be there, but which also doesn't include whatever *is* there in the match. See section 9.3.2 for an example of this construct.)

In contrast, listing 9.16 shows the Java version. You'll notice that the ability to embed comments within the regex isn't really as useful here as it was in Perl, since the comments are actually #-style comments, and they are still terminated by \n"+ at the end of each line.

Listing 9.16   ParseName.java

(See \Chapter9\ ParseName.java)

```java
import java.io.*;
import java.util.regex.*;

public class ParseName
{
  static public void main( String args[] ) throws IOException {
    // BufferedReader lets us read line-by-line
    Reader r = new InputStreamReader( System.in );
    BufferedReader br = new BufferedReader( r );
```

```
String patternString =
  "^\\s*           # Ignore any whitespace at\n"+
  "                # the start of the line\n"+
  "(M(s|r|rs)\\.)  # Match Ms., Mrs., and Mr. (titles)\n"+
  "\\s+            # Space between title and first name\n"+
  "(\\S+)          # First name\n"+
  "\\s+            # Space between first name and last name\n"+
  "(\\S+)          # Last name\n"+
  "\\s*$           # Allow whitespace, but nothing else, \n"+
  "                # after name\n";

int patternFlags = Pattern.CASE_INSENSITIVE|Pattern.COMMENTS;

Pattern pattern =
  Pattern.compile( patternString, patternFlags );

while (true) {
  String line = br.readLine();
  if (line==null)
    break;

  Matcher matcher = pattern.matcher( line );

  System.out.println( line );

  if (matcher.matches()) {
    String title = matcher.group( 1 );
    String firstName = matcher.group( 3 );
    String lastName = matcher.group( 4 );

    System.out.println( "  Title: "+title );
    System.out.println( "  First Name: "+firstName );
    System.out.println( "  Last Name: "+lastName );

    String modernLine = modernize( line );

    if (!modernLine.equals( line )) {
      System.out.println( "  Modernized: "+modernLine );
    }
  } else {
    System.out.println( "  (Doesn't match!)" );
  }
}
}

static public String modernize( String name ) {
  String patternString = "(?<=m)rs\\.";
  int patternFlags = Pattern.CASE_INSENSITIVE;

  Pattern pattern =
    Pattern.compile( patternString, patternFlags );

  Matcher matcher = pattern.matcher( name );

  // StringBuffer to accumulate output of find-and-replace
  StringBuffer sb = new StringBuffer();
```

Regex to parse the name, with comments and white space

❶

Flags are not part of the regex, but are passed into compile()

Conditional: did it match? **❷**

Get the substrings matched by the capturing groups

Modernize the name, if possible

Regex to replace Mrs.

❸ Flags are not part of the regex, but are passed into compile()

```
        // Find first occurrence of target string
        boolean result = matcher.find();
        while( result ) {
            // Replace target string with replacement string
            matcher.appendReplacement( sb, "s." );

            // Find next occurrence of target string
            result = matcher.find();
        }

        // Append unmatched remainder of string
        matcher.appendTail(sb);

        return sb.toString();
    }
}
```

❶ In Java, regex options are bit-fields that can be or'ed together. The resulting value is passed in as the second argument to `compile()`.

❷ Not every match succeeds; `Matcher.matches()` returns a boolean telling whether or not the pattern matches the input sequence. Note that the entire input sequence must be matched for `matcher()` to return `true`.

❸ To carry out the find-and-replace, we use `Matcher.appendReplace()` and `Matcher.appendTail()`. After each call to `find()`, we call `appendReplacement()`, which replaces the matched text and appends it to the `StringBuffer`. `appendReplacement()` also appends any text between the current match and the last one, so that the `StringBuffer` gets the entire string, not just the parts that have been replaced. At the end, we call `appendTail()` to append any remaining characters after the last match.

In this section, we've looked at Java translations of a few common Perl idioms. Next we'll take a look at some programs that have been designed entirely from a Java point of view.

9.4   *Example: HTML templating system*

In this section we'll take a look at a simple HTML templating system. This system allows you to populate a page of HTML with variables; the variable names are replaced with values before the page is sent to the user's browser.

A template looks like this:

```
<title> $title </title>
<h1><center>$title</center></h1>
<h2>$subtitle</h2>
$text
```

Table 9.14 shows a sample set of variable bindings for the variables in the preceding template.

Table 9.14   A set of variable bindings for the instantiation of a template. Each variable on the left, when prefixed with a dollar sign ($), is replaced with the corresponding value on the right.

Name	Value
`title`	Template Test
`subtitle`	An easier way to generate a page
`text`	Using a templating system is much easier than generating each page completely from code.

If we replace the variable references with the values, we get the following HTML:

```
<title> Template Test </title>
<h1><center>Template Test</center></h1>
<h2>An easier way to generate a page</h2>
Using a templating system is much easier than generating each page completely
   from code.
```

We do this all with a class called `Template`. A `Template` object holds the entire contents of a template file, and can be instantiated via the `instantiate()` method, which takes a HashMap as an argument. This HashMap contains the variable bindings that are to be used when instantiating the template.

Listing 9.17 shows the `Template` class.

Listing 9.17   Template.java

(See \Chapter9\Template.java)

```java
import java.io.*;
import java.util.*;
import java.util.regex.*;

public class Template
{
  private String content;

  public Template( File file ) throws IOException {
    // Read the entire file into memory
    FileInputStream fin = new FileInputStream( file );
    byte raw[] = new byte[(int)file.length()];
    int r = fin.read( raw );
    if (r != file.length()) {
      throw new IOException( "Can't fully read "+file );
    }
    fin.close();
```

● **The constructor reads the entire template file into a string**

```
    // Convert the raw data to a string
    content = new String( raw );
  }

  public String instantiate( HashMap mapping ) {
    String instantiation = content;

    for (Iterator it=mapping.keySet().iterator(); it.hasNext();) {
      String var = (String)it.next();
      String value = (String)mapping.get( var );

      Pattern pattern = Pattern.compile( "\\$"+var );
      Matcher matcher = pattern.matcher( instantiation );
      instantiation = matcher.replaceAll( value );
    }

    return instantiation;
  }
}
```

The HashMap argument contains the variable bindings

Apply each variable mapping in turn

Listing 9.18 contains a test program that uses Template. It reads a template file called test.thtml and instantiates the variable bindings from table 9.14.

Listing 9.18   TemplateTest.java

(See \Chapter9\ TemplateTest.java)

```
import java.io.*;
import java.util.*;

public class TemplateTest
{
  static private final String templateFile = "test.thtml";
  static private final String htmlFile = "test.html";

  static public void main( String args[] ) throws IOException {
    Template template = new Template( new File( templateFile ) );
```

Create the Template object

```
    HashMap mapping = new HashMap();
    mapping.put( "title", "Template Test" );
    mapping.put( "subtitle", "An easier way to generate a page" );
    mapping.put( "text", "Using a templating system is much "+
                 "easier than generating each page completely "+
                 "from code." );

    String instantiation = template.instantiate( mapping );
```

Create a set of variable mappings

Instantiate the template using the mappings

```
    FileOutputStream fout = new FileOutputStream( htmlFile );
    PrintWriter out = new PrintWriter( fout );
    out.println( instantiation );
    out.flush();
    fout.close();
  }
}
```

● Write the
result to
a file

In this example, we use the simple `Matcher.replaceAll()` method to do the finding and replacing, rather than the more cumbersome `Matcher.appendReplacement()`/`Matcher.appendTail()` method, because our application is simple. We want to replace *every* occurrence of the variable name with the variable value, and we don't need to do any special processing or evaluation between replacements.

9.5 *Example: a lexical analyzer*

Now we'll consider a program that does lexical analysis. A lexical analyzer (or *lexer*) is the low-level portion of a parser, which breaks an incoming stream of characters into *tokens*. Each token is a basic lexical unit of the language being parsed.

A lexical unit is a unit of a language specification larger than a single character, but smaller than an expression. In Java, lexical units include identifiers (any contiguous sequence of letters and digits, with a non-number at the start), integers (any sequence of digits), {, ++, and so on.

In the Unix world, the tools lex and flex have long been used to create lexers. Such tools read the specification for a lexer and generate a C program that carries out the lexical analysis. Thus, lex and flex are *lexical analyzer generators*. In this section, we will not be creating a lexical analyzer generator, but rather just a lexical analyzer. Such a program reads a specification and a file to analyze, and produces the analysis.

Our lexer uses a specification file that looks like the one in listing 9.19.

Listing 9.19   example.lx

(See \Chapter9\example.lx)

```
whitespace    \s+
whitespace    (^$)
ident         [a-zA-Z][a-zA-Z0-9]+
lparen        \(
rparen        \)
lcbrace       \{
rcbrace       \}
semicolon     ;
comma         ,
```

```
period        \.
equals        =
```

Each line represents a single *rule* of the lexical analyzer, and contains two elements. The second element of the rule is a regex defining a category of token. The first element of the rule is the name of that category. Thus, any substring of the input that matches the regex [a-zA-Z][a-zA-Z0-9]+ is a token of type *ident*.

Actually, not just any substring will be matched thusly. The analysis proceeds from the start of the file, and at each step, the lexer attempts to match each of the regexes to the current string. The regex that matches the longest substring is taken as the correct match, and the matched substring becomes the next token. This continues until the file is exhausted. If, at any point, none of the regexes match the input, this is considered a syntax error, and the analysis is halted.

The configuration file in listing 9.19 is a portion of a simple lexer for Java. Listing 9.20 shows some sample input—nothing too fancy, because our lexer is incomplete.

Listing 9.20   input.txt

(See\Chapter9\input.txt)
```
public LexerRule rule() {
  return rule;
}
```

Let's see what our lexer does with this. The Lexer class has a main() routine that can be used to do a quick lexical analysis of a file. It takes two arguments—the specification file, and the file to be processed:

```
java Lexer example.lx input.txt
```

The main() routine just zips through the file, breaking it into tokens, and printing the tokens to System.out, as shown in listing 9.21.

Listing 9.21   output.txt

(See\Chapter9\output.txt)
```
Parsed example.lx
["public" at line 1, column 1, rule:[ident [a-zA-Z][a-zA-Z0-9]+]]
[" " at line 1, column 7, rule:[whitespace \s+]]
["LexerRule" at line 1, column 8, rule:[ident [a-zA-Z][a-zA-Z0-9]+]]
[" " at line 1, column 17, rule:[whitespace \s+]]
["rule" at line 1, column 18, rule:[ident [a-zA-Z][a-zA-Z0-9]+]]
["(" at line 1, column 22, rule:[lparen \(]]
```

```
[")" at line 1, column 23, rule:[rparen \)]]
[" " at line 1, column 24, rule:[whitespace \s+]]
["{" at line 1, column 25, rule:[lcbrace \{]]
["  " at line 2, column 1, rule:[whitespace \s+]]
["return" at line 2, column 3, rule:[ident [a-zA-Z][a-zA-Z0-9]+]]
[" " at line 2, column 9, rule:[whitespace \s+]]
["rule" at line 2, column 10, rule:[ident [a-zA-Z][a-zA-Z0-9]+]]
[";" at line 2, column 14, rule:[semicolon ;]]
["}" at line 3, column 1, rule:[rcbrace \}]]
```

Each line of the output shows a number of things. First, we have the actual substring of the input file. For example, on the first (boldfaced) line, we have public. This is followed by the location of this string as a line number and a column number within that line. Finally, we have the rule, including the regex that defines it.

Note that the strings at the start of each line contain every character in the file—nothing is left out. Any character that didn't fit into a string matched by one of the lexical rules would be a syntax error, and the lexer never would have gotten past it—the lexer would have reported the error and halted.

It is common in many lexers to ignore white space tokens, but our lexer is relatively simple—we have added a provision for a rule that should be ignored, so the white space is included in the output.

Let's take a look at the source for our lexer. It is made up of three classes:

- LexerRule—A single rule of the lexer (see listing 9.22)
- LexerToken—A single token from an input stream, matched by a LexerRule (see listing 9.23)
- Lexer—The main program that parses the specification file and performs the lexical analysis (see listing 9.24)

Listing 9.22   LexerRule.java

(See \Chapter9\LexerRule.java)

```java
import java.util.regex.*;

class LexerRule {
    // The name of the lexical category that this rule matches
    private String name;

    // The regex used for matching
    private String regex;

    // A pre-compiled Pattern object, kept to save time
    private Pattern pattern;
```

```
/**
 * Create a LexerRule
 */
public LexerRule( String name, String regex ) {
  this.name = name;
  this.regex = regex;
}

/**
 * Return the category name
 */
public String name() {
  return name;
}

/**
 * Return the regex defining the rule
 */
public String regex() {
  return regex;
}

/**
 * Return the Pattern object.  Create one if
 * it hasn't been created already
 */
public Pattern pattern() {
  if (pattern == null) {
    pattern = Pattern.compile( regex );
  }
  return pattern;
}

/**
 * Return a string representation of the rule
 */
public String toString() {
  return "["+name+" "+regex+"]";
}
}
```

A LexerRule combines the category name and the regex that defines it

Only compile the pattern object once, and keep it around

Listing 9.23   LexerToken.java

(See \Chapter9\LexerToken.java)

```
public class LexerToken {
  private LexerRule rule;
  private String text;
  private int line;
  private int column;

  /**
```

```
 * Create a LexerToken
 */
public LexerToken( LexerRule rule, String text,
                   int line, int column ) {
  this.rule = rule;
  this.text = text;
  this.line = line;
  this.column = column;
}

/**
 * Return the rule that matched this token
 */
public LexerRule rule() {
  return rule;
}

/**
 * Return the text matched by this token
 */
public String text() {
  return text;
}

/**
 * Return a string representation of the token
 */
public String toString() {
  return "["+"\""+text+"\""+" at line "+line+", column "+column+",
 rule:"+rule+"]";
}
```

The LexerToken contains the rule, the text, and the location of the text in the file

Listing 9.24   Lexer.java

(See \Chapter9\Lexer.java)

```
import java.io.*;
import java.util.*;
import java.util.regex.*;

public class Lexer
{
  static private final String lxRuleString =
    "^\\s*(\\S+)\\s+(\\S+)\\s*$";

  // Set of rules for this lexer
  private LexerRule rules[] = new LexerRule[0];

  // The current input
  private FileInputStream currentInputStream;
  private LineNumberReader currentReader;
  private String currentFilename;
  private String currentLine;
  private int currentColumn;
}
```

Regex for parsing the specification file

Keep track of our position within the input file

```java
public Lexer( String specfile ) throws IOException {
  loadSpecification( specfile );
}

private void loadSpecification( String specfile )
    throws IOException {
  // Read the specification file line-by-line
  FileInputStream fin = new FileInputStream( specfile );
  InputStreamReader isr = new InputStreamReader( fin );
  LineNumberReader lnr = new LineNumberReader( isr );

  // Pattern for "parsing" each line of the spec file
  Pattern lxRule = Pattern.compile( lxRuleString );

  // Temporarily stores the lists we find
  ArrayList rulesAL = new ArrayList();

  while (true) {
    String line = lnr.readLine();

    // Read until file is exhausted
    if (line==null)
      break;

    Matcher matcher = lxRule.matcher( line );
    if (matcher.matches()) {
      // Add rule to the list of rules
      String name = matcher.group( 1 );
      String regex = matcher.group( 2 );
      LexerRule lr = new LexerRule( name, regex );
      rulesAL.add( lr );
    } else {
      // Syntax error in the specification file
      System.err.println( "Syntax error in "+specfile+" line "+
                          lnr.getLineNumber()+": " );
      System.err.println( "  "+line );
      System.exit( 1 );
    }
  }

  // Don't forget to close the file
  fin.close();

  // Convert the list of rules to an array, and save it
  rules = (LexerRule[])rulesAL.toArray( rules );

  System.out.println( "Parsed "+specfile );
}
public void setSource( String filename ) throws IOException {
  currentInputStream = new FileInputStream( filename );
  InputStreamReader isr =
    new InputStreamReader( currentInputStream );
  currentReader = new LineNumberReader( isr );
```

● **Load rules from the specification file**

● **Each rule is made of a lexical category name and a regex**

● **Tell the Lexer where to get input from**

```
      currentFilename = filename;

      // Position within the file
      currentLine = null;
      currentColumn = 1;
   }
   public LexerToken getNextToken() throws IOException {
      if (currentLine==null || currentLine.length()==0) {
         // If the current line is exhausted, read the next one
         currentLine = currentReader.readLine();

         if (currentLine==null) {
            // If there are no more lines, we're done
            currentInputStream.close();
            currentReader = null;
            currentFilename = null;
            return null;
         }

         currentColumn = 1;
      }

      // Match the next token
      LexerToken token = null;

      // The end of the next token, within the line
      int tokenEnd = -1;

      // The length of the rule that matches the most characters
      // from the input
      int longestMatchLength=-1;

      for (int i=0; i<rules.length; ++i) {
         LexerRule rule = rules[i];

         // The pattern for this rule
         Pattern pattern = rule.pattern();
         Matcher matcher = pattern.matcher( currentLine );

         if (matcher.lookingAt()) {
            int matchLength = matcher.end();
            if (matchLength > longestMatchLength) {
               // This match is the longest so far; save info about it
               longestMatchLength = matchLength;
               String text = matcher.group( 0 );
               int lineNumber = currentReader.getLineNumber();
               token = new LexerToken( rule, text,
                                       lineNumber, currentColumn );
               tokenEnd = matchLength;
            }
         }
      }
      // If we didn't match anything, it's an error
```

Return the next token from the input stream ●

Scan the file line-by-line, and quit when no more lines are left ●

Find the rule that matches the longest substring of the input ➊

```
        if (token == null) {
          System.err.println( "Syntax error in "+currentFilename+
                              " line "+currentReader.getLineNumber()+
                              ", column "+currentColumn+": " );
          System.out.println( "  "+currentLine );
          System.exit( 1 );

          // Never reached
          assert false;

          // For the compiler
          return null;
        } else {
          // We matched something, so we'll return a token.

          // But first, skip past the current token so we're
          // ready to scan for the next one
          currentColumn += tokenEnd;
          currentLine = currentLine.substring( tokenEnd );

          // Now, return the token
          return token;

        }
      }

      static public void main( String args[] ) throws IOException {
        if (args.length != 2) {
          System.err.println( "Usage: Lexer <lxfile> <input>" );
          System.exit( 1 );
        }

        String specfile = args[0];
        String inputfile = args[1];

        Lexer lexer = new Lexer( specfile );
        lexer.setSource( inputfile );

        while (true) {
          LexerToken token = lexer.getNextToken();
          if (token == null)
            break;

          System.out.println( token );
        }
      }
    }
```

Skip past the token we just matched, getting ready for the next match

Return the token we found

❶ We don't just want to find a rule that matches the next characters of the input; we want to match the longest substring of the input that we can. This is called *greedy* lexical analysis, and this is generally how it is done.

To find the longest match, we try every rule against the input. For each match, we note the length, and if it's longer than the previous longest match, we record this one as the longest match. When we're done, we have either the longest match or no match at all.

The `Lexer` program makes use of regexes in a way the previous examples didn't—the regexes are not constants built into the program but are constructed at runtime from strings read from a file. Data-driven parsing is very powerful technique.

This `Lexer` could easily be combined with a Java-based parser to provide a lexer/parser suite not unlike those used under Unix—lex and yacc (or flex and bison).

9.6   *Summary*

The rise of the Web has created a greater demand for systems based on text processing, and regular expressions have become an incredibly important tool. Most large software projects have their own regex system, or make use of a freely available library. With the addition of regexes to the core Java platform, Java programmers should make use of this valuable tool.

The Preferences API

10

This chapter covers

- Purpose and scope of the API
- Comparison with other persistence mechanisms
- Reading and writing data
- Change listeners

The Preferences API, in the `java.util.prefs` package, gives the programmer a convenient way to save and recall configuration information. This information can be saved during one invocation of a program and recalled during a later invocation—that is, the information is *persistent* across invocations. Additionally, this information can be shared between invocations, if desired.

In a sense, the Preferences API could be considered to be misnamed, since it can be used to store any kind of information, not just preference data. However, because of size limitations, and because the Preferences API makes no claims of efficiency, it should not be used as a general database. It is best used for configuration information—small pieces of information that are read and written one or a few times per program invocation, and which need to be saved between invocations. Generally, data stored in the Preferences API consists of a few values that describe the configuration of the program as customized explicitly or implicitly by the user, or the configuration of the software installation itself.

10.1   What the Preferences API is for

Looked at abstractly, the Preferences API is just another way to store data. Java already has a number of ways of doing this, and more are being added all the time. It's important to be clear about what the Preferences API is good for, and what it is not good for.

10.1.1   Simple Preferences API example

Suppose you've written a program that has a number of independent windows, and you want to save their locations on screen as a convenience to the user. That way, once he has arranged the windows the way he likes them, they will be displayed that way the next time he runs the program.

Here is how this can be done with the Preferences API:

```
import java.util.prefs.*;

// ...

Preferences prefs = Preferences.userNodeForPackage( getClass() );
prefs.putInt( "main window x", mainWindowX );
prefs.putInt( "main window y", mainWindowY );
prefs.putInt( "listing window x", listingWindowX );
prefs.putInt( "listing window y", listingWindowY );
```

And here is how these values can be retrieved during a later invocation:

```
Preferences prefs = Preferences.userNodeForPackage( getClass() );
mainWindowX = prefs.getInt( "main window x", 200 );
mainWindowY = prefs.getInt( "main window y", 200 );
```

```
listingWindowX = prefs.getInt( "listing window x", 400 );
listingWindowY = prefs.getInt( "listing window y", 400 );
```

Note that the names of the preference values can have spaces—this is a signal that these names should be thought of as human-readable, and even user-friendly. The Preferences API is to be used for this kind of data.

10.1.2 *Appropriate applications of the Preferences API*

As mentioned previously, the Preferences API can store just about any kind of data. However, it isn't intended for all possible data storage purposes. Data that is being managed using the Preferences API should meet the following criteria:

- The data should be small.
- The data should apply to a single user, or to a single installation.
- The data should need to be stored between invocations.
- The data should only be accessed occasionally.
- The data should not be critical.
- The data should not be essential to the functioning of the application.

Data that meets these criteria is often called *preference* data. This is in contrast to *application* data, which is defined as data that is central to the operation of an application, or that is created or generated by the user in the normal operation of the application.

These criteria are important enough that some elaboration is in order:

The data should be small

This is an intentionally vague statement. The Preferences API specifies a maximum size of 8,192 bytes per value, and so there is a hard limit to what can be stored in a single slot. In addition to this, good judgment should be used. For example, in a word processing program, the Preferences API would be used to store the user's preferred font, but it would not be used to store the contents of a document that is created.

The amount of data should not vary widely during the use of the program. In theory, you *could*, for example, use the Preferences API to store telephone numbers in a Rolodex-style application. But this data could consist of 20 phone numbers, or it could consist of 20 million phone numbers. No existing implementation of this API is capable of dealing efficiently with that much data.

The data should apply to a single user, or to a single installation

The Preferences API is intended to store information that pertains to a particular user, such as changes a user has made to the configuration settings of the program. Thus, in a multiwindow chat program, the positions of the windows might be stored using the Preferences API, but global server log data would be stored in the filesystem.

The data should need to be stored between invocations

This is, in a sense, the whole point. While the API could be used to store data during a single invocation of the program, this would be overkill, since such data could be stored more easily in variables.

It is very common to reach for the Preferences API precisely because you've realized that a particular piece of data, which previously was a regular program variable, needs to be remembered between invocations.

As an example, a game server would not use the Preferences API to store the current scores of players as they are playing the game, but it might store the high-score lists.

The data should only be accessed occasionally

This is another intentionally vague statement. There is, of course, no limit to how often you can access data stored via the Preferences API. However, the API is not intended primarily to be fast. It is only intended to store its data reliably.

It would be common for an application to read configuration data via the Preferences API during startup and never use the API again. Just as commonly, a program might write out changes to configuration values either at shutdown or at the moment the user requests the changes. Some applications, such as servers, might be instructed to reread configuration data from time to time, allowing the applications to be reconfigured without having to shut down and start up again. In other applications, configuration data might be read or written once in a while, such as every time a user connects to the system.

The Preferences API is not intended to store data that is updated thousands of times a second. While a fast enough computer could possibly handle it, such data is really best served by a dedicated database engine or a very fast filesystem.

As an example, a sophisticated web-server logging module might use the Preferences API to store the configuration determining which data should be logged, but it should not use the API to store the actual log data.

The data should not be critical

Applications that store data in the filesystem, or in a database, should continue to do so. These are the places where users and system administrators expect to find data, and the Preferences API is not meant to change that. Corrupted Preferences data should be considered a loss of configuration data, not of application data.

As an example, a program that is used to perform lengthy mathematical calculations might use the Preferences API to store the user's choice of which of several calculation methods to use, but the results of the calculations should be stored in the filesystem, or in a database.

The data should not be essential to the functioning of the application

It is an explicit design goal of the Preferences API that it should not require access to the underlying data store for it to function properly. Configuration information is not considered essential to the functioning of an application. Often, it consists of settings that are entered manually by the user and then remembered for convenience. Such information can be entered again, if necessary. Thus, any data that is central to the execution of the program should not be stored in the Preferences API.

As an example, you might use the Preferences API to store a user's address and phone number if the application were a word processor or spreadsheet, but you would not use it to store such information if the application were an address-and-telephone database.

10.1.3 Design goals of the Preferences API

The following is a list of goals that inspired the design of the Preferences API. These goals distinguish this API from other persistence mechanisms:

- The API should provide a hierarchical, tree-like data store.
- The API should store primitive data types.
- The API should guarantee back-end neutrality.
- There should be no need to remember locations of files.
- The API should not require explicit saving and loading of data.
- The API should be permitted to operate asynchronously.
- Data from different packages or applications should not interfere with each other.
- The API should work in a multithreaded environment.
- The API should work in a multiprocess environment.
- The API should work in a multilanguage environment.

- The API should provide only the minimum concurrency protection.
- The API should work even if the backing store is not available.
- The API should supply per-user data and system-wide data.

We'll take a closer look at each of these goals, because they go a long way toward clarifying when and how this API should be used:

The API should provide a hierarchical, tree-like data store

As we see in section 10.3, the data model used by the Preferences API is *hierarchical*, as opposed to relational or flat. This provides the programmer with the best trade-off between simplicity and flexibility.

The API should store primitive data types

The API provides direct support for storing strings, numerical types (integers, floats, doubles), booleans, and small byte-arrays. There is no support for serialized objects.

The API should guarantee back-end neutrality

It is an explicit and critical feature of the Preferences API that it can and should be implemented differently on different systems. The implementation itself is divided into a system-independent portion that is identical on all systems, and a system-dependent back end.

Unlike most database engines, the Preferences API should behave identically on all systems. This means that any differences in the data-storage capabilities must be hidden by the system-dependent layer. There are no optional methods (but see the discussion of stored defaults in 10.6). Using the API's import/export facility, it should be possible to export a preferences database from one system and import it cleanly into another system.

The repository where the data is actually stored is called the *backing store*. This is distinguished from the Preferences API, or *front end*, which enforces the structures and procedures in a platform-independent way. The backing store might have completely different semantics from the Preferences API, in which case it is the responsibility of the implementation to build the desired semantics on top of the semantics of the back end.

There should be no need to remember locations of files

One of the disadvantages of the older `java.util.Properties` method of storing configuration data is that the programmer was required to find and load the properties files. This made it harder to share configuration data between applications, or to establish conventions for configuration data, because there was no specification telling the applications where the properties files were located.

The Preferences API deals with this by creating a global database whose location is irrelevant to the programmer.

The API should not require explicit saving and loading of data

Using `java.util.Properties`, the programmer would use get and set methods to access data values, and load and store methods to commit these values to disk. In the Preferences API, only the get and set methods are needed—loading and storing are taken care of automatically (although the API provides `flush()` and `sync()` methods—see sections 10.4.15 and 10.4.16).

The API should be permitted to operate asynchronously

The implementation is allowed to defer the writing of data values. The actual API writing calls can return immediately without the actual data being written to the backing store. This allows for backing stores that are slow or only intermittently available.

Data from different packages or applications should not interfere with each other

The user is encouraged by the API to store configuration data separately for each package. However, this is not enforced, which means that it is also easy to share data between packages or applications.

The API should work in a multithreaded environment

The API should be thread-safe.

The API should work in a multiprocess environment

The API should work even if multiple instances of the Preferences API, within multiple JVMs, are accessing the same backing store.

The API should work in a multilanguage environment

The API should work even if programs written in other languages, using other libraries, are accessing the same backing store.

The API should provide only the minimum concurrency protection

Despite the fact that the Preferences API must support the existence of multiple writers to the same backing store, it is not intended to supply sophisticated concurrency mechanisms. There is no support for transactions of any kind. Atomicity is at the level of the single key/value pair. There is no way to ensure that a collection of multiple changes are committed either all together, or not at all.

Within a multithreaded Java program, a sequence of accesses in multiple threads is defined as having the same semantics as they would if they were carried out in a single thread—although the order of these accesses is not specified. This is really just a fancy way of saying that no single access will be interrupted by any other single access, even if the accesses are coming from threads that are active at the same time.

The API should work even if the backing store is not available

It is commonly understood that an application should continue to work even if its configuration files are deleted. In such a situation, the application should run as best it can using a default configuration. The Preferences API is designed to reflect this.

The default implementations that come with the standard JDK packages will likely be such that configuration data is always available to applications. However, it is quite conceivable that the implementation for a small wireless device might store configuration data on a central server. In the event that the device cannot reach the central server, its applications should still be able to run.

The API should supply per-user data and system-wide data

The Preferences API recognizes that some configuration data is configuration for the *system*, and some is for the *user*. Following this distinction, the preferences database consists of a section for system data, and a section for user data. There is a separate user database for each user, and the selection between these is handled automatically and invisibly by the API.

10.2   *Knowing when to use the Preferences API*

As mentioned earlier, there are many ways to save data in Java. The Preferences API isn't even the only way to save preference-style data. However, for most data of this kind, the Preferences API is the new *definitive* method for storing such data. In this section, we look at some competing methods and compare them with the Preferences API.

10.2.1   *Comparison with java.util.Properties*

The Preferences API package is meant to replace "most common uses of Properties," according to the *Preferences API Design FAQ*. In general, you should think of the java.util.prefs package as the new version of the java.util.Properties class.

The main deficiencies of the Properties class, in relation to the Preferences API, are as follows:

- Properties only deals with string data.

- `Properties` requires the programmer to load and save the data to and from a file or stream.

10.2.2 *Comparison with JNDI*

A thorough comparison between the Java Naming and Directory Interface (JNDI) and the Preferences API package is beyond the scope of this book. Suffice it to say that while JNDI can certainly help you accomplish the same goals as the Preferences API, it does so with the conceptual and computational overhead of a sophisticated system consisting of many classes spread through a number of packages. The Preferences API is intended to be available on any platform, no matter how small, and is meant to be easy to use. It is also meant to be used in situations where it's okay if the data isn't available—which may not be the case for your application.

10.3 *Understanding the data hierarchy*

The Preferences API provides a particular *model* for the data it stores. The model is loosely based on a filesystem, but has *names* and *values* rather than *filenames* and *file contents*. The API provides two separate *trees* of data—a system tree and a user tree.

10.3.1 *Tree-like structure*

The Preferences API provides a *tree-like* data model. This is in contrast to other common database structures, such as *relational* and *flat-file*. The database itself is structured as a set of nodes, and each node can contain a set of *key/value pairs*. A node can contain other nodes—a node that contains another node is called the *parent* of that node, and the contained node is called the *child* of the parent node.

As we'll see in section 10.3.3, there are two distinct trees—a *user* tree and a *system* tree.

10.3.2 *Key/value pairs*

Each key/value pair is an *association* between the name (the key) and the value. You can store a value under a name, and then use that name later to retrieve the stored value.

A name must meet the following requirements:

- It must be a primitive Java string
- It cannot be the null string
- It cannot contain the character "/"

A value must be one of the following primitive Java types:

- string (`String`)
- boolean (`boolean`)
- integer (`int`)
- long integer (`long`)
- floating-point (`float`)
- double-precision floating-point (`double`)
- byte array (`byte[]`)

Furthermore, any value that has the potential to be large, such as a string or byte array, must be less than `Preferences.MAX_VALUE_LENGTH` (8,192) bytes in size.

10.3.3 *System vs. user*

As was mentioned previously, the preferences database is divided into two main sections. The *user* tree is used to store configuration data on a per-user basis, while the *system* tree is used to store configuration data on a per-system (or per-installation) basis.

What this means in practice is that a program has access during its execution to two distinct data trees. These trees are functionally identical, with identical APIs. They differ in the kind of data that is stored in them, and in the way they are made available to a particular user.

There is a user tree for every single user on the system. A running program only has access to one of these user trees at a time—the user tree corresponding to the current user. At the same time, the program has access to the system tree. There is only one system tree, and it is shared among all running applications in the system.

It is important to note that the system tree is in no way protected from modification. The user/system distinction does not provide any form of security.

10.3.4 *Definition of a user*

The Preferences API does not specify any kind of formal definition of what a *user* is, nor does it involve itself with any kind of user authentication. It does not even require that a user have a name. All that is required is that the `userNodeForPackage()` and `userRoot()` methods be defined.

It is assumed that "user" will be defined in a system-dependent way, and that there is a way of determining the user at runtime. There are no security protections for this determination except as supplied by the underlying implementation.

10.3.5 Pathnames

As mentioned previously, both the user and system halves of the preferences database are structured like trees, with nodes that can contain key/value pairs and other nodes. This structure is designed to resemble that of a filesystem, and like a filesystem, each element in a tree has an *absolute pathname*, which specifies its precise location within the tree. A node or key/value pair can also have a *relative pathname*, which specifies its location in relation to another node within the same tree.

Figure 10.1 shows an example configuration of nodes and key/value pairs. These nodes and values have the absolute pathnames listed in table 10.1.

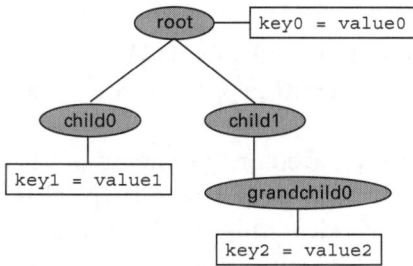

Figure 10.1   An example configuration of nodes and key/value pairs. Nodes are shown as ovals, while key/value pairs are shown as rectangles.

Relative to child1, the nodes and values have the relative pathnames listed in table 10.2.

Table 10.1   Each node in figure 10.1 has an absolute pathname. This pathname describes the location of the node in relation to the root of the preferences tree.

Node	Absolute pathname
root	/
child0	/child0
child1	/child1
grandchild0	/child1/grandchild0

Table 10.2 Nodes also have relative pathnames, which show their
relationship to other nodes, rather than to the root of the tree.

Node	Relative pathname
`child1`	`" "`
`grandchild0`	`grandchild0`

Note that there is no equivalent to the "`..`" found in some operating systems. All relative pathnames go toward the leaves of the tree.

10.3.6 *Per-package subtrees*

The Preferences API encourages the programmer to subdivide the preference trees by package. This helps keep the data for different programs from interfering with each other.

Each package name can be turned into an absolute pathname by changing each "`.`" to a "`/`" and adding a "`/`" at the front of the string. For example, `java.awt.font` becomes `/java/awt/font`. Code within the `java.awt.font` package would then store its subnodes and key/value pairs underneath this node. This is described in more detail in the next section.

Note that this naming convention is just that—a convention. However, as we'll see, this convention is employed by the Preferences API itself, in methods like `user-NodeForPackage()` and `systemNodeForPackage()`, so you should stick to it unless you have a good reason not to.

10.4 *Using the API*

In this section, we'll take a look at the basic usage of the Preferences API. For the most part, the examples in the following sections use the user preferences tree. Unless otherwise noted, the examples work identically when used with nodes from the system tree.

10.4.1 *Traversing the data hierarchy*

Before you can read or write any data using the Preferences API, you must get your hands on a `Preferences` object. This object corresponds to a single node in a preferences tree, and it gives you direct access to the key/value pairs within that node. It also allows you to acquire `Preferences` objects for other nodes, particularly the node's children.

Once you have access to a preferences node, you can read and write values, and use it to get access to children, grandchildren, and so on. Remember that the Preferences API data hierarchy is a lot like a filesystem. When using a filesystem, your application is free to create subdirectories, subsubdirectories, and so on, and to store any data in these directories, using any filenames. Analogously, with the Preferences API, your application is free to create child nodes, grandchild nodes, and so on, and to store any values in these nodes, using any keys. Remember, however, that the Preferences API provides *two* separate data hierarchies—a user hierarchy and a system hierarchy. The former is used for user-specific data, while the latter is used for non-user-specific (or system- or application-wide) data. In this section, we'll take a look at the methods used to get access to different nodes in the data hierarchy.

There are a number of ways of getting a Preferences object. The simplest way is to use the userRoot() method, which provides access to the root of the user preferences tree. We'll look at other methods for getting access to a node later in this section. (All of these methods have analogous system methods.)

```
Preferences root = Preferences.userRoot();
```

This Preferences object corresponds to the path "/".

Once you have your hands on the Preferences object for a particular node, you can use it to gain access to descendants of that node. This is done using the node() method, which takes a relative or absolute pathname and returns a Preferences object.

```
Preferences child0 = root.node( "child0" );
```

Since root corresponds to the path "/", child0 corresponds to the path "/child0". The following line has the same result as the preceding line:

```
Preferences child0 = root.node( "/child0" );
```

You can call the node() method from *any* Preferences object, not just root. By doing this you can use any Preferences object to get access to one of its children:

```
Preferences child1 = root.node( "child1" );
Preferences grandchild0 = child1.node( "grandchild0" );
```

The object grandchild0 corresponds to the absolute path "/child1/grandchild0".

Note that when you use an absolute path, the path of the old object does not matter. The following four lines are equivalent:

```
Preferences grandchild0 = child1.node( "grandchild0" );

Preferences grandchild0 = child1.node( "/child1/grandchild0" );

Preferences grandchild0 = root.node( "/child1/grandchild0" );

Preferences grandchild0 = grandchild0.node( "/child1/grandchild0" );
```

Each package is given its own subtree within the data hierarchy. The most common place for Java code to store its data is in the subtree corresponding to its package, and you can get access to a package's node using the userNodeForPackage() method, which is a static method of Preferences:

```
Preferences prefs = Preferences.userNodeForPackage( getClass() );
```

Note that you must supply a class to this method. userNodeForPackage() gets the package name of the supplied class and turns this into an absolute pathname. This pathname is then used to get access to the preferences node. Thus, the following two code fragments are equivalent:

```
Preferences prefs = Preferences.userRoot().node( "/java/util/prefs" );

package java.util.prefs;
//...
Preferences prefs = Preferences.userNodeForPackage( getClass() );
```

In the second of the preceding code fragments, we use the getClass() method (shown in boldface) to get the Class object corresponding to the class containing this code. This is passed to the userNodeForPackage() method in order to get the Preferences node corresponding to the package containing this class.

However, you can't use the getClass() method if you're writing a static method; in this case, you can use the <Classname>.class syntax to get the Class object associated with a static method:

```
public class MyClass
{
    static private void method() {
      Preferences prefs = Preferences.userNodeForPackage( MyClass.class );
      System.out.println( prefs );
    }
}
```

Just as you can get the user node for a particular package, you can get the system node for that package using systemNodeForPackage():

```
Preferences prefs = Preferences.systemNodeForPackage( getClass() );
```

As mentioned earlier, the system node for a package can be used in the same way as the user node, but it is meant for data that is not user-specific.

In Java, code that is not assigned to a particular package is placed in the *default package*. Within the Preferences API, the absolute pathname for this package is "/<unnamed>".

10.4.2 *Reading and writing values*

Once you have a `Preferences` object, you can use it to read and write values. The following fragment writes an integer to the `Preferences` node for the current class package:

```
int windowX = 250;
Preferences prefs = Preferences.userNodeForPackage( this );
prefs.putInt( "window x", windowX );
```

Getting the value back out later is done as follows:

```
Preferences prefs = Preferences.userNodeForPackage( this );
int windowX = prefs.getInt( "window x", 300 );
```

Note that `getInt()` takes a second argument—this is a *default* value, which will be returned from `getInt()` if there isn't a value for `window x`. Default values are *always* used in any `get()` call. (See section 10.4.7 for more information.)

The same thing can be done with other types:

```
boolean showGrid = false;
Preferences prefs = Preferences.userNodeForPackage( this );
prefs.putBoolean( "show grid", showGrid );

Preferences prefs = Preferences.userNodeForPackage( this );
float gravity = prefs.getFloat( "gravity", 9.8 );
```

There is a `get()` method for each basic type. Note that the values are always stored as strings and that type checking is not performed. Values that are the wrong type, and that therefore cannot be parsed, will trigger the appropriate format exception.

10.4.3 *Allowable types*

Table 10.3 shows the types that are directly supported by the Preferences API, along with the methods that read and write them. Note that all of the types are primitive Java types except for strings (which are objects) and byte arrays (which are arrays).

Table 10.3   The Preferences API has `get()` and `put()` methods for each of the basic types, as well as for string and byte array types.

Type	Java name	Reader method	Writer method
string	`String`	`get()`	`put()`
byte array	`byte[]`	`getByteArray()`	`putByteArray()`
boolean	`boolean`	`getBoolean()`	`putBoolean()`
floating-point	`float`	`getFloat()`	`putFloat()`
double-precision floating-point	`double`	`getDouble()`	`putDouble()`
integer	`int`	`getInt()`	`putInt()`
long integer	`long`	`getLong()`	`putLong()`

10.4.4   Allowable keys

You aren't required to take your key string from the name of the variables being written. The following lines of code are all valid:

```
int windowX = 250;
Preferences prefs = Preferences.userNodeForPackage( this );

prefs.putInt( "windowX", windowX );

prefs.putInt( "window x", windowX );
prefs.putInt( "quiet please", windowX );
```

All that matters is that your application use the same key for reading and writing. A key can be any valid Java `String` with a length less than `Preferences.MAX_KEY_-LENGTH`, which is 80.

10.4.5   Allowable values

For the primitive Java types, any value is valid. String and byte array values must not be `null`.

In some key/value storage systems, storing a particular value is equivalent to removing that value entirely. This is not the case for the Preferences API. In keeping with the semantics of the `java.util.Hashtable` class, storing a value of `null` to a node will throw a `NullPointerException`.

Values must be smaller than `Preferences.MAX_VALUE_LENGTH` (8,192 bytes) in their stored representations. It can safely be assumed that the primitive types (`int`, `boolean`, `float`, `double`, and `long`) always have representations within this limit. String values can be compared against this limit using their `length()`

method, but remember that a Unicode character can require more than a single byte for its encoding.

Byte array values are encoded using the Base64 encoding as specified in RFC 2045, section 6.8, with one change. In practice, this means that the encoding of the byte array will be longer than the length of the byte array, as given by the expression `array.length`. According to the documentation, a byte array must be less than, or equal to, three-fourths of the value of MAX_VALUE_LENGTH. To determine whether a byte array is too long, use the following fragment:

```
if (array.length >= (MAX_VALUE_LENGTH*3/4)) {
  // ...
} else {
  // ...
}
```

Attempting to store a value that will not fit causes an `IllegalArgumentException` to be thrown.

10.4.6 *Allowable node names*

Node names must be smaller than `Preferences.MAX_NAME_LENGTH` (80 bytes) and cannot contain a "/" character. The node name of the root node is the empty string; no other node can have the empty string as a node name. These are the only restrictions on node names.

10.4.7 *Default values*

Each `get()` method takes a default value as the second argument. If the preferences database does not contain a value corresponding to the given key, or if the preferences database is not available, the default value is returned.

In the following example, we assume that the database does not contain a value corresponding to the key "window x":

```
Preferences prefs = Preferences.userNodeForPackage( this );
int windowX = prefs.getInt( "window x", 200 );
```

This code will result in the variable `windowX` containing the value `200`.

Default values are mandatory for *every* `get()` method. This is done to strongly encourage programmers not to assume that preferences will be available, and to ensure that their program works properly in such situations. The burden of creating reasonable defaults is placed on the programmer.

10.4.8 Removing values

Values can be removed entirely from the nodes that contain them by using the remove() method:

```
Preferences prefs = Preferences.userNodeForPackage( this );
prefs.putInt( "window x", 200 );
int windowX = prefs.getInt( "window x", 300 );
prefs.remove( "window x" );
int windowX = prefs.getInt( "window x", 300 );
```

Removing a value is not the same as putting an empty string or zero-valued integer there. Attempting to store a value of null to a preferences object will throw a NullPointerException.

The Preferences API also provides the clear() method. Calling this method is equivalent to calling remove() on all of the keys currently existing in the node:

```
Preferences prefs = Preferences.userNodeForPackage( this );
prefs.putInt( "window x", 200 );
int windowX = prefs.getInt( "window x", 300 );
prefs.clear();
int windowX = prefs.getInt( "window x", 300 );
```

Note that you do not need to specify the type of the value you are removing—the remove() method removes the value regardless of the type that was stored there.

10.4.9 Iterating through the values in a node

The method keys() returns an array containing the keys of all the key/value pairs in the node. This method can be used to iterate through the contents of a node:

```
Preferences uroot = Preferences.userRoot();
String keys[] = uroot.keys();
for (int i=0; i<keys.length; ++i) {
    System.out.println( keys[i]+" "+uroot.get( keys[i], "" ) );
}
```

Even though a node can contain both key/value pairs and child nodes, the keys() method only returns keys of key/value pairs. It does not return node names of child nodes.

10.4.10 Distinguishing between user and system nodes

As was mentioned in section 10.3.3, user and system nodes store information in the same way, and differ only in what they are used for and how they are accessible to different users. In fact, in most implementations, it's safe to assume that both kinds of nodes are implemented by the same Java class, which means you can't necessarily tell them apart by finding out what classes they are implemented by.

As a result, the Preferences API contains a method that allows you to distinguish between user and system nodes. This method is called `isUserNode()`, and it returns a boolean.

Here is an example of its use:

```
Preferences prefs = Preferences.userNodeForPackage( this );
if (prefs.isUserNode()) {
  // ...
} else {
  // ...
}
```

In this example, it is already obvious that the node is a user node, because of the call to `userNodeForPackage`. This will not always be the case, however—there will be some times when a node has been stored or passed to a method that does not know whether the node is a user node or a system node.

There aren't many situations where you would care what kind of node you had—and fewer still where, if you did care, you wouldn't know. You might care if you were writing utility code that dealt with preference data in some way, rather than just reading and writing preference data—such code might take a node as an argument to a method. If, for example, you wanted to impose a policy of only modifying values in user nodes, and treating system nodes as read-only, then you'd need to check the type before you wrote any data.

10.4.11 *Node names and paths*

Every node corresponds to an absolute path. This path can be accessed using the `absolutePath()` method. Each node also has a *node name* that corresponds to the last element in that node's absolute path, and that can be accessed via the `name()` method. (In the following code fragment, the output of each `System.out.println()` line is shown in bold italic following that line.)

```
Preferences root = Preferences.userRoot();
Preferences child1 = root.node( "child1" );
String child1Path = child1.absolutePath();
System.out.println( child1Path );
             //  prints out:    /child1
String child1Name = child1.name();
System.out.println( child1Name );
             //  prints out:    child1
```

The name and path values are meant to be reminiscent of a filesystem.

10.4.12 Getting parent and child nodes

A node that contains another node is called the *parent* of the contained node. The contained node is called the *child* of the containing node. For example, the relationship between parent and child nodes from figure 10.1 can be seen in table 10.4.

Table 10.4 Every node except the root node has a parent.

Parent	Child
/	/child0
/	/child1
/child1	/child1/grandchild0

The Preferences API provides the `parent()` and `childrenNames()` methods to allow you to get the parent or children of a given node.

Every node has exactly one parent, which is returned by the `parent()` method:

```
package a.b.c;
// ...
Preferences prefs = Preferences.userNodeForPackage( this );
Preferences parent = prefs.parent();
Preferences grandParent = parent.parent();
Preferences greatGrandParent = grandParent.parent();
Preferences greatGreatGrandParent = greatGrandParent.parent();
```

Actually, there's one exception: calling `parent()` on the root node returns `null`.

A node can have any number of children, and these children can be discovered via the `childrenNames()` method. A node that has no children will return a zero-length array (as opposed to `null`).

The following code fragment produces the array { "child0", "child1" }:

```
Preferences prefs = Preferences.userRoot();
String childrenNames[] = prefs.childrenNames();
```

In contrast, the following code fragment produces the zero-length array {}:

```
Preferences prefs = Preferences.userRoot().node( "child0" );
String childrenNames[] = prefs.childrenNames();
```

10.4.13 Determining the presence of nodes

You can determine whether a node is present within a preferences tree with the `nodeExists()` method. This method takes a string representing a path, which can be absolute or relative.

In the following code, calls to `nodeExists()` that return `true` are shown in boldface; those that return `false` are shown in italics.

```
Preferences uroot = Preferences.userRoot();
boolean b = uroot.nodeExists( "child1" );
b =          uroot.nodeExists( "/child1" );
Preferences child1 = uroot.node( "child1" );
Preferences grandchild0 = child1.node( "grandchild0" );
b = child1.nodeExists( "grandchild0" );
b = child1.nodeExists( "child1" );
b = child1.nodeExists( "/child1" );
b = grandchild0.nodeExists( "child1" );
b = grandchild0.nodeExists( "/child1" );
```

`nodeExists()` takes a single argument, which is an relative or absolute path. If the path is a relative path, the system attempts to locate the node relative to the given node. If the path is absolute, the system attempts to locate the node relative to the root of the given node; in this case, the only requirement for the node whose `node-Exists()` method is being called is that it be in the same preferences tree as the node in question.

10.4.14 *Removing nodes*

Child nodes can be removed from parent nodes by using the `removeNode()` method. The object that this method is called on is removed from the preferences tree, along with all of its descendants.

```
Preferences uroot = Preferences.userRoot();
Preferences child1 = uroot.node( "child1" );
child1.removeNode();
```

Note that after you've called the `removeNode()` method, you still have a reference to the object in question, which would allow you to continue to call methods on it, or any of its children. Calling any `Preferences` method on these objects, other than `name()`, `nodeExists()`, `flush()`, `isUserNode()`, or `absolutePath()` will result in an `IllegalStateException`. The code shown here in boldface is incorrect, and will throw an `IllegalStateException`:

```
Preferences uroot = Preferences.userRoot();
Preferences child1 = uroot.node( "child1" );
child1.removeNode();
// BAD!  Node has already been removed!
int windowX = child1.get( "window x", 200 );
// BAD!  Node has already been removed!
Preferences grandchild0 = child1.node( "grandchild0" );
```

It is impossible to remove the root node of a tree. Attempting to do so results in an `UnsupportedOperationException`.

10.4.15   *Flushing*

As mentioned in section 10.1.3, an implementation of the Preferences API is not required to write its data to the backing store immediately. Rather, it is allowed to simply make note of the write request, and then schedule a background process to do the writing at some later date.

In order to give the programmer some control over this mechanism, the Preferences API provides the `flush()` method:

```
int windowX = 250;
Preferences prefs = Preferences.userNodeForPackage( this );
prefs.putInt( "window x", windowX );
// ... changes are not permanent yet
prefs.flush();
// ... changes are now permanent
```

It's very important to understand that `flush()` only affects the backing store. The API itself, from the point of view of a Java program, will see any changes *immediately* after they are made. Flushing simply ensures that these changes have been safely saved to whatever medium is holding the permanent representation of the database. This medium is usually the local disk, but could also be a remote server or an intermittently available repository.

For the purposes of flushing, the addition and removal of nodes are considered regular changes—they do not become permanent until they are flushed.

Note that an implementation is not required to operate asynchronously. An implementation can choose to flush changes to the backing store after every single write, after only some writes, or at any other time. A program is not required to call `flush()` before program termination. This is taken care of automatically by the implementation.

10.4.16   *Syncing*

As mentioned in section 10.1.3, the Preferences API is intended to work in an environment where multiple agents are modifying the same backing store. These agents can be multiple threads within a Java Virtual Machine (JVM), or multiple JVMs, or programs written in different languages running on the same system.

Because of this, it is possible that changes made to the backing store by one thread or program will not be visible to another program. However, this other program can remedy the situation by calling the `sync()` method. This method ensures that the given node, and any of its descendants, are up to date with respect to the backing store. Any changes that have occurred to this node within the backing store will be reflected in this node after `sync()` returns.

Figure 10.2 **Two configurations of the interface to a hypothetical IDE application. Users generally need to customize the layout of such applications because there is so much information to see. The Preferences API is a perfect method for storing this customization data.**

The following example demonstrates the interaction between two threads or programs reading from and writing to the same backing store:

```
Preferences prefs = Preferences.userNodeForPackage( this );
prefs.putInt( "window x", 300 );
int windowX = prefs.getInt( "window x", 250 ); // returns 300
// .. Long pause during which another thread or program
// sets this value to 500 in the backing store
windowX     = prefs.getInt( "window x", 250 ); // still returns 300
prefs.sync();
windowX     = prefs.getInt( "window x", 250 ); // returns 500
```

Note that `sync()` also ensures that any unflushed changes to this node within this JVM are flushed to the backing store. That is, `sync()` calls `flush()` before returning. It's not clear from the documentation which happens first—the `sync()` or the `flush()`.

10.4.17 *Example: storing GUI configuration*

A perfect use for the Preferences API is to store user customizations to the GUI of an application. In this example we'll look at the bare bones of the GUI for an integrated development environment (IDE). The interface of our hypothetical IDE has six windows.

IDEs generally have a very crowded interface. Because the interface is so crowded, users generally want to rearrange the windows to suit their needs (figure 10.2 shows two possible window arrangements for the IDE interface). These rearrangements should be saved, because it is very annoying for a user to have to set things up from scratch every time she runs the software.

Listing 10.1 contains a class called `PersistentWindow`, which knows how to store and retrieve its location and size information using the Preferences API. When a `PersistentWindow` is closed via its `remove()` method, or by clicking its close button, it saves its current state so that it can be restored when it is created again.

The `PersistentWindows` class creates all six windows and maintains a list of them. When the program is quit, the windows' `remove()` methods are called so that the state of the entire configuration is saved.

Listing 10.1   PersistentWindows.java

(See \Chapter10\org\jdk14tut\app\PersistentWindows.java)

```java
package org.jdk14tut.app;

import java.awt.*;
import java.awt.event.*;
import java.util.*;
import java.util.prefs.*;
import javax.swing.*;

public class PersistentWindows
{
  private Set windows = new HashSet();
  private Preferences prefs =
    Preferences.userNodeForPackage( getClass() );
  static private final String NAMES[] = {
    "Main", "Source", "Assembly", "Classes", "Watch", "Project" };

  // Default positions of the windows
  static final private Rectangle DEFAULTS[] = {
    new Rectangle( 39, 2, 728, 81 ),
    new Rectangle( 218, 83, 548, 312 ),
    new Rectangle( 218, 396, 547, 125 ),
    new Rectangle( 39, 244, 179, 277 ),
    new Rectangle( 38, 522, 726, 85 ),
    new Rectangle( 39, 83, 179, 161),
  };

  public PersistentWindows() {
    setupGUI();
  }

  private void setupGUI() {                    ❶ Set up the windows
    PersistentWindow pw = null;

    pw = addWindow( 0 );
    pw.getContentPane().setLayout( new BorderLayout() );
    pw.getContentPane().add( new JTextArea(), BorderLayout.CENTER );
    JMenuBar mb = new JMenuBar();
    pw.setJMenuBar( mb );
    JMenu fileMenu = new JMenu( "File" );
```

```
        fileMenu.setMnemonic( KeyEvent.VK_F );
        mb.add( fileMenu );
        JMenuItem exitMI = new JMenuItem( "Exit", KeyEvent.VK_X );
        exitMI.addActionListener( new ActionListener() {
            public void actionPerformed( ActionEvent ae ) {
              removeWindows();
              System.exit( 0 );
            }
          } );
        fileMenu.add( exitMI );
        pw.setVisible( true );

        pw = addWindow( 1 );
        pw.getContentPane().setLayout( new BorderLayout() );
        pw.getContentPane().add( new JTextArea(), BorderLayout.CENTER );
        pw.setVisible( true );

        pw = addWindow( 2 );
        pw.getContentPane().setLayout( new BorderLayout() );
        pw.getContentPane().add( new JTextArea(), BorderLayout.CENTER );
        pw.setVisible( true );

        pw = addWindow( 3 );
        pw.getContentPane().setLayout( new BorderLayout() );
        pw.getContentPane().add( new JTextArea(), BorderLayout.CENTER );
        pw.setVisible( true );

        pw = addWindow( 4 );
        pw.getContentPane().setLayout( new BorderLayout() );
        pw.getContentPane().add( new JTextArea(), BorderLayout.CENTER );
        pw.setVisible( true );

        pw = addWindow( 5 );
        pw.getContentPane().setLayout( new BorderLayout() );
        pw.getContentPane().add( new JTextArea(), BorderLayout.CENTER );
        pw.setVisible( true );
    }

    // Return the window with the given name
    private PersistentWindow getWindow( String name ) {
      for (Iterator it=windows.iterator(); it.hasNext();) {
        PersistentWindow pw = (PersistentWindow)it.next();
        if (pw.name().equals( name ))
          return pw;
      }
      return null;
    }

    private PersistentWindow addWindow( int windowNum ) {
      PersistentWindow pw =
        new PersistentWindow( NAMES[windowNum], DEFAULTS[windowNum] );
```

❷ Add a window, getting its location from Preferences

```
    windows.add( pw );

    return pw;
  }

  private void removeWindow( PersistentWindow pw ) {
    windows.remove( pw );

    // If there are no more windows left, quit
    if (windows.size()==0) {
      System.exit( 0 );
    }
  }

  private void removeWindows() {
    Object ws[] = windows.toArray();
    for (int i=0; i<ws.length; ++i) {
      ((PersistentWindow)ws[i]).remove();
    }
  }

  /**
   * Inner class: PersistentWindow is a JFrame
   * whose position is managed by PersistentWindows
   * class.
   */
  class PersistentWindow extends JFrame {
    private String name;

    public PersistentWindow( String name, Rectangle defaults ) {
      super( name );
      this.name = name;
      setLocation( defaults );
      addListeners();
    }

    public String name() { return name; }

    public void setLocation( Rectangle defaults ) {
      int x = prefs.getInt( name+"_x", defaults.x );
      int y = prefs.getInt( name+"_y", defaults.y );
      int width = prefs.getInt( name+"_width", defaults.width );
      int height = prefs.getInt( name+"_height", defaults.height );
      setLocation( x, y );
      setSize( width, height );
    }

    private void saveLocation() {
      int x = getLocation().x;
      int y = getLocation().y;
      int width = getSize().width;
      int height = getSize().height;
      prefs.putInt( name+"_x", x );
      prefs.putInt( name+"_y", y );
```

❸ **Remove a window**

❹ **Remove all windows**

❺ **PersistentWindow represents a single window**

❻ **Get location info from Preferences**

● **Save location info to Preferences**

```
        prefs.putInt( name+"_width", width );
        prefs.putInt( name+"_height", height );
    }
    private void remove() {      ❼  Remove the
        saveLocation();             window
        setVisible( false );

        // Remove this window from the parent
        // object's list
        removeWindow( PersistentWindow.this );
    }

    private void addListeners() {
        addWindowListener( new WindowListener() {
            public void windowActivated( WindowEvent we ) {
            }
            public void windowClosed( WindowEvent we ) {
            }
            public void windowClosing( WindowEvent we ) {
                // Remove window if the close-button is pressed
                remove();
            }
            public void windowDeactivated( WindowEvent we ) {
            }
            public void windowDeiconified( WindowEvent we ) {
            }
            public void windowIconified( WindowEvent we ) {
            }
            public void windowOpened( WindowEvent we ) {
            }
        } );
    }
}

static public void main( String args[] ) {
    new PersistentWindows();
}
}
```

❶ Each window is initially created using addWindow(), which creates a PersistentWindow. Then each window is decorated with GUI components.

❷ addWindow() creates a PersistentWindow and adds it to the list of windows. This list is maintained so that the program knows when all the windows have been closed, at which point the program can exit.

The windows are indexed by an integer ranging from 0 to 5; this value serves as an index into the names array, which stores the name of each window, as well as into the table of default locations.

❸ removeWindow() maintains the windows list. When there are no more windows, the program can quit.

❹ removeWindows() calls the remove() method of each window. It must call remove() to ensure that the window saves its location information to the Preferences API.

❺ PersistentWindow is a subclass of JFrame so that it can easily be used any place a JFrame is used. This makes it easy to use PersistentWindows throughout your application. Instead of having to explicitly remember the location of every window in your GUI, you can just remember to use a PersistentWindow for each window.

❻ setLocation() attempts to load location and size information from the Preferences API. In the event that the preferences database is not available, it gets this info from the defaults object.

❼ remove() calls saveLocation() before closing the window. After it closes the window, it calls the removeWindow() method of the parent object to make sure it gets removed from the list of windows.

This program illustrates a powerful technique: if each component can be responsible for its own customization information, it becomes easier to add such persistence to an application on an incremental basis. Programmers often avoid saving such customization data because it requires advance planning of a kind that generally isn't given a high priority. The Preferences API makes it very easy to make customizations persistent because it is globally available to all modules in an application, and does not require the assistance of the application's main module.

10.5 *Change listeners*

As was mentioned in section 10.1.3, multiple threads or programs can modify the same backing store, either through the Preferences API inside another JVM, or through another program written in another language, using a completely unrelated interface.

Because multiple agents can write to the same data store, it is desirable that a program be able to receive notice when data values change, and when values or nodes appear and disappear. To this end, the Preferences API provides *change listeners*. These allow your program to register its interest in receiving notice that certain changes have been made to the preferences database.

Note that agents outside the current JVM do not necessarily provide notice of changes they make. Because of the difficulty of implementing such a feature in a platform-independent way, an implementation of the Preferences API is only required to provide updates to changes that originate within the same API as the listener. However, implementations are encouraged to provide updates from other sources if possible.

A node can have any number of listeners attached to it.

10.5.1 *Preference change listeners*

A `PreferenceChangeListener` is an object that wants to receive notification when preference values are added, removed, or changed. Listeners are registered on a per-node basis, which means that a registration only ensures that the listener will receive notice of changes to that particular node.

The `PreferenceChangeListener` interface has a single method, `preferenceChange()`, which receives an object of type `PreferenceChangeEvent`:

```
Preferences prefs = Preferences.userNodeForPackage( this );

prefs.addPreferenceChangeListener( new PreferenceChangeListener() {
  public void preferenceChange( PreferenceChangeEvent pce ) {
    System.out.println( pce.getKey()+" <-- "+pce.getNewValue() );
  }
} );
prefs.putInt( "integer", 10 );
prefs.putInt( "integer", 20 );
prefs.remove( "integer" );
```

The preceding code in boldface produces the following output:

```
integer <-- 10
integer <-- 20
integer <-- null
```

Note the use of the `getNewValue()` method of the `PreferenceChangeEvent`. This method returns the new value of the preference node in question.

10.5.2 *Node change listeners*

A `NodeChangeListener` is like a `PreferenceChangeListener`, except that it is interested in changes to the node structure, rather than changes to the contents of nodes. Each time a child is added or removed from a node that has a listener, that listener is informed of the event via a `NodeChangeEvent` object.

```
Preferences prefs = Preferences.userNodeForPackage( this );
prefs.addNodeChangeListener( new NodeChangeListener() {
  public void childAdded( NodeChangeEvent nce ) {
    System.out.println( "Node added:\n\tparent="+nce.getParent()
                      +"\n\tchild="+
                      nce.getChild() );
  }
  public void childRemoved( NodeChangeEvent nce ) {
    System.out.println( "Node removed:\n\tparent="+nce.getParent()
```

```
                          +"\n\tchild="+
                          nce.getChild() );
    }
} );
Preferences abc = prefs.node( "a/b/c" );
Preferences a = prefs.node( "a" );
a.removeNode();
```

The preceding code in boldface produces the following output:

```
Node added:
    parent=User Preference Node: /<unnamed>
    child=User Preference Node: /<unnamed>/a
Node removed:
    parent=User Preference Node: /<unnamed>
    child=User Preference Node: /<unnamed>/a
```

Note that we don't get "node added" messages for nodes b and c—we haven't installed listeners on the parents of these nodes, so we don't know when they are added.

NodeChangeEvent provides getParent() and getChild() methods. These return the parent and child nodes of the operation that has occurred.

10.5.3 *Example: listening for a GUI change request*

Using listeners to respond to updates in the preference values is an excellent way to communicate customizations to different parts of a program. Normally, when a user customizes some aspect of an application, this change needs to be reflected immediately, and it needs to be reflected in all parts of the program that are affected by the change.

Taking care do this right can be tricky; doing it in full often inspires a listener-like system, so that it can be easy for any part of a program to *listen* for customizations. But why create your own listener-like system, when the Preferences API provides one? In this section, we'll consider a simple example of customization, and we'll use Preferences listeners to implement it.

The interface for our example program is simple. There are two windows. In the main window, there are two buttons that allow you to set the orientation of the secondary window. The two orientations are shown in figure 10.3.

When one of the buttons is clicked, it causes the secondary window to change its position and shape. However, it doesn't do this directly—it does this by setting a preference value. Meanwhile, the program has also registered a listener that listens for changes to this value. When the value change triggers the listener, the listener moves the window.

The advantage of this system is that the code that changes the preference value doesn't have to know which other objects or modules care about the value. Any module can watch for a value change by registering a listener. Additionally, changes made to the preference values from any other process trigger the same results as a change made from within the same process, allowing external tools to control your application.

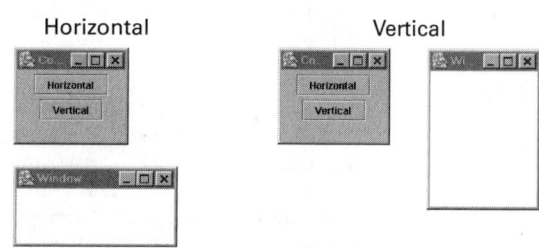

Figure 10.3 **The secondary window changes position in response to clicking the buttons in the main window, and it uses listeners to do so.**

The code for this example is shown in listing 10.2.

Listing 10.2 ListenerExample.java

(See \Chapter10\org\jdk14tut\app\ListenerExample.java)

```java
package org.jdk14tut.app;

import java.awt.*;
import java.awt.event.*;
import java.util.prefs.*;
import javax.swing.*;

public class ListenerExample
{
  private JFrame window;
  private Preferences prefs =
    Preferences.userNodeForPackage( getClass() );
  static private final Rectangle horizontalOrientation =
    new Rectangle( 40, 220, 200, 100 );
  static private final Rectangle verticalOrientation =
    new Rectangle( 220, 40, 80, 200 );

  public ListenerExample() {
    addPrefsListener();
    setupGUI();
    setWindow();
  }

  private void addPrefsListener() {
    prefs.addPreferenceChangeListener(
      new PreferenceChangeListener() {
        public void preferenceChange( PreferenceChangeEvent pce ) {
          System.out.println( "Change: ("+pce.getNode()+") key="+
                              pce.getKey()+" value="+
                              pce.getNewValue() );
          setWindow();
```

● **Listen for a change to the value**

```
      }
    } );
}
private void setupGUI() {
  JFrame controlFrame = new JFrame( "Control" );
  JButton horizontal = new JButton( "Horizontal" );
  JButton vertical = new JButton( "Vertical" );
  Container cp = controlFrame.getContentPane();
  cp.setLayout( new FlowLayout( FlowLayout.CENTER ) );
  cp.add( horizontal, BorderLayout.NORTH );
  cp.add( vertical, BorderLayout.SOUTH );

  controlFrame.setLocation( 40, 40 );
  controlFrame.setSize( 120, 120 );

  window = new JFrame( "Window" );
  cp = window.getContentPane();
  cp.setLayout( new BorderLayout() );
  cp.add( new JTextArea(), BorderLayout.CENTER );

  horizontal.addActionListener( new ActionListener() {
    public void actionPerformed( ActionEvent ae ) {
      setHorizontal();
    }
  } );

  vertical.addActionListener( new ActionListener() {
    public void actionPerformed( ActionEvent ae ) {
      setVertical();
    }
  } );

  controlFrame.setVisible( true );
  window.setVisible( true );
}

private void setHorizontal() {
  prefs.putBoolean( "horizontal", true );
}

private void setVertical() {
  prefs.putBoolean( "horizontal", false );
}
private void setWindow() {
  boolean horizontal = prefs.getBoolean( "horizontal", true );
  Rectangle rect = null;
  if (horizontal) {
    rect = horizontalOrientation;
  } else {
    rect = verticalOrientation;
  }
```

● **Button clicks trigger calls to change Preferences value...**

● **...here**

● **Listener calls this method to move the window**

```
      window.setVisible( false );
      window.setLocation( rect.getLocation() );
      window.setSize( rect.getSize() );
      window.doLayout();
      window.setVisible( true );
   }

   static public void main( String args[] ) {
      new ListenerExample();
   }
}
```

10.5.4 *Example: changing server ports on the fly*

Simple servers and daemons need to be restarted when their configuration changes; more sophisticated ones can change their configuration on the fly. This latter approach is a better solution for critical applications because it increases flexibility and reduces downtime—the less often you have to quit and restart, the better.

The Preferences API provides an excellent way for a server to respond to configuration changes. Not only does it allow configuration values to be changed at any time, it can potentially allow server administrators to use powerful tools to do so: since the preferences values are stored in a system-wide repository, the administrators can use available platform-specific tools to edit these values.

The example in this section uses a simple server called `Server` that listens on a port specified in preferences; additionally, changes to the preferences value cause the server to automatically switch to another port. This all happens within the running server—it does not need to be shut down and restarted.

As we've seen, this change of preference values can be initiated, on some platforms, by another process. However, since this feature is not supported on all platforms, Server uses a simple command-line shell, contained in the `CommandLine` and `ServerCommandLine` classes. There is only one command supported by this shell, which can be entered after you've started the program. The following fragment shows how the user uses the command-line interface—user-entered commands are in boldface:

```
java org.jdk14tut.app.Server
Listening on sun.nio.ch.ServerSocketChannelImpl[/0.0.0.0:5555]
port 5556
Change: (User Preference Node: /org/jdk14tut/app) key=port value=5556
Reopening....
Listening on sun.nio.ch.ServerSocketChannelImpl[/0.0.0.0:5556]
```

The second command, `port 5556`, tells the running server to switch from the current port (5555) to port 5556, which it does.

As in the example in section 10.5.3, this program does not respond *directly* to the user's command. Instead, the user's command sets a preference value, which triggers a listener. This means that the change will happen regardless of whether the preference value is changed from within this process, or, on platforms that support it, from another process.

Listing 10.3 shows the code for Server.java; listings 10.4 and 10.5 show `CommandLine` and `ServerCommandLine`, respectively.

Listing 10.3   Server.java

(See \Chapter10\org\jdk14tut\app\Server.java)

```java
package org.jdk14tut.app;

import java.io.*;
import java.net.*;
import java.nio.*;
import java.nio.channels.*;
import java.util.prefs.*;
import java.util.regex.*;

public class Server implements Runnable
{
  static private final int defaultPort = 5555;
  private int port;
  private Preferences prefs =
    Preferences.userNodeForPackage( getClass() );
  private ServerSocketChannel ssc;

  public Server() {
    port = getPort();
    addPrefsListener();
    new Thread( this ).start();
  }

  public Preferences prefs() {
    return prefs;
  }

  private int getPort() {
    int p = prefs.getInt( "port", defaultPort );
    return p;
  }

  private void addPrefsListener() {
    prefs.addPreferenceChangeListener(
      new PreferenceChangeListener() {
        public void preferenceChange( PreferenceChangeEvent pce ) {
          System.out.println( "Change: ("+pce.getNode()+") key="+
                              pce.getKey()+" value="+
                              pce.getNewValue() );
```

❶ Get port number stored in Preferences

❷ Listen for changes to prefs node

```
          if (pce.getKey().equals( "port" )) {
            try {
              updatePort();
            } catch( IOException ie ) {
              ie.printStackTrace();
            }
          }
        }
      } );
}

private void updatePort() throws IOException {        ❸ Respond to port change
  int p = getPort();
  if (p != port) {
    changePort( p );
  }
}

private void changePort( int port ) throws IOException {    ❹ Close
  this.port = port;                                              ServerSocket
  ssc.close();                                                   Channel
}                                                                when port is
                                                                 changed
public void run() {                ❺ Listen for incoming
  try {                               socket connections
    while (true) {
      // Listen on port <port>, all addresses
      ssc = ServerSocketChannel.open();
      ssc.configureBlocking( true );
      byte anyIP[] = { 0, 0, 0, 0 };
      InetAddress localhost = InetAddress.getByAddress( anyIP );
      InetSocketAddress isa =
        new InetSocketAddress( localhost, port );
      ssc.socket().bind( isa );

      // Accept connections
      while (true) {
        try {
          System.out.println( "Listening on "+ssc );
          SocketChannel sc = ssc.accept();
          dealWithConnection( sc );          ❻ Process incoming
                                                connection
        } catch( AsynchronousCloseException ace ) {
          System.out.println( "Reopening...." );
          break;                                 ❼ ServerSocketChannel
        }                                           is closed when the
      }                                             port is changed
    }
  } catch( IOException ie ) {
    ie.printStackTrace();
  }
}
```

```
protected void dealWithConnection( SocketChannel sc )
    throws IOException {
  System.out.println( "Got connection "+sc );
  sc.close();
}

static public void main( String args[] ) throws IOException {
  Server server = new Server();

  new ServerCommandLine( System.in, System.out );
  }
}
```

❶ The initial port number is read from the Preferences API. Of course, when reading from Preferences, we need a default, which is what the defaultPort value (at the beginning of the code) is for.

❷ We add a listener that listens to changes in preferences for this class. If a value change occurs, and it is a change in the value of the key port, then we call update-Port(), which will reconfigure the server.

❸ updatePort() finds out what the new port value is, and then calls changePort() to reconfigure the server to the new value.

❹ changePort() triggers a reconfiguration of the server by closing the ServerSock-etChannel prematurely.

❺ The run() method contains an infinite loop that does the traditional while-true-accept server inner loop, but with a twist: if the ServerSocketChannel is closed prematurely, this is taken as a signal to reopen on another port.

❻ When a connection comes in, pass it to dealWithConnection(), which, of course, deals with it.

❼ If the ServerSocketChannel is closed prematurely, this is taken as a signal to reopen on another port. This is done by simply exiting the inner while() loop, which sends us back to the top of the outer while() loop, where we prepare a new ServerSock-etChannel on the new port.

The server changes ports in response to a command; the other two classes, CommandLine (see listing 10.4) and ServerCommandLine (see listing 10.5), implement this command-line interface. CommandLine is a generic command-line processing class, and ServerCommandLine is a subclass of CommandLine that knows how to set the server's port number.

Listing 10.4 CommandLine.java

(See \Chapter10\org\jdk14tut\app\CommandLine.java)

```java
package org.jdk14tut.app;

import java.io.*;
import java.util.regex.*;

public abstract class CommandLine implements Runnable
{
  protected BufferedReader in;
  protected PrintWriter out;

  public CommandLine( InputStream in, OutputStream out ) {
    this( new InputStreamReader( in ),
          new OutputStreamWriter( out ) );
  }

  public CommandLine( Reader reader, Writer writer ) {
    this( new BufferedReader( reader ),
          new PrintWriter( writer ) );
  }

  public CommandLine( BufferedReader in, PrintWriter out ) {
    this.in = in;
    this.out = out;
    new Thread( this ).start();
  }

  public void run() {
    try {
      Pattern pattern = Pattern.compile( "\\s+" );
      while (true) {
        // Read each line and do simple parsing:
        // split the line on whitespace
        String line = in.readLine();
        if (line==null) {
          break;
        }

        String command[] = pattern.split( line );

        // Process each command
        boolean ok = processCommand( command );
        if (!ok) {
          System.out.println( "Unknown command: "+line );
        }
      }
    } catch( IOException ie ) {
      ie.printStackTrace();
    }
  }

  // Override this to implement commands
  abstract public boolean processCommand( String command[] );
```

● **CommandLine processes commands**

● **Start a background thread to read**

● **Parse each input line into white-space-separated strings**

● **Pass the parsed command to processCommand()**

Listing 10.5   ServerCommandLine.java

(See \Chapter10\org\jdk14tut\app\ServerCommandLine.java)

```java
package org.jdk14tut.app;

import java.io.*;
import java.util.prefs.*;

public class ServerCommandLine extends CommandLine
{
  private Preferences prefs =
    Preferences.userNodeForPackage( getClass() );

  public ServerCommandLine( InputStream in, OutputStream out ) {
    super( in, out );
  }

  public boolean processCommand( String command[] ) {
    if (command[0].equalsIgnoreCase( "port" )) {
      int port = Integer.parseInt( command[1] );
      prefs.putInt( "port", port );
      System.out.println( "Set port to "+port );
      return true;
    } else {
      return false;
    }
  }

  static public void main( String args[] ) throws IOException {
   new ServerCommandLine( System.in, System.out );
  }
}
```

> Use the same Preferences node that the server uses

> Implement one command, port, which sets the port to the supplied value

> This class can be used standalone ❶

❶ `Server.main()` starts a `ServerCommandLine`, which means that you can type `port` commands at the server's console. A `port` command looks like this:

```
port 5556
```

`ServerCommandLine.main()` also creates a `ServerCommandLine`, which means `ServerCommandLine` can be used as a standalone port-setting tool, setting the port from a separate JVM.

As was mentioned previously, changes made to a preferences value from one JVM might not trigger the `PreferenceChangeListeners` in another JVM; this depends on the implementation. Thus, the standalone `ServerCommandLine` tool may or may not trigger a running server to change ports—you'll have to try it to find out. If the standalone version doesn't cause the server to change ports, it will still store the new port value to the Preferences database.

It is important to note that the approach used here assumes that you will only want to run one copy of the server on your system. If you want to run multiple copies, then it makes sense to create Preferences nodes for each instance. The Preferences database then becomes a kind of instance storehouse, storing configuration values for instances while they run, and also when they are not running.

10.6 *Stored defaults*

The *stored defaults* feature of the Preferences API provides for a mechanism to supply values for keys that haven't been explicitly entered into the preferences database through normal channels. This allows defaults to be specified on a system-wide basis. These values will be present inside the preferences database, and will be returned by calls to the get() methods.

Note that the API does not provide methods for setting stored defaults; it is assumed that the backing implementation has its own method for setting these values. For example, the Preferences API might be implemented on top of some enterprise-wide directory service. In this case, the directory service itself must provide a way to set these values and expose them to the Java API as stored defaults.

When a program writes a value that was previously covered by an existing stored default, this default value is *overridden* by the new value. However, the stored default itself is not changed—it is merely shadowed by the value that was explicitly added.

When a key/value pair is removed for a key that has a stored default, this default value is *uncovered* by this removal. This means that rather than disappearing, the removed key takes on the value of the stored default. The behavior is the same for the clear() method.

10.7 *Importing and exporting*

Since the Preferences API is intended to work with a variety of platform-dependent backing stores, these backing stores will, in general, be incompatible with each other. In order to support the transfer of Preferences data from one system to another, the API provides exportNode(), exportSubtree(), and importPreferences() methods. These methods make use of an XML Document Type Definition (DTD) for the Preferences API, located at http://java.sun.com/dtd/preferences.dtd.

The exportNode() method exports the key/value pairs contained in a single node, but does not export any information about children of that node. exportSubtree() exports both the key/value pairs as well as information about child nodes. These child nodes, as well, are exported. The process is recursive, so that all descendants and their key/value pairs are exported at once.

The importPreferences() method imports the contents of a properly formatted XML file into the node it is called on. This file can contain any combination of key/value pairs and/or child nodes.

To give you an idea of what the preferences format looks like, here is code that dumps the contents of the tree shown in figure 10.1:

```
Preferences uroot = Preferences.userRoot();
Preferences child0 = uroot.node( "child0" );
Preferences child1 = uroot.node( "child1" );
Preferences grandchild0 = child1.node( "grandchild0" );
uroot.putInt( "integer", 10 );
child1.put( "name", "Greg" );
uroot.exportNode( System.out );
uroot.exportSubtree( System.out );
```

exportNode() results in the output shown in listing 10.6; exportSubtree() results in the output shown in listing 10.7.

Listing 10.6   Output of exportNode()

```
<?xml version="1.0" encoding="UTF-8"?>

<!DOCTYPE preferences SYSTEM 'http://java.sun.com/dtd/preferences.dtd'>

<preferences EXTERNAL_XML_VERSION="1.0">
  <root type="user">
    <map>
      <entry key="integer" value="10" />        ● An integer is stored as a string
    </map>
  </root>
</preferences>
```

Listing 10.7   Output of exportSubtree()

```
<?xml version="1.0" encoding="UTF-8"?>

<!DOCTYPE preferences SYSTEM 'http://java.sun.com/dtd/preferences.dtd'>

<preferences EXTERNAL_XML_VERSION="1.0">
  <root type="user">
    <map>
      <entry key="integer" value="10" />        ● An integer is stored as a string
    </map>
    <node name="child0">
```

```
      <map />
    </node>
    <node name="child1">
      <map>
        <entry key="bytes" value="AgMEBQ==" />
        <entry key="name" value="Greg" />
      </map>
      <node name="grandchild0">
        <map />
      </node>
    </node>
  </root>
</preferences>
```

A byte array is stored as a string in Base64 format

A string is stored as a string

XML is an excellent format for importing and exporting, since it is subject to rigorous standardization procedures and is ubiquitously supported.

10.8 *Summary*

The Preferences API is not just another way to sort small-scale data. It is a simple and flexible library for storing preference data that integrates directly with any system-wide preference system that may be available in the underlying operating system. By allowing for easy use of multiple data types and the possibility of stored defaults, the Preferences API is ideal for the kind of non-crucial data that applications need to store to enhance the user experience.

The Java Secure
Socket Extension (JSSE)

This chapter covers

- The Java Secure Socket Extension
- SSL handshaking
- Using keystores and keytool
- Managing keys
- Authenticating clients and servers

The Java Secure Socket Extension (JSSE) provides an abstraction for secure communications using the Java *socket* and *stream* metaphors. JSSE resides in the `javax.net`, `javax.net.ssl`, and `javax.security.cert` packages.

The framework, on its own, can do nothing. Each step in the creation of a secure socket requires the use of one or more security algorithms. These algorithms are supplied by a *security provider*, which, in a sense, "fills out" the blanks in the framework. The JDK 1.4 release comes with the `SunJSSE` security provider, which supplies, among other things, an implementation of the Secure Sockets Layer (SSL) and Transport Layer Security (TLS) security protocols, as well as support for RSA key generation and X.509 key management. The `SunJSSE` provider is used by default, and allows for communications using standard SSL techniques. (According to the documentation, the strength of the cipher suites included with the JSSE distribution in JDK 1.4 requires that it not be possible to change the implementation of the `SSLSocketFactory` and `SSLServerSocketFactory` classes.)

In a certain sense, secure sockets are extremely easy to use, because they work just like regular Java sockets. It is the *creation* of the secure sockets that is complicated, since it involves dealing with security providers and secret keys.

11.1 *Cryptographic terminology*

This section provides a very brief introduction to some of the ideas and terms used later in the chapter.

- *Cryptography* is the practice of keeping data secure through encryption.
- *Plaintext* is any data in its original form. Plaintext is unencrypted data that is readable by anyone.
- *Ciphertext* is data that has been encrypted by some cryptographic system. It cannot be read directly; it must be decrypted—converted back to plaintext—before it can be read. Only the intended recipient should be able to read it, because only the intended recipient can convert it back to plaintext.
- *Encryption* is the process of converting plaintext to ciphertext in order to ensure that only the intended recipient can read it.
- *Decryption* is the process of decoding encrypted data, converting ciphertext back to plaintext.
- A *key* is a piece of data—usually small—used to encrypt or decrypt a piece of user data. All but the most trivial encryption encodes data using keys. There are different kinds of keys for different kinds of cryptography. Secure Sockets Layer (SSL) uses both *public-key cryptography* and *secret-key cryptography*.

- *Public-key cryptography* is cryptography that uses a *public/private key pair*.

- *Secret-key cryptography* is cryptography that uses a *secret key*. Secret-key cryptography is also called *symmetric cryptography*.

- A *public/private key pair* is a pair of keys generated together. Data encrypted by one can be decrypted by the other, and vice versa. The private key is kept private and used only by the owner, while the public key can be given out freely without compromising any data. Each key can be used to decrypt data that has been encrypted by the other key. The private key cannot be derived from the public key, so the fact that the public key may be widely known does not threaten the privacy of the private key. If you encrypt data with your private key, someone else can decrypt it using your public key. Since you are the only person with your private key, a recipient can be sure that the data came from you. If, on the other hand, you encrypt data with someone else's public key, then it can only be decrypted by that person, since only he has his private key. This is how you encode data so that it can be read only by a particular party.

- A *digital signature* is data appended to a message, which authenticates the message and the sender. The signature is generally a digest, or summary, of the message, encrypted with the sender's private key.

- A *secret key* is a key that is used both for encryption and decryption. This is the more traditional kind of code key; it is also called a *shared secret*. Unlike a public/private key pair, a secret key allows you to decrypt data that has been encrypted with that same key. This key must be kept secret to everyone except the two parties involved in the communication, and it is often called a *symmetric key*, because it is used for both encryption and subsequent decryption. The advantage of symmetric cryptography is that it is generally much faster than public-key cryptography. A common technique is to use a slower but more convenient public-key protocol at the start of a data-exchange session to exchange newly generated secret keys, which are then used to encrypt the rest of the data in a session. SSL uses public-key cryptography for authentication and secret-key cryptography for privacy and data integrity.

- *Authentication* is the process of verifying that an entity is who it says it is. For example, when you type your password into a computer, you are *authenticating* yourself to it. The computer can safely assume that you are really you, because you haven't told anyone else your password.*

---

* You haven't, have you?

- A *certificate*, or *signed public key*, is a public key that has been digitally signed in order to prove that it is authentic. Sometimes an entity signs its own public key; this is called a *self-signed public key* or *self-signed certificate*.

- A *certification authority*, or *CA*, is an entity considered to be trusted by all parties participating in the communication. This entity is willing to sign the public keys of other entities. For true security, it's necessary to have your public key signed by a CA—a public key that has been signed by itself isn't particularly convincing because all it tells you is that it was sent by the person who owns that key. The certificate signed by a CA can be used by the originating parties as a kind of calling card, allowing them to prove that they are who they say they are.

11.2 SSL—the Secure Sockets Layer

SSL is a standard for secure communication created by Netscape back in 1994. Since then, the Internet Engineering Task Force (IETF) has taken over management of the standard and renamed it Transport Layer Security (TLS). TLS should really be thought of as the newest version of SSL. TLS version 1.0 is a slight modification of SSL version 3.0.

11.2.1 Components of the default implementation

SSL is not the only form of secure socket communication, which is why JSSE is implementation-neutral. However, SSL is one of the most prominent forms of secure socket communication, so the default SunJSSE provider is basically an implementation of the SSL standard. By default, JSSE uses the standards listed in table 11.1.

Table 11.1 A list of the standard components used by the SunJSSE provider. Each of these components can be replaced by an alternative implementation; JSSE itself is implementation-neutral.

The standard	What purpose it serves
SSL/TLS	The overarching structure
X.509	Key and trust management
JKS (Java Key Store)	Filesystem storage of keys

Each of these aspects of secure socket communication can be implemented in different ways, and you can add new implementations to the system. In the default implementation, keys are stored on disk using the JKS format, but other formats, such as PKCS12, can be used; or the keys can be stored in a secure database or on a central secure-key server.

11.2.2 SSL handshaking

Once a `SSLSocket` (or `SSLServerSocket`) has connected and authenticated, it is used like a regular socket. The authentication process—also called the *handshake*—is the complicated part. Here are the main steps in this process:

1 *Hello*—The client and server agree on the version of SSL to use, as well as what algorithms to use.

2 *Server authentication*—The server sends a signed public key, or *certificate*, to the client, which checks it to make sure the server is who it says it is. This step is technically optional, but it is almost always performed. (The certificate only provides a trusted declaration of the organization's public key. The server is only truly authenticated when it demonstrates knowledge of its private key, which it does by using its private key—which only it knows—to decrypt data that has been encrypted with its public key.)

3 *Client authentication*—This is optional, and not as common as server authentication. In this step, the client authenticates itself by sending a certificate to the server. (Like the server, the client is only really authenticated when it demonstrates knowledge of its private key.)

4 *Client key exchange*—The client generates information for creating a secret key, and encrypts this information using the server's public key. It then sends this information to the server, at which point both the client and the server use this information to derive the same secret key.

5 *Data transfer*—The client and server exchange data, encrypting it and verifying its integrity with the secret key.

This process is taken care of automatically by the SSL code within JSSE and `SunJSSE`. The main thing that the program has to deal with is generating and manipulating the keys.

11.3 Managing keys

The term *key management* refers the process of creating keys, as well as the process of using these keys to create secure sockets. This section will describe the process of creating a Java secure socket, as well as the classes used.

11.3.1 *Creating keys with keytool*

Java provides a standalone program called keytool, which allows the user to create and manipulate keys on disk. For example, keytool lets you create a new public/private key pair:

```
keytool -genkey -alias keyname -keystore filename -keyalg rsa
```

This command creates a new public/private key pair using the RSA algorithm. It stores it in file *filename*, under the alias *keyname*. An *alias* is a name used to distinguish a key from other keys within the same keystore. By default, keytool generates and manipulates files in the JKS format.

keytool will also let you export a public-key certificate into a file:

```
keytool -export -alias keyname -keystore filename -file keyfile
```

This command exports the public key that we just created, and puts it in a file called *keyfile*.

keytool is not specific to JSSE, but rather is used with all facets of Java security. It has a fairly complex set of options, and this section only describes enough for basic use. See the documentation for more information.

11.3.2 *Store keys in a KeyStore*

The java.security.KeyStore class provides access to the keys created by keytool. A KeyStore is created by calling KeyStore.getInstance(), passing in a string describing the type of KeyStore, which in our case is JKS:

```
KeyStore ks = KeyStore.getInstance( "JKS" );
```

You can then load the contents of a JKS-formatted file, which is generally locked with a password, into the KeyStore:

```
ks.load( inputStream, password )
```

The password parameter is used to check the integrity of the data, but data is left encoded within the KeyStore. The password will be needed again later.

KeyStore is not specific to JSSE or SSL; it is part of Java's general security framework, and it resides in the java.security package.

11.3.3 *Creating a KeyManagerFactory*

KeyManagerFactory is part of JSSE proper—it resides in the javax.net.ssl package. A KeyManagerFactory creates KeyManagers, which are used during the process of authenticating this side of a secure connection to the other side of the secure connection.

A `KeyManagerFactory` is created from some source of key material, usually a password-protected `KeyStore` object. Here is how it is typically used:

```
KeyManagerFactory kmf =
    KeyManagerFactory.getInstance( "SunX509" );
kmf.init( keyStore, password )
```

The X.509 implementation is the one most commonly used for key management, and it is currently the only one supported.

11.3.4 Creating a TrustManagerFactory

A `TrustManager` serves the inverse purpose of a `KeyManager`—it is used to authenticate the other side of a secure connection by evaluating the keys that it sends to us. In the case of SSL, the client side uses its `TrustManagers` to authenticate the public-key certificate that has been sent to it by the server.

A `TrustManagerFactory` creates `TrustManagers`; it itself is created much like a `KeyManagerFactory`:

```
TrustManagerFactory tmf =
    TrustManagerFactory.getInstance( "SunX509" );
tmf.init( keyStore );
```

`KeyManagerFactory` and `TrustManagerFactory` generally use two different sets of keys. They can be stored in the same `KeyStore` file, or in separate files. Trust keys (managed by a `TrustManagerFactory`) are generally the public keys of other entities, and so do not require much privacy. Authentication keys (managed by a `KeyManagerFactory`), on the other hand, include private keys, and so should be kept very secure.

11.3.5 Creating an SSLContext

Once you have a `KeyManagerFactory` and a `TrustManagerFactory`, you have all you need. This information is combined into an `SSLContext` as follows:

```
SSLContext sslContext = SSLContext.getInstance( "TLS" );
sslContext.init( kmf.getKeyManagers(), tmf.getTrustManagers(),
                null )
```

The first line creates an `SSLContext` of type `TLS`. You could also use type `SSL`—both of these refer to the same standard implementation. The `init()` method is used to provide key and trust managers. An `SSLContext` has enough information to be able to create a `SocketFactory` or a `ServerSocketFactory`:

```
ServerSocketFactory ssf = sslContext.getServerSocketFactory();
SocketFactory ssf = sslContext.getSocketFactory();
```

These, of course, can be used to create SSLServerSockets and SSLSockets, respectively:

```
ServerSocket serverSocket = ssf.createServerSocket( port );
Socket socket = sf.createSocket( hostname, port );
```

Once you have either of these objects, you can use them as you would a regular Socket or ServerSocket, calling getInputStream() or getOutputStream() in the case of a Socket, or accept() in the case of a ServerSocket.

The steps outlined in this section are fairly complicated, and it's best to see them in context. The next two sections describe programs that use these classes to communicate securely. Each one is accompanied by instructions for creating the keys necessary for the program, and should serve as a template for the process of creating secure applications.

11.4   *Example: a trivial secure web server*

This section presents a simple secure web server. A browser communicates with a secure web server via HTTP, but the data passes through SSL sockets rather than plain sockets. Any time you use your browser to access a URL starting with https: rather than http:, you are using a secure web server.

The web server considered in this section is called THTTPSD, which stands for Trivial HTTP Secure Daemon. It knows how to serve HTML files, text files, and directory listings.

11.4.1   *The authentication model*

The authentication model used in secure web browsing should be considered from the point of view of the user and the browser. A user using her browser wants to surf the Web, but she wants to make sure that the servers she browses are authentic—that they are the sites that they say they are, run by the people who claim to run them. This is especially the case when the user is passing sensitive information, such as credit card information, to the server.

Thus, the browser is trusted, while the web server is not trusted. When the browser connects to a secure web server, it requires that the server authenticate itself. As a regular part of the SSL handshake procedure, the server responds by sending a certificate to the client. (This certificate provides an authoritative declaration of the server's public key. Later on in the connection process, the server will demonstrate that it has the private key corresponding to this public key by using that private key. Only then is the server truly authenticated.)

If the server has a certificate that the browser trusts, as shown in figure 11.1, everything is fine. Each browser comes with a small set of certificates installed from various CAs, such as VeriSign or Entrust; the server's certificate must be signed with one of these CAs, or the browser will not trust it.

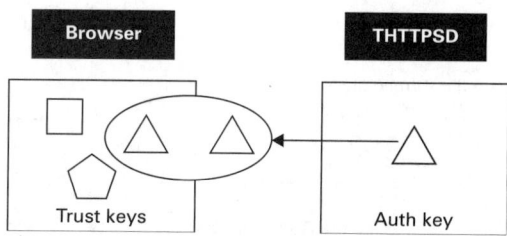

Figure 11.1 The browser has a set of certificates from trusted third parties. If the server has a certificate that the browser trusts, the browser will trust the server.

Figure 11.2 shows a browser rejecting the certificate sent by the server. In this case, the browser might refuse to accept pages from the server, or it might present the user with the option to use the server anyway, knowing that it might be unsafe.

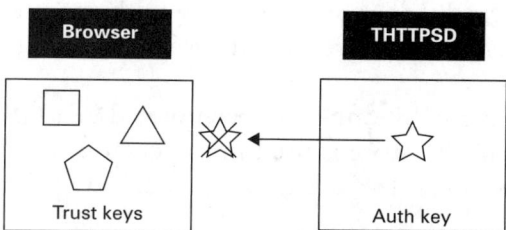

Figure 11.2 The browser has a set of certificates from trusted third parties. If the server does not have a certificate signed by one of these trusted third parties, the browser will refuse to authenticate it.

The THTTPSD web server does not have a key signed by a trusted third party,* so some browsers might not be able to use it. However, newer browsers will allow you to access the server in untrusted mode, or will let you add the certificate to its collection of trusted certificates.

11.4.2 *Generating the key*

The authentication model described in the previous section only uses one key: an authentication key that the server sends to the client, hoping that the client will accept it. For this to work with most browsers, this key would need to be signed by

---

* Hey—signed keys cost money!

a CA, but that is beyond the scope of this chapter. However, we do need to generate the key in the first place, which we can do using `keytool` (the included scripts `thttpsdkeys.sh` and `thttpsdkeys.bat` will generate this key file for you). The `keytool` command is shown in figure 11.3.

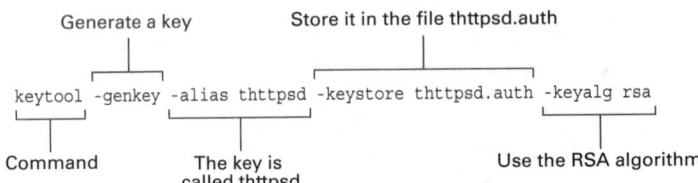

Figure 11.3 **The `keytool` command. This example generates a new key using the RSA algorithm and stores it in a file called thttpsd.auth under the alias `thttpsd`.**

This command creates a public key/private key pair under the alias `thttpsd`, using the RSA key-generation algorithm. The default is for `keytool` to use the DSA algorithm, but many browsers (such as Netscape and Microsoft Internet Explorer) require RSA keys. (`keytool` normally engages in a dialog with the user to gather identity information, but the scripts take care of that for you by using command-line arguments.)

The key pair—which includes a certificate—has been placed in a JKS-formatted keystore called thttpsd.auth. This keystore is used in the creation of the server's `ServerSocketFactory` in the `getServerSocketFactory()` method in listing 11.2 in the next section.

11.4.3 *The configuration file*

THTTPSD uses a configuration file for most of its settings, including the name and password for the keystore file. The configuration file also contains the port number for the server to listen on. The standard port number for a secure web server is 443, but you may not have permission to use that port on your machine, so you can set it here.

In the configuration file included with the source code (see listing 11.1), the port is set to 5555. To access the server running on port 5555 on the machine `mymachine`, use this URL: https://mymachine:5555/. This URL will give you a listing of the directory defined by the document root in the configuration file.

Listing 11.1   thttpsd.cfg

(See \Chapter11\thttpsd.cfg)

```
port=5555
secure=true
docroot=c:/docroot
keyfile=thttpsd.auth
passphrase=thttpsd
```

Note that the docroot is set to c:/docroot—this means that a URL of https://myma-chine:5555/hello/there.txt will bring up the document c:\docroot\hello\there.txt.

On a Unix system, you would use something like docroot=/usr/local/html; the URL shown previously would then correspond to the file /usr/local/html/hello/there.txt.

11.4.4   *The code*

The code for THTTPSD is shown in listing 11.2. Pay special attention to the get-ServerSocketFactory() method, which is where the key is loaded.

Listing 11.2   THTTPSD.java

(See \Chapter11\THTTPSD.java)

```java
import java.io.*;
import java.net.*;
import java.security.*;
import java.util.*;
import java.util.regex.*;
import javax.net.*;
import javax.net.ssl.*;

public class THTTPSD
{
  // The port we will listen on
  private int port;

  // The document root of the server.  All requested filenames
  // are relative to this directory
  private File docroot;

  // Are we running as a secure server or as a regular server?
  private boolean secure = false;

  // All configuration comes from this file
  static private final String configurationFile = "thttpsd.cfg";

  // Configuration variables read from 'configurationFile'
  private Properties properties;
```

```
// Regex for parsing "GET" requests
static private final String getParser =
  "^GET\\s+(.+)\\s+HTTP/[\\d\\.]+$";
static private final Pattern getPattern =
  Pattern.compile( getParser );

// Regex for parsing server config variable names
static private final String serverVarParser =
  "^server\\.([^\\.]+)\\.([^\\.]+)$";
static private final Pattern serverVarPattern =
  Pattern.compile( serverVarParser );

// Size of buffer used to send file contents to a browser
static private final int bufferLength = 1024;

static private SecureRandom secureRandom;

/**
 * Constructor:
 * Configure and start the server
 */
public THTTPSD() throws IOException {
  readConfiguration();
  startServer();
}

/**
 * Read configuration values
 */
private void readConfiguration() throws IOException {
  FileInputStream fin = new FileInputStream( configurationFile );
  properties = new Properties();
  properties.load( fin );
  fin.close();

  // Show the configuration values on the console
  System.out.println( "Configuration: " );
  properties.list( System.out );

  // Get 'port', 'docroot', and 'secure' values from properties
  port = Integer.parseInt( (String)properties.get( "port" ) );
  docroot = new File( (String)properties.get( "docroot" ) );
  if (properties.get( "secure" ) != null &&
      properties.get( "secure" ).equals( "true" )) {
    secure = true;
  }
}

/**
 * Start the server: start a listener
 */
private void startServer() {
  new Listener();
}
```

● **Read the configuration and start a background listening thread**

● **Read configuration variables from thttpsd.cfg**

❶ **Start a Listener, with a background thread, to process incoming connections**

```
/**
 * Deal with a new Socket: create a SocketHandler
 * to process the new connection
 */
private void processSocket( Socket socket ) {
  new SocketHandler( socket );
}
```

❷ **processSocket() is called by the Listener when a new connection comes in**

```
/**
 * Deal with a new connection: parse transaction
 * and respond to it
 */
private void processTransaction( Socket socket,
                                 InputStream in,
                                 OutputStream out )
    throws IOException {
  while (true) {
    String doc = getDocString( in );
    // getDocString() returns null when the connection is closed
    if (doc==null)
      break;

    // Show a log message
    System.out.println( "Request for "+doc+" from "+
                        socket.getInetAddress() );

    // Send the requested document to the browser
    sendDoc( doc, out );
  }
}
```

processTransaction() is called by the SocketHandler that is handling a connection **❸**

● **Read request and send response**

```
/**
 * Send the requested document to the stream, based on
 * what kind of document it is
 */
private void sendDoc( String docString, OutputStream out )
    throws IOException  {
  // Derive the absolute pathname from the relative
  // pathname and the document root
  File doc = new File( docroot+docString );
  if (!doc.exists()) {

    // File doesn't exist
    sendFileNotFound( docString, out );
  } else if (doc.isDirectory()) {

    // File is really a directory
    sendDirectoryListing( doc, docString, out );
  } else if (doc.getName().toLowerCase().endsWith( "html" )) {

    // File is an HTML file
    sendWebPage( doc, out );
  } else {
```

● Decide what kind of document is being requested, and send it

```
    // Default: send as a text page
    sendTextFile( doc, out );
  }
}

/**
 * Send a file-not-found message
 */
private void sendFileNotFound( String url, OutputStream out )
    throws IOException {

  // Build the response message
  StringBuffer message = new StringBuffer();
  message.append( "<!DOCTYPE HTML PUBLIC \"-//IETF//"+
                  "DTD HTML 2.0//EN\">\r\n" );
  message.append( "<HTML><HEAD>\r\n" );
  message.append( "<TITLE>404 Not Found</TITLE>\r\n" );
  message.append( "</HEAD><BODY>\r\n" );
  message.append( "<H1>Not Found</H1>\r\n" );
  message.append( "The requested URL "+url+
                  " was not found on this server.<P>\r\n" );
  message.append( "<HR>\r\n" );
  message.append( "<ADDRESS>THTTPSD/1.0</ADDRESS>\r\n" );
  message.append( "</BODY></HTML>\r\n" );
  message.append( "\r\n" );

  // Send the header and the message
  // Mime type is 'text/html'
  PrintWriter pw = new PrintWriter( out );
  sendHeader( pw, "text/html", message.length() );
  pw.print( message );

  // Make sure all the data gets there, especially because of
  // any buffering that might be used by the encryption
  pw.flush();
}

/**
 * Send directory listing
 */
private void sendDirectoryListing( File directory, String url,
                                   OutputStream out )
    throws IOException {

  // Build the response message
  StringBuffer message = new StringBuffer();
  message.append( "<!DOCTYPE HTML PUBLIC \"-//IETF//"+
                  "DTD HTML 2.0//EN\">\r\n" );
  message.append( "<HTML><HEAD>\r\n" );
  message.append( "<TITLE>"+url+"</TITLE>\r\n" );
  message.append( "</HEAD><BODY>\r\n" );
  message.append( "<H1>Directory: "+url+"</H1>\r\n" );
```

The file doesn't exist—send an error message ●

The file is a directory—list the contents ●

```
    // Add a link for each file in the directory
    File files[] = directory.listFiles();
    for (int i=0; i<files.length; ++i) {
      File file = files[i];
      String name = file.getName();
      String newURL = url+name;
      if (file.isDirectory())
        newURL += "/";
      message.append( "<a href=\""+newURL+"\">"+name+
                      "</a><br>\r\n" );
    }

    message.append( "</BODY></HTML>\r\n" );
    message.append( "\r\n" );

    // Send the header and the message
    // Mime type is 'text/html'
    PrintWriter pw = new PrintWriter( out );
    sendHeader( pw, "text/html", message.length() );
    pw.print( message );

    // Make sure all the data gets there, especially because of
    // any buffering that might be used by the encryption
    pw.flush();
  }
  /**
   * Send HTML page
   */
  private void sendWebPage( File doc, OutputStream out )
      throws IOException {
    // Send the header and the contents of the file
    // Mime type is 'text/html'
    PrintWriter pw = new PrintWriter( out );
    sendHeader( pw, "text/html", (int)doc.length() );
    sendFile( doc, out );
  }
  /**
   * Send text file
   */
  private void sendTextFile( File doc, OutputStream out )
      throws IOException {
    // Send the header and the contents of the file
    // Mime type is 'text/plain'
    PrintWriter pw = new PrintWriter( out );
    sendHeader( pw, "text/plain", (int)doc.length() );
    sendFile( doc, out );
  }
  /**
   * Send HTTP header, including the MIME type and the
   * content-length
```

● **The file is an HTML file—send it**

● **The file is some other file—send it as text**

```
    */
    private void sendHeader( PrintWriter pw, String mimeType,
                             int length )
        throws IOException {
      pw.print( "HTTP/1.1 200 OK\r\n" );
      pw.print( "Content-Length: "+length+"\r\n" );
      pw.print( "Content-Type: "+mimeType+"\r\n" );
      pw.print( "\r\n" );
      pw.flush();
    }

    /**
     * Send the contents of a file
     */
    private void sendFile( File doc, OutputStream out )
        throws IOException {
      byte buffer[] = new byte[bufferLength];
      FileInputStream fin = new FileInputStream( doc );
      while (true) {
        int r = fin.read( buffer );
        if (r==-1)
          break;
        out.write( buffer, 0, r );
      }

      out.flush();
    }

    /**
     * Parse the HTTP header of the incoming request.
     * Return the document that has been requested.
     * Only the GET method is handled
     */
    private String getDocString( InputStream in )
        throws IOException {
      // Create a BufferedReader to read the incoming
      // data one line at a time
      InputStreamReader isr = new InputStreamReader( in );
      BufferedReader br = new BufferedReader( isr );

      // Contains the first line of the request
      String firstLine = null;

      while (true) {
        String line = br.readLine();

        // The request is over if we get a null string,
        // or an empty line
        if (line==null) {
          return null;
        } else if (line.equals( "" )) {
          break;
        }
```

Utility method— send an HTTP header

Utility method—send the contents of a file

Parse an incoming HTTP GET request and return the relative pathname of the requested document

```
      // Save the first line of the request
      if (firstLine==null)
        firstLine = line;
    }

  if (firstLine != null) {
    // Use a regex to find the requested document
    // inside the first line

    Matcher matcher = getPattern.matcher( firstLine );
    if (matcher.matches()) {

      // Yes, we got it
      String doc = matcher.group( 1 );
      return doc;
    } else {

      // No: error, or wrong kind of request, or something
      throw new IOException( "Badly formed request" );
    }
  } else {

    // Return null if no more documents are being
    // requested by this client
    return null;
  }
}

/**
 * Return a ServerSocketFactory.  Return an
 * SSLServerSocketFactory if we're in secure mode,
 * otherwise use the default ServerSocketFactory
 */
private ServerSocketFactory getServerSocketFactory() {            ● Create an
  if (secure) {                                                     SSLServer-
    try {                                                           SocketFactory
      System.out.println( "Running secure" );

      String keyFile =                                            ● Get security properties
        (String)properties.get( "keyfile" );                        from the configuration
      String passphrase =                                           file
        (String)properties.get( "passphrase" );

      // Read authentication keys.  These are used to authenticate
      // ourselves to the client
      KeyStore ks = KeyStore.getInstance( "JKS" );        Read authentication
      ks.load( new FileInputStream( keyFile ),                    keys from       ●
              passphrase.toCharArray() );                      thttpsd.auth

      // The KeyManagerFactory manages the authentication keys
      KeyManagerFactory kmf =
        KeyManagerFactory.getInstance( "SunX509" );
      kmf.init( ks, passphrase.toCharArray() );
```

```
        // Create an SSLContext using our key manager
        SSLContext sslContext = SSLContext.getInstance( "TLS" );
        sslContext.init( kmf.getKeyManagers(), nul
                          secureRandom );
        // Create a ServerSocketFactory
        ServerSocketFactory ssf =
          sslContext.getServerSocketFactory();

        return ssf;
      } catch( GeneralSecurityException gse ) {

        System.err.println( gse );
        gse.printStackTrace();
        System.exit( 1 );

        // Should never reach this
        return null;
      } catch( IOException ie ) {

        System.err.println( ie );
        ie.printStackTrace();
        System.exit( 1 );

        // Should never reach this
        return null;
      }
    } else {

      System.out.println( "Running insecure" );
      return ServerSocketFactory.getDefault();
    }
  }
}

/**
 * INNER CLASS:
 * Listener listens for incoming connections
 */
class Listener implements Runnable {
  /**
    * Constructor: start a background thread
    */
  public Listener() {
    Thread thread = new Thread( this );
    thread.start();
  }

  /**
    * Background thread: listen on a port and accept
    * new connections; The new connections are passed
    * to THTTPSD.processSocket().
    */
  public void run() {
    try {
```

Create an SSLContext using the auth and trust keys ●

● **Create a ServerSocketFactory from the SSLContext**

❹ **Process incoming connections by passing them to THTTPSD.processSocket()**

```
        // Create a ServerSocket from the ServerSocketFactory
        ServerSocketFactory ssf = getServerSocketFactory();
        ServerSocket ss = ssf.createServerSocket( port );

        System.out.println( "Listening on port "+port );

        // Accept connections and process them
        while (true) {
          try {
            Socket socket = ss.accept();
            System.out.println( "Connection from "+
                                socket.getInetAddress() );
            processSocket( socket );
          } catch( IOException ie ) {
            System.err.println( "Listener exception: "+ie );
            ie.printStackTrace();
          }
        }
      } catch( IOException ie ) {
        System.err.println( "Listener exception: "+ie );
        ie.printStackTrace();
      }
    }
  }

/**
 * INNER CLASS:
 * SocketHandler responds to an incoming socket
 */
class SocketHandler implements Runnable {
  private Socket socket;

  /**
   * Constructor: start a background thread
   */
  public SocketHandler( Socket socket ) {
    this.socket = socket;
    Thread thread = new Thread( this );
    thread.start();
  }

  /**
   * Background thread:
   * Call THTTPSD.processTransaction() to process
   * this socket in this background thread
   */
  public void run() {
    try {
      InputStream in = socket.getInputStream();
      OutputStream out = socket.getOutputStream();

      processTransaction( socket, in, out );
    } catch( IOException ie ) {
```

❺ Process client requests by passing the socket to THTTPSD.processTransaction()

```
        }
      }
    }
    /**
     * Pre-initialize the SecureRandom so we can print
     * something about it to standard out
     */
    static private void initializeRandom() {        ❻  Pre-initialize a SecureRandom
      System.out.print(
        "Please wait, initializing random numbers..." );
      System.out.flush();
      secureRandom = new SecureRandom();
      secureRandom.nextInt();
      System.out.println( "done");
    }
    static public void main( String args[] ) {
      try {
        initializeRandom();                    Initialize the random
        new THTTPSD();                         number generator and
      } catch( IOException ie ) {              start a server
        System.err.println( ie );
        ie.printStackTrace();
      }
    }
}
```

❶❷ The main THTTPSD class creates a Listener, which starts a background thread to
❸❹ accept incoming connections. Each time a connection comes in, the Listener
❺ passes it to THTTPSD.processSocket(). processSocket() creates a SocketHandler,
which spawns a background thread to handle that connection. The SocketHandler,
in the background thread, calls THTTPSD.processTransaction() to handle the
requests for web pages.

Thus, separate objects, with their own threads, are spawned to handle listening and
client processing. However, these objects' threads call back to methods in THTTPSD,
because only THTTPSD has the ability to carry out the tasks. Thus, multiple objects in
multiple threads make calls to the processSocket() and processTrans-
action() methods of a single THTTPSD. These methods are thread-safe.

❻ SecureRandom takes a long time to initialize. If you don't create a SecureRandom
object yourself (and pass it into SSLContext.init()), one will be created for you
when the first client tries to connect. The initialization delay can give the impres-
sion that the connection is taking a really long time, so to avoid this, we initialize a
SecureRandom object at the start, and print out messages so that the user will know
what the delay is caused by.

11.5 *Example: a secure credit card authorization system*

The previous section presented THTTPSD, a trivial secure web server. A web server is only half of the client/server equation, though. In this section, we'll look at both halves: the client and server for a credit card authentication system.

11.5.1 *The authentication model*

The authentication model for the secure web server was *asymmetrical*—the web server was required to authenticate itself to the browser, but the browser did not have to authenticate itself to the web server. It was also asymmetrical in the sense that the web server is run by a party that is considered to be trusted, while the browser can be run by anyone with a computer.

In this section, we'll consider a more symmetrical model: the client and server components for a credit card authentication system. Unlike with THTTPSD, we aren't going to need to have any of our keys signed by a trusted third party. The server and client components are considered to be prepared and installed by a single agency (the IT staff of the company offering the service). They communicate via secure sockets not because they might not trust each other, but rather because they want to make sure that they are not dealing with an impostor.

In this model, the client and the server each has its own public/private key pair. Each one also has the public key (or, more precisely, a self-signed certificate) of the other. The certificates verify the public key, but on their own they do not prove anything about the client or the server. Both ends of the connection must demonstrate that they know their own private key, which they do implicitly by using these keys to decrypt information that has been encrypted by the corresponding public keys.

During authentication, the server sends its certificate, and the client verifies this certificate by comparing it to its own copy of the certificate (see figure 11.4). The

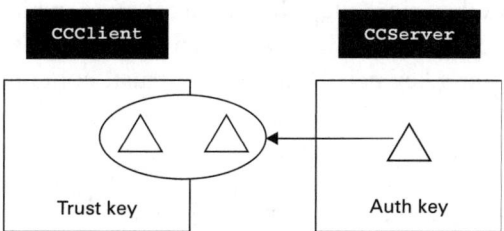

Figure 11.4 The server authenticates itself to the client by sending its certificate, or self-signed public key, and the client verifies this by comparing it to its copy of the certificate.

client then does the same thing—it sends its certificate to the server for authentication (see figure 11.5).

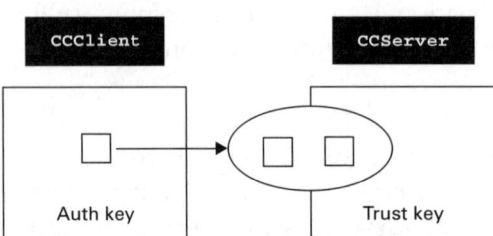

Figure 11.5 **The client authenticates itself to the server by sending its certificate, or self-signed public key, and the server verifies this by comparing it to its copy of the certificate.**

Once both ends are satisfied that they trust each other, the client then generates a symmetric secret key and encrypts this key with the server's public key. It then sends the encrypted key to the server, which decrypts it using its private key. This use of server's private key completes the server's authentication process—only the *real* server knows this key (hopefully).

The symmetric key that has just been sent is then ready to be used for fast encryption and decryption of the socket data sent in both directions. (Technically, the client doesn't send the symmetric key directly. Rather, it sends information that is used by both the client and server to generate the same symmetric key.)

11.5.2 *Generating the keys*

The process of key generation is somewhat more complicated than it was for THTTPSD. The client has its public/private key pair stored in a file called ccclient.auth, and the client sends this public key to the server. It also has a copy of the server's public key (no private key) in a file called ccclient.trust, which it uses to verify the certificate sent by the server. Likewise, the server has two files: ccserver.auth, containing the server's key pair, and ccserver.trust, containing the client's public key.

This is all fairly confusing, so these keys are summarized in two tables. Table 11.2 lists the keys available to the client, and table 11.3 lists the keys available to the server.

Table 11.2   These keys are stored on the client side and are used in various ways in the authentication process.

Key	Stored in	What the client uses it for
Client's public key	`ccclient.auth`	Sent to the server as a certificate.
Client's private key	`ccclient.auth`	Used to decrypt information sent by the server. Since only the client knows this key, this effectively authenticates the client.
Server's public key (certificate)	`ccclient.trust`	Compared against the certificate sent by the server, thereby authenticating the certificate. Also used to encrypt a newly generated secret key, which is sent to the server.

It's important that each side keep its own key pair separate from its copy of the other side's public key, for file-security reasons. Its key pair is extremely sensitive information, since it contains the private key; the other side's public key, on the other hand, is expected to be widely known.

Table 11.3   These keys are stored on the server side and are used in various ways in the authentication process.

Key	Stored in	What the server uses it for
Server's public key	`ccserver.auth`	Sent to the client as a certificate.
Server's private key	`ccserver.auth`	Used to decrypt information sent by the client. Since only the server knows this key, this effectively authenticates the server.
Client's public key (certificate)	`ccserver.trust`	Compared against the certificate sent by the client, thereby authenticating the certificate.

To generate all these key files, we do the following. First, we generate a key pair for the client, into ccclient.auth, which will be included with the client software:

```
keytool -genkey -alias ccclient -keystore ccclient.auth  -keyalg rsa
```

Next, we extract the public-key certificate into a temporary file called ccclient.key:

```
keytool -export -alias ccclient -keystore ccclient.auth -file ccclient.key
```

Finally, we import this public key into ccserver.trust—this file will be included with the server software:

```
keytool -import -alias ccserver -keystore ccserver.trust -file ccclient.key
```

The same process is used to create ccserver.auth and ccclient.trust. The included scripts `cckeys.sh` and `cckeys.bat` will generate all of these key files for you.

11.5.3   *The code*

We'll now look at the code. CCServer, the server, is shown in listing 11.3, while CCClient, the client, is shown in listing 11.4. Again, pay special attention to the getServerSocketFactory() method, which is where the key is loaded.

Listing 11.3   CCServer.java

(See \Chapter11\CCServer.java)

```java
import java.io.*;
import java.net.*;
import java.security.*;
import javax.net.*;
import javax.net.ssl.*;

public class CCServer implements Runnable
{
  // The port number we will listen on
  private int port;

  // Passphrase for the authentication and trust keystores
  static private final String passphrase = "serverpass";

  // Secure random source
  static private SecureRandom secureRandom;

  /**
   * Constructor: start the server socket
   */
  public CCServer( int port ) {
    this.port = port;

    Thread thread = new Thread( this );
    thread.start();
  }

  /**
   * Listen for incoming connections, and hand them off to
   * a SocketHandler
   */
  public void run() {
    try {
      // Prepare ServerSocket
```

● **The main background
thread listens for
incoming connections**

```
   ServerSocketFactory ssf = getServerSocketFactory();
   SSLServerSocket ss =
     (SSLServerSocket)ssf.createServerSocket( port );
```
1 Create a ServerSocket from a ServerSocketFactory

```
   // Request client authorization
   ss.setNeedClientAuth( true );
```
2 Require the client to authenticate itself

```
   // Listen for incoming connections
   System.out.println( "Listening on port "+port+"..." );
   while (true) {
     Socket socket = ss.accept();
     System.out.println( "Got connection from "+
                    socket.getInetAddress() );

     // Handle the socket in a separate thread
     new SocketHandler( socket );
   }
 } catch( GeneralSecurityException gse ) {
   gse.printStackTrace();
 } catch( IOException ie ) {
   ie.printStackTrace();
 }
}
```
3 Handle incoming connections in their own threads

```
/**
 * Handle a transaction: read credit card information,
 * verify it, and send the verification response code
 * back to the client.  This method is called from
 * a SocketHandler object running in a separate thread
 */
private void handleSocket( Socket socket ) throws IOException {
  // Get the streams connected to the client
  InputStream in = socket.getInputStream();
  OutputStream out = socket.getOutputStream();
  DataInputStream din = new DataInputStream( in );
  DataOutputStream dout = new DataOutputStream( out );

  while (true) {
    // Read credit card info
    String ccnumber = din.readUTF();
    String ccexp = din.readUTF();

    // Verify credit card info
    boolean verified = checkCCDatabase( ccnumber, ccexp );

    // Send the verification response code back to
    // the client
    dout.writeBoolean( verified );
    dout.flush();

    // Print a log message
    String message = verified ? "Verified." : "Not verified.";
    System.out.println( "Verify: "+ccnumber+" "+ccexp+": "+
                    message );
```
● Read credit card info, verify it, and send back a result

```
      }
    }

    /**
     * Verify credit card information against some database.
     * This is just a demo, so we'll always return true.
     */
    private synchronized boolean checkCCDatabase( String ccnumber,
                                                 String ccexp ) {
      return true;
    }
```

● **checkCCDatabase() always returns true—it's just a demo**

```
    /**
     * Create secure ServerSocketFactory.
     * Read authentication and trust information from
     * keystore files in local directory
     */
    private ServerSocketFactory getServerSocketFactory()
        throws GeneralSecurityException, IOException {
```

● **Create an SSLServerSocket Factory**

```
      // Read authentication keys.  These are used to authenticate
      // ourselves to the client
      KeyStore authKeyStore = KeyStore.getInstance( "JKS" );
      authKeyStore.load( new FileInputStream( "ccserver.auth" ),
                        passphrase.toCharArray() );
```

● **Read authentication keys from ccserver.auth**

```
      // The KeyManagerFactory manages the authentication keys
      KeyManagerFactory kmf =
        KeyManagerFactory.getInstance( "SunX509" );
      kmf.init( authKeyStore, passphrase.toCharArray() );

      // Read trust keys.  These are used to verify the client's
      // attempt to authenticate itself with us
      KeyStore trustKeyStore = KeyStore.getInstance( "JKS" );
      trustKeyStore.load( new FileInputStream( "ccserver.trust" ),
                        passphrase.toCharArray() );
```

● **Read trust keys from ccserver.trust**

```
      // The TrustManagerFactory manages the trust keys
      TrustManagerFactory tmf =
        TrustManagerFactory.getInstance( "SunX509" );
      tmf.init( trustKeyStore );

      // Create an SSLContext using our key and trust managers
      SSLContext sslContext = SSLContext.getInstance( "TLS" );
      sslContext.init( kmf.getKeyManagers(),
                      tmf.getTrustManagers(),
                      secureRandom );
```

● **Create an SSLContext using the auth and trust keys**

```
      // Create a ServerSocketFactory
      ServerSocketFactory ssf = sslContext.getServerSocketFactory();
      return ssf;
    }
```

● **Create a ServerSocketFactory from the SSLContext**

```
/**
 * INNER Class:
 * SocketHandler handles an incoming connection
 * in a separate thread
 */
class SocketHandler implements Runnable {
  private Socket socket;

  /**
   * Constructor: start a background thread
   */
  public SocketHandler( Socket socket ) {
    this.socket = socket;

    // Start a background thread
    Thread thread = new Thread( this );
    thread.start();
  }

  /**
   * Handle a series of transactions sent over the socket
   */
  public void run() {
    try {

      // Call back to CCServer.handleSocket
      handleSocket( socket );

    } catch( IOException ie ) {
    } finally {
      try {
        socket.close();
        System.out.println( "Closed "+socket.getInetAddress() );
      } catch( IOException ie ) {
        System.err.println( "Problem closing socket: "+socket );
        ie.printStackTrace();
      }
    }
  }
}

/**
 * Pre-initialize the SecureRandom so we can print
 * something about it to standard out
 */
static private void initializeRandom() {
  System.out.print(
    "Please wait, initializing random numbers..." );
  System.out.flush();
  secureRandom = new SecureRandom();
  secureRandom.nextInt();
  System.out.println( "done");
}
```

❸ Create a ServerSocketFactory from the SSLContext

❹ Call back to CCServer.handleSocket

● Pre-initialize a SecureRandom object

```
/**
 * Verify arguments, init the random number generator,
 * and start the server
 */
static public void main( String args[] ) {
  if (args.length != 1) {
    System.err.println( "Usage: java CCServer <port>" );
    System.exit( 1 );
  }

  int port = Integer.parseInt( args[0] );

  initializeRandom();

  new CCServer( port );
  }
}
```

❶ The `ServerSocketFactory` has been configured to create `SSLServerSockets` that do their authentication using the keys in ccserver.auth and ccserver.trust.

❷ Normally, only the server is required to authenticate itself. This is because it is generally the server that is performing some sensitive action, such as taking a credit card number, and the client can be anyone, anywhere on the Internet. This way of distributing the burdens of authentication is appropriate for web browsers, FTP clients, and the like.

Our application, however, is a highly sensitive system. Additionally, we can expect that the clients' installations are under the control of the organization running the server, and so it is not unreasonable to expect that each client should go to the trouble of acquiring the keys necessary for authentication. Thus, we require client authentication.

Of course, this is just a text example, and so we are using keys generated locally and shared between the server and the client. No external authority is being used in this process.

❸ ❹ `SocketHandler` takes a `Socket` object and spawns a background thread to process the transactions coming from it. The `run()` method of the `SocketHandler` just repeatedly calls `CCServer.handleSocket()` to actually process each transaction coming from this `Socket`.

Thus we have multiple `SocketHandlers` calling the `handleSocket()` method of a single `CCServer` object. The reason we call back into the `CCServer` object from the `SocketHandler` is because only `CCServer` knows how to authenticate; `SocketHandler` is only here to spawn a background thread.

Listing 11.4   CCClient.java

(See\Chapter11\CCClient.java)

```java
import java.io.*;
import java.net.*;
import java.security.*;
import javax.net.*;
import javax.net.ssl.*;

/**
 * Client for secure credit card verification system
 */
public class CCClient
{
  // Hostname and port of the verification server
  private String hostname;
  private int port;

  // Streams connected to the server
  private DataInputStream din;
  private DataOutputStream dout;

  // Passphrase for the authentication and trust keystores
  static private final String passphrase = "clientpass";

  // Secure random source
  static private SecureRandom secureRandom;

  /**
   * Constructor: set up the connection, and start
   * reading credit card info from standard in
   */
  public CCClient( String hostname, int port ) {
    this.hostname = hostname;
    this.port = port;
  }

  /**
   * Process a series of credit cards read from
   * the command-line
   */
  private void process() {
    setupConnection();
    verifyFromStandardIn();
  }

  /**
   * Make connection to server, and get
   * a stream pair to communicate with it
   */
  private void setupConnection() {
```

```
   try {
     SocketFactory sf = getSocketFactory();
     Socket socket = sf.createSocket( hostname, port );

     InputStream in = socket.getInputStream();
     OutputStream out = socket.getOutputStream();

     din = new DataInputStream( in );
     dout = new DataOutputStream( out );
   } catch( GeneralSecurityException gse ) {
     gse.printStackTrace();
   } catch( IOException ie ) {
     ie.printStackTrace();
   }
 }

/**
 * Read credit card information from standard in,
 * and verify it via the server
 */
private void verifyFromStandardIn() {
   try {
     // Get a BufferedReader for reading standard in one
     // line at a time
     InputStreamReader isr = new InputStreamReader( System.in );
     BufferedReader br = new BufferedReader( isr );

     while (true) {
       // Read credit card number
       System.out.print( "Enter CC number: " );
       System.out.flush();
       String ccnumber = br.readLine();

       // Read expiration date
       System.out.print( "Enter CC expiration date: " );
       System.out.flush();
       String ccexp = br.readLine();

       // Verify on remote server
       boolean verified = verify( ccnumber, ccexp );

       String message = verified ? "Verified." : "Not verified.";
       System.out.println( message );
     }
   } catch( IOException ie ) {
     ie.printStackTrace();
   }
 }

/**
 * Send credit card info to server, and get
 * verification in response
 */
```

1 Create a Socket from a SocketFactory

● Get streams connected to the server

● Read credit card info from standard in, and verify it via the server

● Read credit card info from standard in

● Verify credit card info via the server

```
private boolean verify( String ccnumber, String ccexp )
    throws IOException {
  dout.writeUTF( ccnumber );
  dout.writeUTF( ccexp );
  dout.flush();
  boolean ok = din.readBoolean();
  return ok;
}
```

● Send the credit card info, and send back a response

```
/**
 * Create secure SocketFactory.
 * Read authentication and trust information from
 * keystore files in local directory
 */
private SocketFactory getSocketFactory()
    throws GeneralSecurityException, IOException {
```

● **Create an SSLSocketFactory**

```
  // Read authentication keys.  These are used to authenticate
  // ourselves to the server
  KeyStore authKeyStore = KeyStore.getInstance( "JKS" );
  authKeyStore.load( new FileInputStream( "ccclient.auth" ),
                    passphrase.toCharArray() );
```

● **Read authentication keys from ccclient.auth**

```
  // The KeyManagerFactory manages the authentication keys
  KeyManagerFactory kmf =
    KeyManagerFactory.getInstance( "SunX509" );
  kmf.init( authKeyStore, passphrase.toCharArray() );

  // Read trust keys.  These are used to verify the server's
  // attempt to authenticate itself with us
  KeyStore trustKeyStore = KeyStore.getInstance( "JKS" );
  trustKeyStore.load( new FileInputStream( "ccclient.trust" ),
                    passphrase.toCharArray() );
```

● **Read trust keys from ccclient.trust**

```
  // The TrustManagerFactory manages the trust keys
  TrustManagerFactory tmf =
    TrustManagerFactory.getInstance( "SunX509" );
  tmf.init( trustKeyStore );

  // Create an SSLContext using our key and trust managers
  SSLContext sslContext = SSLContext.getInstance( "TLS" );
  sslContext.init( kmf.getKeyManagers(),
                  tmf.getTrustManagers(),
                  secureRandom );
```

● **Create an SSLContext using the auth and trust keys**

```
  // Create a SocketFactory
  SocketFactory ssf = sslContext.getSocketFactory();
  return ssf;
}
```

● **Create a SocketFactory from the SSLContext**

```
/**
 * Pre-initialize the SecureRandom so we can print
 * something about it to standard out
 */
```

```
static private void initializeRandom() {  ● Pre-initialize a SecureRandom object
  System.out.print(
    "Please wait, initializing random numbers..." );
  System.out.flush();
  secureRandom = new SecureRandom();
  secureRandom.nextInt();
  System.out.println( "done");
}

/**
 * Verify arguments, init the random number generator,
 * and start the client
 */
static public void main( String args[] ) {
  if (args.length != 2) {
    System.err.println(
      "Usage: java CCServer <hostname> <port>" );
    System.exit( 1 );
  }

  String hostname = args[0];
  int port = Integer.parseInt( args[1] );

  initializeRandom();

  CCClient ccc = new CCClient( hostname, port );
  ccc.process();
}
}
```

❶ The SocketFactory has been configured to create SSLSockets that do their authentication using the keys in ccclient.auth and ccclient.trust.

11.6 *Summary*

The JSSE packages, along with the SunJSSE security provider, provide a complete implementation of secure socket communication using the SSL/TLS standard. JSSE makes it easy to communicate with other SSL-enabled entities, such as secure web servers, as well as SSL-enabled versions of common Internet applications, such as FTP.

JSSE uses the familiar *socket* and *stream* metaphors so familiar to Java programmers. These classes are used in exactly the same way as their regular, unencrypted versions. The difficult part of using JSSE is in managing security keys, but the complexity of this is inherent to security practices in general. JSSE, along with keytool, supports common key formats and is interoperable with existing SSL software and techniques.

index